Livelihood Diversities in Mountain Economy

About the Author

I.C. Awasthi, a Ph. D. (Economics) from the Jawaharlal Nehru University, New Delhi is presently Senior Faculty at the Institute of Applied Manpower Research (Planning Commission, Government of India) Delhi. He received specialised training on Manpower Planning from the Institute of Employment Studies, University of Sussex, United Kingdom. He is alumnus of Indian Institute of Management (Ahmedabad) and International Programme of Development Evaluation Training (Carleton University, 2009). He works in the areas of labour, employment, decentralised planning and human resource development. He has contributed over 3 dozen papers in the professional journals and published two co-authored and three edited books. He is Member, Governing Council of International Organisation for Collaborative Outcome Management in South Asia (IOCOMSA).

Livelihood Diversities in Mountain Economy

Constraints and Opportunities

I.C. Awasthi

CONCEPT PUBLISHING COMPANY PVT. LTD.
NEW DELHI-110059

ISBN-13 : 978-81-8069-836-1

First Published 2012

Published and Printed by

Concept Publishing Company Pvt. Ltd.
A/15-16, Commercial Block, Mohan Garden
New Delhi-110059 (India)
T: 25351460, 25351794, *F*: 091-11-25357109
E: publishing@conceptpub.com, W: www.conceptpub.com
Editorial Office: H-13, Bali Nagar, New Delhi-110 015, India.

Cataloging in Publication Data--*Courtesy:* D.K. Agencies (P) Ltd. <docinfo@dkagencies.com>

Awasthi, I. C. (Ishwar Chandra), 1955-
Livelihood diversities in mountain economy : constraints and opportunities / I.C. Awasthi.
p. cm.
Includes bibliographical references (p.) and index.
ISBN 9788180698361

1. Rural development—India—Uttarakhand. 2. Uttarakhand (India)—Economic conditions. 3. Rural industries—India—Uttarakhand. 4. Manpower policy, Rural—India—Uttarakhand. 5. Labor supply—India—Uttarakhand. I. Title.

DDC 307.1412095451 23

Foreword

Mountain regions of India are, by and large, characterised by subsistence economies. With a limited and environmentally fragile resource base, people in these regions are mostly engaged in food crop cultivation and animal husbandry. Commercial activity is limited, confined to some horticulture, local material based tiny enterprises and handicrafts. With relative inaccessibility to markets, there is very limited scope for expansion of these activities. As a result, the hill and mountain regions are facing the major challenge of widespread and persistent poverty further aggravated by food deficits, adverse terms of trade and exploitative linkages with other regions, gender inequity and human drudgery and environmental degradation. Development interventions brought about through various programmes and projects by the national and local governments, non-government organisations and international agencies, have so far met with limited success in alleviating poverty and improving the livelihoods of people in these regions. The primary reason for their failure has been attributed to inappropriate approaches and strategies in which the mountain perspectives were entirely missing as, most often, development initiative has been based primarily on the knowledge and experience of development in plainlands.

The present study by Dr. I.C. Awasthi clearly establishes the need for incorporation of the physical, environmental and social specificities of the mountain regions in development policies and strategies. Based as it is on a thorough review of past studies on development of mountain areas, specially of the region under study, detailed analysis of official secondary data and an extensive field survey in the hill districts of Uttarakhand state, it highlights the limitations of the conventional development models and approaches and the need to use a mountain perspective framework for hill and mountain area development.

Unemployment has been observed as one of the serious problems in the region : while labour force growth has been quite high, the long-term employment growth has been very low. Adequate employment opportunities cannot be generated unless productive base of the economy is enhanced. Gender biased work structure, female drudgery, out-migration, low incomes and chronic poverty are among the other socio-economic maladies afflicting the hill people. Not only the long-term growth of employment, growth of aggregate and sectoral output and income levels has also been lower in the state as compared to the all-India average. This productivity in the major economic sectors in the state compares very unfavourably with the all-India level. The proportion of poor below the poverty line is alarmingly high in the state, with rural poverty at 41 per cent, lower only than in the poorest states of India, namely Orissa, Bihar, Chhatisgarh and Jharkhand. Industrial activities are limited and are confined to plains areas only.

In order to tackle these basic problems of the state, the study argues that mountain areas should primarily focus on the niche products of the region in which they have comparative advantage rather than producing those products that do not have any distinct advantage in terms of product and price competitiveness. However, there is a need for evolving special policies and support mechanisms to promote the micro and small enterprises taking into account the complexity and constraints in the region. This would require sector-specific development strategies and infrastructural development utilising approaches and technologies that integrate environmental, economic and social dimensions of sustainable development. For this, detailed planning is a prerequisite in the region and within region at the micro level, due to enormous diversity in terms of nature and suitability of land and other natural resources.

This book brings out some of the major issues that have wider ramifications for policy formulation and implementation with a view to improving the livelihoods in the hill region. Some of the results have direct implications for immediate policies and programmes while others should become the basic elements of a long-term policy for sustainable livelihood security and raising the living standards.

I hope this book will help understand the nuances of hill perspectives and concerns for sustainable development of mountain economies. As such it will prove useful to the policy-makers, development agencies, researchers, NGOs, and all others who are concerned with and involved in the task of development of these regions.

January, 2011

T. S. Papola
Professor, Institute for Studies in Industrial Development (ISID), New Delhi
and
Former Division Head, International Center for Integrated Mountain Development (ICIMOD), Kathmandu

Preface

Despite the increasing interventions brought about in the mountain regions through various programmes and project approaches by the national Governments and donor agencies, and increasing environmental and sustainability concerns expressed by the international agencies; the mountain regions have by and large remained at the lowest ebb of development trajectory barring a few cases. The primary reason for this failure is inappropriate development strategy in which the mountain perspectives was missing and, most often, development has been undertaken from the outside flatlanders or mainstream institutions, who have lesser understanding of the peculiarities of hill-specific problems.

This book grew out of an in-depth study carried out in the Uttarakhand State as part of the research work undertaken at the Jawaharlal Nehru University, New Delhi. The formation of an independent Uttarakhand State has helped to focus on the developmental problems in the region and some positive results are visible in terms of increased accessibility, communication and development works, but unless the developmental issues are dovetailed within the hill perspective, most of the real issues will remain distant objectives. Unemployment has been one of the serious problems in the region and the long-term employment growth has been abysmally low. Adequate employment opportunities cannot be generated unless the productive base of the economy is sufficiently enhanced.

Agriculture is increasingly becoming an uneconomic family enterprise, and employment opportunities outside agriculture are extremely limited. Within farm sector there is a huge incidence of underemployment in terms of unutilized labour time. Majority of the rural households are forced to diversify their activities as a part of their survival strategy to cope with the seasonality and uncertainty of production.

The work structure is highly gender-biased in rural areas of the state as women mostly work in agriculture related occupations while their male counterparts work in non-farm occupations. A very low share of female employment in the non-agriculture sector shows a complete dichotomy and segmentation of work activity due to various socio-economic factors that inhibit females to participate in the labour market outside cultivation despite the fact that over the years their literacy levels have improved considerably. From the policy perspective this has far-reaching implications for their employability outside the agriculture.

Multiple economic activities are most pervasive and widespread among different groups of population in the survey areas in Uttarakhand, manifesting symptoms of backward economy. Migration has been a common phenomenon in the hill region of Uttarakhand and is closely related to the economic backwardness of the region. In fact, out-migration and economic underdevelopment reinforce one another and produce a vicious circle that further accentuates the process of underdevelopment. Out-migration is not an unusual event but a constant response to uneconomical agriculture enterprise, fragile resource base (land and forest), environmental degradation, limited employment opportunities, and hence, livelihood insecurity.

In spite of the relatively distinct resource base for development of numerous non-farm activities and enterprises in the state, its potential has not been exploited fully within the constraints of fragile environment. It is therefore necessary to formulate a mountain-specific framework that incorporates growth with equity and addresses the issues such as mountain agriculture, persistent poverty, sustainable livelihood, environment sustainability and gender dimension. Such perspectives would call for an integrated approach towards development by adequately encompassing the mountain specificities for achieving the desired objectives.

The book has been structured into nine chapters. The first chapter discusses the broad features and development issues in mountain economies across the world, mainly Alps mountain regions of European countries, Andean mountain ranges in the South America and Hindu Kush Himalayan (HKH) region countries in the South Asia.

This is followed by issues and diversity of development experience of Indian hill economies, mainly in ten hill states, which is presented in chapter two. Chapter three reviews the literature on the non-farm sector from the theoretical perspective and from empirical realities. In the end, the chapter describes the objectives, hypotheses, study area, sampling method, and tools used. Chapter four analyses the patterns and trends of rural non-farm sector utilising secondary sources of data, primarily from the NSS and Census. Chapter five to eight present empirical findings based on primary survey. Chapter five presents broad features of socio-economic and demographic characteristics of sample households. Chapter six reports the evidences of employment and livelihood diversities in the region. Chapter seven examines the pattern of non-farm employment and rural enterprises, and Chapter eight analyses migration patterns and linkages. The concluding chapter (Chapter nine) summarises the main conclusions and reports policy imperatives.

The present study brings out some of the major issues that have wider ramifications for policy formulation and implementation with a view to improving the livelihoods in the hill region. Some of the results have direct implications for policies and programmes based on evidences thrown by the survey results that have great underpinning to evolve a long-term policy for sustainable livelihood security and raising the living standards of the people of the hill region.

I express my immense gratitude to Professor Ravi S. Srivastava, my supervisor at the Jawaharlal Nehru University, for his constant guidance and unstinted support.

I am deeply grateful to Professor T.S. Papola who has been kind enough to write the Foreward of this book. Professor Papola, a leading development economist in the country, has closely studied the development issues in mountain regions and his work has been widely acclaimed in the development literature of mountain and hill regions. I have drawn heavily from his development framework.

I have also been enormously benefited from the ideas evolved as a result of discussion and comments from the faculty at the Centre for the Study of Regional Development, Jawaharlal Nehru University, New Delhi. Comments received from Professor Ramesh Chand,

Director, National Centre for Agricultural Economics and Policy Research, New Delhi and Professor A.K. Singh, Director, Giri Institute of Development Studies, Lucknow have been extremely helpful in improving the quality of my research work. These observations and comments helped me re-look at and synthesise the arguments brought forward in this study. I put on record my profound gratitude to all of them.

My long and arduous field-work over three dozen villages in the Uttarakhand hills gave me opportunity to understand the problem facing the hill people and helped me to refine my research instruments. I have been benefited from discussions with many village people which provided me the first-hand information regarding the research problem.

I am thankful to all my friends and well-wishers in the Institute and outside who have constantly encouraged me and helped me in various ways. My special thanks to Sh. Anup Karan who helped me in data processing and evolving the framework of the field data analysis.

I am thankful to my wife Kamla, my son Bhartendu and my daughter Mansi for their constant support and endurance. My children, who are economists in their own right, have constantly kept me informed about the recent developments in the area, whatever they learnt at the Delhi School of Economics and Tata Institute of Social Sciences, Mumbai respectively.

I dedicate this work, however small, to my parents with whose blessings I could accomplish this work.

Finally, I am immensely grateful to Shri Ashok Kumar Mittal of Concept Publishing Company Pvt. Ltd., for taking personal interest in bringing out this book in time. However, the onus of all omissions and errors lies with me alone.

January, 2011
New Delhi

I.C. Awasthi

Contents

List of Tables

List of Figures

List of Annexures

1

Features and Development Issues in Mountain Economies

I. Introduction

All mountain areas share certain common physical attributes such as steep slopes, instability and ecological complexity which make them extremely vulnerable to environmental disturbance that has strong influence on human living. Mountain areas cover 24 per cent of the earth's land surface (Kapos *et al.*, 2000) which contain 12 per cent of the global population (Huddleston *et al.*, 2003), and further 14 per cent of the global population is estimated to live in their vicinity (Meybeck *et al.*, 2001). These mountain regions have huge economic potentials such as fresh water resources, hydro-power, forests, minerals, tourists' interests etc., but most of them are politically and economically marginalised and isolated. Thus, mountain populations are at a clear disadvantage in comparison to other non-mountain regions. There is widespread poverty among mountain inhabitants and loss of indigenous knowledge (Chapter13, Earth Summit, 1992). The importance of mountain economies had been by and large neglected until 1992 when the global importance of mountains was recognised at the United Nations Conference on Environment and Development, held at Rio de Janeiro (Brazil). Chapter 13 of Agenda 21, "Managing Fragile Ecosystems: Sustainable Mountain Development", was included in this key global document endorsing commitment for action by the heads of States or governments of most of the countries in the world. The global recognition of the importance of mountains was further emphasised by designating the year 2002 as the International Year of Mountains (IYM) by the General Assembly of the United Nations.

The mountain or hill regions across the countries are characterised by certain common features or specificities (Price, 1981; Ives and Messerli, 1989; Allan *et al.,* 1988). The important specificities are inaccessibility, fragility, marginality, and diversity or heterogeneity. The other related specificities are natural suitability and adaptive human mechanisms. The first four specificities have been termed as first-order specificities and the next two as the second-order specificities. The second-order specificities are different from the first ones in the sense that they are the responses or adaptive mechanisms to first-order specificities (Jodha, 1992). Inaccessibility, fragility and marginality are constraints in a given situation, while diversity and human adaptation represent opportunities. Inaccessibility is related to slope, altitude, terrain and consequential hazards. These factors produce isolation, sparse habitation, and limited links, communication and mobility which in turn affect the activity and livelihood patterns of the mountain population. Topographical factors not only reduce accessibility but also increase the cost of infrastructure and maintenance. Fragility is related to delicate economic system, vulnerable resources and changing livelihood patterns, which often is a resultant process of inaccessibility. Fragility occurs due to excessive use or exploitation of resources ignoring resource conservation, management and recycling. Inaccessibility results in marginality or exclusion from the mainstream in terms of areas, location, activity and people which leads to unfavourable terms of trade for such locations. Diversity or heterogeneity is a dominant phenomenon in all the mountain economies due to peculiar landscape and spatial dimensions, which results in different kinds of adaptation and socio-economic patterns across different locations and habitations. Spatial dimensions result in diversity in terms of resources, products and activities which provide comparative advantage to the specific location or area. This advantage may be in the form of production of unique or niche products such as fruits, vegetables, flowers, medicinal plants, seeds etc. Harnessing such resources ensures optimal livelihood security to the communities, whereas their overuse can have an adverse impact on the sustainability of resources. The adaptation mechanism, in a broader sense, includes human interaction with environment for sustainable livelihood which has helped in sustainable use and conservation of resources over time. The adaptation mechanism (traditional knowledge and wisdom) has evolved over a long period of time through trial and error methods to win over the constraints and hazards generated by the specificity characteristics. These specificities are interrelated and have multidimensional features having direct bearing on the bio-physical and socio-economic aspects of mountain life. These specificities may differ across different locations or countries and also may have different implications (positive as well as negative) for the resources and activities of the mountain regions.

II. Development Trajectory of Mountain Economies

The mountain habitat shares certain similar bio-climatic features and concerns across the world (see Annexure-I.1), whether these are the Alps mountain regions of European countries or Andean mountain ranges in the South America (Venezuela, Columbia, Ecuador, Peru, Bolivia, Chile, and Argentina) or Hindu Kush Himalayan (HKH) region countries in the South Asia (Afghanistan, Pakistan, India, China, Nepal, Bhutan, Bangladesh and Myanmar). These relate primarily to the changing mountain environment due to degradation of resources owing to their excessive use. This has resulted in reduction in biomass production, marginalisation and low human welfare. Many of these mountain regions are prone to natural hazards (landslides, earthquakes, avalanches, diseases etc.) (Li Tianchi, 1998). Human conflict and wars also concentrated in many of the poor regions (Libiszewski and Bachler, 1997) making the life of the mountain people more vulnerable. The minority inhabitants in certain mountain regions suffered not only from the resources exploitation but also from ethnic conflict, violence and wars (Ives, *et al.,* 1997). But then, there are major differences in the mountain economies of the developed countries of Europe and that of Andean regions and HKH regions in respect of their development trajectories. Mountain regions of European countries (Alps) had much similar situations during the 18th Century to what exists today in the mountain regions of Andean or HKH regions. These Alpine inhabitants, for instance, had witnessed high poverty, out-migration, malnutrition and even outright starvation during Little Ice Age (1500 to 1850 AD) (Ives, 1997). European mountain regions developed fast primarily because of their strong external linkages with the developed regions experiencing industrial revolution, and in this process, mountain regions benefited significantly from this strong linkage effect (Messerli, 1984). Development of transports – both navigation and railways – had facilitated long distance trade. Large-scale out-migration helped in reducing the demographic pressure, and unlike most developing countries today, Europe at that time experienced faster growth of income than the population, thereby improving their standard of living. The potato, railway development after the mid-19th Century and later mass tourism and large-scale winter sports helped these economies to transform rapidly (Ives, 1997). Industrialisation in the Alps has been closely related to the development of hydro-power-based industries, and today, more than 50 per cent of the population lives in urban areas. The tourism industry in Alps is most dynamic and competitive. Also, mountain-peasants in these countries receive large sum of subsidies from the governments and other institutions to encounter the limited incomes from mountain agriculture. Many countries (Austria, Switzerland, Germany, France, UK and Norway, for example) have some sorts of institutional mechanisms and state protection in place with considerable political will to ameliorate the in-built inequalities in the mountain economies.

The strong linkages with the economically growing areas have thus been the main driving force for development of these mountain economies, and it is argued that further boost in linkages would have far-reaching positive impact on these regions. However, this assumption has been questioned by some scholars (Batzing *et al.*, 1996) who maintain that the development has rather concentrated in a few favourable locations, and a large part of Alpine Zone is loosing its productive potential with rising disparities. Therefore, they argue, mountain regions must continue to receive special treatment. Some areas of French and Italian Alps, for example, are still holding traditional agricultural system with little or no alternative development possibilities (*e.g.* industry or tourism), and they are still helped through subsidies. In spite of some aberrations, these regions are far ahead than the other least developed mountain regions in terms of development, welfare and opportunities.

In the least developed mountain regions, the most common economic activities include subsistence land-based activities (crop production combined with animal husbandry, horticulture, forestry, etc.), traditional enterprises drawing upon local raw material, using rudimentary technology, limited use of external inputs and resources. Low availability of resources including land, human drudgery, infrastructural bottleneck and emigration are the other adverse features of such economies. These features exhibited a closed system of limited trade, exchange and surplus. By and large, such a subsistence nature of economic activities provided the base for sustenance of the mountain people. This has led to a sustainable development and management of resource use and activities, even though with low productivity and low pay-offs.

However, over the years there has been rapid population growth, thereby putting increasing pressure on the limited cultivable land necessitated by the increasing demand for food. The growing demand for food-crops led extension from the hitherto cultivated areas to the marginal land and forest land. This process has had its adverse effect on the land and forest resources making them economically unsustainable leading to environmental degradation. Conscious efforts to develop mountain areas and bringing them into the mainstream development trajectory (mainly through government) have evoked new hopes and aspirations among the people. Government played a key role through various interventions such as infrastructural development in the form of transport and communication that provided access to these areas, which has opened new vistas of development. Various sectoral development programmes in the field of agriculture, education, health and other non-agriculture-based activities brought about closer interactions with the rest of the world. These trends have, however, far-reaching implications for the mountain economies in terms of improved livelihood patterns, sensible use of resources and their sustainability.

III. Commonalities and Complementarities

Despite several interventions brought about in the mountain regions through various programmes and project approaches by the national governments and donor agencies, and increasing environmental and sustainability concerns expressed by the international agencies, the mountain regions have by and large remained at the lowest ebb of development trajectory, barring a few stray cases. The primary reason for this failure is that the development has been undertaken from the outside flatlanders or mainstream institutions, and most often in these endeavours the mountain perspectives were either missing or absent. It is, therefore, necessary to incorporate essential prerequisites for attaining the long-term goal of sustainable development (Ives *et al.*, 1997). The hurdles in the way to sustainable development in the poor countries are much more rigorous than the mountain regions of industrialised countries. The major challenges and concerns in the poor countries have been:

1. Mountain Specificities
2. Subsistence Agriculture and Food Deficits
3. Persistent Human Poverty
4. Adverse Terms of Trade and Exploitative Linkage Relations
5. Gender Inequity and Drudgery
6. Environmental Degradation.

1. Mountain Specificities

Mountain specificities have often been neglected at the time of designing and implementation of development programmes, and in most cases, several sectoral projects are designed in the non-mountain context. Such macro decisions have been found to be unrelated to micro level realities, and often inter-sectoral linkages are neglected. As a result, the effectiveness and relevance of such projects remain abysmally low. The main reason behind this is disregarding the mountain perspectives which have been defined as "explicit or implicit consideration of specific mountain conditions and characteristics and their operational implications while conceiving, designing, implementing and assessing interventions in mountain areas" (Jodha *et al.*, 1992). There are evidences of large infrastructural projects (dam and hydro-power projects, mineral exploration, for instance) coming up in the region disregarding the fragility and associated environmental hazards. Also, owing to lack of linkages (ancillary activities) in such projects, most of the benefits (water, irrigation facilities, power etc.) flow to the lowland areas without making major improvements in highland agriculture and other non-agricultural activities. There are successful evidences across the countries where mountain specificities have been incorporated in the development policies and planning, and as a result, the region has seen rapid transformation from the traditional cropping system to diversified market oriented products utilising location specific diversity in the HKH Region (Jodha *et al.*, 1992). The prime examples in the HKH Region are the horticulture products in Himachal Pradesh (India); Technology development and diffusion models of Lumle and Pakhribas Agricultural Centres (Nepal); Aga Khan Rural Support Programme (AKRSP) in North Pakistan and Agro-based cottage industries in Western Sichuan (China).

The case of Himachal Pradesh provides a unique example of transformation from the traditional agriculture to one of the leading horticulture-producing regions, through harnessing the resource niche having comparative advantages. Indeed, the government has played a key role by promoting infrastructure (road network, communication, hydro-electric projects etc.) and by providing institutional support (credit, marketing, price support, processing and development of ancillary activities). All this has far-reaching implications for the diversification process in the rural economy – from farming traditional cereal crops to horticulture crops along with dairy development – which has significantly improved the livelihood options and income levels of the people. Nonetheless, this process has also been accompanied by sustained ecological and resource degradation (land and forest, for example) along with inter-regional inequities (Bhati, 1990). Another example is of Nepal, which is not only land-locked but a vast area of the country is still backward and underdeveloped. With increasing pressure of population and its adverse effect on the natural resource use, the country has been facing the problem of food deficiency and pervasive poverty. The experiments of Lumle and Pakhribas Agricultural projects were truly pioneering in transforming the western and eastern development regions of the country. The Lumle Project had grown from the strong foundation laid at the Lumle Agricultural Centre (LAC), which integrated the institutional, technological and participatory approach with a view to disseminating the relevant technologies to farmers. It had built-up a strong linkage with research, technology, extension, training and other inputs, and involved farmers at every stage with comprehensive understanding of the field conditions that favoured development of overall farming system. This project had successfully demonstrated that the mountain farming could provide sustainable livelihoods to its population (Pound *et al.*, 1992). Likewise, Pakhribas Agricultural Centre (PAC) was established in the eastern development region with a view to carrying out multi-disciplinary farmer-oriented research activities, utilising local resource for sustainable farming, evolving appropriate technologies suiting local conditions, and involving communities so that long-term sustainable farming system could be developed. The Pakhribas Project has developed suitable technologies for crop production, indigenously bred varieties, fodder and firewood and overall farming system (Chand *et al.*, 1992). These projects have not only proved to be sustainable in the hill farming context but highly replicable to other HKH region. The success of these types of projects largely relied on external funding, autonomous working environment, flexibility, strong linkages, participatory approach and a zeal to transform, but the lack or absence of these attributes might not have produced the desired results by these pioneering projects. Yet another example is from the Northern-most districts of Pakistan where the Aga Khan Rural Support Programmes (AKRSP) with its sustained efforts had created village level institutions combining the productive physical infrastructure and resource management which made a significant impact in the village economies in terms of increased opportunities of incomes and livelihoods (Husain, 1992). It is one of the finest examples of how the subsistence and rather static village economies in the region saw transformation into the economies of opportunities and well-being of the people. Thus, it truly represents a community development project based on strong institutional foundation. But how far such institutional innovations would continue to evolve and spread in village economies in a fast changing environment largely dictated by the market, remains a key question. The other notable example in the region is Western Sichuan (China), which possessed enormous diversity of resource base (plant, animal, agro-cottage) that has provided the region an advantage of developing variety of cottage industries, which helped to transform the subsistence economy into a commodity producing and exchanger economy (Zhaoguang, *et al.*, 1992). Of course, the locational advantages were also associated with constraints posed by the inaccessibility to the road network, market and other support services that had produced considerable bottleneck in the way to reap the full benefits.

However, the above innovative examples are neither many in the regions nor these have been replicated to the extent desired. As a result, the economies in the regions, by and large, suffer from food deficiency, human poverty and degradation of natural resources thereby posing serious threats to the sustainability of mountain economies. Thus, there are few lessons to be learned within the regions, and numerous lessons to be unlearned from within the regions, which clearly show why certain projects succeeded and why others could not even be designed or evolved.

2. Subsistence Agriculture and Food Deficits

Mountain agriculture includes all land-based activities such as crop farming, horticulture, animal husbandry and forestry carried out in an integrated manner. Agriculture base has generally been at a low or subsistence level employing traditional technology and localised inputs with very little output meant for the markets. Such system had extensive linkages to all the land-based activities using traditional adaptation mechanisms with little or no external linkages. Over the years, there have been changes in land use, cropping pattern, input use, production, and livestock composition because of increasing population, accessibility (transport and communication), state interventions and market network. Generally, there has been stagnation in growth in the area under cereal crops, but an increase in productivity in several areas, through crop diversification and use of chemical fertilisers, and a decline in high-value cash crops and spurt in micro livestock dairies (Tulachan, 2000). Increasing pressure of population also led to extensive use of land resources in marginal and forestlands thereby putting strain in existing land resource with adverse effects on ecology. Despite the intensification of production with expansion of cropped area, the foodgrain production is not enough to meet the growing demands of population, and therefore, people have to resort to multiple livelihood strategies to eke out their livings. Mountain agriculture is thus becoming more and more unsustainable due to fragmentation of landholdings, displacement of marginalised farmers, landlessness, natural disaster accompanied by ever increasing burden of young age population.

3. Persistent Human Poverty

Human poverty is a consequence of various forces that work in a complex mountain specificities' context, which produces cumulative and causative effects that keep a large number of people in a state under continued human poverty. In China, for example, out of 80 million poor people (reported in 1993), a great majority were from the mountain minority people. Some of the poorest mountainous countries in the region are Nepal, Bhutan, and Afghanistan. Mountain regions of Uttarakhand (India), Northern Pakistan and Xizang in China presumably have very high proportion of poor people, as they tend to be invisible because of aggregating census data (Ives, 1997). More than 60 per cent of rural Andean population lives in extreme poverty (Denniston, 1995). The Philippines is yet another example where mountain area has abysmally low rate of human development index (0.410) than the national capital region (0.871) – the life expectancy being 55 years, and more than 55 per cent people live in poverty compared to 15 per cent in the national capital region (UNDP,

1996). It is also observed that mountainous/landlocked countries are often among the poorest ones in the world (*e.g.*, Nepal, Ethiopia, Bolivia); mountain regions in less developed countries are generally among the poorest regions in these countries (for Uttarakhand in India, Yunnan and Xizang in China, and northern Pakistan); and mountain regions even in developed economies such as Austria and Switzerland are comparatively less affluent than the lowland areas of these countries (Ives, 1997).

Human poverty is closely related to the basic activities in which vast population is engaged in – primarily agriculture – which is not only at subsistence level but also a low productive activity. Subsistence agriculture on scattered and uneconomical holdings, being entirely under rainfed conditions with limited scope for the technological improvements resulted in a large region as food deficit which led to increasing dependence on import of foodgrains. This is the main cause of widespread poverty that compels a large majority of households to resort to a variety of livelihood activities within off-farm and non-farm sectors. Pluriactivity is most common in such economies as a coping mechanism. Out-migration is also an offshoot of household livelihood strategy that takes place to a considerable extent from such depressed regions. This kind of outflow has obvious implications for the place of origin, which suffers not only from the shortage of able-bodied men for carrying out agricultural activities, but also forces the burden of cultivation on women thus creating extraordinary drudgery for women. Not only this, inaccessibility results in lack of publicly provided goods and services, particularly at distant locations, and also increases the cost of living due to prevailing high price levels. Often, the usual poverty surveys based on consumption levels show lower intensity of poverty levels (headcounts) in the mountain areas than the better areas in non-mountain areas (India, Nepal and Pakistan, for example). However, such surveys do not take into account the hill specificities that require more energy levels in terms of calorie intake, warm clothing and permanent shelter. If higher calorie needs, warm clothing, permanent shelter including higher prices prevalent in these areas is taken into account, the poverty ratio in the hill region would be much higher than what is arrived at by the conventional surveys (Papola, 2002).

4. Exploitative Terms of Trade and Exploitative Linkage Relation

Mountain economies have certain distinct advantages than the flatland economies in terms of natural resources (e.g., water, forest, mineral resources, tourism amenities services, and other niche products such as herbs, flowers, seeds, fruits, and vegetables) which are the fundamental basis for linkages between the high and lowland economies. This unequal endowment base between the two economies generates flow of goods, services and resources, and terms of trade. Owing to hill specificities (inaccessibility, fragility and marginality), it becomes difficult for the mountain economies to harness these niche resources and engage them in the external trade. This in turn perpetuates them to remain marginal entities in their economic interactions with the mainland economies (Jodha, 1997; 2000). This kind of interaction develops a relationship between the mountains and the plains as of a hinterland-metropolis type, in which former acts as supplier of resources (raw material) to the latter. The lowland economy therefore acts as suction pumps, pulling in the resources from the highland economy for the benefits of their own with little or no value additions to the highland economy. Extraction of timber, water and mining resources from the highland are the prime examples of this interaction. On the other hand, flow of goods and services from the lowland to highland has been in the form of consumer goods – mainly foodgrains, and in any case, the volume of such trade from the lowland to highland has been low. This kind of trade has largely been remained unidirectional (from highland to lowland also) making the former as net looser from such extractive trade. The other kinds of flows from lowland to highland relate to investment in development activities mainly in infrastructure development. However, the infrastructure development has both positive and negative implications for the highland economy. It has provided supplementary means of subsistence and greater interactions to the markets in the plains and also aroused the aspirations of people through demonstration effects. Also, construction of road and communication network has eased the inaccessibility. But providing infrastructure facilities do not induce the growth process automatically – rather it leads to backwash effects, primarily because the infrastructural development in the highland fails to generate indigenous momentum of development through linkage effect (Papola, 1996). Large-scale infrastructural development has often taken place at the cost of negating the ecological, environmental and human aspects of the hill region that has caused more harm to the sustainability of mountain resources. This kind of infrastructural development has actually made possible more vigorous extraction of mountain resources either by government or by the private contractors. Extraction of resources required new skills, enterprise and capital, which was more easily seized by the private entrepreneurs from the lowland, and not by the locals. A fast growing contractor-business class regime has exploited the forest and mineral wealth indiscriminately. Development administration has been insensitive to the needs of the hill people. Their movements from the mountain regions are a clear sign of the neglect of their aspirations and lack of a sustainable development of the hill economy (Joshi, 1995; 1999). The deliberate extractive policy of these resources by private contractors and the government has led to rapid resource degradation from the highlands to the lowlands without adequate compensatory mechanisms. The large projects like erecting dams, hydro projects, and mining activities has severe negative implications for the local economy, since there are little or no local economic linkages of these large projects. Also, they cause huge dislocation and disruptions of habitats, while the benefits of these projects flow to the lowland economies. Not only this, a large flow of out-migration from the highland to lowland areas is happening uninterruptedly, primarily because of low economic base and lack of opportunities. This outflow is a drain of human resources for the local economy and costs enormously in terms of drudgery to the women, though it generates cash income for mountain families. However, the net gains from out-migration in terms of monetary resources are quite mixed. This kind of development generates backwash rather than the spread effects of development, and the terms of trade becomes highly unequal and against the highland economies. These inequitable linkages have shown worsening economic and environmental impacts on the highland economies, and have much wider policy implications.

Therefore, there is a need to evolve a compensatory mechanism that brings more gains to mountain areas, which often flow to the lowlands rather than the highlands. It is being increasingly felt that the economic linkages between the highlands and lowlands, and the development of either cannot be carried out in isolation from the other. Hence, there is an urgent need for an integrated approach to highland-lowland development (Jodha, 1997). Even in the context of liberalisation, the highland economies, particularly in Andes and Himalaya, are unlikely to benefit from it because these economies seldom enjoy absolute cost advantage either in agriculture or at industry. Subsistence nature of agriculture with high population growth may even further increase their disadvantage and exacerbate the inequalities. However, such adverse effect will be less severe in the case of western Alps, where the population growth is relatively low, and tourism and amenity industry is better developed (Rieder and Wyder, 1997).

5. Gender Inequity and Drudgery

Women are the principal agents of production in mountain agriculture and central to all the household activities. They undertake most of the agricultural operations barring ploughing; they bring fodder and water from distant places and undertake numerous household activities such as cooking, washing, childcare, etc. The most arduous tasks are bringing fuel-wood, fodder and water. Because of environmental degradation, they have to walk down further, which involves more time and drudgery. They are overburdened with all activities in the household. Yet, they have little or no access and control over resources (e.g., land), and most of the household decisions are taken by the male members – whether it is related to sale and purchase of assets, children's education or even to migrate. Out-migration of male members put additional burden on the women and increases the hardship of women-headed households, as they have to perform the tasks which men traditionally used to do. They have limited access to labour market and worse, the socio-cultural factors inhibit women to seek employment beyond a limited segment of the labour market. Moreover, women suffer from social discrimination which has adverse effects in terms of poverty, access to food, health and nutrition, educational facilities and workloads. This kind of gender discrimination seems to be entrenched and pervasive in many parts of the HKH Region.

6. Environmental Degradation

Environmental degradation is a resultant process of many factors that has adverse impacts on environmental capital consisting of species, habitats, eco-system and stock of natural resources. This process of degradation is a natural phenomenon and also attributed to human activities carried out either for subsistence, development or commercial purposes. Historically, rise in population led to expansion of cultivated areas in marginal land and subsequently in forest areas, primarily to meet food requirements. This process involved clearing of forests. Further, increased requirement of fuel and fodder, uncontrolled grazing, and increasing demand for other natural resources also put pressure on forest areas. Timber being the most important forest produce from the point of view of commercial purposes, cutting of trees by the unscrupulous traders and contractors or even by the government agencies have taken a heavy toll on forest resources. Upstream damage as a result of reckless deforestation severely affected the downstream habitats as well (e.g., floods). The recurrent disasters like landslides, earthquakes, forest fires and other hazards have been increasing in the mountain economies. Large-scale unplanned construction activities have serious environmental consequences owing to lack of understanding of mountain construction approaches. Government policies, large development projects and commercial interests, implemented without taking into account the environmental aspects, have also added to environmental degradation. All these factors have serious repercussions on the sustainability of environment and on the livelihood of mountain population. Key challenge of sustainable development is the interaction between economic growth and natural environment that supports it, lies at the core of sustainable development. Economic growth contributes to higher levels of human well-being, and provides the resources to address a range of environmental objectives. Economic growth can however also lead to excessive degradation of natural and environmental resources, when incentives for their use are inappropriate, and external effects are not internalised. Historically, economic growth has meant transforming much of societies' stock of natural resources into other forms of capital. Today, maintaining functioning ecosystems that can support economic and social development is recognised as crucial for development to last, especially when no substitutes are available" (OECD, 2001).

IV. Conclusion

There are commonalities in mountain areas in terms of bio-physical characteristics, greater environmental concerns, subsistence agriculture, lack of development and marginalisation of population. However, these areas have certain distinct advantages in terms of forest wealth, water resources, tourist amenity services and other niche products, etc. in which they have comparative advantages than the non-mountain regions. Some regions or areas have been able to harness these resources up to their advantage using appropriate development strategies, whereas many areas could not do so mainly because of lack of infrastructure development and other developmental activities. The development trajectory, therefore vary across mountain regions because of differences in growth drivers.

During the 18th Century, the mountain region of Europe had similar conditions as many mountain regions of poor HKH or Andean regions have today. The mountain region of Europe developed during the late 18th and early 19th Centuries credited to strong external linkages from the regions experiencing industrial revolution, and fast agricultural growth. Industrial revolution had changed the production relationship that had benefited mountain region significantly. Development of transport (railways and navigation) had facilitated trade and out-migration from the mountain regions, which helped to reduce demographic pressures to certain extent. External linkages to the areas experiencing fast growth in employment and incomes had favoured the growth of mountain areas in terms of infrastructural development, employment opportu-nities, education, skill and tourism development, while linkages in the Andean and HKH regions have been mostly to the regions or areas which are marginally better-off than the mountain areas (Banskota, 2000). The population growth in these regions is significantly higher and this had an adverse effect on the environment and ecology. Infrastructure development is still at a nascent stage in these regions with limited internal linkages. The tourism industry has been promoted in many parts of HKH Region but environmental considerations are neglected and internal linkages are often found weak. Many mountain economies in Alps are helped by the national economies in the form of subsidies and greater flow of funds to ameliorate the inequalities. Development strategies in Austria, France, Slovenia, Switzerland are more 'proactive', targeted at a new mountain economy organised around tourism industry, quality agricultural products and agro-tourism, transport facilities, and in some cases, high-tech industries and certain activities in the services sector (e.g., health care, spa's) (Mountain Areas in Europe, 2004).

The ultimate objective is to achieve what has aptly described in the world summit on sustainable development that "sustainable management of mountain resources means enabling mountain populations to earn a livelihood, providing protection against natural hazards, enhancing conservation of natural resources, safeguarding social and cultural traditions, and supporting development that takes account of the special features of mountain regions, and ensures that the interests of both mountain and lowland populations become equal parts of a fundamental social contract" (WSSD, 2002). It is, therefore, necessary to formulate a mountain perspective framework that incorporates growth with equity and addresses the issues like mountain agriculture, persistent poverty, sustainable livelihood, environment protection and gender dimension. Such perspective would call for an integrated approach to development dovetailing the mountain specificities adequately, in order to achieve desired objectives.

2

Issues and Diversity of Development Experience of Indian Hill Economies

I. Problems of Hill Economies

Historically, heavy dependence on subsistence agriculture, lack of transport, communication and other development activities had kept the hill economies largely at a subsistence level. This type of economy has been closely knitted to the social structure based on mutual obligation and livelihood security. Along with subsistence agriculture, certain types of traditional village industries developed based on the locally available raw material and specialisation. The nature of village industries was largely linked to rural economy which produced mostly for final consumption. There was little surplus for reinvestment, and at best, these village industrial units were operating at a low margin of subsistence. Primary processing activities dominated these industries. The system of mutual obligation and social security resulted in some kind of trading. However, the trade was not meant for the market but for subserving largely the social and economic needs of the community based on exchange and barter system. In any case, trade was minimal for the market primarily because of subsistence nature of the economy. Whatever little trade took place was limited to generate cash requirements for meeting household needs (i.e. non-food items). Such trade primarily occurred not to produce surplus but often to meet the compulsion of cash requirements. To a large extent, such cash requirements were met through remittances particularly by the out-migrants.

Due to distinct geo-physical structure and location-specific problems of these areas, region-specific plan strategies have been formulated keeping in view the basic needs of the people, and priorities of the concerned state governments. From the Fifth Five Year Plan onwards, hill areas started getting increasing attention under the special hill area development programme and with higher allocation of resources made to improve the development activities in the region. Later, Hill Sub-plan, Tribal Area Sub-plan, Tribal Development Agency projects, Western Ghats Development Programme, Border Area Development and North-Eastern Council were formulated. The Central Government has been supplementing the efforts of the state governments in this direction through special Central assistance for special area programmes.

These states have been receiving liberal grants-in-aid from the Central Government under various schemes. The Hill Area Development Programme (HADP) continues to be funded through Special Central Assistance on 90 :10 Centre : State basis.

Also, in certain cases, some states got special financial packages from the Central Government to alleviate special problems facing the state governments. With an increasing focus on infrastructural development, numerous development activities spurt in the region mainly in the form of road, communication, electricity, expansion of education, health, commerce and introduction of new technology in agriculture. Many other sectoral development schemes (such as agriculture, horticulture, irrigation, animal husbandry, social welfare, industry, forestry, etc.) were also started to promote developmental activities. Owing to increased accessibility, spurt in development activities and induction of modern technology, there has been widespread awareness among the people about the new economic options and opportunities that are being offered by the significant changes occurring in the development front. A whole range of new initiatives has been undertaken with a view to improving farming practices and for better options of livelihoods. Several NGOs have emerged in the scene in recent years to supplement the government efforts in this direction. Indeed, all these efforts have helped in improving the livelihood opportunities. However, the results of these development initiatives have been varied or mixed, and most often without much significant impacts. The development efforts have helped, in particular, to those who have relatively better resource base (i.e., land, assets, education and skills), have proximity to road head and access to markets and other inputs. A large majority of the people has thus remained marginalised in the development process.

The hill economy has increasingly confronted with the challenges and problems concerning to sustainable livelihoods, mountain agriculture, persistent poverty, fragile environment, and female drudgery. Traditionally, hill people are meeting their food and other non-food requirements through crop cultivation, livestock rearing and collection of forest produce. Increasing population along with rising aspiration of people due to expansion of development activities and better livelihood options has led to increasing pressure on land and other limited traditional resources. The cultivable land being scarce is getting further fragmented with the increase of population, and it has hard-pressed the people to look for alternative livelihood strategies. The alternative strategies consisted of the extension of cultivation on hitherto uncultivated marginal land (though limited), improvement in quality of livestock, diversification of agriculture into high value crops such as horticulture and non-food crops for the market. But these coping strategies have limitations in providing food security to the people on a sustainable basis because of low productivity of resources and the problems associated with the hill specificities on the one hand, and increasing population on the other. The limited resources, low bargaining strength, lack of appropriate institutional mechanism for the access to market, credit and other inputs have severely restricted expansion of livelihood opportunities. The mountain agriculture, therefore, could not ensure food security and, instead, increased the vulnerability of the people. The numerous development activities have both positive and negative impacts on the hill economy. The inaccessibility, for example, has been reduced through development of road transport linking to different parts of the region, but the fragility factor has severely restricted road transport to penetrate beyond certain areas as it involves high risk in development of transport network and other infrastructure. Positive effects have been in terms of relatively increased mobility of people and resources within the region and exposure to outside the region; whereas the negative effects have been in terms of increased outflow of men and resources, and breakdown of traditional livelihood security. Not only this, increased transport and other linkages between the hills and the plane areas have led to higher access to the natural resources of the former.

The natural resources (viz., timber, minerals and minor forest-products) are being gradually exploited and even overexploited by the unscrupulous contractors, traders and other agencies to meet the growing demands from the plane areas. This kind of unidirectional trade from the hill to plane areas has generated value addition to the latter at the cost of the former, and the benefits thereof have been mostly accrued to the plane areas. This led to the drain of hill resources and adverse environmental effects, which in turn, produced adverse terms of trade in the region. One of the direct manifestations of this kind of development process is the increased out-migration of people in the towns and cities in search of jobs and livelihoods, which has resulted in adverse implications to the village economy in terms of unfavourable sex ratio, increased women's drudgery, diminishing yields from alternative livelihood options and greater dependency on remittance. This process accentuated further as links to outside region increased. Increasing exposure aroused the aspirations of the people on the one hand, and the limited potential for development made it difficult to provide sustainable livelihood opportunities on the other. Improvements in agriculture technology elsewhere did not help much the hill economy due to the problems associated with hill specificities. Although there has been some diversification from cereal-growing to horticulture (mainly fruits and vegetables) over a period of time, yet it is limited to certain pockets of the economies that are well connected through road transport. Overall, there has been an insufficient food supply within the mountain region which has increased the dependence on food imports from outside region. The preconditions of agriculture growth, such as intensification of resource use, input absorption capacity, infrastructural back up and economies of scale do not exist in the hill region due to the conditions of fragility and marginality (Jodha, 2000). Also, relatively low accessibility results in limited mobility and high cost of inputs, which severely restricts the possibility of promoting staple or chief commodity and exploiting other niche products in the region. This in turn, inhibits the trade and specialisation to grow for the market, mainly because, neither surplus is produced nor do the hill specificities permit trade to develop in a wider scale. In any case, trade in the region is minimal for the market due to subsistence nature of the economy. The manufacturing base, in any case, is miniscule barring *tarai* areas, which have relatively favourable industrial climate. No large industries can be set up in the hilly region due to conditions like fragility, lack of transportation network (rail), markets, power and economies of scale. Village and household industries based on livestock, food processing and natural resource have been promoted, but it could not generate self-reinforcing and self-sustaining forces owing to small scale operation, little quantity, dispersed production and lack of access to appropriate institutions (Papola, 2000). Over a period of time, the base of these industries has weakened. Moreover, these industries have been subjected to increasing competition from the similar products from plane areas that are superior in terms of quality, and their prices are much cheaper than the local products. This has made an adverse impact on the local economy. The weak agriculture and industrial base would obviously have far reaching implications for the hill economies. The volume of trade would be low, and even it would have adverse impact in the areas where the region might have absolute or comparative advantages (say, tourism, forest products and other niche products). This is a clear sign of minimal or no trade. Ironically, when trade does not occur, it has positive effects on the region. The trade related exploitation is minimal or not experienced at all. Therefore, in case of no-trade or minimal trade, the advantages as well as disadvantages occurring from trade is the least. The features of isolation, fragility and marginality thus produce a circular constellation of forces in the region so as to keep the economy more or less at subsistence level. Another important feature is diversity. Diversity is widespread not only within the region but also across sub-regions, villages and within villages. This diversity can be seen in terms of culture, dialects, human adaptation, living pattern, indigenous knowledge and local resources. Diversity also results in negative as well as positive effects. Negative effect in the sense that no single solution can be found to overcome the problems of development in a situation of diversity. However, often micro solutions are helpful and easier than the macro solutions for tackling the problems relating to diversity, which can have the positive effects. This diversity, if properly understood and dovetailed in the planning process, can help develop certain activities, which might have absolute or comparative advantages (say, herbs and medicinal plants and use of other local resources). Diversity can also have profound positive effects on promoting, protecting and conserving environment through traditional methods.

The development trajectories of the hill states have generally been viewed from the perspective of subsistence nature of the economy, wherein a large majority of people are engaged in agriculture based activities for sustenance. Industrial base is generally weak, and services sector largely represents amorphous government aided activities. Too much dependence on Central Government for grants and weak financial base for internal resource mobilisation have put these economies in a vulnerable position. The development is largely support-based driven by the exogenous factors rather than generating indigenous momentum of growth. The dilemma is that, though these economies possess good amount of natural resources and also have comparative advantages in certain products, many of these states have not been able to harness their niche resources, and consequently, remained largely at the lowest ebb of development trajectories. In spite of certain commonalities in terms of bio-physical characteristics, there exists a wide diversity among hill states in respect of resource base, potentialities and socio-cultural differentiations. The development strategies therefore require to be distinct in different hill economies in view of regional specificities (Papola, *et al.*, 1983). Nevertheless, it would be useful to look into some of the development indicators that might throw some light in the relative performances.

II. Diversity and Development Problems

1. Demographic Profile

The Himalayan Region covers 10 states, namely, Jammu & Kashmir (J&K), Himachal Pradesh, Uttarakhand, Sikkim, Arunachal Pradesh, Nagaland, Manipur, Mizoram, Tripura, Meghalaya and Darjeeling district of West Bengal, and Karbi Anglong and North Cachar districts of Assam. Population growth in the hill states has been generally higher than the national average with considerable variations in terms of population density. Out of these 10 states, the population growth in seven states during 1991-01, and that in six states during 2001-11, are more than the national average. Nagaland, Sikkim and Manipur have not only recorded the highest growth rate but also saw an increase in growth rate during 1991-01. Barring Arunachal Pradesh, Mizoram and Tripura, where the population growth has substantially declined in 1991-01, in other states population has still recorded very high growth. Population growth declined significantly in most of the hill states barring Uttarakhand which registered small decline during 2001-11. Nagaland is the only state which has recorded a small negative growth after very high growth in the previous decade. The density of population is sparse ranging from a minimum of 17 in Arunachal Pradesh to 350 in Tripura, and all the hill states have lower density than the national average. A high degree of variation is observed in the levels of urbanisation across different states ranging from 10 per cent in Himachal Pradesh to about 51.5 per cent in Mizoram in 2011. The growth of urban population has been phenomenal in certain states, particularly in Sikkin, Nagaland and Tripura during 2001-11. Manipur however shows erratic pattern during 1991-2001. Probably, the decline in urban population is due to the fact that many villages which were parts of urban areas in earlier census has now been declassified as rural. Urbanisation in most of the hill states has been lower than the national average except in Mizoram (Table 2.1). The more populous states like Himachal Pradesh, J&K and Uttarakhand have generally shown a steady pattern of urbanisation over the years. However, the less populous states show an occasional spurt in the growth of urban population stretching upon the existing few urban centres.

2. Social Development

Hill states have generally performed better in attaining higher level of literacy. Barring Arunachal Pradesh and J&K most of the states have achieved much higher level of literacy rates than that of the country as a whole. Mizoram has achieved a remarkable progress with over 91.6 per cent literacy, being the second highest performing state in the country after Kerala. Tripura, Himachal Pradesh and Mizoram have achieved over 90 per cent male literacy rates. The J&K is the only state where higher level of gender disparity is noted. In other states, disparity is lower than the All-India level (Table 2.2).

Table 2.1 : Demographic Profiles of the Hill States

State	*Percentage decadal growth*		*Population density per sq. km.*	*Percentage of urban population*		
	1991-01	*2001-11*	*2011*	*1991*	*2001*	*2011*
J&K	29.43	23.71	124	23.83	24.81	27.21
Himachal Pradesh	17.54	12.81	122	8.69	9.80	10.04
Uttarakhand	20.41	19.17	189	22.97	25.67	30.55
Sikkim	33.06	12.36	86	9.10	11.07	24.97
Arunachal Pradesh	27.00	25.92	17	12.80	20.75	22.67
Nagaland	64.53	-0.47	119	17.21	17.23	28.97
Manipur	24.86	18.65	122	27.52	25.11	30.21
Mizoram	28.82	22.78	52	46.10	49.63	51.51
Tripura	16.03	14.75	350	15.30	17.06	26.18
Meghalaya	30.65	27.82	132	18.60	19.58	20.08
India	**21.54**	**17.64**	**382**	**25.71**	**27.81**	**31.16**

Source: *Registrar General of India, Census of India, 2001 and 2011 (Provisional Population Totals Paper 1 and 2).*

Table 2.2 : Literacy Rates

State	*Literacy Rates, 2001*			
	Person	*Male*	*Female*	*Gender gap*
J&K	68.74	78.26	58.01	0.74
Himachal Pradesh	83.78	90.83	76.60	0.84
Uttarakhand	79.63	88.33	70.70	0.80
Sikkim	82.20	87.30	76.43	0.87
Arunachal Pradesh	66.95	73.69	59.57	0.81
Nagaland	80.11	83.29	76.69	0.92
Manipur	79.85	86.49	73.17	0.84
Mizoram	91.58	93.72	89.40	0.95
Tripura	87.75	92.18	83.15	0.90
Meghalaya	75.48	77.17	73.78	0.95
All India	**74.04**	**82.14**	**65.46**	**0.79**

Source: Registrar General of India, Census of India, Provisional Population Totals Paper 1, 2011

3. Poverty Levels

Poverty in the hill context has generally been explained within the resource bias thesis or highland-lowland linkages relationship, which essentially looks at the resources being extracted for the use of lowland's priority interest and neglecting the interests of mountain people. This kind of explanation, however, gives a subordinate role to the peoples' centrality approach in poverty analysis in contrast to sustainability approach that gives the central place to people than the resources.

There are certain problems with regard to poverty data in the hill states. In most cases, poverty data in individual states are aggregated, and not reported separately, primarily because relatively very low levels of population inhabit mountain areas. The NSSO – the data-generating agency – does not give adequate representation to smaller states due to their size and sparse population. Secondly, the poverty line in the north-eastern states is identical because poverty levels in Assam are used for all other states in that region, and therefore, poverty data do not indicate the differentiation, hence their accuracy is often doubted. This problem is referred to as 'statistical invisibility'. Moreover, there are problems of comparability in these estimates over time. Percentage of population below poverty line in 2004-05, for instance, is not comparable with that in 1999-2000 based on uniform recall period, but can be compared with 1993-94 and earlier rounds. Likewise, proportion of population below poverty line in 2004-05 is, roughly but not strictly, comparable with that in 1999-2000 based on mixed recall period.

If poverty data are assumed to be reliable, then half of the hill states (namely, Sikkim, Arunachal Pradesh, Nagaland, Tripura and Meghalaya) had higher level of poverty levels in rural areas compared to national average in 1993-94 albeit with very low intensity of urban poverty in all the states. In 2004-05, poverty levels at All-India levels declined by about 7.7 percentage points, and rural and urban poverty declined by 9 and 6.7 percentage points respectively over 1993-94. Barring Uttarakhand, most of the hill states saw rapid decline in the rural poverty levels. North-eastern states recorded almost 23 percentage points' decline in the poverty levels. Poverty estimates in the North-eastern Region are based on the consumer expenditure data collected by the NSS relating to Assam. Price variations of rural-urban population shares are only considered, which influence state-specific estimates. Studies show that there are marked difference in the nature of poverty levels between the planes and the hills (North-eastern Region: Vision 2020). Similarly, J&K and Himachal Pradesh have about 26 percentage point's and 20 percentage point's decline in rural poverty levels, respectively during 1993-94 and 2004-05, which are much higher than the All-India average. Urban poverty levels are also very low in these states except Uttarakhand, which shows about 11 percentage point's higher urban poverty as compared to All-India average.

Uttarakhand is a peculiar hill state where proportion of poor below poverty line is alarmingly high at 39.6 per cent (combined) with rural poverty at 40.8 per cent and urban poverty at 39.8 per cent.* It is one of the poorest states after Orissa, Bihar, Chhattisgarh and Jharkhand.

Table 2.3 : Populations Below Poverty Line

State	*Population below poverty line*					
	1993-94			*2004-05*		
	Combined	*Rural*	*Urban*	*Combined*	*Rural*	*Urban*
J&K	25.17	30.34	9.18	5.4	4.6	7.9
Himachal Pradesh	28.44	30.34	9.18	10.0	10.7	3.4
Uttarakhand	NA	NA	NA	39.6	40.8	36.5
Sikkim	41.43	45.01	7.73	20.1	22.3	3.3
Arunachal Pradesh	39.35	45.01	7.73	17.6	22.3	3.3
Nagaland	37.92	45.01	7.73	19.0	22.3	3.3
Manipur	33.78	45.01	7.73	17.3	22.3	3.3
Mizoram	25.66	45.01	7.73	12.6	22.3	3.3
Tripura	39.01	45.01	7.73	18.9	22.3	3.3
Meghalaya	37.92	45.01	7.73	18.5	22.3	3.3
All India	**35.97**	**37.27**	**32.36**	**27.5**	**28.3**	**25.7**

Source : Based on uniform recall period (30 days), Planning Commission, Government of India

* BPL survey conducted by the Rural Development Department (BPL Survey, 2002) in the state estimated the proportion of BPL families at 47.20 per cent, which are similar to the estimates presented by the Planning Commission.

4. Human Development Indicators

A comparative picture of the status of human development in various states and the Union Territories is presented in the National Human Development Report 2001, brought out by the Planning Commission in March, 2002. The Human Develop-ment Index (HDI), as considered in this Report, is a composite of variables capturing attainments in three dimensions of human development, namely, economy, education and health. These have been considered on the basis of (a) per capita monthly expenditure adjusted for inequality; (b) a combination of literacy rate and intensity of formal education; and (c) a combination of life expectancy at 1 year of age and infant mortality rate.

The Gender Disparity Index is estimated as a proportion of female attainments to that of male for a common set of variables. It can be seen that the relative positions of J&K, Sikkim, Arunachal Pradesh, Tripura and Meghalaya are at the lower end of performance, however, the relative ranking of Himachal Pradesh, Nagaland, Manipur and Mizoram are better and below half way.Also, the latter states have performed better in reducing gender disparity except Nagaland (Table 2.4).

Table 2.4 : Human Development Index, 1991

State	*1991*		
	Value	*Rank*	*Gender disparity index rank*
J&K	0.402	21	25
Himachal Pradesh	0.469	13	4
Uttarakhand	NA	NA	NA
Sikkim	0.425	18	20
Arunachal Pradesh	0.328	29	18
Nagaland	0.486	11	21
Manipur	0.536	9	3
Mizoram	0.548	7	6
Tripura	0.389	22	29
Meghalaya	0.365	24	12
All India	**0.381**	**0.676**	

Note: Such a composite index is not available in respect of the hill states for the recent years.

Sources : National Human Development Report, Planning Commission, 2001

5. Consumption Expenditure

Average level of consumption expenditure is an important indicator for assessing the well-being of the people. While generally the per capita consumption expenditure has shown an improvement during 1994 to 2005, the states like Arunachal Pradesh, Manipur, Tripura and Uttarakhand have either recorded lower per capita consumption or closer to national average, particularly in the case of urban areas. In terms of annual growth, there has been a perceptible decline of per capita expenditure both in rural and urban areas in 2004-05 over 1999-2000. In 1994-2000, two states in rural areas (Tripura and Meghalaya) and six states in urban areas (J&K, Himachal Pradesh, Sikkim, Arunachal Pradesh, Tripura and Meghalaya) had recorded lower growth rate as compared to all-India average. In 2004-05, the situation has worsened as four states in rural areas (Nagaland, Manipur, Mizoram and Tripura) (Tripura with negative growth) and all the hill states in urban areas slipped into lower per capita consumption expenditure growth compared to all-India average. Clearly, the welfare in terms of consumption expenditure has lowered in recent years (Table 2.5).

Increase in per capita consumption expenditure may not necessarily reflect the increase in the well-being of different deciles of population, particularly if distribution of consumption expenditure is not taken into account in rural and urban areas. Such inter-inequalities in rural and urban areas are captured by the Gini-coefficient ratios. It is observed that rural inequality in per capita consumption expenditure has declined in most of the states except in Sikkim, Nagaland, Manipur, and Mizoram, where inequality has increased during 1994-2000. But, during 2000-05, inequality has increased sharply in most of the hill states in rural as well as urban areas barring Arunachal and Manipur. Inequalities are more pronounced in rural areas of J & K, Himachal Pradesh, Sikkim and Nagaland, and urban areas of Tripura and Meghalaya. The lowest rural-urban inequalities have been observed in Sikkim and J & K, and the highest in Tripura in 2004-05 (Table 2.6).

Table 2.5 : Per Capita Consumption Expenditure (Rs./month)

State	*1993-94*		*1999-2000*		*2004-05*		*ACGR 1994-2000*		*ACGR 2000-05*	
	Rural	*Urban*	*Rural*	*Urban*	*Rural*	*Urban*	*Rural*	*Urban*	*Rural*	*Urban*
J&K	363.31	541.58	677.23	952.85	793.16	1070.12	10.94	9.87	3.21	2.35
Himachal Pradesh	350.63	746.92	684.50	1242.93	798.11	1390.07	11.79	8.86	3.12	2.26
Uttarakhand	NA	NA	NA	NA	647.15	978.26	—	—	—	—
Sikkim	298.72	518.44	531.68	905.69	688.53	1106.79	10.09	9.74	5.31	4.09
Arunachal Pradesh	258.11	458.60	648.00	762.00	771.53	881.10	16.58	8.83	3.55	2.95
Nagaland	441.45	510.02	941.30	1242.39	1010.81	1498.47	13.45	16.00	1.44	3.82
Manipur	299.57	319.55	537.79	707.77	614.20	726.38	10.24	14.17	2.69	0.52
Mizoram	389.55	549.51	721.83	1056.64	778.35	1200.51	10.83	11.51	1.52	2.59
Tripura	343.93	489.94	528.41	876.59	487.63	1000.54	7.42	10.18	-1.59	2.68
Meghalaya	356.98	530.55	563.64	971.87	655.30	1190.09	7.91	10.61	3.06	4.13
All India	**281.40**	**458.00**	**486.08**	**854.96**	**558.78**	**1052.36**	**9.54**	**10.96**	2.83	4.24

Source : Consumer Expenditure Surveys, various NSS rounds.

Table 2.6 : Gini Ratio of Per Capita Consumption Expenditure

State	*1993-94*		*1999-2000*		*2004-05*	
	Rural	*Urban*	*Rural*	*Urban*	*Rural*	*Urban*
J&K	0.234	0.282	0.184	0.223	0.237	0.244
Himachal Pradesh	0.275	0.435	0.236	0.298	0.295	0.318
Uttarakhand	NA	NA	NA	NA	0.279	0.320
Sikkim	0.207	0.249	0.221	0.256	0.263	0.257
Arunachal Pradesh	0.300	0.275	0.292	0.298	0.272	0.243
Nagaland	0.153	0.195	0.155	0.206	0.209	0.233
Manipur	0.149	0.153	0.192	0.216	0.158	0.175
Mizoram	0.165	0.174	0.188	0.237	0.194	0.244
Tripura	0.236	0.279	0.189	0.294	0.215	0.338
Meghalaya	0.271	0.239	0.149	0.205	0.155	0.258
All India	**0.282**	**0.340**	**0.258**	**0.341**	**0.297**	**0.373**

Source : Consumer Expenditure Surveys, various NSS rounds.

6. Growth Rates

Analysis of Net State Domestic Product (NSDP) gives some indication of economic performance in the hill states. It can be seen that the performance in most of the hill states has been quite low in comparison with the national average during 1994-05. Barring Himachal Pradesh, Tripura and Meghalaya, all the states have recorded lower growth rates than the all-India average. Though the performance improved in 2004-05 as compared to 1994-2000, yet J&K, Himachal Pradesh, Arunachal and Manipur had still recorded lower growth rate as compared to national average.

Most of the hill states have therefore achieved a lower rate of growth in NSDP indicating poor economic growth performance. One of the main reasons for such a poor performance are that many states have been suffering from disturbed law and order condition due to insurgency. The J&K, Nagaland, Manipur and Tripura have been suffering from these disturbances for a long time, which have taken their toll in developmental activities. Tripura, despite facing insurgency has however shown better performance which is quite intriguing (Table 2.7).

Table 2.7 : Growth of NSDP

State	*Per Capita NSDP (Rs.) (1993-94)*			*ACGR*
	1993-94	*1999-2000*	*2004-05*	*1993-94 to 2004-05*
J&K	6543	7384	8075	1.93
Himachal Pradesh	7870	11051	13471	5.01
Uttarakhand	6896	7256	10584	3.97
Sikkim	8402	9874	12637	3.78
Arunachal Pradesh	8733	8890	10348	1.55
Nagaland	9129	8726	12292*	2.74*
Manipur	5846	7097	8015	2.91
Mizoram	NA	NA	NA	NA
Tripura	5534	7968	11136**	6.56**
Meghalaya	6893	8996	11278	4.58
All India	**7690**	**10071**	**12416**	**4.45**

*Pertains to 2002-03; ** Pertains to 2003-04.
Source : Central Statistical Organisation, 2006.

7. Labour Force Participation Rates

Labour Force Participation Rates (LFPR) in majority of states barring Nagaland, Mizoram and Sikkim have shown declining trends during 1993-94 to 1999-2000 (Table 2.8). The declining trend in labour force is also observed at the all-India level. Female labour force has declined at a faster rate than the male labour force during the period. One of the reasons for such changing dynamics and decline in labour participation rate could be due to demographic transition and delayed entry in the world of work. Low work participation may possibly take place because of the students pursuing higher level of education and training. Indeed, pursuance of higher education has been one of the main factors responsible for decline in the work participation rate. However, NSS survey results (2004-05) show a sharp increase in the LFPR in all the states and the female LFPR, in particular, saw a substantial jump. A large part of such employment opportunities have come up in the unorganised sector including agriculture sector, which can be regarded as low productive employment.

Table 2.8 : Persons in the Labour Force (%)

State	*1993-94*			*1999-2000*			*2004-05*		
	Male	*Female*	*Person*	*Male*	*Female*	*Person*	*Male*	*Female*	*Person*
J&K	NA	NA	NA	NA	NA	NA	55.7	23.5	40.5
Himachal Pradesh	58.6	49.4	54.1	54.5	44.5	49.6	57.2	49.3	53.3
Uttarakhand	50.8	47.2	49.1	45.2	33.9	39.5	53.5	36.2	44.8
Sikkim	56.8	18.9	39.1	52.3	24.2	39.1	56.9	30.6	44.6
Arunachal Pradesh	50.9	36.9	44.4	42.1	27.3	35.1	49.5	35.0	42.6
Nagaland	44.0	19.8	32.6	51.4	41.3	46.6	54.6	47.1	51.0
Manipur	47.6	28.9	38.9	50.1	24.8	37.5	51.8	32.2	42.1
Mizoram	51.3	29.3	40.8	52.6	35.4	44.3	54.3	36.2	45.5
Tripura	53.0	13.8	34.0	50.9	7.7	30.0	60.6	14.3	38.1
Meghalaya	59.9	43.8	52.0	52.9	37.8	45.5	55.2	44.6	49.9
All India	**55.6**	**28.7**	**42.7**	**54.1**	**26.0**	**40.5**	**55.9**	**28.9**	**42.9**

Source : National Sample Survey, various rounds.

8. Distribution of Main Workers

Vast majority of workforce ranging from 44 per cent to 68 per cent are engaged in the primary sector. Half of the hill states have comparatively higher share in the primary sector than the All-India average. Secondary sector employment is lower in all the hill states as compared to All-India average. Again, tertiary sector employment is quite higher and almost all the states show higher share in tertiary sector than the all-India figures (Table 2.9). The share in the secondary sector is lower in all the hill states as compared to national average indicating the lack of industrialisation, which is one of the main reasons for lack of development. Nagaland, Mizoram and Meghalaya accounts for less than 10 per cent share of the workforce. In services sector, the workforce share is higher in almost all the states ranging from 25 per cent in Nagaland to 42 per cent in J&K as compared to national average of 26 per cent.

Table 2.9 : Distribution of Main Workers, 2001

State	*Primary sector*	*Secondary sector*	*Tertiary sector*
J&K	44.28	13.47	42.25
Himachal Pradesh	59.14	11.85	29.01
Uttarakhand	55.86	14.40	29.75
Sikkim	55.06	12.04	32.90
Arunachal Pradesh	62.51	11.41	26.08
Nagaland	67.88	6.67	25.45
Manipur	52.37	13.01	34.62
Mizoram	61.05	8.19	30.76
Tripura	51.09	12.02	36.89
Meghalaya	66.76	7.16	26.07
All India	57.46	16.65	25.89

Source : Registrar General of India, Census of India.

Proportion of workers to total population in most of the states is higher than the national average except J&K, Uttarakhand and Tripura. The share of female workers is higher in almost all the states except Tripura compared to the national levels indicating huge female drudgery. Cultivators constitute a large share among the total workforce ranging from 40 to 69 per cent, with Tripura showing exceptionally low share (27 %) compared to national average of 32 per cent (Table 2.10).

Table 2.10 : Percentage Distribution of Workers, 2001

State	*Person*	*Male*	*Female*	*Cultivators*
J&K	37.01	35.14	42.67	42.40
Himachal Pradesh	49.24	54.62	43.67	69.01
Uttarakhand	36.92	46.14	27.33	50.10
Sikkim	48.64	57.44	38.57	49.90
Arunachal Pradesh	43.98	50.63	36.54	57.84
Nagaland	42.60	46.70	38.06	64.74
Manipur	43.62	48.12	39.02	40.17
Mizoram	52.57	57.29	47.54	54.87
Tripura	36.25	50.62	21.08	27.02
Meghalaya	41.84	48.34	35.15	48.14
All India	**39.10**	**51.68**	**25.63**	**31.65**

Source : Union Primary Census Abstract, 2001.

Distribution of main workers shows that half of the states (namely, Himachal Pradesh, Arunachal Pradesh, Nagaland, Mizoram and Meghalaya) have higher proportion of workers in farm sector and only J&K, Manipur, Tripura, Uttarakhand and Sikkim have higher proportion of workers in the non-farm sector, but Uttarakhand and Tripura have marginally higher share compared to national average (Table 2.11).

Table 2.11 : Distribution of Main Workers, 2001

Sates	*Farm sector*	*Non-farm sector*
J&K	40.31	59.69
Himachal Pradesh	57.30	42.70
Uttarakhand	52.11	47.89
Sikkim	51.80	48.20
Arunachal Pradesh	59.15	40.85
Nagaland	66.87	33.13
Manipur	49.69	50.31
Mizoram	58.96	41.04
Tripura	46.13	53.87
Meghalaya	62.78	37.22
All India	**53.39**	**46.61**

Source : Union Primary Census Abstract, 2001.

9. *Growth of Employment*

A striking feature of employment growth in the economy is that there has been significant fall in the employment growth during 1990s in comparison with that in 1980s. This is true in the case of all hill states as well. Majority of hill states have recorded abysmally low overall employment growth during 1993-94 to 1999-2000 barring Sikkim, Nagaland and Mizoram which have recorded higher growth than national average. Nagaland has recorded an exceptional growth rate of 11 per cent. Himachal Pradesh, Uttarakhand, Arunachal Pradesh and Tripura have recorded negative growth rates, and females in particular, saw sharp decline in employment opportunities (Table 2.12).

Employment growth during 1999-2000 to 2004-05 shows substantive gain in employment growth as compared to earlier periods. Barring Mizoram, all the hill states show higher employment growth than the all-India average. Interestingly, female employment growth outstrips the male employment growth in most of the states (Table 2.12).

Table 2.12 : Growth of Employment (UPSS) (%)

State	1993-94 to 1999-2000			1999-2000 to 2004-05		
	Male	Female	Person	Male	Female	Person
J&K	2.2	-1.2	1.1	-	-	-
Himachal Pradesh	0.2	-0.3	-01	2.5	3.0	2.7
Uttarakhand	-.03	-2.8	-1.4	4.6	1.8	3.5
Sikkim	0.9	7.3	2.6	3.5	6.3	4.4
Arunachal Pradesh	-0.7	-2.4	-1.4	4.8	6.9	5.6
Nagaland	7.6	18.4	11.3	3.6	5.1	4.2
Manipur	2.1	-0.9	1.0	2.3	7.0	3.9
Mizoram	2.7	5.8	3.8	2.4	2.1	2.3
Tripura	0.9	-7.4	-0.4	2.8	5.0	3.5
Meghalaya	0.5	0.2	0.4	2.4	5.0	3.5
All India	**1.5**	**0.4**	**1.1**	**2.4**	**3.7**	**2.8**

Source : Various NSS rounds.

10. Incidence of Unemployment

Increasing labour force and declining growth in employment cause increased incidence of unemployment. It can be observed from Table 2.13 that the incidence of rural unemployment in majority of hill states has been on the rise until 1999-2000 for both sex barring Mizoram and Tripura. Mizoram albeit shows a marginal decline while Tripura shows a substantial decline. In 2004-05, incidence of unemployment though somewhat declined in five states as compared to 1999-2000, yet male unemployment continued to rise in majority of states as compared to all-India average. Tripura indeed shows an exorbitantly high rate of unemployment.

Incidence of unemployment in urban areas seems to be much pronounced than in the rural areas as most of the states have higher unemployment rates – Tripura showing an exceptionally high rate (28 %) during 2004-05. Urban unemployment rates have generally increased in majority of states in 1999-2000 as compared to 1993-94. However, in 2004-05, most of the states show decelerating trends. Female unemployment is consistently registering very high rate in all states as compared to males indicating their vulnerability in the labour market (Table 2.14).

The post-reform period shows a perceptible increase in unemployment rates, more so in rural areas and such a situation might have serious repercussion in the long run. Therefore, the principal concern of development planning ought to be an employment policy with greater emphasis on inclusive and shared benefits.

In order to ensure that growth is broad-based and inclusive, there is a need to implement effective public policies and strategies that bring more people into mainstream, promote increased participation of poor men and women in economic decision-making, reduce poverty and disparities, and promote equitable access to the benefits of growth. It is now increasingly realised that development goals need to be expressed in explicit and real terms so that fruits of development are widely shared. This ought to be an important policy objective, especially for the hill states, which suffer from locational disadvantages.

11. Sectoral Composition Plan Expenditure

Investment in social sector and infrastructure is the key to economic prosperity and well-being of the people. In all the states, social sector investments are showing continuous increase over the years barring J&K, which has shown a decline in 1990s. In certain cases, social sector investments have assumed quite a large proportion. In spite of huge investments in social sectors, relative rankings of J&K, Arunachal Pradesh, Manipur and Mizoram have been low while the rankings of Sikkim, Tripura, Meghalaya and Nagaland have been high. Sectoral allocation for infrastructure development, on the other hand, has either declined or stagnated in 1990s except in the cases of J&K, Manipur and Mizoram. There has been a sharp fall in the sectoral share in infrastructure for Nagaland during 1990s. This trend has widespread

Table 2.13 : Incidence of Unemployment (Rural) (%)

State	*1983*			*1993-94*			*1999-2000*			*2004-05*		
	Male	*Female*	*Person*	*Male*	*Female*	*Person*	*Male*	*Female*	*Person*	*Male*	*Female*	*Person*
J&K	0.6	0.2	0.5	0.9	0.5	0.8	1.2	1.0	1.1	1.7	1.3	1.5
Himachal Pradesh	1.4	0.5	1.0	0.9	0.1	0.6	1.8	0.6	1.3	1.6	2.0	1.8
Uttarakhand	NA	NA	NA	NA	NA	NA	NA	NA	NA	2.0	0.4	1.3
Sikkim	1.0	0.7	0.9	0.6	1.4	0.8	3.3	1.9	2.8	2.8	1.5	2.4
Arunachal Pradesh	-	-	-	1.4	0.3	0.9	0.7	0.2	0.5	1.1	0.6	0.9
Nagaland	-	-	-	2.2	0.0	1.5	2.6	2.1	2.4	2.2	1.4	1.8
Manipur	0.6	0.0	0.4	1.2	0.4	0.9	2.1	1.6	2.0	1.4	0.7	1.1
Mizoram	0.1	-	0.1	1.5	0.4	1.1	1.4	0.3	0.9	0.5	0.1	0.3
Tripura	1.4	14.7	2.8	1.5	6.4	2.4	0.9	3.6	1.2	9.6	32.0	13.3
Meghalaya	0.4	0.1	0.3	0.4	0.0	0.2	0.4	0.3	0.4	0.1	0.5	0.3
All India	**1.4**	**0.7**	**1.1**	**1.5**	**0.8**	**1.2**	**1.7**	**1.1**	**1.5**	**1.6**	**1.8**	**1.7**

Source : Various rounds of NSS.

Table 2.14 : Incidence of Unemployment (Urban) (%)

State	*1983*			*1993-94*			*1999-2000*			*2004-05*		
	Male	*Female*	*Person*	*Male*	*Female*	*Person*	*Male*	*Female*	*Person*	*Male*	*Female*	*Person*
J&K	3.2	7.6	3.8	8.2	9.0	8.4	4.4	9.2	4.9	3.7	10.9	4.9
Himachal Pradesh	7.6	7.6	7.6	3.5	0.4	2.7	6.4	8.4	6.8	1.7	10.1	3.8
Uttarakhand	NA	NA	NA	NA	NA	NA	NA	NA	NA	4.2	10.2	5.4
Sikkim	9.9	6.9	9.4	1.4	8.2	2.5	6.4	13.2	8.0	3.6	4.3	3.7
Arunachal Pradesh	-	-	-	0.8	5.5	1.4	1.7	8.6	3.0	1.1	2.8	1.2
Nagaland	0.4	0.0	0.3	6.9	5.9	6.7	9.3	8.9	9.2	4.6	7.2	5.5
Manipur	0.5	0.1	0.3	4.8	2.8	4.2	7.0	6.0	6.7	5.2	6.3	5.5
Mizoram	1.1	1.0	1.1	0.4	0.5	0.4	3.3	2.3	2.9	1.6	2.6	1.9
Tripura	6.8	29.0	10.8	5.9	17.6	8.4	5.3	8.7	5.8	16.6	56.8	28.0
Meghalaya	8.4	9.2	8.6	1.0	3.6	1.7	3.4	6.9	4.5	3.5	3.5	3.5
All India	**5.0**	**5.2**	**5.1**	**4.1**	**6.6**	**4.6**	**4.5**	**5.9**	**4.8**	**3.8**	**6.9**	**4.5**

Source : Various rounds of NSS.

Table 2.15 : Sectoral Composition of Actual Plan Expenditure (%)

States	*Social Sector*				*Infrastructure*			
	1981-82	*1991-92*	*1997-98*	*Rank*	*1981-82*	*1991-92*	*1997-98*	*Rank*
J&K	30.79	33.31	28.86	23	32.74	37.04	41.19	8
Himachal Pradesh	22.95	32.64	35.24	13	45.06	32.78	31.41	23
Uttarakhand	NA	NA	NA	NA	NA	NA	NA	NA
Sikkim	19.83	28.09	45.38	4	41.42	47.07	32.90	21
Arunachal Pradesh	24.59	25.90	29.65	21	45.46	47.07	46.37	6
Nagaland	26.65	24.38	36.73	12	39.33	30.42	19.87	31
Manipur	29.07	24.58	32.44	17	32.44	29.93	38.57	14
Mizoram	26.54	25.68	30.35	20	45.93	35.38	41.1	10
Tripura	28.69	30.16	43.18	5	27.53	26.11	22.34	29
Meghalaya	28.97	29.32	37.83	9	45.09	38.99	33.58	19

Note : Actual plan expenditure by major heads has been clubbed as per the following :

Social sector: Education, Health, Water Supply & Sanitation, Urban Development, Information, Welfare & Labour.

Data for1981-82 is an average of 1980-82, 1991-92, and average of 1990-93 and 1997-98 an average of 1996-98.

Source : Tenth Five-Year Plan, 2002-07, Planning Commission, Government of India.

ramification to the economic base of different sectors of economy (Table 2.15).

12. Credit-Deposit Ratio

The Credit-Deposit ratio (CD) in all the hill states is lower as compared to the all-India average. This ratio has declined in all the states (in some states rather sharply) between 1994 and 2001. In 2006, this ratio has substantively increased, but still the hill states lag far behind the All-India level. In the north-eastern states (including Assam), the CD ratio is 39 per cent, which is lowest among all the regions. This abysmally low CD ratio in the hill states is an indication of poor utilisation of bank deposits for development work. High deposits with low credit might have adverse effect on entrepreneurship activities, which in turn retard development activities in the private sector. For stimulating development activities in the hill states, it is necessary to encourage private entrepreneurship; otherwise, large deposits might take recourse to lowland development activities. All efforts are needed to stimulate development activities, which could attract private investment from the lowland rather than reverse flow of savings (Table 2.16).

Table 2.16 : Credit-Deposit Ratio: All Scheduled Commercial Banks

States	1994*	2001*	2006**
J&K	38.74	38.3	44.9
Himachal Pradesh	47.93	22.6	40.5
Uttarakhand	NA	NA	25.8
Sikkim	23.24	15.6	45.3
Arunachal Pradesh	14.10	17.3	25.1
Nagaland	42.07	13.9	22.3
Manipur	65.21	38.9	50.6
Mizoram	24.51	25.5	51.4
Tripura	58.63	23.0	31.6
Meghalaya	17.39	16.8	39.3
North-eastern region	**38.89**	**28.1**	**39.3**
All India	**54.29**	**58.5**	**72.5**

Sources : * Tenth Five-Year Plan, 2002-07, Planning Commission, Government of India

** Data for the year 2006 (as per sanction) are based on BSR 7 Survey.

13. Diversity in Development Patterns

In spite of similar bio-physical attributes among all the hill regions, the development patterns vary across the hill states in terms of various development indicators.

The case of Himachal Pradesh provides a unique example among all the hill states. The transformation of the region from subsistence agriculture to one of the leading horticulture-producing region is worth emulating. The development strategy gave primacy to development of transport network (mainly, roads), communication and hydroelectric projects. The government provided institutional support for diversification from traditional cereal crops to horticulture crops along with dairy development. The state also adopted an appropriate land use pattern with a view to optimising the returns. This has significantly improved livelihood options and income levels of the people. Health and education sectors have shown an impressive growth. The forests have been exploited to produce mainly timber and resin that contributes to about 35 per cent from the state (Negi, *et al.,* 2004). In industry, emphasis is being laid on setting up of industrial units, which are environment-friendly and based on local raw material and niche products. The industrial sector contributes nearly 15 per cent of GDP. Some of the leading industrial houses have been attracted to set up industrial units in the state. The introduction of single window clearance for medium and large-scale sectors has facilitated promotion of industrial units. Sustainable tourism industry has been promoted without disturbing ecology and environment. Various types of tourism is being promoted in the state such as pilgrimage, adventure sports, wildlife and cultural heritage, primarily to provide employment and income. The state is endowed with vast potential of hydropower – about 20,392 MW of which 6,045 MW has been so far harnessed. The state is one of the most socially progressive states in the country. It has recorded the lowest decadal population growth after Tripura (Table 2.1); highest literacy rate next to Mizoram (Table 2.2) and lowest poverty levels after J&K (Table 2.3). It has performed better in terms of human development indicators, and has substantially higher per capita consumption expenditure (second highest in the urban areas) with lower inequality of per capita expenditure (Tables 2.5 and 2.6). The state has highest per capita NSDP in 2004-05 and is one of the fastest growing hill economies recording 5.1 per cent growth per annum during 1999-2000 and 2004-05 (Table 2.7). Although employment growth has substantively increased, yet unemployment rate recorded an increase in 2004-05 in rural areas as compared to 1999-2000.

Performance of Jammu & Kashmir, on the other hand, does not seem to be that encouraging as in the case of Himachal Pradesh. The state has recorded relatively higher decadal population growth (Table 2.1), lowest overall and female literacy rates (Table 2.2), and highest gender disparity among all the hill states. Though poverty level is lowest (5.4 % in 2004-05) in the state, yet per capita NSDP is lower (about 2 %) than the national average (4.5%) during 1993-2004. The infant mortality rate (IMR) is estimated at 108 per thousand. In spite of a large natural and human resource base, the state lags behind in industrial development. The state possesses immense potential for development of the power sector, but the performance is not commensurate with the possibilities – only 10 per cent of the total potential has so far been harnessed. In terms of road length per 1000 sq. km, the state ranks the lowest (127/1000 sq. km) as compared to Himachal Pradesh (542/1000 sq. km) and Assam (872/1000 sq. km) in 1996-97. Also, the inter-district variations in accessibility of roads are very sharp. For example, in terms of road length per 100 sq. km, Budgam district has the highest road density of 81.84 km and the districts of Leh, Kargil and Doda have poor accessibility with road density of mere 2.58, 4.82 and 5.24 km respectively (Sadhu, *et al.*, 2004). Tourism has been the major economic activity of the state but due to insurgency within the valley since 1989, tourist inflow received a major setback. The state has not made any concerted efforts for tourism diversification. The area under fruit and vegetable cultivation has increased marginally though there is immense potential for growing horticulture crops, vegetables, floriculture and medicinal herbs. There are also good potentials for promoting handicrafts and handlooms industries.

Uttarakhand is a new state (carved out from Uttar Pradesh in

2000) and the database for the independent state is not that robust as it is in the case of other hill states. However, some of the aggregate indicators available point to the state of the economy. Population growth has declined from 2.4 per cent in 1981-91 to about 1.9 per cent per annum during 1991-01; literacy rates are impressive (72%) with relatively lower gender gap but very high poverty ratio (39.6%) – highest among all the hill states, which is 12 percentage points higher than the national average (2004-05). The share of farm sector workers among the main workers is low – about 52 per cent as per 2001 Census. The NSDP growth has been lower (3.9% per annum) as against 4.5 per cent of national average during 1993-94 to 2004-05. One of the main reasons for this type of poor performance is that the state failed to incorporate mountain-specific development plans as was in the case of Himachal Pradesh. Such development specificity has been by and large found missing in Uttarakhand (Pokhriyal, 2004). Although there are good potentials for certain products in which Uttarakhand is supposed to have advantage, such as hydro-electricity, wool processing, forest produce, horticulture, and tourism and amenities (Awasthi, *et al.*, 2005), yet many of these activities could not be developed primarily due to lack of appropriate development strategy. For instance, the estimated potential of power generation is about 20,450 MW in the state of which only 11 per cent could be harnessed till 2007. There is a huge gap between the industrial activities in plane areas and hills, owing to some critical constrains facing the latter. Recent Industrial Policy (2008) in particular, addresses the economic development in the hills where industrial activities have generally been considered dormant.

People, particularly at a higher altitude, have traditional skills and technology who have been producing wool and woollen products for market either in exchange of commodities or for money since long time. But now, this home-based activity is mostly obliterating. Likewise, the region is well known for Hindu pilgrimage, famous glaciers, trekking fields, and outing places which offer potentials for development of tourism industry. However, the linkages of tourism industry within local economy are found to be extremely weak.

The north-eastern states present somewhat a mixed pattern in development front.

> "The trauma of partition, political evolution and insurgency combined with the geographic allocation, transport bottlenecks, natural calamities, etc., have hindered the progress of the North East, and the region has experienced relatively slower economic growth compared to the rest of the country" (Planning Commission, 2002).

Most of the states still have very high rate of population growth, though declined considerably during last two decades, which is much higher than the national average except in the case of Tripura. Literacy has improved significantly over the years, yet it is still lower in Arunachal Pradesh and Meghalaya as compared to the all-India average. However, the gender gap in literacy is lower as compared to other hill states. Rural poverty was alarmingly high (45 per cent) in these states, much higher (8 percentage points) than the national average until 1993-94. Surprisingly, poverty ratio has fallen sharply from 45 per cent in 1993-94 to 22 per cent in 2004-05, which raises serious doubts whether poverty has actually declined to such an extent. Annual growth in per capita expenditure has fallen substantively during 1999-2000 to 2004-05 both in rural as well as urban areas. NSDP growth in most of the states has been lower than the all-India average during 1993-94 and 2004-05. Unemployment rate in Tripura (in rural as well as urban areas) is extraordinarily high, and in Nagaland and Manipur, urban unemployment rate is about 5.5 per cent which is higher than the national average. Income inequality measured by gini-coefficient has widened in most of these states in recent years barring Arunachal Pradesh and Manipur. Primary sector still constitutes the bulk of the labour force in all the hill states of the region, and secondary sector has remained stagnant. In some cases, the hill economies are experiencing some sort of de-industrialisation (Das, *et al.,* 2004). The decline in the share of primary sector is being compensated by the rise in that of the tertiary sector. And, the rise in the share of public expenditure is the reason behind the growth of the share of the tertiary sector. The economic development in these economies is yet to be rooted in self-sustaining process (Das, *et al.,* 2004). In Sikkim, poverty levels and unemployment rates continue to be significantly higher, and sustainability of major livelihood options (agriculture crops) in which most of the poor depended are declining or stagnating in terms of productivity levels, despite an impressive performance shown by the state in economic and social indicators (Papola, 2003).

Efforts made by the government to promote horticulture and cash crops as a strategic intervention to replace shifting cultivation has however failed to completely replace it. Agricultural transformation through horticulture and cash crops has raised social, economic and environmental problems. Such transformation has failed to satisfactorily deliver the promised economic returns. Conversion to settled agriculture has increased vulnerability and eroded self-reliance hitherto inherent in upland agriculture (Choudhury, 2004). This is because land management is the most neglected part of the development policy and planning of this region (Maithani, 2004). Increasing number of rural households with no cultivable land in the region (except in Manipur and Meghalaya) and disproportionately rising small and marginal farmers have added constrains in livelihood in rural areas (Das, 2004).

Being 'special category' states, they receive 90 per cent grant and 10 per cent loan from the Central Government. Because of these assured central assistance, they do not make any efforts to mobilise their own resources. This has resulted in increasing dependence on Central resources. For instance, for the year 2001-02, average per capita Central assistance for state plans for all the states in the region taken together was Rs.1,546 as compared to Rs. 356 for the country as a whole (Planning Commission). Own revenue receipts as a percentage of total expenditure varies from about 6.5 per cent in Mizoram and Nagaland to 22 per cent in Assam, while all other states' share put together is about 43 per cent in 2003-04. The Central Government's contribution to north-eastern region state budget varies from about 41 per cent in Sikkim to about 86 per cent in Arunachal Pradesh. For all other states, this share is about 34 per cent in 2002 (Sachdeva, 2000). Various indicators show that all the hill states of North-East come under 'very low' category in overall development except Manipur, which is under 'low' category (Goswami and Gogoi, 2004).

In all the north-eastern states including other hill states, industrialisation gets a low priority – it forms a small part of total outlay (ranging from 1 to 5%) barring Nagaland and Manipur, where it is between 8 to 12 per cent. Health allocation is also low, in most of the states it is between 3 to 6 per cent (Annexure II.1).

III. Conclusion

Despite having similar bio-physical characteristics, the development patterns vary across the hill states in terms of various development indicators.

Himachal Pradesh provides a notable example of the transformation process from a traditional cereal crop producing region to one of the leading horticulture producing regions. Himachal Pradesh has made considerable progress in terms of high literacy rates, almost universal enrolments at primary level, availability of schooling facilities, expansion of health care facilities and physical infrastructure. In several aspects, the state has become the role model for the other hill states of the country. Focused public interventions, greater participation of women and strong local institutions have been supportive policy measures, notwithstanding, the state has issues of concerns that need to be addressed (Himachal Pradesh Human Development Report, 2002). It has huge potentials for hydro-power, tourism, and has excellent agro-climatic diversity for value adding agro-business. The state has formulated comprehensive framework for creating investor-friendly environment to ensure sustainable industrial development.

Jammu & Kashmir has the lowest poverty ratio among all the hill states and relatively better natural resource base, but it lags in industrial development. The social indicators, in particular, gender discrimination in education and infant mortality are still very high. The state has immense potentials for tourism and hydel power. It offers vast scope for horticulture production and has unique climate for cultivation of saffron. It also has suitable climatic conditions for floriculture, aromatic and medicinal plants. But these resources have not been harnessed to the extent desired. There are also good potentials for promoting handicrafts and handlooms industry. However, strained Indo-Pak relations and continued insurgency in the state has created a major setback in the development goal of the state.

Uttarakhand has recorded an impressive literacy rate with relatively lower gender gap, but very high poverty ratio – highest among all the hill states. Although there are good potentials for hydro-electricity, tourism and amenities, horticulture, wool processing, forest produce, yet these resources have not been harnessed due to lack of economic infrastructure and institutional support. Recent economic indicators, however, show much better performance in terms of sectoral growth and other development indicators in the state.

North-East Region has remained industrially the most backward region. Decadal population is still very high in majority of the states (Nagaland, Mizoram, Meghalaya, Arunachal Pradesh and Manipur) as compared to all-India average. Per capita income is lower than the national average. North-East Region continues to be the net importer of foodgrains. Bulk of labour force is engaged in agriculture and allied activities with high unemployment rates, particularly among youth.

Most of the hill states have good potentials for development particularly in horticulture, hydro-power generation, tourism and other location-specific products. The region has also good potentials for petroleum and natural gas resources. Despite good resource base, there is acute deficiency of critical economic infrastructure in the region. There is need for creating institutions and building capacity in order to spur development activities.

3

Rural Employment in the Context of the Hill Economy :

The Theoretical Framework and Empirical Evidences

I. Theoretical Foundations and Empirical Evidences

1. Labour Transfer Model

The problems of development in the developing countries have generally been analysed within the frame of dualistic nature of economy – a low productive, labour surplus rural economy with a predominantly agriculture based high productive modern industrial urban sector. The key issue has been how to transform the rural economy characterised by the excessive labour supply and low productivity in the predominant agriculture sector. The dual economy model originally developed by W. Arthur Lewis (1954), and later by John Fei and Gustav Ranis (1964) has shown that with the development of modern sector, the surplus labour from agriculture (backward) sector would be gradually absorbed into modern sector as development takes its roots. The basic premise of this formulation was that in the subsistence sector, the wages are determined by tradition, subsistence need and other non-economic factors; while the urban wages are determined by marginal productivity. Since rural wage is higher than labour productivity or marginal product of labour, there will be no incentive to raise the wage until the labour productivity is enhanced sufficiently to equal the wage. Thereafter, as the marginal product or labour productivity continues to rise, the wage will go up. Therefore, in the Lewisian framework, there is unlimited supply of labour in the modern sector at the subsistence wage rates until they ceased to be underemployed in the agriculture sector. Therefore, in the early phase of industrial development, the income generated would be wholly accrued by the industrial capitalist class. This surplus is critical for industrial development that facilitates faster labour transfer and modern sector employment growth.

The labour transfer model however failed to generate adequate employment and the key assumptions of his theory did not fit in well with the realities or empirical foundation of agrarian economies. Experiences show that the labour absorption capacity in the industrial sector has been quite limited owing to higher capital intensity and fast industrial restructuring that tend to displace existing labour with capital. The wage constancy assumption in the industrial sector even for underemployed rural labourers seems to be quite unreasonable, untenable and does not borne out by the facts (Sen, 1966, 1975; Lal, 1976; Rosenzweig, 1978; Bardhan, 1979). Unlike in industrial economies, a large volume of workforce in the developing countries is engaged in self-employment activities (agricultural and in the informal economy) where the productivity is low, and neither Lewisian price mechanism seems to operate nor the rural to urban migration thesis based on wage differentials adequately explains the empirical findings of agrarian economies. Push factors often seem to dominate in the migration process, which is governed by various reasons such as seasonality, erosion of assets, landlessness and poverty, particularly in the context of backward economies. Many micro-evidences corroborate this thesis (Lipton, 1980; Oberai and Singh, 1983; Breman, 1985; Bora, 1996). Lewis himself realised the limitations of his theory when he revisited and observed the following major constraints such as: large size of traditional sector, pervasiveness of labour saving innovations, and vulnerability of small-scale enterprises (Lewis, 1979).

The static equilibrium assumption derived from the neo-classical theory holds that the working of economic forces will cause spatial differences to be narrow, also does not fit in the realities of backward economies, where institutional and structural rigidities retard the growth process. It was therefore argued that the principal reason for lagging growth in developing countries or the geographic regions can be explained by the cumulative causation hypothesis (Myrdal, 1957), and not by the unrealistic stable equilibrium assumption. This hypothesis relates to geographic dualism or regional inequalities applicable to nations, and regions within nations, that show very wide differences in terms of industrialisation, income, trade, employment and levels of unemployment. Myrdal argues that the process of migration, capital movements, trade and other means of development retard the growth process of backward regions through strong backwash effects and weak spread effects that eventually slow down the growth of the whole region or the country. Migration from the backward region, for instance, denudes that area of human capital and entrepreneurs, depress the demand for goods and services, and factors of production; while the developed regions experience an increase in the demand for goods and services, enterprises, factors of production, and economic and social infrastructures. Myrdal's description of resource transfer from the backward areas to developed ones works to the advantage of later, and this kind of exploitative relation also holds true to some extent in the backward hill regions, which act as the resource supplier of the plain areas and themselves remain heavily dependent on the developed regions of the country. Myrdal's hypothesis also asserts that at the initial stage, migration will be selective (skilled and educated) but later it will be less selective, and the spread effects would be more powerful. However, this hypothesis has not been validated in the context of backward economies. It is often observed that out-migration is not that selective in backward economies, particularly in the hill regions, primarily because of the subsistence nature of economy and low industrial base. In such economies, the spread effects remain weak even after a substantive period mainly because of the regional specificity that compels the economy to remain a marginal entity in the development process.

2. Trade-Induced Development Argument

In the classical and neo-classical framework, trade was viewed as a propelling force of development. Classical economists viewed comparative advantage as the key to efficient resource allocation where the country can enjoy higher income by specialising production according to its comparative advantage and trading. The export-led growth theory further suggests that the country could even vent for surplus through exporting raw material or primary products (staple) in which they enjoy comparative advantage that would induce higher rates of growth and strengthen the linkage effect with other sectors, and eventually enhance employment and incomes. Staple theory (along processing) in a way is closer to Rostow's leading sector analogy, which can act as a prime mover and a propelling force for the rest of the economy (Meier, 1975). However, the trade theory is built upon factor-price equalisation theorem and assumption of immobility of factors of production, especially labour which instead of stimulating growth perpetuates in cumulative causation and results in inequality in the lagging regions (Myrdal, 1957); whilst, the backward economies with peculiar regional specificity (e.g. hill regions) have shown strong patterns of out-migrating to lowland areas caused by the differing opportunities or amenities between the two distinct areas, and more so have been carried out as a coping mechanism. Though many such backward areas have certain resource advantages in terms of niche products, yet the resources cannot be used intensively due to specificity characteristics (viz., inaccessibility, fragility and marginality) that keep the region at a disadvantaged position. There are thus obvious limitations both in the Lewisian theory and export-led theory, which suggest venting surplus to the backward economies through exporting labour and trade theory and through exporting staple resources.

3. Industrialisation Strategy

It is argued that the backward economies suffer from low equilibrium trap and to get out from this state of underdevelop-ment, the prerequisite is to have 'critical minimum efforts' and the need for a 'big push' in the form of planned large-scale investment, what has been known as a doctrine of balanced growth (Rosenstein-Rodan, 1943). This theory essentially looks into the problem of underdevelopment or backwardness in terms of scale of investment necessary to overcome indivisibility on both the supply and demand sides. Supply side bottlenecks are lumpiness of capital that needs huge investment in large number of activities simultaneously, which can take advantage of external economies; and the demand side indivisibility refers to the limitations posed by the size of the market. If numbers of activities are established simultaneously, each will provide market for others. The theory thus recognises the indivisibility of supply side and complementarities of demand side, and emphasises striking a balance between different sectors of economy, namely, agriculture and industry. The theory very rightly assumes the criticality of large-scale investment to overcome underdevelop-ment. However, it has been observed that large-scale investment does not automatically results in employment and income generating activities as has been postulated in this theory, but often such investment in hill economies leads to ecologically unsustainable development primarily by ignoring the regional specificity (e.g. vital bio-physical system). The mountain specificities pose constraints on development activities and are generally not suitable for highly diversified economic structure (Papola, 1996). Infrastructure development instead of inducing the momentum of growth, create vast degradation of resources (due to excessive use) and the fact remains that greater accessibility helped outflow of resources (natural and human) uninterruptedly, whereas the gains from the development have gone mostly to the plane areas. The complementarities of supply and demand side activities are often missing in the hill regions because of lack of focus on incorporation of the hill specificities (ecology and environment) while conceptualising and operationalising the infrastructural development (Jodha, 1992).

4. Regional Growth Theory Argument

The regional growth theory suggests that a good resource base and locational advantage are the prerequisites of the growth process to unleash. The regional growth has been promoted typically by the ability of the region to produce goods and services that are demanded by the national economy and outside the national economy. For growth process to take-off, it is necessary that the region must ensure the expansion of resource in relation to its demand. The demand for the goods and services (derived from resources) must exhibit a high-income elasticity. The other important aspect is that the resources (or goods and services) must create locationally forward and backward linkages in order to generate multiplier effects and to create markets. To a large extent, such linkages would depend upon how returns from the goods and services demanded by the outside region could generate active demand for regionally produced goods and services (Perloff and Wingo Jr., 1964). As the regional markets expand, it creates conditions for self-reinforcing and self-sustaining regional growth pattern. For such growth to occur, the most critical factor or the prime mover for successive stages of development is strong manufacturing base. But in the backward region, and typically in the hill region, the "economic relationships between the mountains and plains have been of to hinterland-metropolis, in which the highlands served as a source of primary products (raw material) for the mainstream lowland economies and societies, with all the structural and operational inequities associated with such relationships" (Jodha, 1997). Seldom have the activities carried out based on hill products generated momentum of internal linkages, and the benefits of resources have by and large accrued to outside hill economy. The mountain economies even after a considerable period of state interventions, with a view to promoting development activities, have remained poor and the developed parts/centres of the country, unlike usual regional growth trajectory as visualised in the early stages of development, still acts as ".... suction pumps, pulling in more dynamic elements from the more static regions. The remainder of the country is thus relegated to a second-class, peripheral position placed in a quasi-colonial relationship to a centre experiencing net outflows of people, capital and resources, most of which redound to the advantage of the centre where economic growth will tend to be rapid, sustained and cumulative" (Friedman and Alonso, 1964).

5. *Agricultural Strategy*

Many countries during 1960s and 1970s crafted their policies around the centrality of the Lewisian Model with a view to achieving faster development of urban industrial sector and greater resource allocation (rather, deliberately) that was made to favour the urban areas at the cost of rural sector. As a result of overriding priority accorded to industrialisation policy, agriculture sector received relatively smaller share of national resources. The experiences of development planning until mid-1970 have amply shown that the policies promoting industrialisation helped urban areas but benefits thereof did not trickle down to the rural areas. The critiques of industrialisation strategy detected urban bias in development strategy which led to the formulation of alternative strategy widely known as "agriculture first strategy" credited to Lipton (1968) and Mellor (1976), who explained the causes of continued rural poverty and unemployment as the primacy given to the capital-intensive industrialisation. Mellor brought out to the fore the virtuous linkages of consumption and production sides of agricultural growth, and envisaged that the fast agriculture growth would in turn produce non-farm linkages as the road to rural industrialisation (Mellor, 1976; 1986). The empirical evidences suggest that the agricultural development has a positive impact on the growth of non-farm sector through various linkage effects (Bhalla, 1993; Papola, 1987; Unni, 1991). Punjab and Haryana are the prime examples of such virtuous linkages where fast agricultural development led to the growth of non-farm sector through ploughing back the agricultural surpluses into the non-agriculture sector.

However, in the context of hill economy, such linkages are often weak due to subsistence nature of agriculture and other difficult agricultural conditions that hardly produce any surplus for the market. In spite of being agriculturally backward, these regions have certain distinct advantages over others in terms of agro-climatic features enabling the growth of a variety of high value cash crops and enterprises based on mountain niche products.

Such enterprise-based activities have been developed in certain parts of hilly region – in the Hindu Kush Himalayan Region – based on niche products. The most widely known example is Western Sichuan (China), where over two-dozen products have been developed based on mountain specific resources. The other areas where specific products (rather limited one) have been developed are apple cultivation in Himachal Pradesh, vegetable farming in Garampani area in Nainital district, Ginger and Pineapple in Meghalaya and other parts of the north-eastern states, tea plantation and processing in Ilam district in Nepal, livestock and dairy development in areas closer to Kathmandu, and apple cultivation in Arunachal Pradesh (Papola, *et al.*, 2005).

In the context of hilly region, enterprise-based activity can take different forms – diversification from cereal-based products to high value horticultural products to simple processing, and other enterprise-based activities such as livestock, forest (non-timber), artisan and tourism industry.

There are case studies which amply demonstrate that agricultural transformation based on high value crops has increased food security and improved living conditions. However, for successful transformation, accessibility to wider market network and strong R&D institutions are critical (Sharma, 1996; Sharma, 1997; Sharma and Sharma, 1997; Tulchan, 1997; Badhani, 1998).

Himachal Pradesh is a case in point that diversified into high value crop, in particular, apples that have brought about virtuous production and consumption linkages, which helped attain higher levels of growth of employment and income (Sharma, 2005). This has also increased opportunities for non-farm employment (Chand, 1995). Uttarakhand also holds considerable potentials for development of horticulture and other niche products such as micro-hydel plants, tourism and other amenity services, minor forest products and wool processing.

6. Rural Non-Farm Sector

It was clearly recognised that the problem of rural unemployment and underemployment could not be solved because of inherent structural problems associated within agriculture sector. Evidently, this sector has been characterised by low productivity (as a consequence of large volume of labour employed), iniquitous distribution of land and diminishing land-man ratio, the provision of productive employment to burgeoning labour force within agriculture sector was conceived as a difficult proposition. The Rural Non-Farm sector

(RNF), on the other hand, has gained considerable significance as an alternative strategy for employment generation, poverty reduction and higher rate of growth. The rationale behind attaching importance to the rural non-farm sector rested on the following premises. Firstly, the labour absorption capacity in agriculture sector is limited, particularly in land-scarce countries. Moreover, it has been found to be difficult to bring about deep-rooted redistributive land reforms (Saith, 1992). Secondly, out-migration to urban areas cannot be assumed to be capable of providing adequate livelihood opportunities for all those unable to make living in agriculture. Also, out-migration has serious implications on both the urban areas (in terms of pressure on scarce urban infrastructure) and rural areas (in terms of skill drain). Thirdly, expansion of rural non-farm activities has significant spin-off effects on agricultural development. Relatively low labour cost and low capital intensity in numerous non-farm activities tend to have positive linkage effects on rural economy. Finally, these activities offer income potential during slack season and provide means to cope/ survive when farming fails (Gordon and Craig, 2001).

Empirical evidences suggest that there has been considerable deceleration of agriculture employment growth in rural areas during the 1980s and 1990s. It registered 0.5 per cent growth during 1983 to 1987-88 and then picked up to 2.16 per cent during 1987-88, but again plummeted to 0.20 per cent during 1993-94 to 1999-2000. Such a catastrophic fall in the growth of agriculture employment indicates inability of this sector to absorb further labour force. However, in spite of such significant decline in agriculture employment growth, the RNF sector registered 2.0 per cent growth during 1987-88 to 1993-94 and 2.3 per cent during 1993-94 to 1999-2000. Though employment in the non-farm activities increased, albeit marginally during 1993-94 to 1999-2000, yet there has been substantial reduction in poverty (Bhalla, 1998).

The growth in rural non-agriculture employment during 1983 to 1987-88 was however significantly higher (5.2 per cent) and this growth has helped absorb the excess labour from the agriculture sector, though temporarily, as a large volume of employment was generated through construction activities as a part of coping with severe drought situation. The proportion of rural non-agriculture employment increased from 16.6 per cent in 1977-78 to 23.8 per cent in 1999-2000. The share of males increased relatively much faster (7.2 percentage points) than the females (2.8 percentage points) during 1977-78 to 1999-2000. Activities like construction, trade and transport have expanded while manufacturing activities stagnated. The share of employment for males increased relatively faster in the tertiary sector, while for females, the increase was higher in the secondary sector. The picture across states varies significantly. States like Bihar, Kerala, Assam and Himachal Pradesh have shown faster growth in later half of the 1990s while states like Karnataka, Maharashtra and Andhra Pradesh show slower diversification (Sharma *et al.*, 2001).

The NSS round (2004-05) results, however, show significant up-trends in the employment growth of agriculture and non-agriculture sectors. Agriculture sector employment grew at about 1.7 per cent per annum during 1999-2000 to 2004-05 and non-agriculture employment recorded an all-time high both in terms of share and growth during this period. Non-agriculture sector recorded 5.7 per cent per annum growth rate during 1999-2000 to 2004-05, and its share has gone up to about 27.4 per cent in 2004-05.

This newfound interest in the rural non-farm sector has generated a large body of literature from numerous regional level studies (disaggregated to state and district levels) to village level studies – identifying and analysing the causes and determinants of the growth of non-farm sector. The first set of studies mostly relied upon secondary data from NSS and Census, while village level studies utilised the field data collected from the households. These studies were both analytical in nature using quantitative techniques, and were descriptive types as well. Most of these studies have tried to disentangle the alternative hypotheses postulated in the literature (Unni, 1991; 2000). These hypotheses are related to three major arguments put forth for the growth of rural non-farm sector, namely, agriculture growth induced argument, prime movers outside agriculture, and residual sector hypothesis.

(i) Agriculture Growth Linkage Hypothesis

It was postulated that the accelerated growth of agricultural sector, consequent upon the green revolution technologies, would enhance farm productivity and income levels that in turn would help in the expansion of both agriculture and non-agricultural sectors through demand-led growth. This growth would occur through consumption and production linkages of agriculture sector with that of non-agricultural sector (Mellor, 1976; 1986). Consumption linkages emanate from the increased farm incomes that result in increased demand for non-farm sector goods and services produced in the nearby villages and towns. Also, increased farm productivity would push the real wages upwards and the labourers also would demand more farm and non-farm output. The production linkages occur within agriculture sector both from input side (backward) as well as from output side (forward). Backward linkages typically originate from agriculture and then move to non-agriculture sector in the form of increased demand for agricultural inputs such as farm implements and machineries etc., while the forward linkages necessitates processing of agricultural outputs (food products, edible oils, tobacco etc.) that would spring up agro-processing units. This demand-led growth would promote various non-agriculture employment and income opportunities and would in turn help the rural industrialisation process. This hypothesis has been empirically validated by numerous studies (*see* in particular: Papola, 1987; Dev, 1990; Hazell and Haggblade,1991; Unni, 1991, 1994; Bhalla, 1993; Chadha, 1994).

(ii) Prime Movers Outside Agriculture Hypothesis

Empirical validation of agriculture-led growth model recognised the importance of other prime movers outside agriculture, which were identified as important factors for the growth of non-farm sector, and agriculture as a sole prime mover for the growth of non-farm sector, was countered (Bhalla, 1993; 1997). While the growth of agriculture was acknowledged for the expansion of non-farm sector activities, the role of prime movers outside agriculture, such as growth of urbanisation, infrastructure development, rural development programmes, and education and skill formation assumed increasingly significant aspects for workforce diversification. Bhalla (1993), while analysing the district level data from the census, argues that the shift in consumer taste in favour of urban products and agricultural inputs has made a significant impact on the growth of non-farm sector particularly in agriculturally prosperous districts. Also, increasing links with the urban centres provide an impetus for rural workforce diversification, particularly in corridor districts (Bhalla, 1997). Studies by Unni (1991), Jayaraj (1994), Eapen (1995), and Srivastava and Dubey (2002) have found significant positive influence of urbanisation on rural non-farm growth. These urban towns also provide increasing income opportunities to rural population through commuting (Vaidyanathan, 1986; Basant., *et al.*, 1998).

Also, the activities which generate strong linkages with the rural areas in terms of employment and income generation to the rural population irrespective of their locations seem to be occurring important space dimension of the rural non-farm sector growth (Saith, 1992). Small towns in rural hinterland have been playing extremely important roles in creating employment and income opportunities in the non-farm sector for the nearby villages through generating backward and forward linkages. Productivity and income levels in the non-farm enterprises have been found to be generally higher where such towns are more widely dispersed than the cases of a few towns which are concentrated (Papola, 1992).

Rural infrastructure (particularly roads, telecommunications and electricity) is another prime mover that has been facilitating growth of non-farm sector in terms of providing employment and income opportunities through self-employment and wage employment. Hazell and Haggblade (1991) underscore the importance of rural infrastructure in enhancing the income multipliers of agriculture growth for the non-farm sector. Harris (1991) did recognise the importance of agriculture growth as a necessary condition for the expansion of rural non-farm sector, however, he observed that it was not a sufficient condition, and highlighted the need for an improved rural infrastructure. Similarly, studies by Jayaraj (1994) and

Narayanmoorthy *et al.*, (2002) underscore the importance of transport infrastructure in promoting rural non-farm employment. Likewise, Shukla (1992) also observed the beneficial impact of good roads on rural trading and non-household manufacturing activities. But then, development of roads and communications can also result in backwash effects to the rural economy – it may find an easy market for cheap urban goods thereby producing obliterating effects on the rural traditional enterprises, and thus may lead to out-migration of rural youth rather than contributing to development of local rural non-farm sector (Reardon 1999; Islam, 1997). Numerous other activities tend to agglomerate where the infrastructure is adequate and eventually the non-farm sector gets benefited (Binswanger *et al.*, 1989). Infrastructure development also helps people to have an access to new opportunities by commuting to nearby towns.

Education is also considered another important factor that influences the growth of rural non-farm growth in villages and small rural towns (Islam, 1997; Chadha, 1997; Lanjouw, 1999). Eapen (1994) also notes the importance of education in the context of Kerala that helped in shifting employment from farm to non-farm sector. However, job preference of the educated persons in Kerala has been towards salaried jobs rather than self-employment (Mathew, 1995). Likewise, Jayaraj (1994), Basant (1993) and Narayanmoorthy (2002) observed a positive relationship between literacy and rural non-farm sector employment. Also, the role of government programmes and public expenditure in rural development programmes have been an important contributory factor for promoting non-farm sector activities. In fact, the rising public expenditure during 1980s was the major factor for growth of non-farm sector, and also, deceleration in non-farm employment during early 1990s was attributed to the drop in public expenditure (Ghosh, 1995; Sen, 1996, 1997).

Apart from the role of specific factors influencing the growth of non-farm sector, a number of studies have also identified the influence of composite factors on the expansion of non-farm activities (*see* in particular: Harris, 1991; Eapen, 1995; Vaidyanathan, 1994; Basant, 1993;Visaria and Basant, 1994).

(iii) Residual Hypothesis

Contrary to the broad development perspective envisaged in the structural change thesis that is followed by prosperity (induced through urbanisation, modernisation of agricultural growth and infrastructural development) which leads to diversified occupational structure (Kuznets, 1966) and eventually helps increase the demand for labour in non-agricultural sector. It is argued (McGee, 1971) that such transformation of surplus labour from agriculture to industry is mere a distress-induced phenomenon that ultimately gets transformed into low productive service occupations rather than in the industry that has limited absorption capacity. In other words, the central issue in the context of non-farm activities is whether diversification of workforce is demand-induced or merely acts as a sponge for surplus labour in the farm sector. This debate has probably excited most discussion in the literature of non-farm sector.

The residual sector hypothesis was credited to Vaidyanathan (1986) who noted a positive correlation between the non-farm sector growth of employment and unemployment rate, and postulated that non-farm sector absorbed surplus labour from agriculture when the absorption capacity of farm sector in urban areas is limited. The non-farm sector employment acts as a sponge for the growing labour force. A large number of studies have however contested this hypothesis by empirical validation. Evidences at macro level suggest that the earning levels in non-agriculture activities have been significantly higher than the agricultural activities (Papola, 1992). Evidence also suggests that productivity and wage rates in non-farm sector are significantly higher than in the agriculture sector (Bhalla, 1998). The decade of 1980s amply shows that sharp fall in poverty in rural areas (with rising real wages) was largely due to dynamism in diversification of rural economy into non-farm activities, despite the fact that employment growth in agriculture was slowest (Ghosh, 1995; Sen, 1997). The post-1987-88 scenarios (i.e. up to 1993-94) however, show a reversal of trend in this diversification process, more particularly for females (Chadha, 1997). The deceleration of such diversification of workforce is largely attributed to fiscal compression of economic reforms process (Chadha,

1997; Sen, 1998). The state-wise analysis during the decade of 1970s and 1980s clearly brings out the fact that those states which have done fairly well in agriculture have also done better in diversification into non-agriculture sector, thus strengthening the argument of the virtuous linkages of farm and non-farm sector (Chadha, 1997). This thesis has been widely accepted by other scholars like Vaidyanathan (1986); Vyas and Mathai (1978); Unni (1998).

It is also important that a large section of workforce is engaged in self-employed activities in the non-agricultural sector, and wage rate as such does not seem to influence the supply of workers in this segment. It is highly unlikely to discard the residual hypothesis on the basis of wage rates. One cannot therefore completely rule out the possibility of residual hypothesis in certain areas or segment of population. Higher levels of employment in non-farm activities have been observed to co-exist with high incidence of rural poverty in many of less developing countries, and diversification is merely transitory phenomenon associated with stress (Seth, 1992). Although employment in terms of man-days may appear to have increased in the non-farm sector, yet in terms of earnings the distress seems to be apparent (Chadha, 1994). Some of the studies found weak production inter-linkages between farm and non-farm sectors (Dev, 1990; Unni; 1991). Sometimes, the distress push the processes work strongly in some region (Verma, *et al.,* 1995). Also, some part of the region seems to have stronger linkage effect while other part still shows the distress-induced effects (Singh, 1994). The rural non-farm (RNF) activities may create distress situation in case of supplementary workers who actually have no main occupation and whose employment is of subsidiary nature, and those who are engaged in secondary activities (Bhalla, 1990).

(iv) Limitations of Existing Literature in the Context of the Hill Economy

Available literature (*see* Unni, 1998 for detailed review) suggests various alternative positions for growth of non-agriculture sector, which analyses the relationship between various indicators and the non-agricultural employment. But the context of analysis in most of these studies has been restricted to non-hill economy. The constraints posed by the terraced type cultivation do not lend much support to the Mellorian type of linkages for the growth of non-farm sector. Not only this, lack of development in general raises the issues of low productivity which results in mushrooming of numerous types of non-farm activities. How sustainable are they? Do their existence represent a dynamism or it is merely an involutionary growth? When agriculture and manufacturing are at precarious situations, relatively faster growth of tertiary segment needs a detailed probe with the help of other prime movers outside agriculture (Bhalla, 1993). The case of hill economy presents a typical example of rather unexplored and relatively less researched area. As the experts have aptly concluded that "it is not obvious how readily the emergence of vibrant rural non-farm employment can be engineered in a remote, agriculturally backward and sparsely populated area, i.e. lack of case examples" (World Bank, 2000). Literacy rate is comparatively much higher in the hill areas and the share of rural non-farm employment has also shown an increasing trend over the years. This line of causation seems to be undisputed as scholars have shown that high level of education helps the movement into non-farm activities (Chadha, 1997; Lanjouw, 1999). But in the context of hill region, significantly large number of educated persons out-migrate in search of jobs outside. Such level of flight of human capital has an obvious effect on the local economy. In addition to the level of education, there are other factors such as caste, gender and size of landholdings which also influence the employment opportunities in the hill areas (Lanjouw and Shariff, 1999).

II. Economic Characteristics of Uttarakhand

Mountain economies pose some specific problems and within it there exists wide diversity and variability both in terms of resource endowments, development potential as well as constraints. The Uttarakhand state is characterised by economic backwardness. It is predominantly a hilly and mountainous region with undulating topography, varied climate, limited arable land and difficult agricultural conditions. This has resulted in a low economic base. The habitants are sparsely populated and widely scattered. The declining forest cover and its environmental consequences on the land and water resources also pose serious problems. Increasing population pressure coupled with heavy dependence on low productive agriculture, industrial backwardness, lack of social services, inadequate infrastructure and harsh geographical features are the challenges facing the development of the region. Also, long gestation period of projects and relatively higher per unit cost of infrastructure development, and low returns on investment resulted in limited income earning opportunities.

The dominant characteristics of the region's backwardness are closely related to its mountain specificities viz. inaccessibility, fragility and marginality. Although, agriculture is the main occupation of the hill people yet it suffers from several inherent maladies. Landholdings are small, fragmented and scattered. Preponderance of cultivators in tiny size of land parcels is most common barring the *tarai* region—Dehradun, Udham Singh Nagar and Hardwar districts. Marginal holdings account for about 70 per cent and small holdings for about 18 per cent of the total holdings in the state. Irrigation facilities are very low and agriculture is mainly rainfed. Net irrigated area as a percentage of net cropped area in the state is 45 per cent in 2008-09. Out of this, hill area has the share of only about 18 per cent, and there is a wide variation between hill and non-hill districts. The share of net irrigated area in the hills is about 26.5 per cent while for the planes it is 73.5 per cent in 2008-09. Traditional agriculture practices are predominant and any drastic changes can hardly be made due to several constraints. The use of fertiliser is abysmally low (2%) in the hill districts while four plane districts use 98 per cent of total fertiliser consumed. This has resulted in low productivity and low returns from agricultural crops. All these factors lead to limited food availability, and hence food insecurity, which is a common feature in many parts of the hill districts in the state (IDFC, 2002). Agriculture is the primary occupation of the people but the specificities of land-use pattern differ considerably from place to place. For instance, in the higher altitude, agro-pastoralism is dominant while in the lower altitude, settled agriculture on terrace slope is practiced. In the valleys, intensive agriculture is widely prevalent (Farooque and Rawat, 1997). These factors greatly influence the production, consumption and livelihood patterns. The other components of agriculture are livestock production and horticulture. The livestock is central to agricultural development as it helps in cultivation, and provides milk, meat, wool, skin, etc. The livestock increased marginally during 1983-98 with a decline in the growth of sheep, and cattle, and relatively high growth of poultry, and buffalo stock. The proportion of scrub cattle is large in the livestock reserve. The quality of cattle is generally poor with low productivity. There is a demand for improved variety of livestock but lack of good fodder supplies, poor marketing and infrastructure for animal has hampered the livestock growth on commercial lines. Also, over the years, pressure on land has resulted in degradation of pastures and erosion of common grazing land. Horticulture (fruits and vegetables) has potential for high returns but technological and other constraints have severely restricted the scope of expansion. Agriculture is largely based on traditional methods with little diversification to potential areas according to its land capability (Shah, 1996). The manufacturing base is very low, large industries are almost non-existent and the share of employment in manufacturing sector is very low (2.5%) in the hilly districts. Household manufacturing base, in particular, is observed to be disappearing fast. The shift of workforce from the primary to tertiary sector largely constitutes the proliferation of 'other services', which comprises of government activities rather than growth of trade, transport, storage and commerce. While in general, there has been substantial inter-sectoral movement of workforce from agriculture to other sectors of economy, in value terms, the level of development in manufacturing, services and industrialisation has been negative for all hilly districts in Uttarakhand and their relative ranking is in the bottom rung of 369 districts in the country chosen for study by S.C. Gulati (quoted in Bora, 2000). Per capita NDDP in the plain districts is generally higher (higher than the state average) compared to the hill districts. The various indicators of development in the state show low levels of development with marked inter-district disparities. The plane districts (namely, Dehradun, Udham Singh Nagar and Hardwar) are relatively better off as compared to other hilly districts in the state (Annexure III.1).

Lack of productive employment has forced people to seek multiple livelihood strategies as the main coping mechanism to meet increasing food and cash requirements. Unemployment among adult males has led to a large-scale out-migration in search of livelihood and employment. The migrants in turn have been supporting back their families through remittance. This phenomenon is sometimes termed as 'money-order economy'. The movement of people from the region is closely related to its backwardness. In all the hilly districts of the state, out-migration exceeds immigration. Micro level studies also show high rate of out-migration particularly among the educated youth. By and large, push factors motivated to a large number of migrants (70%) and pull factors did so for smaller magnitude (19%). Also, the region suffers net loss due to out-migration (Bora, 1996). This has not only resulted in drain of human resources, but also entailed enormous burden on the women. The hill women perform all activities except ploughing, and suffer extremely from heavy workload and drudgery. They work about 14 to 16 hours per day (Planning Commission, 1985). Surprisingly, backwardness exists in tandem with high literacy rate. As per 2011 Census, literacy rate in Uttarakhand has increased to 79.6 per cent (88.3 % for males and 70.7% for females). Higher literacy rate further accentuates the out-migration process. This drain of educated youth is primarily due to low productive base of the economy. Also, in the hill region, caste factor plays an important role in determining the level of education and livelihood. Labour relation and caste linkages greatly influence the employment and earnings. The development interventions since the Fifth Five Year Plan, when special hill area development programme was initiated, have been in the nature of the general strategy of development. Never the development of hill area was conceived in terms of formulation of region-specific development strategy (Papola, 1983). This has produced undesirable socio-economic and cultural gap in the state. Planners and policy-makers often failed to understand the hill specificities that have put an adverse effect on the carrying capacity of the system. A fast growing contractor-business class regime has exploited the forest and mineral wealth indiscriminately. Development administration has been insensitive to the needs of the people. The people's movements (e.g. *chipko andolan and* demand for a separate hill state) were the clear manifestation of the neglect of aspiration of the people and lack of a sustainable development of the hill economy (Joshi, 1995; 1999).

From the long-term development perspective, agriculture-field crops have limited scope for increased productivity, employment and incomes due to limitations posed by the hill agriculture. However, the region offers potentials for development in view of its specific resource endowments and relative advantages such as forest wealth, water resources, tourist amenities services, mineral resources and cultivation of high value non-food crops (fruits, vegetables, seeds, medicinal plants, exotic flowers, mushroom, etc.). There has been considerable increase in the growth of the area under fruits and vegetables over the years. Production of vegetables increased from 508 mt. to 692 mt., vegetables increased from 388 mt. to 461 mt. during 1996-97 to 2005-06. Studies show that Himachal Pradesh, which presents a similar case of hill region, has diversified into vegetables and fruit cultivation and attained higher levels of growth of employment and income. This has also increased opportunities for non-farm employment (Chand, 1995). Uttarakhand also hold considerable promise for development of horticulture. Area study in Uttarakhand shows that incomes as well as employment are much higher in the case of vegetable crops than conventional crops. Commercialisation of agriculture also tends to check out-migration (Badhani, 1998). Another area study (Chand, 1996) shows how irrigation is a critical factor for high return off-season vegetable crops that have been proved highly remunerative as compared to traditional crops. Another area where there is a large scope of development is animal husbandry, and sheep and goat rearing for woollen products. This is primarily because of the large land area under forests and pastures. Forest is the most important resource in Uttarakhand. Forest area covers 65 per cent of the reported area in 2009-10. It has a wealth of forest produce including minor forest produce. It contributes quite significantly to the earnings of the state government. Most of the benefits of this resource in the past have however gone to the plane area. As it is well known, timber is taken out from the hill region in unprocessed form and the real value addition occurs in the plane areas. A small fraction of it accrues to local people in the form of wage component (Joshi, 2001).

There were 1,210 khadi udyog/gramodyog units and 35,955 SSI units employing 3,750 and 1,42,780 persons respectively during 2009-10. There are 203 large industries employing 79697 persons in 2009-10. Industrial sickness is quite high as more than 36 per cent units involving 22.7 per cent of industrial employment are closed. Government has taken series of measures to revive and rehabilitate the sick units (Government of Uttarakhand, 2003). Major small-scale industries in Uttarakhand are Khadi, handicrafts, handloom fabrics and food products. Industrial activity is highly skewed in the State of Uttarakhand. Most of the industrial activities are concentrated in the planes, and hills are bereft from industrialisation. Dehradun, Hardwar, Nainital and Udham Singh Nagar have about 89 per cent of the factories set up in Uttarakhand and 94 per cent of all the employed in the state (Mittal *et al.*, 2008).

Integrated Industrial Development Policy, 2008 was launched in February especially for the industrial development of hilly and remote areas in the state. While Nainital and Dehradun ranked among the top 15 industrially developed districts in erstwhile Uttar Pradesh; four districts, namely, Chamoli, Pithoragarh, Uttarkashi and Almora, were among the 15 industrially most backward districts in that state (Singh, 1997).

Hill districts offer vast potential for development of tourism industry. In 2010 alone, 309.7 lakh domestic tourists and 1.4 lakh foreign tourists visited different tourist's spots in Uttarakhand, which is one of the key GDP drivers. The region offers an unique environment for various types of pollution-free and precision-based enterprises (e.g. electronics) and amenities services like hotels, resorts and tourism, which offer vast scope for promoting new concepts of tourism. The region is rich in water resources with a niche for generation of hydro-electricity. However, about 11.0 per cent potential has been harnessed presently as against the estimated potential of 25,450 MW power generations. The region can utilise this huge potential to meet the growing domestic power needs and export the surplus to other states. This may be one of the important sources of revenue generation. Development of micro and mini projects would be environmentally most appropriate for utilising water resources. With greater involvement of private sector the resources can be utilised more efficiently and optimally.

All these activities have considerable prospects for providing sustainable livelihoods. As the hill economy gets diversified and commercialised, the employment and income would be enhanced within area or at a commuting distance thereby reducing the forced migration.

III. Rural Non-Farm Employment in Uttarakhand

Uttarakhand now comprises of 13 districts (seven in Garhwal region and six in Kumaon region).* Total population of the state in 2011 is 101.16 lakh comprising of 51.54 lakh males (51%) and 49.62 lakh females (49%). Annual growth of population declined from 2.04 per cent during 1991-2001 to 1.9 per cent during 2001-11. Workforce participation (main workers) in 1991 was 35.17 per cent (47.33 % cent males and 22.19 % females) which declined sharply at 27.96 per cent (37.08% males and 18.68% females) in 2001. Main and marginal workers together show that there has been a steep increase in the percentage of marginal workers in the 1990s. Percentage of marginal workers almost doubled from 4.8 per cent in 1991 to 10.51 per cent in 2001 in the state. Gender-wise, Worker Participation Rate (WPR) of male (marginal) workers increased by more than five times (from 1.5% to 8.8%) during the period 1991-2001. The share of female population as marginal workers is still very high as compared to their male counterparts, which also increased by about 4 percentage points during the decade 1991-2001 (Table 3.1). As per census, the share of

---

* Garhwal region consists of Chamoli, Rudraprayag, Dehradun, Garhwal, Tehri Garhwal, Uttarkashi and Hardwar districts and Kumaon region consists of Almora, Bageshwar, Nainital, Udham Singh Nagar, Pithoragarh and Champawat districts. Hardwar district has been added and remaining twelve districts have been carved out from erstwhile eight districts.

Table 3.1 : Work Participation Rate in Uttarakhand

Area/Sex	*Main*			*Main plus marginal*		
	1981@	*1991*	*2001*	*1981@*	*1991*	*2001*
Rural						
Person	37.07	36.8	28.40	42.97	42.81	41.44
Male	46.85	46.65	34.73	48.71	48.48	45.35
Female	27.94	26.74	22.27	37.93	37.06	37.65
Total						
Person	36.19	35.17	27.96	41.13	39.94	38.47
Male	47.69	47.33	37.08	49.24	48.78	45.91
Female	24.21	22.19	18.68	32.7	30.5	30.89

Note : @ Excludes Hardwar district.
Sources: 1. Census of India, *Primary Census Abstract, Uttar Pradesh,* 1981-1991.
2. Census of India, 2001.

the agricultural and allied sector in employment (main workers) in the state decreased from 71 per cent in 1981 to 67 per cent in 1991, and further to 55 per cent in 2001. The share of the secondary sector employment declined marginally from 8.8 per cent in 1981 to 8 per cent in 1991 and 13.3 per cent in 2001 (Table 3.2). Almost an entire shift in employment from primary sector, particularly in 1980s, has been absorbed by the services sector in the state, which accounted for one-fourth of employment in the state in 1991. In 2001, there has been a relatively faster diversification of workforce from agriculture sector. Surprisingly, the share of rural women workforce in agriculture is highest (cultivators + agricultural labourers + livestock, fishing, etc.). Their share was 97.94 per cent in 1971, 97.77 per cent in 1981, 96.74 per cent in 1991 and 92 per cent in 2001 – a decline of 1.2 percentage points during the 20 years (1971-1991) is an evidence of structural stagnation. Their high participation in agricultural activities is marked by their low productivity and increasing vulnerability.

A noteworthy feature, however, is that the pace of diversification of rural workforce from agriculture to non-agriculture has accelerated in the 1990s, as there has been a decline by 5.4 percentage points (excluding Hardwar) during the decade 1991-2001 (Tables 3.2 and 3.4). Across districts, the share of rural non-farm employment is

Table 3.2 : Structural Shifts in Main Workforce in Uttarakhand*, 1981-2001

Sector/Industry	*1981**			*1991**			*2001*		
Rural	*Person*	*Male*	*Female*	*Person*	*Male*	*Female*	*Person*	*Male*	*Female*
Cultivators	74.72	62.54	95.55	70.11	54.73	93.08	60.33	46.34	85.68
Agricultural labourers	5.85	8.17	2.00	6.82	9.17	3.3	7.57	10.09	2.99
Livestock, fishing, forestry, etc.	1.53	2.32	0.22	1.9	2.94	0.36	3.01	2.82	3.36
Mining and quarrying	0.23	0.37	0	0.19	0.31	0.02	1.31	1.67	0.65
Manufacturing – household	1.3	1.76	0.53	0.83	0.99	0.58	1.90	2.15	1.45
Manufacturing – other than household	2.41	3.29	0.25	2.36	3.72	0.33	3.71	5.42	0.63
Construction	2.36	3.75	0.1	1.93	3.16	0.11	4.24	6.40	0.33
Trade and commerce	2.13	3.38	0.04	2.72	4.46	0.13	3.90	5.86	0.33
Transport, storage and communication	1.15	1.84	0.01	1.2	1.99	0.03	2.21	3.37	0.10
Other services	8.34	12.57	1.3	11.93	18.53	2.06	11.82	15.88	4.48
All									
Cultivators	63.77	49.61	89.87	58.13	41.33	89.34	45.77	32.22	78.37
Agricultural labourers	5.54	7.22	2.1	6.4	7.99	3.37	6.11	7.45	2.90
Livestock, fishing, forestry, etc.	1.61	2.28	0.25	2.2	3.14	0.43	2.77	2.54	3.30
Mining and quarrying	0.27	0.39	0.01	0.19	0.27	0.02	1.21	1.44	0.64
Manufacturing – household	1.49	1.86	0.73	0.86	0.93	0.72	1.96	2.04	1.78
Manufacturing – other than household	4.27	6.1	0.5	4.21	6.1	0.6	6.11	8.07	1.39
Construction	3.07	4.49	0.16	2.93	4.37	0.2	5.28	7.27	0.49
Trade and commerce	4.78	7.02	0.16	5.79	9.41	0.4	7.66	10.51	0.81
Transport, storage and communication	2.04	3.01	0.04	2.16	3.25	0.08	3.43	4.76	0.24
Other services	13.15	18.02	6.18	17.13	23.21	4.84	19.70	23.69	10.08
Total	100.00	100.00	100.00	100.00	100.00	100.00	100.00	100.00	100.00

Note: * Excluding Hardwar district.
Source : Census of India.

substantially higher in three districts, namely, Dehradun (51%), Hardwar (42.6%) and Nainital (32%), whereas in the remaining districts, it ranges between 18 to 30 per cent – the larger share of rural non-farm employment being mainly in construction, trade and government services. This wide variation in the share of rural non-farm employment (sector-wise) among the districts is mainly due to their urban base – the three districts with highest shares of rural non-farm employment have highest degree of urbanization in the state, which provide employment opportunities to the rural workforce mainly through commuting daily to nearby urban centres (Table 3.4). The NSS data do not show any remarkable changes in the structure of employment in rural areas as there has been hardly any significant decline (about 3.9 percentage points) in the share of agriculture in employment during the past 18 years, i.e. 1987-88 to 2004-05. Construction is a dominant activity in rural areas as it employs about 6.10 per cent of the rural workforce in the state. Public services are the next largest employer accounting for about 5.0 per cent share in rural employment (Table 3.3). It also emerges that whatever has been the degree of structural changes in employment, it has been limited to male workers, and more so among the rural males (Awasthi, *et al.*, 2005).

As per the Economic Census (1998), there are about 2.05 lakh non-farm enterprises in the state comprising 1.43 lakh own account enterprises and 0.62 lakh establishments. About 58 per cent of these units (56% own account and 62% establishments) are concentrated in three plane districts (Dehradun, Nainital and Hardwar), and over 91 per cent of registered units are located in these districts, which are agriculturally and industrially well endowed (Table 3.5). Most of the units in these districts are located in urban areas (78%). These districts are well developed in terms of infrastructure, connectivity, market links and urbanisation, which caused relatively faster growth of non-farm enterprises while hill districts are at disadvantaged positions due to its peculiar geographical settings that impede the growth of these enterprises. The proportion of these units in the hill districts is as low as 3.6 per cent in Uttarkashi to 11 per cent in Pithoragarh district, while in the plane district, the share ranges from16 per cent in Dehradun to 22 per cent in Nainital (Table 3.5). The pattern of change

Table 3.3 : Percentage Distribution of Workers (UPSS) by Industrial Category in Uttarakhand

Industry	*1987-88*	*1993-94*	*1999-2000*	*2004-05*
		Rural		
Agriculture etc.	82.29	84.42	79.49	78.40
Mining & quarrying	0.07	0.27	0.00	0.00
Manufacturing	5.80	1.52	3.49	3.40
Electricity, water etc.	0.04	0.10	0.25	0.20
Construction	5.07	4.51	7.71	6.10
Trade, hotel and restaurant	1.91	1.52	2.06	4.40
Transport, etc.	0.37	0.75	2.00	2.00
Fin. inter, business act. etc.	0.20	0.38	0.54	0.50
Pub. admin., edu., etc.	4.26	6.36	4.36	5.00
Total	100.00	100.00	100.00	100.00
Agriculture etc.	72.75	75.62	64.46	61.69
Mining & quarrying	0.06	0.32	0.00	0.00
Manufacturing	6.51	2.74	5.50	5.54
Electricity, water etc.	0.44	0.23	1.06	0.48
Construction	5.62	4.25	8.23	7.16
Trade, hotel and restaurant	4.61	3.66	6.75	10.06
Transport etc.	0.80	1.63	2.43	3.33
Fin. inter, business act. etc.	0.74	0.94	1.70	1.05
Pub. adm., educ., etc	8.47	10.45	9.87	10.66
Total	100.00	100.00	100.00	100.00

Source : NSSO, Households Unit Record Data for various rounds.

between the period 1990 and 1998 shows that these units (both own account as well as establishments) are declining in Dehradun and Nainital (rural and urban) and increasing in Hardwar district, while urban areas in all the hill districts show a consistent increase with a marginal decline in rural areas in three districts (Chamoli, Pauri Garhwal and Pithoragarh). The concentration of own account units in the rural areas of the hill districts is declining (except a marginal increase of 1 per cent in Uttarkashi) probably because of various constraints facing these units both from supply and demand sides (Table 3.6). Sectoral distribution of non-farm enterprises show that trade and commerce (45%) and services (28%) dominated in the state but more than half of the manufacturing (51%), trade and

Table 3.4 : District-wise Percentage Distribution of Workers by Industry Division (Main plus Marginal), 2001

District	*Total*					*Rural*					*Total*
	Cultivators	*Agri. labour*	*Sub-total*	*Household industry*	*Other workers*	*Cultivators*	*Agri. labour*	*Sub-total*	*Household industry*	*Other workers*	
Almora	74.77	1.38	76.16	1.18	22.66	79.48	1.47	80.95	1.18	17.87	100.00
Bageshwar	69.91	2.01	71.92	1.61	26.46	77.33	2.09	79.42	1.56	19.01	100.00
Chamoli	64.36	1.38	65.74	1.82	32.44	70.35	1.41	71.77	1.70	26.53	100.00
Champawat	74.67	3.07	77.74	1.88	20.38	76.20	3.12	79.31	1.87	18.81	100.00
Dehradun	18.64	7.01	25.65	2.22	72.13	36.25	13.07	49.31	2.57	48.12	100.00
Garhwal	67.06	1.55	68.62	1.15	30.24	73.85	1.68	75.53	1.10	23.37	100.00
Hardwar	22.63	19.06	41.69	3.98	54.33	31.44	25.97	57.41	4.29	38.30	100.00
Nainital	42.03	8.60	50.64	1.85	47.51	56.69	11.51	68.19	2.03	29.77	100.00
Pithoragarh	67.70	1.17	68.86	3.86	27.27	72.94	1.26	74.20	3.62	22.18	100.00
Rudraprayag	75.78	0.53	76.31	0.92	22.77	76.85	0.54	77.39	0.92	21.69	100.00
Tehri Garhwal	69.85	1.20	71.05	0.85	28.10	76.43	1.31	77.74	0.89	21.37	100.00
Udham Singh Nagar	29.72	25.63	55.35	3.30	41.35	40.13	32.83	72.96	2.20	24.83	100.00
Uttarkashi	75.10	1.91	77.00	1.42	21.57	79.01	2.01	81.02	1.45	17.53	100.00
Uttarakhand	49.77	8.26	58.03	2.23	39.74	61.75	9.75	71.50	2.07	26.43	100.00
Uttarakhand excl. Hardwar	54.04	6.56	60.60	1.96	37.44	65.88	7.54	73.42	1.77	24.81	100.00
India	31.71	26.69	58.4	4.07	37.52	42.14	31.2	73.34	3.77	22.9	100.00

Source : Registrar General of India (2002), *Census of India, 2001, Workers and Non-workers,* (Electronic Data), New Delhi.

Table 3.5 : Number of Non-farm Enterprises in Uttarakhand

District	*Own account enterprises*		*Establishments*		*All*	
	Number	*Percentage*	*Number*	*Percentage*	*Number*	*Percentage*
Uttarkashi	4791	3.36	2562	4.11	7353	3.58
Chamoli	10038	7.04	4433	7.11	14471	7.06
Tehri	9340	6.55	3427	5.49	12769	6.33
Dehradun	18116	12.70	13643	21.87	31759	15.49
Pauri	8960	6.28	3818	6.12	12778	6.23
Pithoragarh	12820	8.99	3969	6.36	16789	8.19
Almora	17123	12.01	5669	9.09	22792	11.12
Nainital	30243	21.20	14569	23.36	44812	21.87
Hardwar	31189	21.87	10283	16.49	41472	20.23
Total	**142620**	**100.00**	**62373**	**100.00**	**204995**	**100.00**

Source : Economic Census, 1998, Economics and Statistics Division, State Planning Institute, Lucknow.

Table 3.6 : Percentage Distribution of Non-farm Enterprises in Uttarakhand

District	***1990***		***1998***		***2005***	
	Rural	*Urban*	*Rural*	*Urban*	*Rural*	*Urban*
Uttarkashi	4.98	1.44	5.36	1.58	4.91	1.91
Chamoli	11.60	3.18	10.36	3.32	10.61	3.33
Tehri	4.98	2.22	9.66	2.34	8.00	2.22
Dehradun	8.97	26.99	7.99	24.00	8.58	23.43
Pauri	10.46	4.89	7.41	4.90	8.61	4.10
Pithoragarh	11.06	3.45	11.05	4.95	12.16	5.79
Almora	16.25	4.08	17.03	4.42	13.87	4.26
Nainital	16.10	31.72	14.45	30.22	17.92	30.83
Hardwar	11.10	22.03	16.69	24.27	15.34	24.13
Total	**100.00**	**100.00**	**100.00**	**100.00**	**100.00**	**100.00**

Sources : (i) Economic Census, 1990 and 1998, Economics and Statistics Division, State Planning Institute, Lucknow.
(ii) Economic Census, 2005 (Quick Results) Economic and Statistical Directorate, Uttarakhand.

commerce (63%), and services enterprises (58%) are concentrated in the three plane districts (Table 3.7).

Quick results of Fifth Economic Census (2005) show that total number of non-farm enterprises increased from 2.05 lakh in 1998 to

Table 3.7 : Percentage Distribution of Non-farm Enterprises in Uttarakhand

District	*Mining & quarrying*	*Manuf-acturing*	*Constru-ction*	*Trade and com-merce*	*Hotel and restau-rant*	*Trans-port, storage etc.*	*Services*	*Total*
Uttarkashi	6.90	4.68	8.24	2.58	4.45	7.19	3.79	3.59
Chamoli	-	8.13	7.38	5.85	9.79	6.67	7.73	7.06
Tehri	5.17	6.21	34.19	5.10	7.39	9.83	6.24	6.23
Dehradun	12.07	10.92	10.19	17.61	13.49	15.47	15.13	15.49
Pauri	-	4.71	1.14	6.68	6.76	4.73	6.51	6.23
Pithoragarh	12.07	9.90	0.05	7.65	9.12	7.84	8.28	8.19
Almora	56.89	15.95	4.95	9.37	17.12	14.40	9.51	11.12
Nainital	6.90	18.97	5.52	23.26	18.60	16.16	23.34	21.86
Hardwar	-	20.53	28.34	21.90	13.18	17.71	19.47	20.23
Total	**100.00**	**100.00**	**100.00**	**100.00**	**100.00**	**100.00**	**100.00**	**100.00**

Source : Economic Census, 1990 and 1998, Economics and Statistics Division, State Planning Institute, Lucknow.

about 2.92 lakh in 2005. Three plane districts (namely, Hardwar, Dehradun and Udham Singh Nagar) account for about 43 per cent of the total non-farm enterprises providing 52 per cent employment.

1. *Typology of Rural Non-Farm Activities*

Conceptually, rural non-farm sector constitutes a large number of activities outside agriculture sector (crop cultivation) such as auxiliary, off-farm activities, rural industrial sector, services and non-agricultural labour in creating of public infrastructure (Saith, 1992). Such a broader definition of rural non-farm sector encompassing all non-agricultural activities excluding crop husbandry is desirable, as this would capture all aspects of rural diversification (Papola and Sharma, 2005). In rural non-farm sector, self-employment is the dominant category, and regular and wage employment in the public or government sector are minuscule and is likely to shrink further. Therefore, a large part of employment has necessarily to come in the form of self-employment and casual employment from the unorganised sector. Enterprises are the main sources of employment creation that consist of variety of household and non-household activities in rural setting. Heterogeneity is widespread in rural enterprises in terms of capital use, product groups, productivity and production relations. The duality within enterprises is often discernible; a large number of enterprises have linkages to local economy using locally available raw material, traditional skills and low degree of technology, and a substantial part of output is meant for final consumption in the local economy. Such enterprises use mostly family labour with little surplus and majority of them are operating at low margin of subsistence. Seasonal enterprises, artisan-based and caste-based enterprises fall in this category. Without technological improvements, skill development and product diversification, the existing traditional household and tiny/small units would gradually obliterate and liquidate (Islam, 1987).

The other types of enterprises are those that use improved technology, hired labourers, and have linkages outside the local economy. Such enterprises are operating more or less on a stable basis with surplus as a prime motive for growth of enterprises. These enterprises have been providing most of the employment outside agriculture to the rural population either on regular basis or seasonal basis. However, many of these enterprises face numerous structural problems, which make them increasingly difficult to survive in a competitive environment. There is a need to look into the problems of these enterprises both from supply as well as demand sides and make the policy environment conducive for the growth of these enterprises. Notwithstanding, in a changed economic environment, most of the employment is likely to be generated in small and micro enterprises in the unorganised sector. It is therefore critical to promote such enterprises through formulating of appropriate strategies and policies to overcome them.

As discussed in the preceding section, Uttarakhand (hill districts) is characterised by the subsistence agriculture and any drastic transformation within cereal-based agriculture has obvious limitations due to the problems associated with hill agriculture. In any case, traditional agriculture with its low productive base and increasing pressure of population on limited cultivable land does not seem to be a viable and a sustainable option for providing employment and livelihood any longer. Also, the industrial base is precarious in the hill districts and it does not offer much scope for sustained employment and incomes. The large-scale industrial activity is neither possible nor desirable in view of ecological and environmental considerations. Wherever such activities have been undertaken, it had disastrous effects on the ecology and environment and caused greater human sufferings (e.g. mine extracting activities and construction of large dams). It is therefore important that while choosing any activity for development, its impact on ecology and environment has to be taken into consideration on the one hand, and sustainability of activities in providing employment and incomes to the local population, on the other. Also, owing to mountain specificities, only certain kinds of activities can be considered which are based on niche resources or have comparative advantage in the area concerned. Such activities could be developed and specialised through commercialisation and trade (Papola, 1996).

(i) Enterprise-based Activities

Enterprise-based activities are critical for sustainable employment generation and enhancing of income levels which in turn can help improving the living standard of the people. Factors like typical hill specificities (inaccessibility, fragility and marginality), limited and thinly spread resource base, lack of infrastructural facilities, distant markets, low entrepreneurial base, and lack of appropriate policy support severely constrict enterprise-based activities, particularly in the hilly region. Also, ecological and environmental considerations pose acute limitations to the large-scale enterprise development. As a result, entrepreneurial activity is mostly concentrated in the plane districts, which do not have many handicaps that are usually associated with the hilly region. Though the region possesses certain mountain-specific resources, which have potential for being developed as niche products having comparative advantage to the region, yet there are not many examples of harnessing these unique resources into tradable products and services for the wider markets. Traditionally, hill districts have developed numerous tiny and household-based activities utilising locally available resources and skills, mostly for sub-serving the needs of local economy through trade and exchange under mutual obligation system, but very little of them meant for external trade. These kinds of enterprise-based activities have however limited product lines carried out on a small scale with little surplus for reinvestment. But over the years these enterprises are languishing and operating at a low equilibrium trap with little product diversification and surplus. The major reasons for sickness of these enterprises can be attributed to both the supply and demand side aspects. Supply side constraints are lack of credit, training, market support, availability of appropriate technology, power, shrinking local resource base, and other structural bottlenecks. And, demand side constraints are lack of product competitiveness (hence low internal and external demand), increasing competition in the product market from the plane areas, limited linkages and integration to other directly productive segments of economy, etc.

In the context of hill region, enterprise-based activity can take different forms – diversification from cereal-based products to high value horticultural products to simple processing, and other enterprise-based activities such as livestock, forest (non-timber), artisan and tourism.

(a) Natural resource-based enterprises

The amount of land available for cultivation in the state, particularly in the hill districts, is very limited as it constitutes only 12.4 per cent of the total reported area with significant variation in the land utilisation pattern between the hill and plane districts. The plane districts (Hardwar and Udham Singh Nagar) have as high as 53 per cent of net sown area while the hill districts have as lowest as 3.7 per cent of net sown area in Uttarkashi district. Per capita availability of agricultural land is quite low in the state (0.09 hectare as compared to 0.17 hectare in India during the year 2000). Also, lack of irrigation hinders the use of improved agricultural practices such as high yielding varieties of seeds, and use of fertilisers and pesticides resulting in very low agricultural productivity in hill districts. This, in turn, imposes severe limitations on the part of the state to meet its food requirements for the increasing population resulting in persistent food deficits in all the hill districts barring Nainital (IDFC, 2002). It is, therefore, important from the long-term perspective to diversify the cereal crop-based activities in high value horticultural crops (fruits, vegetables and medicinal plants) for which the state has comparative advantage. Harnessing the niche-based farming products can eventually help to achieve food security through direct use of products or trade in such products (Jodha, 1992). Developing such high pay-off activities would have positive impact on livelihood security and also on the ecology without degrading the resources. There are case studies which amply demonstrate that agricultural transformation based on high value crops have increased food security and improved the living conditions. However, for successful transformation accessibility to wider market network, strong R&D institutions are critical (Sharma, 1996; Sharma, 1997; Sharma and Sharma, 1997; Tulchan, 1997; Badhani, 1998). Such diversification has helped in restricting out-migration (Badhani, 1998). It is observed that income accrual from the sale of primary products (horticultural) is generally very low due to lack of processing and value addition activities in the region. The major reasons for lack of enterprise activities are small scale and dispersed production, lack of transport and institutional mechanism that does not allow processing to be viable in the region. However, with appropriate policy interventions it is possible to develop enterprise-based activities that would provide higher income through processing and value addition, and help develop upstream and downstream linkages necessary to generate internal momentum of growth. Such enterprise-based activities have been developed in certain parts of hilly region– in the Hindu Kush Himalayan Region– based on niche products. The most widely known example is Western Sichuan (China), where over two-dozen products have been developed based on mountain-specific resources. The other areas where specific products (rather limited one) have been developed are apple cultivation in Himachal Pradesh, vegetable farming in Garampani area in Nainital district, Ginger and Pineapple in Meghalaya and other parts of north-eastern states, tea plantation and processing in Ilam district in Nepal, livestock and dairy development in areas closer to Kathmandu, and Apple cultivation in Arunachal Pradesh (Papola, *et al.*, 2005).

Though the area under commercial crops in the state is comparatively low (one-fifth of the net cropped area), yet there has been a significant growth in the area in production of vegetables, particularly, potato crop. Fruit crops production has also increased albeit lower than the vegetable crops. It has been found that the average yield of fruit and vegetable crops is comparatively higher than that of the traditional foodgrain crops, which has witnessed an increasing trend over the years. However, lack of processing and enterprise-based activities within hill districts, the benefits largely accrued to the enterprises in the plane areas. The hilly districts, therefore, act as a supplier of the primary products and the benefits thereof redound to the advantage of the plane areas, where processing takes place.

The experience of Himachal Pradesh with a similar landholding pattern shows how agriculture could be made more remunerative through diversification into horticulture crops and can create more employment and better income opportunities– clearly, a lesson to be learnt.

In addition, there are other products based on natural resources such as flowers, medicinal plants, herbs, tea, mushroom, bamboo-based products, honey, spices, and minor forest produce, etc. which can be promoted and developed for wider market. Value addition through processing can enhance income levels of the people, but it would require input support of various kinds in an integrated manner.

(b) Livestock-based enterprises

Livestock is central to crop-based activities as it helps in numerous ways: provides draught power for ploughing the field, milk and milk products, meat, skin, hides and wool. Livestock activities form an important supplementary source of income particularly for the poor households. It acts as an insurance against vulnerability, especially when crop fails or entitlements are lost or severely eroded. Some of the livestock activities form the basis of enterprises in the hill districts such as animal rearing, dairying, wool and woollen-based products, etc. However, most of the activities suffer from numerous handicaps: demand constraints, access to market, lack of quality, lack of linkages and other support services. Increasing the value of the products by moving them up for the wider market with higher quality and higher unit value remains a major challenge for the enterprise development. It has been observed that some of the traditional enterprises such as wool-based enterprises are languishing primarily because of increasing competition from the plane areas and apathy of government agencies to promote these activities. However, there is a good scope for promoting some of these activities, particularly having distinct advantage for external trade (viz. woollen products), while others can create increasing market for local economy (viz. dairying products).

(c) Traditional skill-based enterprises

Many traditional skill-based activities have come up autonomously over time in the hill region that became central to their subsistence economy. Some skills developed in view of the availability of forest-based resources (viz. rope making, broom making, wood products, etc), some skills are based on livestock resources (viz. manufacture of woollen products, tannery), while some are based on *jajmāni* system (black- smithy, tailoring, priest services, ploughing, etc.) and in some cases handicrafts products. However, some of these traditional skills have either vanished or are gradually disappearing or languishing owing to various reasons. There is an urgent need to revive them through promotional and support mechanism. Some of the products have the potential for meeting the demand of higher echelons of the society and thus can cater to niche market (viz. handicrafts).

(d) Tourism and amenities-based enterprises

The hilly region offers a unique environment for various types of pollution-free and precision-based enterprises (e.g. electronics) and amenities services like hotels, resorts and tourism. There is a vast scope foı promoting new concepts of tourism like pilgrimage tourism, health tourism, wildlife tourism, cultural tourism and trekking, adventure sports, river rafting, skiing, angling and aero-sports, winter sports, etc. Tourism and amenities services assume one of the main economic drivers and lead sectors for many hill economies that contribute substantively to their GDP. It contributes not only directly (tourist flow) but also indirectly through developing and supporting many tourist related activities (e.g. vegetable production, raising poultry, handicrafts, etc). Though income originating from tourism has been impressive over the years, yet the gain from it has been minimal for the local economy due to low retention capacity of this income. This is primarily due to poor linkages generated by the tourism industry to the local production base; as a result, large part of income flows outside the local economy for procuring goods and services. It is often argued that tourism industries in the mountain economies generate considerable leakages rather than strengthening linkages (Sharma, 2000).

Obviously, there are constraints in promoting enterprises in the hilly region where resources are limited and dispersed (with low possibility of resource-use intensification), limited access to market, inputs, infrastructural bottlenecks, lack of appropriate institutional mechanism and suitable policy environment to support enterprise-based activities (Papola *et al.,* 2005). However, there is immense potential for enterprise development in the hill region based on niche products in which the region possesses comparative advantages. There is therefore a need for according high priority to enterprise development in the region by creating a favourable economic condition and conducive policy environment, keeping in view the constraints and potentials (hill perspective) of the region.

2. Nature of Linkages

Most of the household-based enterprises are linked to limited local economy, drawing upon local resources and skills, and catering to the needs of local economy with little or no surplus for expansion and productivity improvement. These are related to manufacturing agricultural implements, collection of forest products, construction of houses, etc. In a way, they are subsisting at a low level of margin with little or no possibilities of further employment and income in the existing scale of operation. Though some activities are linked beyond the local economy and have potential for increased employment and incomes, such as woollen products, handicrafts and furniture etc.; yet due to lack of technological improvements, product diversification and market support, most of these activities confront with numerous handicaps. There are some activities which have social linkages to certain social classes under *jajmani* system (mutual obligation). For example, the scheduled castes households manufacture agricultural implements and provide certain services (ploughing) to the upper castes households (Brahmin and Khastriya) in lieu of a fixed quantity of foodgrains. This system has been providing social security to lower social group (SCs) since very long time. However, this system has significantly eroded over the years. In certain areas, numbers of new products are coming up based on local resources having distinct locational advantages, such as medicinal plants, herbs, seeds, floriculture, mushrooms, fruits and off-season vegetables that have linkages to wider markets outside the local economy. These resources can be promoted as enterprise-based activities that would provide greater value additions and employment opportunities. Linking these specialised products with the urban market and strengthening the rural-urban linkages through greater infrastructural development, improved communication and market network would help these enterprises to forge linkages for sustained growth. Tourism is yet another important industry that can be promoted through introducing new concepts and greater linkages to the production segments and other services that impinge directly on the expansion of tourism related activities. These mountain products have immense potential for employment and income generation through enterprise development.

IV. Need for the Study

It is widely known that rural households and individuals derive their incomes from diverse and multiple sources of activities. Often, large official surveys provide little or no information about the informal nature of activities, in particular, secondary sources of employment and incomes. Yet, understanding this aspect is very important to comprehend the extremely complex and heterogeneous character of this sector. In view of certain limitations of the aggregative nature of data provided by the census and the NSS, it is essential to carry out micro level studies in order to capture the nuances and dynamics of various non-farm sector activities so as to have a fuller picture and better perspective of the hill economy. Though the regional aggregate data help to understand the macro evidences, yet it does not help understand the micro realities and processes involved through which individual household diversifies activities (Unni, 2000). To be more precise, these aggregate sources of data do not capture the following aspects of the nature of study being proposed (Vaidyanathan, 1997):

(i) Employment conditions across different social classes, their educational/training background and incomes;
(ii) Linkages between farm and non-farm activities;
(iii) Migration pattern (seasonal or long-term) among different social groups and its impact on the place of migration and analysis of the motivational factors for migration;
(iv) Identification of activities having prospects of becoming lead sectors in view of the resource base; and
(v) Impact assessment and the role of various government policies/programmes in generating employment and skill base.

V. Objectives

Within the above broad framework, the study attempts to understand the nature, growth and pattern of employment in the hill region. In particular, the study focuses on non-farm activities. The specific objectives of the study are as follows:

(i) To examine the livelihood diversities and income patterns of the people in farm and non-farm sector by gender, social groups and educational levels across spatial entities.

(ii) To understand the nature and trends of occupational diversification of workforce.
(iii) To analyse the pattern of non-farm employment and incomes by household features and its linkages to rural enterprises.
(iv) To analyse the migration flows, remittance patterns and linkages among different social groups; and
(v) To analyse the policy implications and evolve development strategies in the perspective of hill economy.

VI. Hypotheses

(i) Small parcels of landholdings with ecologically fragile region offer limited potential for labour absorption in the field crops for a growing labour force.
(ii) Diversification of agriculture into high value horticultural crops and development of other potential segments promotes employment and incomes of the people.
(iii) Growth of diversified non-farm sector restricts out-migration and stop drainage of human resources from the hill economy.
(iv) Relatively higher share of workforce in the non-farm sector in Uttarakhand translates into higher income levels at household/region levels; and
(v) Education and skill development among males and females are linked to disparities in employment opportunities in the non-farm sector.

VII. Methodology

The study is mainly based on primary survey. However, some important sources of secondary data have also been used from the NSSO and Census to supplement the primary sources of data. Findings of the NSS and Census have been put together and are presented in Chapter 4.

In all, 40 villages and 400 households have been selected across four hill districts and eight development blocks for detailed investigations.

(i) Sampling

The Uttarakhand State has two administrative regions – the Kumaon Region with six districts and the Garhwal Region with seven districts. In both the regions, four hill districts has been chosen – two hill districts in each region namely, Almora and Pithoragarh in Kumaon Region and Tehri Garhwal and Uttarkashi in Garhwal Region (Annexure III.2). The districts having entire or substantial area falling in the plane areas have not been considered since they do not reflect the distinct features of hill economy. The rationale for selection of the districts is based on the following variables:

* Percentage of rural non-farm workers to total workforce;
* Percentage of urban population to total population;
* Area under non-food crops;
* Percentage of area under horticulture.

(a) Selection of district

All the districts have been ranked separately in each region based on their relative shares in the above variables. In each region, two districts have been chosen – one with the highest value of composite index and another with the lowest value of composite index.*

(b) Selection of blocks

Similarly, in each selected district, all the blocks falling in the district are ranked using the above variables. Again, one block with the highest

---

* Actual value-minimum value/maximum value-minimum value. The formula applied gave scale-free values for each of the variables. Composite index was derived by taking the average value of the index of the four variables.

value of composite index and another block with the lowest value of composite index have been selected.

(c) Selection of villages

All the villages in the selected blocks have been stratified on the basis of distance criteria from the block headquarters. Villages have been selected nearer to the block (up to 5 km), middle distant villages (more than 5 km but up to 15 km) and very far-off villages (more than 15 kms.). In each block, five villages have been selected drawing two villages each from the middle distant and very far-off villages, and one village from nearer to the block in order to capture the nuances of village economies. In all, 40 villages have been selected which are spread over eight developmental blocks.

(d) Selection of households

In each village, 10 households have been chosen following stratified random sampling procedure. First, the list of households in a village has been stratified on the basis of social groups, and then all the social groups have been proportionately represented in the sampling frame. In the hill area, the number of households in a village generally is small and they are thinly spread. Ten households in every village form about 20 to 30 per cent of sample size.

(ii) Survey Tools

The primary data have been collected through structurally designed questionnaires (household, village schedule and enterprise survey) eliciting information on various aspects of household economy, village economy, and about enterprises. The household questionnaire covered information on household particulars such as age, education level, occupation (principal and subsidiary), employment status, migration status, etc. Particulars on land and other productive assets have also been collected which have profound impacts on the livelihood pattern of rural population. Employment pattern and income from agriculture and animal husbandry have also been gathered. Migration is a significant phenomenon in the hill region of the state, where large number of people out-migrate in search of livelihoods for varying durations. Information has been collected on migratory pattern and its implications on the region. Apart from this, information has also been collected on the different segments of non-farm employment. A special survey on rural enterprises has been conducted in order to understand the nature and types of enterprises, employment, incomes and their linkages to the local economy. Information about villages in terms of various social and economic infrastructure and amenities has been collected through village schedule in order to comprehend diversities in village economies (Annexure III.3).

Focus Group Discussions (FGD) technique was also used to generate a profile of the people's perceptions. One village from each block was selected for FGD. The FGD was carried out in eight villages which were randomly selected. The discussions were designed to elicit responses pertaining to the villagers' perceptions of livelihood issues – assets, vulnerability, peoples' perceptions for improvement in access to livelihoods and employment opportunities available (Annexure IX.1). Also, Participatory Rural Appraisal (PRA) exercise was undertaken in selected villages through social mapping and wealth ranking in order to understand the physical characteristics and socio-economic conditions of the community (Annexure IX.2).

(iii) Analytical Tools

Most of the results are presented in the form of bi-variate and multi-variate tables. Compound Annual Growth (CAG) and Coefficient of Variation (CV) have been used to show the trend and variations and measure of inequality over time. The CAG is used for calculating an annual growth rate whose value fluctuates widely from one period to another. The coefficient of variation represents the ratio of the standard deviation to the mean largely measuring the extent of inequality or comparing the degree of variation from one data series to another, even if the means are pretty same or different concerned variables.

The exact formulae can be written as follows:

$$\text{CAG: } A = P\,(1 - r/100)^{n}$$

Where; A = Value after n years; P = Initial value; r = Rate of growth; n = Number of years.

CV: The CV expresses the variation as a percentage of the mean, and is calculated as follows:

$$CV\% = (\sigma/\mu)^{*}\ 100$$

$$\sqrt{\sigma = \sum 1/n - \sum_{i=1}^{n} (X_1 - \mu)}$$

where; σ = standard deviation; μ = arithmetic mean

(iv) Models

In order to show causality between dependent and independent variables, multiple regressions and logistic models have been used. Logistic regression model is used for prediction of the probability of occurrence of an event that makes use of several predictor variables that may be either numericals or categories.

(a) Multiple regression model

In the present exercise multiple regressions have been fitted in order to compute degree of causality between household income and non-farm employment along with other controlling factors. The model uses Ordinary Least Square (OLS) method.

$$y = \beta_0 + \beta_1 x_1 + \beta_2 x_2 + \ldots\ldots\ldots\ldots + \beta_k x_{k} + \mu$$

where; y is the dependent variable Monthly Per Capita Income (MPCI)

$x_1, x_{2, \ldots\ldots\ldots}\ x_k$ are the k independent variables and

$\beta_1, \beta_{2, \ldots\ldots}\ \beta_k$ are the corresponding regression coefficients.

β_0 is the constant term.

μ is stochastic error term.

Values of β coefficients of multiple regression models show the extent of impact of predictor variables on criterion variable.

(b) Logistic regression model

Logistic model is a class of binary response models in the form:

$$P(y = 1/X) = G(\beta 0 + \beta_1 x_1 + \beta_2 x_2 + \ldots\ldots\ldots\ldots + \beta_k x_k) = G(\beta_0 {}_+ X\beta)$$

where G is a function taking on values strictly between zero and one 0<G(z)<1, for all real numbers z. X is the vector of independent variables and β is the corresponding vector of the regression coefficients.

In the Logit model, G is the logistic function:

$$G(z) = e^z / 1 + e^z = \Lambda(z),$$

$$Y(P) = \frac{1}{1 + e^{-z}}$$

Y = Probability of happening the event; P = 1, when event happens; P = 0, when event does not happen; e = Base of natural logarithms.

This is the cumulative distribution function for a standard logistic random variable.

4

Rural Non-farm Sector Employment in Uttarakhand : Trends and Patterns

I. Overview

One of the characteristic features of backward regions is a relatively large workforce engaged in the agriculture sector. These regions have a vast traditional agriculture sector with low level of technical progress and low productivity per man. In general, subsistence agriculture is characterised by huge underemployment in terms of unutilised labour time and low productivity.

The central problem facing such backward regions is a structural one in nature. It has been argued that any structural transformation is considered successful when it is accompanied by corresponding changes in the structure of the workforce. In spite of perceptible changes in the share of GDP, there has not been any substantial change in the structure of workforce over the years (Chakravarty, 1988). For instance, the proportion of the workforce dependent on agriculture has declined from about 74 per cent in 1972-73 to about 57 per cent in 2004-05, while the share of national income originating from agriculture has declined from about 45 per cent to about 18 per cent during the same period. This kind of structural change has resulted in low productivity in the agriculture sector.

In the literature it is argued that agriculture alone cannot provide productive and sustainable employment in the long- run primarily because of limited absorption capacity of agriculture in the face of increasing pressure on limited cultivated area, on the one hand, and burgeoning labour force on the other. While there has been substantial decline in the share of Gross Domestic Product (GDP) contribution to agriculture sector over the years, the share of employment has not declined correspondingly.

Therefore, the most strategic option suggested is the diversification from agriculture to non-agriculture activities, which would help to provide better employment opportunities and higher wages. Diversion of workforce to non-agriculture would also help in increasing the level of productivity and wages in agriculture sector.

The Rural Non-Farm sector (RNF) has, therefore, gained considerable significance as an alternative strategy for employment generation, poverty reduction and for higher rate of growth. The rationale for attaching an importance to the rural non-farm sector is well documented in the literature (Islam, 1987; Saith, 1992; Chadha, 1993). The empirical evidence amply shows that though there is a significant decline in agriculture employment growth, yet rural non-agricultural employment registered much higher growth rates. While agriculture employment growth rates (UPSS) plummeted from about 2.2 per cent to about 0.2 per cent during 1987-88/1993-94 to 1993-94/1999-2000, the non-agricultural employment registered improvement from about 2.0 per cent to 2.3 per cent during the same period. In terms of RNF share, it increased from about 16.6 per cent in 1977-78 to about 23.8 per cent in 1999-2000. The NSS Round (2004-05) results, however, show significant up-trends in the employment growth of agriculture and non-agriculture sector. Agriculture sector employment grew at about 1.7 per cent per annum during 1999-2000 to 2004-05, and non-agriculture employment recorded an all-time high — both in terms of share and growth during this period. Non-agriculture sector recorded 5.7 per cent per annum growth rate during 1999-2000 to 2004-05, and its share has gone up to about 27.4 per cent in 2004-05. The earning levels in non-agriculture activities have been significantly higher than agricultural activities (Papola, 1992; Bhalla, 1998) and the impact of RNF sector has been generally positive in terms of rise in real wages and reduction in poverty. But, distress driven non-farm employment evidences cannot be ruled out in certain regions (Vaidyanathan, 1986; Singh, 1994; Verma, *et al.,* 1995; Sharma, 2001).

The decade of 1980s saw a series of events which led an all-round progress in rural economy (Chadha, 1997). There has been a fast structural shift of workforce from agriculture to non-agriculture, both for males and females. Not only this, the process was accompanied by a number of healthy trends in rural economy. Poverty levels declined fast, real wages increased, and agriculture performed better; though employment growth in agriculture and organised sector was slowest. Then, early 1990s saw an opposite trend in this process and registered a shift of workforce to non-agriculture sector. Employment growth slowed down in almost every agricultural activity and female workforce had a sharp fall. In rural areas, the trend generated concerns as the proportion of agriculture workforce remained almost at the same level (at about 78.3%) between 1987-88 and 1993-94. During this period, employment growth rate in every activity slowed down barring community and personal service, both for males and females. The early 1990s had, in fact, shown even a reverse shift of workforce from non-agriculture to agriculture sector in rural areas that has been termed as structural retrogression (Bhalla, 1998).

The post-1994 period, however, presents a slightly improved situation for employment growth in non-agriculture sector in rural areas, as compared to the earlier period (i.e. 1987-88 to 1993-94). But the growth has fallen sharply from what it had recorded during 1977-78 to 1987-88. During 1993-94 to 1999-2000, agriculture sector saw a sharp fall in employment growth, both for males and females. Females in particular saw a catastrophic fall and recorded a negative growth. Barring manufacturing and construction, all the sectors recorded deceleration in female employment growth. Males recorded a significant employment growth in manufacturing, construction, transport and communication and financial services. Throughout the period starting from 1987-88, females seem to have suffered most in shrinking employment opportunities in contrast to earlier periods, when they had grabbed most of such employment opportunities. Hence, the decade of 1990s saw fluctuating trends with initial downturn and then started picking up.

The major explanation of rising share of non-agricultural workforce during the 1980s has been attributed to the increasing share of public investment during this period. Also, the declining workforce share has been linked to the reduction of government expenditure during 1990s (Ghosh, 1995; Sen, 1997; 1998). The construction activity under rural employment programmes received a big jolt; the reduction of subsidies and rising prices of foodgrains under PDS with cuts in social sector expenditure and high price rise had played major roles in their misery. Not only this, fiscal compression had an adverse impact on public spending in rural infrastructure, irrigation and other agriculture related development works. The broad trend experienced during 1980s and 1990s, therefore, shows sharp dissimilarities in rising and declining of rural non-agricultural workforce.

The NSS results (2004-05), as noted, show substantive up-trends in the share and growth of non-agriculture employment (UPSS) in 2004-05 as compared to 1999-2000. Construction and financial sectors saw a faster growth recording a little over 11 per cent and 10 per cent per annum, respectively. Trade, hotel & restaurant posted 6.7 per cent and transport, etc. grew over 6.4 per cent per annum. Female employment grew at a higher rate than their male counterparts in almost every activity barring mining & quarrying and construction. Female employment in transport recorded almost 25 per cent growth; financial services over 11 per cent and construction close to 10.5 per cent. In public utilities, the growth has been over 9 per cent and in manufacturing it has been about 5.6 per cent per annum. Females recorded a much higher growth than males. Even in agriculture, female employment grew over 3 per cent, while male employment recorded less than 1 per cent during this period. State level trends also broadly correspond to macro evidences at all-India level.

II. Pattern of Rural Employment in Uttarakhand

The State of Uttarakhand has 13 districts, of which 10 are hill districts and more than 85 per cent of the population in these hill districts lives in rural areas. The hill economy is characterised as subsistence farming economy, and rural households are predominantly dependent on subsistence agriculture for their livelihoods. Agriculture is by and large a low-paid sector with huge incidence of underemployment in terms of unutilised labour time. Industrial activity is highly skewed in the State of Uttarakhand, as most industries are located in the plane districts, and hill districts are bereft of any major industry. Industrial base in the hill region is very low. Large industries cannot be set up due to lack of economies of scale and infrastructural constraints. Also, ecological formations do not permit large industrial set-up in the region. Micro and household enterprises are obliterating fast due to limited linkages effects within the local economy and unfavourable institutional and market mechanisms. Their inaccessibility in terms of lack of access to infrastructure, markets, technologies, and information further accentuates the process of underdevelopment in the region. All these factors resulted in a low productive base, which in turn, created a tendency of distressed diversification of workforce into low productive employment in unorganised non-agricultural activities. A large number of males out-migrated for earning cash income and females replaced their labour, thereby increasing their overall labour force participation.

1. Labour Force Participation Rates (LFPRs)

Labour force constitutes the economically active population and is a measure of labour supply at a given point of time. The size of labour force is primarily affected by the demographic factors that frame its formation and growth; and the social, economic and institutional factors determine the size of labour force. These factors affect the rates of economic activity by age and sex which in turn depend upon the level of economic development and economic structure, as well as, upon the employment policy and the system of education. As economy grows, LFPR generally tends to decline over a period of time, particularly in a developing economy, and this phenomenon is governed by various factors. LFPR declines primarily because of increasing participation of children in educational institutions and withdrawal of aged population from the labour force due to improved economic conditions. Also, a high LFPR may be indicative of poverty driven phenomenon particularly in a subsistence economy.

Similar to all-India pattern, the LFPR has been observed to be declining from 1983 to 1999-2000, both for males and females in

Uttarakhand revealing a relative shrinking of labour supply. It is important to note that the female LFPR in the state is significantly higher and the male LFPR is substantively lower as compared to all-India pattern during this period.

The NSS Round (2004-05), however, shows a significant up-trend over the previous rounds, both at all-India and in the state. It is important to note such significant changes in the structure of labour force in recent years. The overall LFPR in rural areas in the state is about 49.6 per cent and for males and females, the LFPR stands out at 52.6 and 46.8 per cent respectively in 2004-05 (Table 4.1). As

Table 4.1 : Labour Force Participation Rate in Uttarakhand and in India (UPSS)

Location/ year	*Uttarakhand*			*India*		
	Person	*Male*	*Female*	*Person*	*Male*	*Female*
Rural						
1983	52.40	51.64	53.17	44.90	55.24	34.17
1987-88	52.19	53.97	50.57	44.30	54.90	33.10
1993-94	53.23	51.77	54.62	44.90	56.09	33.04
1999-2000	43.48	45.44	41.69	42.35	53.99	30.19
2004-2005	49.63	52.65	46.85	44.61	55.51	33.30
Urban						
1983	33.42	54.06	6.83	35.82	53.80	15.87
1987-88	28.41	47.94	8.07	35.64	53.40	16.18
1993-94	32.65	47.55	14.45	36.34	54.30	16.50
1999-2000	28.75	44.82	10.27	35.35	54.20	14.74
2004-2005	36.21	56.06	14.60	38.25	57.03	17.82

Note : Excludes Hardwar district.
Source : NSSO, household unit record data on employment and unemployment, various rounds.

compared to rural India, the LFPR in the state is higher by 5.0 per cent, and for males it is lower by 2.8 per cent, while for females it is substantively higher by about 13.5 per cent. The noticeable feature in rural areas in the state is a very high LFPR among females as compared to all-India level. Though the LFPR among females in the rural area has substantively declined over the years, yet it is about 13.5 per cent higher as compared to all-India in 2004-05. The main reason for

Fig. 4.1 : Trends in Rural Labour Force Participation Rate in Uttarakhand.

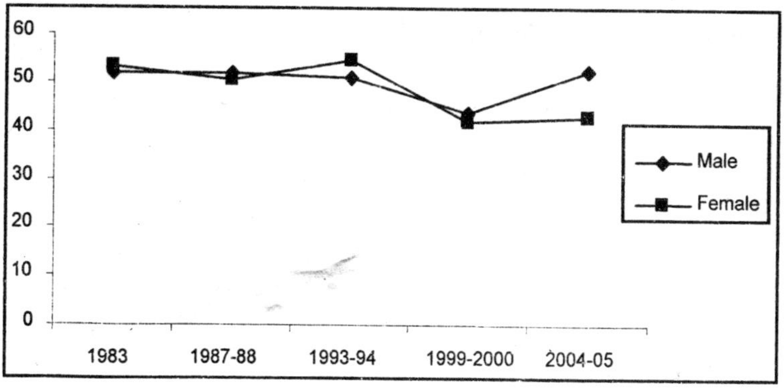

such a high LFPR among females is subsistence nature of agriculture economy that provides the only source of employment, since there are limited opportunities of employment outside agriculture. In the urban areas, male and female LFPRs are lower by about 1 and 3 per cent, respectively as compared to the all-India rate.

The long-term trend of LFPR in rural area does not show any perceptible variation for males and females at the all-India level during 1983 to 2004-05. It remained at 55-56 per cent for males and 33-34 per cent for females. The trend in the state, however, does show a declining trend for females but with a negligible variation for males during the same period. The female LFPR declined to about 6.3 per cent points and the male LFPR either marginally increased or remained almost constant during the period. Some departure is clearly noticed in this trend in 1999-2000 when the LFPR declined both at all-India level and in the state.

The most distinguishable feature of LFPR in rural areas is, therefore a disproportionately high female LFPR by UPSS as compared to the national average. One of the reasons for this substantively higher rate of LFPR among the females is not a demographic phenomenon, rather it is purely an economic phenomenon where a large percentage of males out-migrate for earning cash income and females replace their labour, thereby increasing their overall participation rate.

2. Work Participation Rates (WPRs)

(i) National Sample Survey

Work Participation Rate (WPR) is an important indicator of development showing the proportion of working population to total population in an economy. It is generally believed that the higher WPR is an indication of well-being of population and rightly so. Conversely, it is also observed that in a poor region, WPR is generally higher among the population which does not necessarily an indication of improved economic status and well-being, rather indicates a poverty driven phenomenon. In poor regions, people do not have perennial source of employment and they are engaged in multiple activities for short duration at low wage rates. Such pluri-activity is often most common in such regions to cope with the livelihood uncertainty. It is, therefore, important to consider the qualitative dimension of WPR in terms of pattern and nature of employment, its duration, work conditions and wages.

In Uttarakhand, similar to the all-India pattern, there has been a steady decline in WPR across sexes from 1983 to 1999-2000. The decline of WPR in the case of Uttarakhand is, however, much sharper than the all-India average during 1993-94 and 1999-2000, for both males and females. The decline in the case of females is staggeringly high (13.4%). Yet, another important feature is a relatively low male WPR in the state and a very high female WPR as compared to the all-India average throughout this period (Table 4.1A).

Table 4.1A : Workforce Participation Rate in Uttarakhand and in India (UPSS)

Year	*Uttarakhand*			*India*		
	Person	*Male*	*Female*	*Person*	*Male*	*Female*
1983	48.43	51.62	45.02	41.92	53.63	29.58
1987-88	45.62	50.17	41.35	41.21	53.15	28.51
1993-94	48.26	49.33	47.19	41.96	54.48	28.55
1999-2000	38.58	43.57	33.75	39.67	52.73	25.99
2004-05	45.57	51.89	39.55	42.01	54.69	28.67

Note : Excludes Hardwar district.

Source : NSSO, household unit record data on employment and unemployment, various rounds.

A steady decline in WPR in the state, both by UPS and UPSS across sexes and locations, has been noted from 1983 to 1999-2000 (Table 4.2). The decline in WPR has been significantly higher (12.3% and 9.7% by UPS and UPSS,respectively) in 1999-2000 over 1993-94, and for females the decline is extraordinarily high (18.8% and 13.4% by UPS and UPSS, respectively). In rural area, the decline in WPR for males has been comparatively lower (6.5%) but for females there has been sharp fall (20.9%) according to UPS during the same period.

There has been an absolute decline of 3.10 lakh workers (UPSS) in rural areas — females registering a decline of about 2.18 lakh and males recording a fall of 0.91 lakh workers in 1999-2000 over 1993-94 (Annexure Table IV. 4). However, no such decline has been observed in case of urban workers. There has been a fall of 7 percentage points WPR (UPSS) in case of rural males and 13 percentage points for rural females (Table 4.2). For rural females, there has been a much sharper fall in WPR in 1999-2000 over 1993-94 as compared to males.

But the evidence of 61st NSS Round shows a substantive gain in WPR, both for males and females, over 55th Round. There has been an absolute gain of 4.77 lakh rural workers (males constituting 2.71 lakh and females 2.06 lakh) and 1.90 lakh urban workers (males constituting 1.50 lakh and females 0.40 lakh).

Table 4.2 : Workforce Participation Rate in Uttarakhand

Location/ year	*UPS*			*UPSS*		
	Person	*Male*	*Female*	*Person*	*Male*	*Female*
Rural						
1983	49.16	48.30	50.05	52.36	51.56	53.17
1987-88	43.00	44.11	42.00	51.16	51.80	50.57
1993-94	47.52	48.11	46.96	52.72	50.73	54.62
1999-2000	33.46	41.55	26.09	42.61	43.68	41.64
2004-2005	40.60	48.14	33.75	48.90	51.37	46.63
Urban						
1983	31.74	51.21	6.66	32.08	51.81	6.66
1987-88	24.40	41.60	6.50	26.91	45.02	8.07
1993-94	28.75	43.47	10.76	31.04	44.62	14.45
1999-2000	25.80	41.81	7.38	27.75	43.31	9.85
2004-2005	32.39	52.81	10.16	34.26	53.51	13.30

Note : Excludes Hardwar district.

Source : NSSO, household unit record data on employment and unemployment, various rounds.

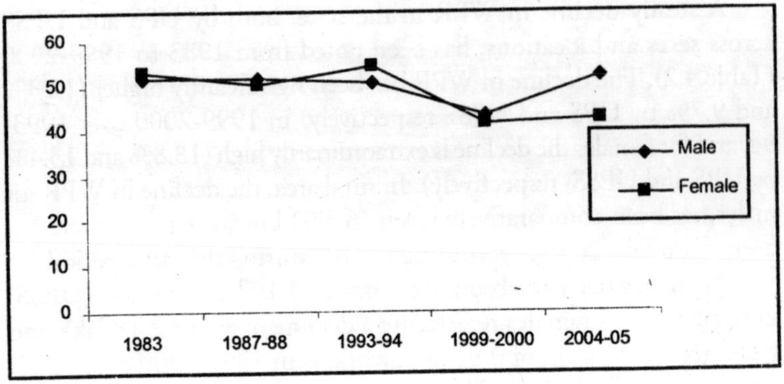

Fig. 4.2 : Trends in Rural Workforce Participation Rate in Uttarakhand

(ii) Workforce Participation Rate by Population Census

The Population Censuses also corroborate the faster decline of WPR in the state as compared to all-India average, both for male and female population. The decline is more pronounced in the decade 1990s than in the 1980s. Yet, another important feature clearly discernible is high WPR among females with low WPR among males as compared to the national average (Table 4.2A).

High female WPR in rural areas of the hill region is a distinct phenomenon where women plays the central role in earning livelihood mainly through labouring in cultivation and allied activities. Table 4.2B below clearly shows that female WPR in rural areas of the hill region is extraordinarily higher (44.5%) than the plane areas of the region (17.4%).

(iii) NSS Evidences

The NSS (61st Round, 2004-05) results, however show an improvement in the participation rates over earlier round (55th), both in India and in the state as well across both sexes. The improvement is substantive, particularly in the state as compared to all-India average. The increase in the WPR for males in rural area is observed to be much higher (6.6% by UPS and 7.7% by UPSS) as compared to females (7.7% by UPS and 5.0% by UPSS). In urban areas also the

Table 4.2A : Workforce Participation Rate in Uttarakhand and in India, 1981-2001

Area/Sex	*Main*			*Main plus marginal*		
	*1981**	*1991*	*2001*	*1981**	*1991*	*2001*
				Uttarakhand		
Rural						
Person	37.07	36.8	27.77	42.97	42.81	39.63
Male	46.85	46.65	36.09	48.71	48.48	45.99
Female	27.94	26.74	19.5	37.93	37.06	33.32
Total						
Person	36.19	35.17	27.39	41.13	39.94	36.94
Male	47.69	47.33	38.13	49.24	48.78	46.42
Female	24.21	22.19	16.24	32.7	30.5	27.09
				India		
Rural						
Person	34.76	35.36	31.02	38.87	39.99	41.97
Male	52.62	51.27	44.51	53.81	52.48	52.36
Female	16.00	18.40	16.77	23.18	26.67	30.98
Total						
Person	32.56	33.79	30.55	36.70	37.50	39.30
Male	50.25	50.47	45.34	52.60	51.60	51.90
Female	13.63	15.79	14.68	19.70	22.30	25.70

Note : *Excludes Hardwar district.
Source : Census of India, 1981-2001.

Table 4.2B : Workforce Participation Rate (All) in Hill and Plane Regions of Uttarakhand, 2001

Region	*Area*	*Person*	*Male*	*Female*
Hills	Total	42.35	44.72	40.06
	Rural	44.35	44.15	44.54
	Urban	30.46	47.69	9.10
Planes	Total	31.48	47.90	13.12
	Rural	33.57	48.32	17.44
	Urban	28.71	47.36	7.22
Uttarakhand	Total	38.47	45.91	30.89
	Rural	41.44	45.35	37.65
	Urban	29.36	47.49	7.91

Note : Excludes Hardwar district.
Source : Population Census, 2001.

up-trend for males is substantive — WPR for males increased by 11.0 per cent by UPS and 10.2 per cent by UPSS. For females, the increase is relatively small (2.8% by UPS and 3.4% by UPSS).

In fact, WPR for males recorded an all-time high since 1983, both in rural and urban areas. Such an up-trend of employment in recent years warrants a possible explanation.

Age-specific analysis of WPR throws some light on the changing structure of employment, particularly, the substantive fall and rise in WPR during 1994-2000 and 2000-05 respectively. Looking at the age-specific WPR between 1993-94 and 1999-2000, the fall has been observed in most of the population segments for rural males barring the age-group 55-59 where a marginal increase has been noted (0.20%). For rural females, the decline has been noted in all the age groups. For rural males, the decline in WPR is significantly higher at the younger age groups, more so in the age groups 15-19 and 20-24. There has been 6.44 per cent decline of WPR in the age group 10-14, 19.50 per cent in 15-29, and 16.10 per cent fall in 20-24 age groups (Table 4.3). Also, there has been a sizeable decline in WPR in the age groups 59 and above, (accounting for about 17.85%). In other segments, the fall has not been that much significant.

During 2000-05, there has been a substantial increase of male WPR (10.2%), while the female WPR recorded an increase of about 5.0 per cent. The huge decline of male WPR observed during 1999-2000 (over 1993-94) in the age groups 10-14, 15-19 and 20-24 has largely been offset by corresponding increase in WPR during 2000-05. The WPR has not improved in the age groups 25 to 49 which are prime working age, and in fact, there has been a decline in the participation rates. There has also been a huge increase of WPR at the age 59+ (a reversed trend observed during 1994-2000) indicating a retrogressive phenomenon.

For females, most of the increase has been noticed in the age groups 15-19, 30-34, 55-59 and 59+ during 2000-05.

The evidence set up by the recent survey results show a sudden spurt in WPR at younger age groups and at older age groups, and shrinking employment opportunities at prime working age groups which is a cause for concern. Whether school/college-going and older-

Table 4.3 : Age-wise Distribution of WPR (UPSS) in 1993-94 to 2004-05 in Rural Uttarakhand

Age-group	*5-9*	*10-14*	*15-19*	*20-24*	*25-29*	*30-34*	*35-39*	*40-44*	*45-49*	*50-54*	*55-59*	*59+*	*Total*
Rural Males													
1993-94	0.67	9.79	40.92	79.42	97.62	99.14	97.36	100.0	100.0	96.79	97.80	74.21	50.73
1999-2000	0.00	3.35	21.42	63.32	96.34	97.95	98.55	100.0	100.0	89.75	98.00	56.36	43.68
Difference (1994-2000)	-0.67	-6.44	-19.50	-16.10	-1.28	-1.19	-1.19	0.00	0.00	-7.04	0.20	-17.85	-7.05
2004-05	0.00	5.32	33.77	70.28	90.28	97.55	97.52	99.56	98.06	95.85	92.38	78.18	51.37
Difference (2000-05)	0.00	1.97	12.35	6.98	-6.06	-0.40	-1.03	-0.44	-1.94	6.10	-5.62	21.82	7.69
Difference 1993-94 to 2004-05	-0.67	-4.47	-7.15	-9.14	-7.34	-1.59	0.16	-0.44	-1.94	-0.94	-5.42	3.97	0.64
Rural Females													
1993-94	1.05	25.85	70.91	79.06	90.54	77.63	92.73	86.61	84.72	88.91	84.16	62.32	54.62
1999-2000	0.00	4.37	26.26	72.73	74.36	71.18	76.52	80.70	84.36	81.25	61.07	41.23	41.68
Difference (1994-2000)	-1.05	-21.48	-44.65	-6.33	-16.18	-6.45	-16.21	-5.91	-0.36	-7.66	-23.09	-21.09	-12.94
2004-05	0.00	5.25	45.74	77.52	79.53	81.12	77.53	75.26	77.09	78.87	87.44	55.54	46.63

Notes : (i) No figures reported in the age group of 0-5, (ii) Excludes Hardwar district.
Source : Various Rounds of NSSO.

age (59+) population have actually reverted back to labour market under duress conditions seems to be the most worrying factor.

The decline in the WPR in younger age-groups has been generally regarded as beneficial in the process of development, as it indicates higher attendance in the middle, secondary or even higher level of education (Sundaram, 2001). Nevertheless, it would be in order to look other factors as well before reaching to any conclusive evidence in the case of Uttarakhand. The other influencing factors could be the change in the student-population ratio, rate of unemployment, and shift in age-structure of population over the years.

Generally, there has been a huge decline in WPR extending all the age groups during 1993-94 to 1999-2000, both for males and females in the rural area, and then a clear up-trend is observed in 2004-05 over 1999-2000. The overall decline in WPRs between 1994-2000 for rural males is reported as :-7.05 and for females as -12.94 percentage points, which is expressed in terms of difference between WPRs during the above period; but the fall in WPRs varies across the age groups, both for males and females. For males, WPR in the age groups 15-19, 20-24 and 59 and above recorded the highest decline; while for females, the decline is substantive in the age-groups 10-14, 15-19, 35-39, 55-59 and 59 and above registering around 15 per cent decline. The difference between the overall unemployment rates has increased by 1.9 per cent during the said period, yet unemployment rate turned out to be a staggeringly high for males in the age-group 15-19 (29.14%), while for females, it is very low. How such a huge decline in the WPR can be explained during 1993-94 to1999-2000?

There has been an across-the-board gain in school/college attendance, both for males and females, which is a significant outcome of educational achievements during this period. The most notable gain in attendance has been in the age-group 15-19 for girls and 20 to 24 age groups for boys (over 30%). The decline in WPR in the age groups 5-9 and 10-14 can be solely attributed to the increase in school attendance among boys. In the age group 20-24, there has been a huge decline of male WPR (16%) and also a substantive gain (30%) in attendance in higher education during the period. Also, in the age group 25-29, the increase in attendance in higher education is reported to be much higher than the decline in WPR. In these age groups, no increase in unemployment rate have been reported (Table 4.5). It can be argued that a large part of fall in WPR is offset by increasing attendance in schools/colleges, which can be regarded as a positive indicator.

But, it is quite unconvincing to forward the same argument for the young age group (15-19) among boys recording a substantial decline in WPR (19.50%) solely due to higher attendance in school education. This is primarily due to a huge increase in the unemployment rate of about 29.14 per cent in this age group and a relatively slower gain in school attendance (7.7%) during this period (Tables 4.4 and 4.5). The fall in WPR in this young age group is probably due to the dropping out of a large number of students from the school system at different stages, who are forced to enter in the labour market at an early age without any marketable skills, and are ultimately accommodated in the informal economy in low productive activities, which is a cause of serious concern.

In the higher age-groups (30-34 and above), fall in WPR is due to fall in employment opportunities. This is particularly so in the case of agriculture sector where labour absorption capacity has severely shrunk due to its being a highly uneconomical enterprise, as a result of which, labour is gradually getting out of cultivation activities and entering into the unorganised labour market for better option of livelihood. But, somehow, they are not reported as usually unemployed. This has been corroborated by the fact that there has been a substantive fall of workforce in the share of agriculture and allied activities (8.3 percentage points), mining & quarrying (0.6 percentage points) and public services (4.8 percentage points) in 1999-2000 over 1993-94 (Table 4.12). There has been also a fall of 17 per cent WPR in the age group 59 and above, which might be attributed, to some extent, to the retirement and voluntary withdrawal from the labour market as a result of enhanced earnings of the younger population.

Even then, these factors are discounted (withdrawal of children and aged from the labour market), since there has been a significant fall of workers in 1999-2000 over 1993-94. Such a huge fall in the UPS workers clearly indicates the shrinking of job opportunities in the state and this process might result in either resorting to low productivity jobs in the informal sector or pushing them to out-migrate under duress conditions.

The situation is still far worse for rural females as there has been quite a sharp fall in the WPR (12.94%) extending to all the age groups. In the younger age groups (10-14 and 15-19), there is a significant fall of WPR and this fall could be attributed to the increasing participation in the educational institutions as there has been an impressive growth of school education of girls in the state. There has been a perceptible improvement in the student-population ratio from 1993-94 to 1999-2000; the increase is reported by about 17.0 per cent in the age group 10-14, and 34.6 per cent in the age group 15-19 during this period (Table 4.4). Even in the age group 20-24, there has been an increase of student-population ratio (5.1%). How one can explain the huge fall of WPR in other female population segments?

The possible explanations for such a significant fall in WPR could be the withdrawal from agriculture as a result of uneconomical enterprise, displacement from non-farm activities owing to an increasing competition from their male counterparts in the limited segment of labour market, intermittent involvement in subsidiary activities, and out-migration along with their male members. The sectoral share of female workforce shows that there has been a fall in agriculture (1.5%), and the share of manufacturing; trade, hotels & restaurants and finance, real estate & business has fallen down to zero during 1993-94 to 1999-2000 (Table 4.12). Barring agriculture, construction and public services, females do not have any access to other segments of non-farm sector. In the context of rural areas in the state, females are engaged in multiple activities such as cultivation, animal husbandry, fetching water, collection of firewood & fuels and child care activities, and therefore it becomes extremely difficult to extricate themselves and opt suitable employment. Precisely, this is the reason why they are not reporting as usually unemployed. But then, the NSS report evidence (2004-05) indicates substantive up-trend in the WPRs, both for males and females.

It is quite surprising that during 1993-94 to 1999-2000, there has been a consistent fall in WPRs in the younger age groups - both for boys and girls, which was regarded a positive sign for increasing school/college going population. In 2000-05, the trend appears to be altogether a reversal showing an increase in the WPRs, more so in the case of boys than the girls. There has been an increase of WPRs in the age groups 10-14 (1.97 percentage points), 15-19 (12.35 percentage points) and 20-24 (6.98 percentage points) for boys, and 19.48 percentage points increase for girls in the age group 15-19. Such a huge increase in WPRs in the younger age groups indicates a compulsion to enter into the labour market as a result of discontinuing and dropping out from educational institutions. Looking at the school attendance population, it becomes clear that the attendance among boys has declined to about 2.92, 13.56 and 3.66 percentage points respectively in the age groups 10-14, 20-24 and 25-29 during 2000-05. Similarly, the attendance for girls declined for the age groups 15-19 and 20-24 (Table 4.4). This is a major trend reversal as a growing number of youth are not being retained in educational institutions. Also, the incidence of unemployment increased for males in the age groups 25-29 and 30-34, and relatively higher incidence of unemployment has been noted for females in the age groups 20-24 and 25-29 (Table 4.5). Increasing unemployment at the prime working age groups characterises the vulnerability of households that has widespread ramifications to the livelihoods options in a limited segment of labour market. Yet another conspicuous feature noted is the increasing WPR for males and females in the older age group (59 years and above), which probably indicates a compulsion on the part of old aged population to search for employment under duress conditions. This contravenes the earlier trend (during 1994-2000) of withdrawing from labour market which might be attributed to some extent to the retirement and voluntary withdrawal from the labour market as a result of enhanced earnings of younger population. The increasing pressure in the labour market and the elderly entering into it is not a healthy trend.

3. Intensity of Subsidiary Employment

Another distinct feature noted is that an overwhelmingly large majority

Table 4.4: Attendance in School/College Education in Rural Area, 1993-94 to 2000-04 %.

Age-group	*1993-94*			*1999-00*			*2004-05*		
	Male	*Female*	*Person*	*Male*	*Female*	*Person*	*Male*	*Female*	*Person*
0-4	2.04	3.04	2.53	14.66	13.62	14.17	11.97	4.45	7.95
5-9	73.40	70.93	72.22	86.17	79.92	83.29	89.44	88.16	88.76
10-14	92.73	69.82	81.10	97.82	86.78	92.11	94.90	91.06	93.02
15-19	63.90	24.94	44.82	71.66	59.51	65.28	76.70	58.51	68.06
20-24	11.40	4.28	7.32	41.42	9.38	23.44	27.86	7.44	16.87
25-29	0.00	1.53	0.82	5.80	1.05	2.83	2.14	3.40	2.85

Note : Excludes Hardwar district.
Source : Various rounds of NSSO.

Table 4.5 : Unemployment Rate (UPS) in 1993-94 to 2004-05 in Uttarakhand

Age-group	*10-14*	*15-19*	*20-24*	*25-29*	*30-34*	*35-39*	*40-44*	*45-49*	*50-54*	*55-59*	*59+*	*Total*
Rural Males												
1993-94	0.00	4.22	9.55	2.38	0.86	0.00	0.00	0.00	0.00	0.00	0.00	2.02
1999-2000	0.00	33.36	9.13	2.31	1.98	0.00	0.00	0.00	0.00	0.00	0.00	3.88
2004-05	0.00	9.32	6.72	5.72	2.05	0.00	0.39	0.00	0.00	0.00	0.00	2.45
Difference (1994-2000)	0.00	29.14	-0.42	-0.07	1.12	0.00	0.00	0.00	0.00	0.00	0.00	1.86
Difference (2000-05)	0.00	-26.70	-4.08	2.12	-0.31	0.00	0.33	0.00	0.00	0.00	0.00	-1.91
Difference 1994-2005	0.00	2.44	4.50	2.05	0.81	0.00	0.33	0.00	0.00	0.00	0.00	-0.05
Rural Females												
1993-94	0.00	0.00	0.00	0.00	0.00	0.00	0.00	0.00	0.00	0.00	0.00	0.00
1999-2000	0.00	0.00	0.00	0.80	0.00	0.00	0.00	0.00	0.00	0.00	0.00	0.12
2004-05	0.00	0.00	1.61	1.81	0.00	0.24	0.00	0.00	0.00	0.00	0.00	0.46
Difference (1994-2000)	0.00	0.00	0.00	0.80	0.00	0.00	0.00	0.00	0.00	0.00	0.00	0.12
Difference (2000-05)	0.00	0.00	1.54	0.86	0.00	0.22	0.00	0.00	0.00	0.00	0.00	0.31

Source : Various rounds of NSSO.

Notes : (i) No figures reported in the age-groups of 0-5 and 5-9, (ii) Excludes Hardwar district.

of rural females in the state work as subsidiary capacity (11.9% in 2004-05) indicating their marginalisation and vulnerability. As regards, severity of subsidiary employment in the state, the gap between the share of UPS and UPSS workers has increased from about 2.6 per cent in 1983 to about 6.1 per cent in 2004-05; while at the all-India level, this gap declined albeit marginally from 4.6 per cent to 4.1 per cent.

The gap in rural area of the state increased which is significantly higher as compared to urban area. However, at the all-India level, this gap has declined both for males and females during 1983 to 2004-05. In rural area of the state, the gap for male subsidiary workers remained almost at the same level (3.2%) while for females this gap increased by about four times (3.1% to 12.9%) during the same period. In urban area, this gap increased marginally for males (0.6% and 0.7%) but for females, it increased significantly (0.0% to 3.1%). At the all-India level however this gap has generally declined for males as well as for females - both in rural and urban areas, except for urban females which increased marginally (Table 4.2).

While the NSS Round (61st) shows a substantive gain in WPR, marginalisation of the workforce in the state continues to be abated. The share of female subsidiary workers though declined, yet it is still very high at about 12.9 per cent, and that of male subsidiary workers recorded a marginal increase at 3.2 per cent. Even in urban areas of the state, marginalisation process is on the increase.

Female subsidiary workers have increased alarmingly high, particularly in 1999-2000. There has been an increase of 4.66 lakh subsidiary workers in the rural areas in 1999-2000, of which 88 per cent increase was recorded alone for females (Annexure Table IV.1). Most of the increase in the female employment was in agriculture sector (95.5%), followed by construction (4.2%) and a minuscule increase (0.1%) was in public services. For males, almost all the increase in subsidiary employment was in agriculture sector (99%) and the remaining increase (1%) was noted in public services. The similar trend is also noted in NSS 61st round results (2004-05) where there has been an increase of 4.49 lakh subsidiary workers in the rural areas, of which female accounted for about 80.5 per cent (Annexure Table

IV.2). Agriculture is the most predominant activity for subsidiary employment, both for males and females. For females, such a huge increase in the subsidiary capacity employment was solely due to low productive sectors that are regarded as the last resort.

While in rural areas of the state, females are increasingly forced to resort to subsidiary nature of employment, mostly in agriculture and construction, and their male counterparts are probably competing for better opportunities in the non-farm segments. Males are trying to get slightly better kinds of jobs within the hierarchy of rural job markets, thereby giving space to female workers by vacating less preferred jobs. It can be observed that female participation (UPSS) in the rural labour market is limited to agriculture and allied activities (96.5%), public administration (1.6%) and manufacturing (1.1%); while males are visible in almost every branch of non-farm sector (Table 4.12). For females, marginalisation process has precipitated over the period but for males this process has however slackened. Even in the urban area, the gap increased both for males and females indicating their vulnerability in the urban labour market. The severity has however dampened in late 1990s.

4. Growth in Employment

One of the distinct patterns of employment during 1993-94 to 1999-2000 has been the fast deceleration of employment growth. While at all-India level employment grew at about 1.0 per cent, in Uttarakhand there has been a catastrophic fall in employment, particularly in the rural area recording a negative growth for both the sexes (Table 4.6). While the urban area recorded a positive growth (1.20%) the female employment continued to have a huge negative growth (-3.22%). During 1993-94 to 1999-2000, employment in rural area recorded an absolute decline with a negative growth (-1.96%) and females in particular were the worst hit. Clearly, the fall in employment was more pronounced among females than males. The period 2004-05 saw a sharp up-trend in employment growth (over 1999-2000), and this trend has been noticed in all the segments - both at all-India and state levels. Interestingly, employment growth in the state is observed to be higher than all-India (barring rural female) and male employment growth, in particular, saw a substantial gain during this period.

In spite of substantial gain in employment growth in recent years, the long-term employment growth (1983 to 2004-05) in rural Uttarakhand continues to record a much lower growth (0.28%) than the all-India average (1.01%) and females in particular saw an abysmally low growth (0.15%). The urban area too recorded a lower employment growth compared to all-India level. While male employment grew at a much slower pace, female employment grew at a much higher rate in the state as compared to all-India.

All through (1983 to 2004-05) employment growth was abysmally low in Uttarakhand and rural areas suffered the most, and the females in particular have a negligible share in employment growth.

Table 4.6 : Employment Growth in Uttarakhand and All-India during 1983 to 2004-05

Period/Area	*Uttarakhand*			*All-India*		
	Person	*Male*	*Female*	*Person*	*Male*	*Female*
Rural						
1983-88	0.68	1.19	0.17	0.71	1.01	0.20
1988-94	2.42	1.54	3.31	2.44	2.53	2.27
1994-2000	-1.96	-1.10	-2.81	0.67	0.94	0.16
2000-05	3.01	4.44	1.42	2.87	2.39	3.75
1983-05	0.28	0.40	0.15	1.01	1.18	0.71
Urban						
1983-88	0.25	-0.43	6.08	1.85	1.76	2.19
1988-94	5.31	3.54	14.84	4.73	4.65	5.01
1994-2000	1.19	2.22	-3.22	2.34	2.71	0.91
2000-05	5.50	5.20	6.98	3.75	3.28	5.57
1983-05	1.77	1.42	4.35	2.09	2.14	1.87

Source : Various rounds of NSSO.

The census data also reveal a declining employment growth from 1981-1991 to 1991-2001 and the decline has been much faster during the decade 1991-2001 recording a negative growth rates for main workers. The decline has been both for males and females, but it is more pronounced among females than males. In fact, there has been an absolute decline in main workers (from 2.16 million to 1.97 million) during this period and the decline is noted only in the rural area. However, total workers (main and marginal workers combining together) show positive growth rates which is solely due to the increase in marginal workers. Clearly, stable employment opportunities in the state have declined and marginalisation process got intensified in the 1990s, which largely reflects the short duration and uncertain nature of employment in the labour market (Table 4.6A).

Table 4.6A : Annual Compound Growth of Workers in Uttarakhand, 1981-2001

Area/sex	*Main workers*		*Main plus marginal workers*	
	*1981-91**	*1991-2001*	*1981-91**	*1991-2001*
Rural				
Person	1.80	-1.28	1.99	0.55
Male	1.38	-1.17	1.45	0.74
Female	2.46	-1.47	2.65	0.33
Total				
Person	2.10	-0.65	2.25	1.07
Male	1.84	-0.45	1.89	1.22
Female	2.61	-1.12	2.78	0.81

Note : *Excludes Hardwar.
Source : Censuses of India.

The sectoral pattern of employment growth during 1990s witnessed an absolute decline in cultivators and thus recording a negative growth (-0.42%). Agriculture labour too had very low growth (0.20%) thereby squeezing overall employment opportunities in agriculture sector. Mining & quarrying posted the highest growth (15.4%) followed by household manufacturing (9.4%) and construction (8.0%). Manufacturing and construction recorded a reasonably higher growth; trade & commerce and transport; storage & communication posted between 4 to 5 per cent annual growth. The rural area too had a high growth of employment in manufacturing and construction but a huge fall in employment in agriculture sector was hardly enough to push them in non-agriculture sector. Thus rural employment growth recorded very low growth (0.75%) as compared to urban area (2.5%) (Table 4.6B).

Table 4.6B : Sectoral Growth in Employment, 1991-2001 (ACGR)

Sector	*Rural*	*Urban*	*Total*
Cultivators	-0.36	-4.94	-0.42
Agriculture labour	0.53	-3.92	0.20
Livestock and forestry	4.28	-5.80	2.06
Mining and quarrying	16.42	10.24	15.45
Manufacturing (household)	9.67	8.35	9.39
Manufacturing (non-household)	9.46	3.86	6.56
Construction	10.09	4.76	7.93
Trade and commerce	5.28	3.50	4.19
Transport, storage and communication	6.44	3.07	4.65
Other services	-2.29	2.30	0.01
All	**0.75**	**2.50**	**1.08**

Source: Census of India, 1991 and 2001.

5. *Broad Sectoral Analysis*

In Uttarakhand, there has been virtually no movement of workforce from primary to other sectors until 1993-94, rather the share of employment in primary sector increased gradually throughout this period indicating a considerable structural rigidity. The share increased from about 73 per cent to 76 per cent during 1983 to 1993-94, while secondary sector's share increased marginally (1.40 percentage points) and the share of services declined by 4.5 percentage points. But then, there has been a relatively faster movement of workforce from primary to other sectors from 1993-94 to 1999-2000. The primary sector's share in employment declined by about 11.6 percentage points and corresponding increase has been noted in secondary and tertiary sectors. The share in secondary sector's employment doubled (from 7.24% to 14.79%) and tertiary sector's employment increased by 4 percentage points (Table 4.7). In 2004-05, the process of occupational diversification slowed down. The share in primary sector employing bulk of workforce did not show any diminution, rather it increased

(4.5 percentage points) whereas the secondary and tertiary sectors registered a decline (4.0 and 0.5 percentage points, respectively).

Table 4.7 : Employment Structure in India and in Uttarakhand, 1983 to 2004-05 (UPSS)

Years	*Primary*	*Secondary*	*Tertiary*
		All India	
1983	68.70	13.30	18.00
1987-88	64.80	15.50	19.70
1993-94	64.60	14.20	21.20
1999-2000	61.70	15.80	22.50
2004-05	59.05	17.57	23.36
Change in 1980s (1983-1988)	-3.90	2.20	1.70
Change in 1990s (1994-2000)	-0.20	1.60	1.30
Change during (2000-05)	-2.65	1.77	0.86
		Uttarakhand	
1983	72.92	5.85	21.22
1987-88	74.49	10.24	15.27
1993-94	76.07	7.24	16.69
1999-2000	64.46	14.79	20.75
2004-05	68.92	10.83	20.25
Change in 1980s (1983-1988)	1.57	4.39	-5.95
Change in 1990s (1994-2000)	-11.61	7.55	4.06
Change during (2000-05)	4.46	-3.96	-0.50

Note: Excludes Hardwar district.
Source: Compiled from various rounds of NSS on employment and unemployment.

While there has been a relatively faster structural shift of workforce from primary sector at all-India level and in most of the states during the decade of 1980s; conversely in Uttarakhand, the trend has been observed to be opposite. The share of employment in primary sector increased by about 1.6 percentage points during 1980s and the share of secondary sector increased by 4.39 per cent while share of services declined by about 6 percentage points. The increase in the share of employment in secondary sector is largely due to the increased employment in construction activities; and the decline in services sector employment owes to the fall in employment in public administration, education, health and others. During 1990s, while there has been a slowdown in workforce movement from primary to other segments at all-India level and in other states, Uttarakhand saw a faster movement of workforce from primary to other sectors. There has been a perceptible decline in the share of primary sector employment (11.61%), and the share of employment in secondary sector doubled (7.24% to 14.79%). The services sector also noted an increase by about one-fourth during 1990s (1993-94 to 1999-2000). The reason for this increase in the secondary sector employment is due to a steep rise in construction activities and also in manufacturing employment, while the increase in tertiary sector is largely due to the rise in the share of trade. Occupational diversification of workforce in recent years (1999-2000 to 2004-05) seems to have significantly slowed down in the state and the decline particularly in the share of secondary sector is a cause of concern.

6. Trends in Employment Status

An important dimension of employment is its composition in terms of status of workforce (though not necessarily measures the quality of employment). Total employment is generally disaggregated into self-employment, regular employment and casual employment. Regular paid employment is generally considered secure and self-employment as fairly secure, even though incomes from certain types of self-employment activities might be highly irregular, inadequate and even uncertain. But for typical casual workers, neither the duration of employment nor the income is certain.

A long-term shift in the structure of employment in rural areas shows that the self-employment base has eroded systematically during 1983 to 1999-2000, both for males and females, at all-India level. A distinct sign of increasing casualisation has also been noticed and it has been more conspicuous among females than among males (Table 4.8). The share of regular employment has declined for males and it has marginally increased for females. In urban areas, however, a somewhat different trend has been noticed for both males and females. The share of self-employment has remained more or less constant for males and females. The share of regular employment has declined and that of casual employment has increased for males, while for females the share of regular employment has increased and that of casual employment has declined over the period.

As regards the status of employment in Uttarakhand, self-employment opportunities have generally shrunk during 1983 to 1999-2000 except in the case of urban females, where it has shown an improvement, though it has recorded a sharp fall between 1993-94 and 1999-2000, solely due to a fall in agriculture and allied activities. Casualisation among rural females has become most conspicuous in terms of growth, while regular employment shows an improvement more so among females (Table 4.8).

The 61st NSS Round (2004-05) results at the all-India level show an improvement (over 55th Round) in the share of self-employment and regular employment, both for males and females in the rural areas and recorded a decline in the share of casual employment. A substantial gain in the share of self-employment among females, both in rural and urban areas, and males in the urban areas has been noted - an all-time high since 1983. In the urban areas, the share of regular employment declined for males (by a little over 1 percentage point) and for females, the share registered an improvement by over 2 percentage points.

In Uttarakhand, self-employment has been the principal mode of livelihoods for males as well as for females. But for rural females, it is indeed the sole source of employment as an overwhelmingly large majority of workforce (94%) is engaged in it - primarily in cultivation activities.

Table 4.8 : Status of Employment (UPSS) in All-India and in Uttarakhand

			All India		
Rural	*1983*	*1987-88*	*1993-94*	*1999-2000*	*2004-05*
Male					
1. Self-employed	60.50	58.60	57.90	54.90	58.13
2. Regular	10.30	10.00	8.30	8.85	8.98
3. Casual	29.23	31.40	33.88	36.25	32.88
Female					
1. Self-employed	61.97	60.82	58.50	57.36	63.67
2. Regular	2.72	3.70	2.78	3.08	3.71
3. Casual	35.31	35.50	38.65	39.56	32.62

Urban					
Male					
1. Self-employed	40.95	41.70	42.10	41.68	44.78
2. Regular	43.70	42.10	42.16	41.69	40.63
3. Casual	15.43	14.60	16.22	16.85	14.58
Female					
1. Self-employed	45.81	47.10	45.40	45.30	47.69
2. Regular	25.74	27.50	28.60	33.27	35.59
3. Casual	28.44	25.40	26.20	21.36	16.72
			Uttarakhand		
Rural	*1983*	*1987-88*	*1993-94*	*1999-2000*	*2004-05*
Male					
1. Self-employed	68.41	72.71	72.21	69.96	72.79
2. Regular	12.69	12.77	12.21	13.73	13.61
3. Casual	18.90	14.52	15.58	16.31	13.60
Female					
1. Self-employed	98.24	97.35	97.72	90.44	93.50
2. Regular	0.19	0.60	0.63	1.78	1.68
3. Casual	1.57	2.05	1.65	7.78	4.82
Urban					
Male					
1. Self-employed	43.46	45.94	38.12	40.96	53.19
2. Regular	43.73	51.74	57.54	51.72	40.85
3. Casual	12.80	2.32	4.34	7.32	5.96
Female					
1. Self-employed	23.44	48.54	65.41	37.11	49.03
2. Regular	37.92	45.37	33.32	62.89	43.21
3. Casual	38.64	6.09	1.27	0.00	7.76

Note : Excludes Hardwar district.

Source : NSSO, household unit record data on employment and unemployment, various rounds.

Self-employment opportunities in the rural areas show an improvement in 2004-05 over 1999-2000, yet such opportunities have generally shrunk as compared to pre-1999-2000, both for males and females. Regular employment for males as well as females have generally declined albeit marginally during 1999-2000 to 2004-05. The share of casual employment has also declined for males and females but the decline is sharper for females as compared to that of males. It clearly appears that the restructuring process has halted and those who have moved on to non-agriculture sector earlier, seems to have been reverted back to agriculture sector. In urban area, the share of self-employment increased but regular employment declined significantly for males as well as females, but there has been a huge increase of casual employment for females.

The rise and fall in the share of self-employment over the years in rural area has been largely due to the increase and decrease in the share of employment in agriculture, forestry and fishing. It is not due to the fact that there have been institutional and technical improvements in agriculture sector that increased the labour absorption. In fact, there are structural constraints in bringing out such improvement in hill agriculture. The fact remains that due to limited employment opportunities outside agriculture, agriculture sector still acts as a sponge for the burgeoning labour force.

In absolute terms, there has been an increase of about 1.67 lakh persons (females recorded a decline of 0.12 lakh, while males posted an increase of 1.79 lakh) in 2004-05 over 1993-94 (Table 4.9). Out of the total fall reported among female workers, self-employed workers registered a sharp decline. Although, regular and casual employment among females shows substantive increase (in percentage terms) during 1993-94 and 2004-05, yet the overall gain in employment in absolute terms is minuscule as compared to the sharp fall in self-employment. In the case of male employment, a large part of the increase has occurred in self-employment pursuits.

Table 4.9 : Status of Rural Workers (UPSS) in Uttarakhand, 1993-94 to 2004-05

Status	*1993-94*		*1999-2000*		*2004-05*		*% change 1993-94 to 2004-05*	
	Male	*Female*	*Male*	*Female*	*Male*	*Female*	*M*	*F*
Self-employed	877435	1291725	786107	997487	1015425	1223942	15.72	-5.25
Regular	148366	8328	154277	19632	189860	21992	27.97	164.07
Casual	189315	21811	183268	85808	189721	63095	0.21	189.28
Total	1215116	1321864	1123652	1102927	1395006	1309029	14.80	-0.97

Notes : 1. Figures have been worked out using interpolated population and corresponding WPRs (UPSS).
2. Excludes Hardwar.

Females seem to be displaced from self-employment, which is more of a stable kind of employment, and are largely taking refuge in casual nature of employment, which is uncertain both in terms of days of employment and wages. Such casualisation process has long-term adverse implications in enhancing their entitlements in the labour market. If the employment is casual and temporary, then the persons depending on such type of employment would have little or no chance to improve their skill base.

What is distinct in the pattern of status of employment in Uttarakhand as compared to that of all-India? Few facts which are discernible are as follows:

First, the share of self-employment in rural Uttarakhand is significantly higher and it is much higher in the case of females as compared to rural India — constituting mostly agriculture and allied activities. The decline in this share has been slower in Uttarakhand. In urban area, male share broadly corresponds to that of all-India but for females, there has been a sharp fall in the share of self-employment in 2004-05 over 1993-94, primarily due to a sharp fall in the share of agriculture and allied activities (Annexure Table IV.3). Occupational shift of workforce in rural Uttarakhand has lagged far behind that of rural India but for urban area, the pace of shift corresponds to that of urban India in recent years.

Secondly, while regular employment opportunities have shrunk for males and increased for females, albeit marginally, at all-India level, in Uttarakhand such opportunities have generally declined across rural and urban areas for both sexes, and urban area in particular, has experienced a huge fall of such employment. Owing to limited employment opportunities outside agriculture, public administration, education, health & others have larger share in employment in Uttarakhand as compared to that of all-India levels barring rural females.

Finally, the share of casual employment is much lower in the state as compared to that of all-India. Lack of general economic development has limited such opportunities in the state. Urban female share in casual employment has been rising in the state, while regular employment opportunities have dampened significantly.

7. Unemployment Trends

Unemployment rate in the state is about 2.2 per cent of the labour force, which is slightly lower than the national average (2.3%) in 2004-05. Male unemployment rate in the state is reported to be higher and female unemployment rate is much lower as compared to the corresponding all-India rates in 2004-05 (Table 4.9A). Male

Table 4.9A: Unemployment Rate in Uttarakhand and in India (UPS)

Area/Year	*Uttarakhand*			*India*		
	Person	*Male*	*Female*	*Person*	*Male*	*Female*
Rural						
1983	0.08	0.15	0.00	1.14	1.42	1.66
1993-94	0.96	2.02	0.00	1.20	1.43	0.79
1999-2000	1.99	3.88	0.12	1.48	1.71	1.04
2004-2005	1.47	2.45	0.46	1.67	1.60	1.79
Urban						
1983	4.01	4.16	2.54	5.04	5.09	4.86
1993-94	4.94	6.16	0.00	4.52	4.05	6.24
1999-2000	3.48	3.36	4.10	4.75	4.51	5.71
2004-2005	5.38	4.54	8.89	4.49	3.81	6.88
All						
1983	0.60	1.0[illegible]	0.07	1.91	2.29	1.17
1993-94	1.50	2.89	0.00	1.90	2.07	1.54
1999-2000	2.28	3.73	0.42	2.20	2.44	1.69
2004-2005	2.16	2.98	1.12	2.31	2.18	2.56

Note: Excludes Hardwar district.

Source : NSSO, household unit record data for 38th, 43rd, 50th, 55th and 61st rounds.

unemployment situation in the rural area is much severe in the state and it has increased from 0.15 per cent in 1983 to 3.88 per cent in 1999-2000, while female unemployment situation is minuscule (0.12%). Male unemployment rate has throughout been higher from 1993-94 to 2004-05 in rural area of Uttarakhand as compared to the corresponding rate at the all-India level, and in 1999-2000, unemployment rate grew at a much faster pace (2.2 times). However, female unemployment rates were much lower in the state as compared to all-India. In the urban area, unemployment rate has generally been lower in the state than all-India, both for males and females from 1983 to 1999-2000 barring urban males in 1993-94 that shows an up-trend of 2 percentage points. In 2004-05, unemployment rate in the state is reported to be higher as compared to all-India, particularly for urban females, which shot up slightly above two times. Some of the distinct patterns of unemployment in the rural area are noted in the State of Uttarakhand. Firstly, unemployment rate among males is consistently higher in the rural area in the state, and pace of unemployment rate is much faster as compared to corresponding rates at all-India. Secondly, female unemployment rate is reported to be virtually negligible, primarily because females generally do not report themselves available for work in typical hill set-up.

The reasons for high and low incidence of unemployment for males and females respectively in the rural areas are altogether different. Open unemployment in Uttarakhand is a male-specific phenomenon. The reason for high rate of unemployment is primarily due to lack of regular employment opportunities and also intermittent employment opportunities that would otherwise have engaged them in a subsidiary capacity. The incidence of educated unemployment rate is very high in the rural area, since they do not find any regular employment opportunities. As a result, either they remain usually unemployed or get accommodated in low productivity employment in the unorganised sector. An offshoot of this kind of unemployment leads to out-migration, which is more conspicuous in the hill economy.

Female unemployment is quite low which is also reflected in terms of their high WPR. In fact, from 1983 to 1993-94, none of the female was reported as unemployed by usual status. This seems obvious as hill women are preoccupied with cultivation and other household chores and generally do not report as unemployed. There is a high intensity of underem-ployment, particularly in agriculture sector in terms of unutilised labour time and inadequate levels of income despite higher work participation; especially in the case of rural female workers, that is generally not captured in open unemployment. Unemployment by Current Daily Status (CDS), which captures underemployment intensity more precisely, throws consistently higher rate of unemployment, both for males and females, indicating a huge unutilised labour time. Although the overall unemployment rate by CDS is lower in Uttarakhand as compared to all-India, yet in the rural area the unemployment rate among males has been higher during 1993-94 to 1999-2000. Female unemployment rate in rural area is consistently registering low rates not because of the fact that they remain fully employed but largely because of their engagement in low-paid agricultural activities that do not allow them to report as either available or seeking for work. In urban area, unemployment rates are lower, both for males and females, as compared to all-India rates (Table 4.9B). Recent results (2004-05), however, show some decline in unemployment rate among rural males but reported an increase in unemployment rate for females as compared to earlier rounds. Conversely, in urban area, the unemployment rate has increased and female unemployment, in particular, has registered a huge increase (Table 4.9B).

Table 4.9B : Unemployment Rate in Uttarakhand and in India—CDS

Area/Year	*Uttarakhand*			*India*		
	Person	*Male*	*Female*	*Person*	*Male*	*Female*
Rural						
1993-94	6.48	7.76	0.00	5.62	5.64	5.55
1999-2000	4.92	7.51	0.94	7.14	7.19	7.01
2004-2005	4.85	6.34	2.15	8.20	8.00	8.70
Urban						
1993-94	1.70	3.28	0.00	7.43	6.72	10.52
1999-2000	4.10	4.34	2.60	7.66	7.29	9.39
2004-2005	7.32	7.89	6.23	8.30	7.50	11.60

Note : Excludes Hardwar district.
Source : NSSO, household unit record data for 50th, 55th and 61st rounds.

III. The Rural Non-Farm Sector

In the rural India, overall share of non-farm sector employment is estimated to be around 27.3 per cent — male constituting 33.5 per cent and females 16.8 per cent in 2004-05. Diversification of rural employment to secondary and tertiary sectors has been observed to be highest in 2004-05 (over 1999-2000) accounting 3.4 percentage points' rise in the total rural workforce, which is marginally higher than what was recorded during 1983 and 1987-88 (3.2 percentage points) (Table 4.10). The process of diversification slowed down in1993-94 but picked up slightly in 1999-2000. The recent period

(2004-05) saw a relatively faster movement of workforce from primary to secondary and tertiary sectors.

The reasons for rise in the share of non-farm sector workforce during the two periods, however, differ entirely. Explanation to the sudden rise in the share of non-farm workforce during 1987-88 is often associated with severe drought experienced, when many workers moved on from agriculture sector to secondary and tertiary sectors temporarily. This was the period when secondary sector, due to increased construction activity, showed a sudden jump of more than 2 per cent, both in case of male as well as female workers. The period 2004-05 evincing upturn of overall economy, primarily because of the better management of macro-economic policy and series of policy reform measures initiated at sectoral levels that has seen a faster movement of workforce.

It may be noted that the share of non-farm employment has been increasing steadily for males from 1983 to 2004-05 albeit faster movement noted in 2004-05, but for females there has been rather an unsteady pattern recording a faster movement in 1987-88 (over 1983), but then it saw a decline in the share till 1999-2000 as compared to 1987-88. The share in recent years (2004-05) however experienced a rise over 2 percentage points. The declining trend of female employment in non-farm sector from 1993-94 to 1999-2000 is regarded as a phenomenon of structural rigidity when the employment in agriculture sector, after consistent fall during 1980s, started increasing. The reasons for the decline in manufacturing employment and subsequent increase in agricultural employment are due to structural retrogression of agriculture workforce in rural area during 1988-94 (Bhalla, 1997; 1998).

1. Size of Rural Non-Farm Employment in Uttarakhand

Total rural employment in Uttarakhand is estimated to be around 27.04 lakh, of which 5.63 lakh is in the non-farm sector constituting 5.11 lakh males and about 0.51 lakh females in 2004-05 (Annexure Table IV.4).

The share of rural non-farm sector workers in Uttarakhand is estimated to be 19.7 per cent, which is lower by 7.6 percentage points corresponding to all-India share in 2004-05. The share of male workforce is about 35.8 per cent, which is 2.3 percentage points higher than the all-India level and the share of females is abysmally low at 3.4 per cent, recording about 13.3 percentage points lower corresponding to all-India level in 2004-05 (Table 4.10).

Table 4.10 : Broad Sectoral Distribution of Rural Workers (UPSS) in India and in Uttarakhand, 1983 to 2004-05

Years	*Primary**	*Secondary*	*Tertiary*	*Rural non-farm sector*
All India - Rural Person				
1983	81.5	9.0	9.4	18.4
1987-88	78.3	11.3	10.3	21.6
1993-94	78.2	10.2	11.5	21.7
1999-2000	76.1	11.3	12.5	23.8
2004-2005	72.7	13.7	13.6	27.3
All India - Rural Male				
1983	77.5	10.2	12.2	22.4
1987-88	74.5	12.3	13.4	25.7
1993-94	74.1	11.3	14.7	26.0
1999-2000	71.4	12.7	16.0	28.7
2004-2005	66.5	15.5	18.0	33.5
All India - Rural Female				
1983	87.5	7.4	4.8	12.2
1987-88	84.7	10.0	5.3	15.3
1993-94	86.2	8.3	5.6	13.9
1999-2000	85.4	8.9	5.7	14.6
2004-2005	83.3	10.2	6.6	16.8
Uttarakhand - Rural Person				
1983	82.4	4.2	13.4	17.6
1987-88	84.6	8.6	6.8	15.4
1993-94	84.6	6.4	9.0	15.4
1999-2000	79.3	11.8	8.9	20.7
2004-2005	80.29	8.49	11.21	19.71
Uttarakhand- Rural Male				
1983	65.7	8.3	26.0	34.4
1987-88	69.6	17.3	13.1	30.4
1993-94	69.9	12.8	17.3	30.1
1999-2000	61.6	21.6	16.8	38.4
2004-2005	64.22	15.23	20.56	35.78
Uttarakhand -Rural Female				
1983	99.1	0.0	0.9	0.9
1987-88	98.6	0.5	0.9	1.4
1993-94	97.7	0.7	1.6	2.3
1999-2000	96.2	2.3	1.5	3.8
2004-2005	96.55	1.68	1.78	3.45

Notes : (i) *Excludes mining & quarrying, (ii) Excludes Hardwar district.
Source : Compiled from various rounds of NSS on employment and unemployment.

There has been a fall in the share of male non-farm employment from 34.4 per cent in 1983 to 30.1 per cent in 1993-94, and thereafter a substantive increase in the share has been recorded. This share rose up to 38.4 per cent in 1999-2000 and slipped to 35.8 per cent in 2004-05. The reasons for these fall and rise in the share of non-farm workers in the two periods are altogether different.

The reason for the decline in the share of male non-farm workforce during 1983 to 1993-94 is an increase in the share of cultivators — probably those who moved on to other sectors temporarily and might have reverted back to cultivation (retrogression effect), and a sharp fall in the share of employment in public administration, education, health & others (7.7 percentage points). Though there has been an increase (about 3.9 percentage points) in the secondary sector employment, primarily due to a rise in construction activities, but then the increase was nullified by the decline in services and subsequent rise in the number of cultivators (Table 4.12).

The period of 1999-2000 saw a steep rise in the share of non-farm employment among males as compared to 1993-94 that has happened primarily due to a sharp fall in the share of cultivators (8.3 percentage points), a rise in construction (3.8 percentage points), transport (2.5 percentage points) and trade (1.2 percentage points) (Table 4.12). Surprisingly, for females, there have been very little movement of workforce into the non-agriculture sector over a long period (16-17 years) as the share is abysmally low (3.8%). Their share however showed an increase at a relatively faster pace during 1990s as compared to 1980s, but the employment in secondary and tertiary sectors solely constituted by the construction activities and public administration, education, health and others. The process of the fast movement of workforce seems to have halted in 2004-05 as compared to 1999-2000. There has been a decline of one percentage point in the overall share of non-farm employment in 2004-05 over 1999-2000. The share of primary sector workers increased by about 1 percentage points, that of secondary sector declined by 3.3 percentage point and a corresponding increase has been noted in tertiary sector (mainly in trade, transport & restaurant and transport, storage & communication). The share of male workers in the non-farm sector declined (2.6 percentage points) and a huge decline has been observed in the share of manufacturing and construction workers. Primary sector workers' share increased by 2.6 per cent and tertiary sector workers' share also increased by 3.8 percentage points (mainly in trade, hotel and restaurant). Such a substantive fall of workers in the manufacturing and construction activities might have pushed many male workers either in agriculture sector back or petty trading activities. Surprisingly for females, the share has declined from 3.8 per cent to 1.8 per cent during 1999-2000 to 2004-05 (Tables 4.10 and 4.12).

The work structure is highly gender biased in the rural areas of the state as women overwhelmingly work in agriculture related occupations, while their male counterparts work in the non-farm occupations (Awasthi, 2009). Such a low share of female employment in non-agriculture sector shows a complete dichotomy and segmentation of labour market that inhibit women to seek employment outside a limited segment of labour market (outside cultivation) despite considerable improvement in their literacy levels over the years. From the policy point of view, this raises the issue of yet another kind as how to increase their productivity within agriculture and non-agricultural activities through various skill development programmes that would help increase their productivity and enable them to enter into the labour market.

2. Growth of Non-farm Employment

Performance of employment growth in the state has been dismal and rural areas in particular saw an abysmally low growth of employment over the years. The decade 1990s registered a much lower employment growth as compared to 1980s. The overall farm sector employment growth has turned out to be negative (-4.06 %), while non-farm sector employment growth recorded a fairly high growth (4.71%) per annum during 1994-2000 (Table 4.11). In rural areas too, non-farm employment performed much better than farm sector. While farm sector recorded a negative growth (-3.65%), non-farm sector registered a much better growth (5.34%) during 1994-2000. Labour absorption capacity in agriculture sector has severely shrunk during 1990s as compared to 1980s. The NSS round results (61st Round, 2004-05) have registered a substantive gain in the overall employment growth (4.53%) reverting the negative growth (-1.61%) in the earlier round (1999-2000). Farm sector has achieved a dramatic up-trend (4.82%) which is higher than non-farm sector growth (3.96%). Employment in rural area registered 3.96 per cent growth, non-farm sector 3.51 per cent growth and farm sector registered 4.08 per cent growth per annum.

Table 4.11: Compound Annual Growth Rates of Employment in Farm and Non-Farm Sector in Uttarakhand

Sector	*1988-94*	*1994-2000*	*2000-2005*	*1994-2005*
Rural				
Farm	1.78	-3.65	4.08	-0.21
Non-farm	-0.53	5.34	3.51	4.51
All	1.44	-2.15	3.96	0.58
Urban				
Farm	17.57	-23.81	38.83	0.08
Non-farm	3.73	4.07	5.09	4.53
All	5.45	1.27	7.06	3.86
All				
Farm	2.12	-4.06	4.82	-0.12
Non-farm	1.47	4.71	3.96	4.36
All	1.96	-1.61	4.53	1.13

Notes: (i) Growth rate has been worked out using interpolated population and corresponding WPR (UPSS).
(ii) Excludes Hardwar.

It is important to note that, though there has been a significant deceleration in the growth of employment in rural areas during 1994-2005 (less than 1%), yet non-farm sector employment grew by 4.51 per cent.

During 2000-05, the overall RNF employment grew at 3.51 per cent per annum, which is lower by 1.8 percentage point from 1994-2000, yet the sub-sectoral growth trend reveals a distinct pattern of changes. The agriculture segment after registering a negative growth

(-3.65%) in 1994-2000, has a dramatic recovery (4.08%) in 2004-05. However, some of the growing segments in the earlier round have either posted a negative growth or decelerated. For example, electricity and construction segments have registered a negative growth. Growth of electricity, construction, transport, storage & communication and financial services slowed down, but there has been a huge increment in trade, hotels & restaurants and public administration, education, health & others (Annexure Table IV.5).

For females, there was a broad-based sectoral employment growth during 1987-1994, but then, there has been a major trend reversal afterwards. During 1994-2000, females recorded a very high employment growth rate in construction, which was evidently the principal source of non-farm employment. Then, in 2004-05, employment in construction slipped and turned out to be negative. The only segment that picked up fast growth for females has been public administration, education, health & others.

For males, employment growth in trade, hotels & restaurants and public administration, education, health & others have registered an improvement while manufacturing, electricity, transport, storage & communication; finance, real estate & business have decelerated in 2004-05 as compared to 1999-2000 (Annexure Table IV.5).

3. Sectoral Composition of Rural Non-farm Employment

The distinct feature of rural non-farm sector in Uttarakhand is that it is a highly gender-biased labour market; while males virtually dominated the non-farm occupations, females have a minuscule share in these activities. Females are grossly under-represented in the rural non-farm sector, primarily due to their over-representation in agriculture and allied activities (Table 4.12). The share of males in the rural non-farm sector is about 35.8 per cent, while for females it is 3.4 per cent in 2004-05. For males, the major sources of non-farm employment have been construction (10.6%); trade, hotel and restaurant (7.3%); public administration, etc. (8.5%) and manufacturing (4.2%), but for females, opportunities in non-farm sector employment are minuscule (3.4%). Their share in public administration is highest (1.6%) followed by manufacturing (1.0%) and construction (0.5%) (Table 4.12).

Table 4.12 : Sectoral Distribution of Workers (at one digit level) in Rural Uttarakhand, 1983 to 2004-05 (UPSS)

Sector/Sex	*1983*	*1987-88*	*1993-94*	*1999-2000*	*2004-05*
Rural Person					
Agriculture and allied	82.15	84.56	84.58	79.29	80.29
Mining & quarrying	0.28	0.02	0.27	0.00	0.00
Manufacturing	2.84	3.47	1.52	3.89	2.66
Electricity	0.05	0.04	0.10	0.25	0.23
Construction	1.27	5.11	4.51	7.61	5.60
Trade, hotels & restaurants	1.35	1.91	1.52	2.06	3.66
Transport, storage & communication	1.47	0.37	0.75	2.01	1.95
Finance, real estate & business	0.31	0.20	0.38	0.53	0.50
Pub. Adm., education, health & others	10.28	4.34	6.36	4.36	5.10
All	100.00	100.00	100.00	100.00	100.00
Rural Male					
Agriculture and allied	65.05	69.58	69.92	61.63	64.22
Mining & quarrying	0.57	0.03	0.57	0.00	0.00
Manufacturing	5.69	6.89	2.72	7.97	4.19
Electricity	0.09	0.08	0.21	0.51	0.43
Construction	2.55	10.31	9.27	13.13	10.61
Trade, hotels & restaurants	2.56	3.82	2.99	4.21	7.26
Transport, storage & communication	2.94	0.77	1.60	4.11	3.80
Finance, real estate & business	0.62	0.41	0.54	1.09	0.96
Pub. Adm., education, health & others	19.92	8.12	12.20	7.34	8.54
All	100.00	100.00	100.00	100.00	100.00
Rural Female					
Agriculture and allied	99.14	98.56	97.67	96.14	96.55
Mining & quarrying	0.00	0.00	0.00	0.00	0.00
Manufacturing	0.00	0.27	0.46	0.00	1.11
Electricity	0.00	0.00	0.00	0.00	0.03
Construction	0.00	0.24	0.27	2.33	0.54
Trade, hotels & restaurants	0.16	0.12	0.21	0.00	0.03
Transport, storage & communication	0.00	0.00	0.00	0.00	0.09
Finance, real estate & business	0.00	0.00	0.24	0.00	0.03
Pub. Adm.,education, health & others	0.70	0.81	1.16	1.52	1.63
All	100.00	100.00	100.00	100.00	100.00

Notes : Excludes Hardwar district.
Source : NSSO, household unit record data on employment and unemployment, various rounds.

There has been a steady increase in the share of non-farm

employment, both for males and females during 1983 to 1999-2000. Most of the non-farm activities showed a perceptible increase in the share during the period, but the recent years (2004-05) saw a clear downturn.

During 1983 to 1999-2000, there has been a gradual increase in every branch of non-farm activities for males. Manufacturing, electricity, construction, trade, hotels & restaurants, transport, storage & communication, and finance, real estate & business - all sub-sectors grew and among these, construction sector grew fastest during this period. The only sub-sectors that saw a decline in the share of employment are mining & quarrying, and public services. For females, construction and public services turned out to be the only segments that provided employment in the non-farm sector. The reason for an increase in the share of public services and construction seems to be altogether different. Reservation seems to be the prime reason for increasing the share in public services, while in construction, the vulnerability along with coping with the need for cash income appears to be the main reason, particularly in the absence of any other alternative option of earning an income.

Many activities that had noted a substantive gain in the share in 1999-2000 over 1993-94 saw a clear downturn in 2004-05. The share of male workers declined from 38 to 36 per cent during 1999-2000 to 2004-05. Barring trade, hotels & restaurants, and public administration most of the activities saw a fall in the share of male workers. The share of manufacturing, and construction declined between 3.8 and 2.5 per cent, respectively. The only segment which grew fastest is trade, hotels & restaurants, which increased from 4.2 to 7.3%). For females, the share declined from 3.8 to 3.4 per cent during the same period. Manufacturing saw a significant increase in the share (1.1%), while the share in construction virtually collapsed (2.3% to 0.5%) and noted only a marginal gain in public services, etc.

4. The Growing Sub-sectors

Overall, rural employment growth turned out to be negative during

1993-94 to 1999-2000. However, some of the segments have shown better performance in terms of employment growth. Manufacturing of food products and beverages, textiles, wood & wood products, construction, retail trade except motor vehicle, etc, land transport, post & telecommunication, health & social work, and manufacturing of rubber & plastic products have registered a fairly reasonable growth. While agriculture, forestry & logging, manufacturing of wearing apparel, chemicals, machinery and equipment, public administration and education recorded a negative growth. Construction, education, public administration, and private household segments have been important sources of employment for females.

Some of the segments outside agriculture have been emerging with good potential for employment. It is also important from the policy point of view to promote these segments with all necessary support system. However, this kind of employment structure also indicates highly male-dominted work structure where females have no access barring education sector. This has important policy inplications as well and such disparities are closely linked to ecucation and skill levels of the female workforce.

5. Non-Farm Informal Sector

Most of the employment is being generated in the unorganised sector primarily because of declining employment in the organised sector. However, the duration of employment is uncertain, condition of work is generally precarious and wages are depressed. In spite of all these adverse work conditions, unorganised sector is regarded the future source of employment. There are certain segments within informal or unorganised sector that are doing relatively better in terms of employment and productivity, but a large part of this sector is operating at a low margin of subsistence and creating the employment of last resort.

In rural Uttarakhand, maximum share of enterprises are in trade segment followed by manufacturing and construction, and minimum share being in financial intermediation and services. In terms of employment per unit, the major sectors are transport, storage & communications and manufacturing, while the minimum employment intensive sectors are financial intermediation and construction. Financial intermediation, transport, storage & communication, hotel and restaurant are the major contributors in terms of productivity, while manufacturing and services have the lowest productivity (Table 4.13). Within these sectors, there are certain segments that have performed better in terms of employment per unit and productivity, which needs to be promoted from policy point of view. In the manufacturing sector, textiles (2.2%), non-metallic minerals (2.0%), machinery and equipments (2.9%) and electrical machineries (6.8%) are the most promising segments, where not only per unit employment is above the average employment size (1.6%) in manufacturing sector, but also the productivity per worker in textiles (Rs.16,524) and machinery and equipments (Rs.15,738) segments is higher than the average productivity in this sector (Rs.13,489) (Annexure Table IV.6). Similarly, within the trade sector, sale, maintenance and repair of motor vehicle (2.4%) and wholesale trade and commission trade (2.4%) segments have higher employment per unit in comparison to overall employment per unit in trade (1.2%). Within the services sector, education segment has much higher employment per unit (2.9%) as compared to overall service sector in the rural area (1.5%). Even in the health and social services segment, per unit employment is slightly lower but productivity is almost double (Rs.28,407) the overall service sector (Rs.14,373). From the long-term perspective such segment of informal economy, where employment and productivity is higher, needs to be promoted with a view to creating productive employment.

In the urban area, both per unit employment and productivity are higher as compared to the rural area in the state. Construction is the most booming segment showing not only the highest per unit employment but also have maximum productivity as compared to all other segments. The other employment intensive sectors are manufacturing, and services and trade, where employment per unit is higher than average employment per unit. Trade is yet another sector where employment is equal to that of the average employment size but productivity is higher than the average productivity in this sector. Within manufacturing, manufacturing of food and beverages (2.6%),

Table 4.13 : Proportional Share of Employment and Gross Value Added (GVA) and Labour Productivity in Different Unorganised Sub-sectors in Rural Uttarakhand, 1999-2000.

Industry group	*Enterprise*	*Worker*	*GVA (Rs.)*	*Enterprise %*	*Workers %*	*GVA %*	*Worker/ Enterprise*	*Produ-ctivity (Rs.)*	*Rank*
Manufacturing	29654	46385	625693957	22.42	26.38	18.14	1.6	13489	7
Construction	23726	25669	407436969	17.94	14.60	11.81	1.1	15873	5
Wholesale, retail trade, etc.	43720	51717	1022863936	33.05	29.41	29.65	1.2	19778	4
Hotel & restaurant	13849	18896	373841071	10.47	10.75	10.84	1.4	19784	3
Transport, storage and communications	11441	19164	751789663	8.65	10.90	21.79	1.7	39229	2
Financial intermediation	1699	1749	91913577	1.28	0.99	2.66	1.0	52543	1
Services	8182	12251	176084700	6.19	6.97	5.10	1.5	14373	6
Total	132271	175831	3449623873	100.00	100.00	100.00	1.3	19619	

Source : Annexure Table IV. 6

wearing apparel (2.00%), electric machineries (2.4%) and furniture (2.3%) have higher average per unit employment (1.8%). Productivity in manufacturing of food and beverages (Rs.29,485), wearing apparel (Rs.15,432) and furniture (Rs.32,802) is higher and it is much higher in the cases of food and beverages, and furniture than the average productivity in this sector (Rs.14,856) (Table 4.14). In trade sector, sale, maintenance and repair of motor vehicles are the most efficient segments both in terms of employment per unit (5.1%) as well as in terms of productivity (Rs.40,827) as compared to that of the average trade sector (1.6% and Rs.30, 827 respectively). In financial intermediation, renting machineries and equipments, and education in services sector have performed much better both in terms of employment per unit and productivity (Annexure Table IV. 6).

6. *The Rural Unorganised Manufacturing*

The rural unorganised manufacturing consists of three different sets of enterprises. At the lower end of hierarchy remains 'Own Account Manufacturing Enterprises' (OAME) using mostly family labour and hiring a few workers occasionally. The other two types of enterprises that hire at least one worker on long-term basis is 'Non-Directory Manufacturing Establishment' (NDME) employing up to five workers, and 'Directory Manufacturing Establishment' (DME) employing more than five workers.

There has been a fairly high growth of enterprises (3.5% per annum) and employment (4.4% per annum) during 1994-95 to 2000-01, but there has been an abysmally low growth of GVA (0.68% per annum) resulting in a decline in productivity (-3.55% per annum) (Table 4.15).

OAME has an overwhelming presence in rural areas and it contributes significantly in terms of employment and value addition. The share of OAME in terms of number of enterprises, workers and GVA is 92 per cent, 67 per cent and 48 per cent, respectively in 2001. The share in terms of employment remained at the same level over 1994-95, but there has been a significant fall in terms of employment and GVA during this period (Annexure Table IV.7). The major enterprises in OAME category have been manufacturing of food

Table 4.14 : Proportional Share of Employment and Gross Value Added (GVA), and Labour Productivity in different Unorganised Sub-sectors in Urban Uttarakhand, 1999-2000

Industry group	*Enterprise*	*Worker*	*GVA (Rs.)*	*Enterprise %*	*Workers %*	*GVA %*	*Worker/ Enterprise*	*Produ-ctivity (Rs.)*	*Rank*
Manufacturing	15920	28267	419945693	16.57	17.96	10.09	1.8	14856	7
Construction	1491	7547	308101735	1.55	4.79	7.40	5.1	40827	1
Wholesale, retail trade, etc.	46592	72344	2230180438	48.48	45.96	53.57	1.6	30827	3
Hotel & restaurant	3709	4745	125127942	3.86	3.01	3.01	1.3	26369	4
Transport, storage and communications	4530	5978	146595206	4.71	3.80	3.52	1.3	24523	6
Financial intermediation	818	1231	39466187	0.85	0.78	0.95	1.5	32072	2
Services	10990	20072	503424238	11.44	12.75	12.09	1.8	25081	5
Total	96096	157404	4162766907	100.00	100.00	100.00	1.6	26446	

Source : Annexure Table IV. 6.

products (35%), manufacturing of wood & wood products (34%), manufacturing of non-metallic mineral products (19%) with higher shares in terms of employment (38, 23 and 24% respectively) and GVA (66, 18 and 6% respectively) as well in 1994-95. However, in 2000-01, the share of enterprises in manufacturing of wood & wood products declined sharply from about 34 per cent to about 12 per cent, the employment share declined from 23 per cent to about 10 per cent, and GVA from 18 to 15 per cent. The share of enterprises in non-metallic mineral products also declined drastically from about 19 to 4 per cent and employment from 24 to 6 per cent, and GVA from 6 to 2.5 per cent. However, the share of manufacturing of textile products rose steeply from about 4.6 to 42 per cent, workers' share increased from 5 to 31 per cent and GVA's share rose from 2.4 to 19.5 per cent in 2000-01 (Annexure Table IV.7). The other emerging segment is manufacturing of metal products and parts, except machinery and equipment.

In NDME, the dominating segments are manufacturing of food products and wood & wood products in terms of enterprises, workers and GVA in 1994-95, but in 2000-01 the share of food products declined sharply and the share of textiles emerged as an important segment. In DME, the share of food products and non-metallic mineral products increased steeply, while the share of wood & wood products declined sharply during 1994-95 to 2000-01 (Annexure Table IV.7).

Table 4.15 : Trends of Rural Unorganised Manufacturing in Uttarakhand

Year	*Enterprise*	*Employment*	*Enterprise per worker*	*GVA**	*Productivity*
1994-95	43,725	99,498	2.28	729,368,524	7,331
2000-01	53,780	128,755	2.39	759,596,702	5,900

Notes : See Annexure Table IV.7. * constant (1993-94) prices.
Source : NSS, 51st and 56th rounds of unorganised manufacturing.

IV. Productivity and Income

1. Sectoral Composition of Income

Economic structure is an important indicator of development that shows the process of structural transformation in the economy over the years. Income is generally considered as an important parameter of such structural changes. However, changes in income alone may not be a sufficient condition for any successful structural transformation. It is therefore important for any successful transformation that changes in the structure of income should be accompanied by corresponding changes in the structure of workforce or employment. But, in spite of significant changes in the structure of income in primary sector, employment structure has not shown the desired changes over the years. For instance, in the State of Uttarakhand, about 62 per cent workforce in the primary sector is contributing about 28 per cent income while 38 per cent workforce in secondary and tertiary sectors is contributing about 72 per cent wealth.

Table 4.16 presents the income structure, to be more precise, the Gross State Domestic Product (GSDP) structure of the state as also that of all-India in terms of the standard tri-sectoral classification, viz., percentage share of primary, secondary and tertiary sectors, at two points of time i.e.1993-94 and 2004-05.

As may be observed, in Uttarakhand, the reliance on primary producing sectors was higher than that of all-India; though the share has declined from 1993-94 to 2004-05, yet this gap still continues. However, in the secondary sector, Uttarakhand has recorded a higher share than all-India average by about 3.2 per cent in 2004-05, but a large part of increase has come through construction activities. In terms of tertiary sector, the gap has widened between Uttarakhand and all-India over the period (Table 4.16).

Table 4.16 : Share of GSDP in Uttarakhand and India (1993-94 prices)

Sector	*Uttarakhand*			*All India*		
	1993-94	*1999-2000*	*2004-05*	*1993-94*	*1999-2000*	*2004-05*
Primary	40.10	38.30	28.32	33.54	27.37	22.81
Secondary	23.36	20.39	27.95	23.69	24.30	24.78
Tertiary	36.54	41.31	43.73	42.77	48.33	52.40
	100.00	100.00	100.00	100.00	100.00	100.00

Source : Central Statistical Organisation.

2. *Sectoral Pattern of Productivity*

Productivity is an important measure of growth in real terms. Per worker income in primary sector is generally very low as compared to other sectors indicating a low productivity, primarily due to an overcrowding in this sector. The relative sectoral productivity is therefore an important indicator for change in the structure of economy.

It can be observed from Tables 4.17 and 4.18 that growth in per worker GSDP in all sectors in the state is below that of all-India during 1994-2000, barring the primary sector which achieved a respectable growth. In secondary sector, every branch registered a negative growth in the state. The tertiary sector posted a positive growth in productivity (4.95%) in the state, bulk of which appears to

Table 4.17 : Distribution of GSDP per Worker and Growth of Major Industry in Uttarakhand at 1993-94 Prices

Industry	*Per worker GSDP (Rs.)*			*ACGR growth in per worker GSDP (%)*		*GSDP growth (%)*	
	1993-94	*1999-2000*	*2004-05*	*1994-2000*	*2000-05*	*1994-2000*	*2000-05*
Agriculture & allied activities	8430	12042	10669	6.12	-2.39	2.33	1.81
Mining & quarrying	69090	-	11559190	0.00	-	3.75	29.18
Primary Sector	**8707**	**12534**	**12102**	**6.26**	**-0.70**	**2.38**	**3.58**
Manufacturing	76470	34147	56547	-12.57	10.61	-4.52	13.99
Electricity, gas & water supply	135989	41484	201011	-17.95	37.11	2.00	20.42
Construction	26238	23913	55426	-1.53	18.31	8.46	19.23
Secondary Sec.	**49801**	**28901**	**60845**	**-8.67**	**16.05**	**0.87**	**17.18**
Trade, hotels & restaurants	30702	22357	21282	-5.15	-0.98	1.19	10.39
Transport, storage & communication	37994	41255	56113	1.38	6.35	5.39	16.28
Banking & insurance	172614	177550	344363	0.47	14.17	6.92	7.87
Community and social services	19026	34717	51307	10.54	8.13	6.01	12.81
Tertiary Sector	**32290**	**43156**	**52883**	**4.95**	**4.15**	**5.30**	**11.30**
All	**16113**	**21194**	**27577**	**4.67**	**5.41**	**3.17**	**10.03**
Per capita income	***7654***	***8254***	***12095***	***1.27***	***7.94***		

Source : Annexure IV.8.

Table 4.18 : Distribution of GDP Per Worker and Growth of Major Industry at All-India at 1993-94 Prices

Industry	*Per worker GDP (Rs.)*			*ACGR growth in per worker GDP (%)*		*GDP growth (%)*	
	1993-94	*1999-2000*	*2004-05*	*1994- to 2000*	*2000-05*	*1994-2000*	*2000-05*
Agriculture & allied activities	10115	11956	11957	2.83	0.00	2.88	1.52
Mining & quarrying	72810	125788	129729	9.54	0.62	5.22	4.10
Primary	**10830**	**12975**	**13144**	**3.06**	**0.26**	**3.07**	**1.76**
Manufacturing	31428	43885	46829	5.72	1.31	7.34	5.57
Electricity, gas & water supply	132445	252736	262574	11.37	0.77	6.94	3.36
Construction	33979	33673	29832	-0.15	-2.39	6.35	5.00
Secondary Sec.	**34716**	**44793**	**44887**	**4.34**	**0.04**	**7.08**	**5.24**
Trade, hotels transport, & communication	38352	46313	59066	3.19	4.98	9.24	8.05
Banking & insurance	246796	301307	249852	3.38	-3.68	8.36	5.12
Community and social services	26030	46416	52176	10.12	2.37	8.57	4.30
Tertiary	**42380**	**59606**	**69899**	**5.85**	**3.24**	**8.82**	**6.31**
All	**20884**	**28881**	**32923**	**5.55**	**2.65**	**6.63**	**4.42**
Per capita income	**8742**	**11438**	**13787**	**4.58**	**3.81**		

Source : Annexure IV.9.

have come from the community and social services sub-sector, reflecting essentially the pace of change of wages/salaries in that sector rather than an effective measure of the degree of efficiency. This pattern of productivity change in the state stands in marked contrast to the all-India level in major segments of the economy. Even per capita income in the state was lower by 28 per cent, and GDP growth also turned out to be far below as compared to all-India in 1999-2000. The later period (2000-05), however, saw a perceptible increase in sectoral growth in terms of per worker GSDP in the state. Barring the primary sector, every segment of economic activities saw a substantive improvement in sectoral performance as compared to all-India. The secondary sector has shown a dramatic improvement in productivity and registered a whopping growth in per worker GSDP

(16% per annum). In fact, every segment of secondary sector showed an impressive performance. Sectoral performance in terms of per worker GSDP growth in the state has been far better than all-India. The overall GSDP growth per worker, per capita income and GDP growth in the state has doubled as compared to all-India during the later period. In spite of a perceptible performance in the state during 2004-05, per worker GSDP (absolute terms) in primary and tertiary sectors and per capita income have been much lower throughout during 1993-94 to 2004-05 as compared to all-India.

3. Wages

The indicators of judging the quality of employment are income levels, labour productivity, status of employment and wage rate. We have earlier seen that self-employment is the principal mode of employment and the recent round (61st) also indicates an increase in self-employment, both in rural and urban areas, over the earlier round (55th). In rural areas, most of the employment has occurred in self-employment, both for males and females, which by and large indicate a low productive agriculture sector. While the share of regular employment has declined for males and remained constant for females, the share of casual employment increased for males but declined for females in 2004-05 as compared to 1999-2000 (Tables 4.8 and 4.9). The share of GDP in agriculture sector has been declining over time (Table 4.16) and the increase in self-employment is manifestation of overcrowding in this sector.

Growth in per worker GSDP in all sectors in the state was below the all-India average during 1994-2000, barring the primary sector which achieved a respectable growth. In the secondary sector, every branch registered a negative growth in the state. However, in the latest period (2000-05), there has been a perceptible increase in sectoral growth in terms of per worker GSDP in the state, barring the primary sector that saw a substantive improvement in the sectoral performance as compared to all-India. In spite of the perceptible performance in the state during 2004-05, per worker GSDP (absolute terms) in primary and tertiary sectors, and per capita income have been much lower throughout during 1993-94 to 2004-05 as compared to all-India (Tables 4.17 and 4.18).

Table 4.18A shows the trend in wages (constant prices) over time. Rural wages tend to show an increasing trend, both for regular and casual employment across both the sexes during 1999-2000 to 2004-05. This has reversed the earlier trend of falling of regular wages that continued for both the sexes during 1993-94 to 1999-2000, and overall casual wages remained almost stagnant. The pace of growth in real wages has been equal for males and females but casual employment wages have moved much faster for males as compared to females during 1999-2000 to 2004-05. However, in urban area, real wages have declined both for regular and casual workers during 1999-2000 to 2004-05. The fall in regular wages was substantially higher for females (36%). Such a fall in real wages accompanied by the increasing employment manifests sort of a low productive employment for urban workforce which is a matter of serious concern.

Table 4.18A : Daily Wages (Rs. per day) in Uttarakhand at Constant Prices according to Employment Status (Base 2004-05)

Location/ status	*1993-94*	*1999-2000*	*2004-05*	*1993-94*	*1999-2000*	*2004-05*	*1993-94*	*1999-2000*	*2004-05*
Rural		**Male**			**Female**			**Person**	
Regular/salaried	172	160	194	173	112	135	172	154	187
Casual workers	58	57	70	44	54	56	57	57	68
Urban									
Regular/salaried	167	219	213	126	213	137	161	218	198
Casual workers	79	81	70	51	NA	60	77	81	69

Source : NSS various rounds.

V. Factors Determining Rural Non-farm Employment (RNFE)

There are several factors that determine the growth of rural non-farm employment. Generally, education and skill levels of workers, land distribution and other asset pattern across rural households, availability of infrastructure and credit, etc. have been identified as the important determinants of the RNFE. However, these factors are often differently positioned in terms of their motivating powers to engage in different types of non-farm employment activities at individual and household level in rural economy.

1. Education and Skills

There are strong arguments, theoretically as well as empirically, that strengthening education — particularly primary and secondary education — has enormous beneficial effects pouring out to the society and industry (Islam, 1997; Reardon, 1997; Lanjouw, 1999). It enhances productivity, flexibility, increases mobility and provides the very foundation on which further skill and acumen can be built upon. Education is thus considered a crucial dimension of human resource development, which has an innate relationship with labour market conditions and is viewed as a means of improving skills and competencies required by jobs thrown up in the labour market. Education and skill levels facilitate the access to non-farm employment opportunities, and as the level of education and skill improves the incidence of casual employment declines both in agriculture and non-agriculture sectors (Chadha, 1997). Another large household survey corroborates the findings and observes that the educational levels improve the prospects of better non-farm employment, particularly, in well-paid regular non-farm occupations (Lanjouw and Shariff, 2002).

In Uttarakhand, literacy has achieved an impressive growth over the year and has helped in improving the access to non-farm employment, both within and outside the state mainly through out-migration mechanism. In spite of tremendous progress made in the provision of school and higher education, there are certain issues with regard to inequity in the accessibility of education across different classes in the society and inter- and intra-district variation in terms of accessibility, affordability and quality. The progress of educational facilities also need to be assessed in terms of qualitative measures, such as pupil-teacher ratios, drop-out rates, examination results, infrastructural facilities, trained teachers, etc. Though these are the basic measures, yet to some extent indicate the quality of educational facilities made available in the state.

The skill levels in the rural economy are very low which also has restricted their access to the local labour market as well as outside local labour market, particularly for females. There has been a proliferation of educational institutions (including higher educational institutions) but so far as appropriate and marketable skills are concerned, very few institutions are actually providing these skill training. Technical courses like ITIs and Polytechnics suffer from obsolete trades, poor infrastructure and weak industry-education linkages. Many other professional courses are mushrooming in the state in recent years, but without corresponding to the emerging demand of economy in terms of skill and competency levels, they remain qualitatively at sub-optimal levels causing unemployment, depressed wages and low-income levels. Such a situation might result in low returns which would not be a viable form of investment in the long run; and this kind of situation needs to be corrected by setting some standards and benchmarking with a view to improving the quality of these institutions. From the policy point of view, it is a prerequisite to promote vocational and technical education with marketable skills that have demand within local economy as well as outside local economy. There are numerous opportunities for development, particularly in the niche segments where the economy has comparative advantages (viz., tourism, power generation, and cultivation of medicinal plants and herbs, etc.) which can have enormous skill demands, if these sectors are promoted optimally to the advantage of the economy.

It can be seen from Table 4.19 that rural non-farm employment generally shows an increasing trend with higher levels of education and the opposite is also true in the case of non-literate category.

The trend, however, does not seem to be clear over the years, both for males and females, particularly in the middle and above educational categories. This is due to the small sample size that does not capture the nuances fully over time, particularly before 2004-05, when Uttarakhand was a part of Uttar Pradesh.

In 1993-94, the share of males showed a consistently rising trend with higher levels of education, and particularly at the graduate and above level, the share is very high. Also, for females, the up-trend is clearly noted in all categories barring the middle level. In 1999-2000, while the overall share in the non-farm sector has increased, it has declined in the categories of higher secondary, and graduate and above categories. The fall in the case of graduate and above is not that high, but in the category of higher secondary, the share has declined sharply. Two sets of arguments can be put forward as the possible reasons for decline in the share of non-farm sector in these two educated categories. The first argument is related to migration. In the hill region, migration is an important phenomenon and those who are better educated and skilled out-migrate for better employment and income opportunities. The second argument is related to the strength of local economy in providing gainful employment to the educated youth. In the later case, the local employment avenues particularly the regular jobs are limited for educated persons and they probably prefer to engage themselves in agricultural activities rather than in low pay-off non-farm activities.

Table 4.19 : Percentages of Rural Workers Engaged in Non-Farm Sector by Education Levels, 1994-2005

Education/ category	*1993-94*	*1999-2000*	*2004-05*	*1993-94*	*1999-2000*	*2004-05*	*1993-94*	*1999-2000*	*2004-05*
Rural		**Male**			**Female**			**Person**	
Not literate	21.35	26.08	29.41	1.44	3.71	1.52	6.97	8.88	9.80
Up to primary	22.41	35.02	32.98	1. 81	1.63	3.76	15.02	21.26	19.17
Middle	30.18	45.19	33.65	0.00	0.00	3.50	21.32	33.68	23.04
Secondary	36.69	44.54	28.75	21.10	3.95	1.99	33.51	35.02	20.45
Higher secondary	43.73	24.51	46.75	38.76	13.33	8.26	42.94	21.89	32.50
Graduate and above	82.91	77.86	61.42	44.07	44.76	35.70	78.90	71.06	56.36
Total	30.14	38.37	35.78	2.33	3.86	3.45	15.43	20.71	19.71

Note : Excludes Hardwar district.
Source : NSS, 50th, 55th and 61st rounds.

2. Land Size Classes and Rural Non-farm Employment

Land is the most important asset in rural setting along with livestock assets. It has been documented that poor and landless people often resort to non-farm activities, particularly so in low pay-off non-farm activities (Basant, 1993; Thorat, 1993; Thorat *et al.*, 2005; Islam,

1997; Reardon *et al.*, 1998; Reardon *et al.*, 2000). Larger landholdings help provide access to higher wage occupations in the non-farm employment, though not necessarily to non-farm earnings (Lanjouw and Shariff, 2002).

In Uttarakhand, over 70 per cent landholdings are marginal, which have become highly uneconomical for cultivation. In any case, cultivation does not ensure food security beyond a few months in a year for majority of the households. Multiple activities within farm and non-farm sector are a dire necessity for survival.

Over the years, concentration of small and marginal landholding has increased due to fragmentation of family landholdings and increase in population. Consequently, dependence on the non-farm employment has gone up over the period.

It can be observed from Table 4.20 that the landless and sub-marginal landholdings households depend considerably on non-farm employment. Almost 91 per cent among landless households depended on non-farm employment in 1999-2000, and this share has gone up from 72 per cent in 1993-94. The dependence on non-farm employment both for males and females increased substantively over the period. However, dependence on non-farm employment in the higher size land-class is very low witnessing an inverse relationship between the land size-class and their participation in the non-farm employment. Larger landholding sizes require more labour use, particularly in a typical hill traditional farming, which has virtually little or no scope for bringing about technical progress.

Table 4.20 : Share of Rural Non-farm Sector by Land Size Class

Land category (ha)	*1993-94*			*1999-2000*		
	Male	*Female*	*Total*	*Male*	*Female*	*Total*
Landless	77.42	54.68	72.19	93.47	82.79	90.69
>0< = 0.40	34.70	1.78	16.52	51.54	1.59	24.28
> 0.40< = 1	15.67	0.00	6.42	15.40	1.17	7.66
>1< = 2	15.88	0.00	6.96	12.82	0.00	5.98
>2< = 4	15.45	0.00	9.09	11.26	0.00	4.68
>4	13.01	3.58	9.39	13.03	0.00	7.84
Total	30.14	2.32	15.40	35.59	2.50	17.95

Source : NSS, 50th, 55th rounds.

3. Gender and Social Group

Gender and social class is yet another important dimension that influences the access to participation in non-farm activities in rural areas. There are societal norms that largely shape the economic options available to them. These norms constrict the participation of women and certain social groups in certain types of activities, and also certain types of activities are exclusively in the domain of specific social category or gender. Apart from social and cultural inhibitions, women's low work participation is caused due to 'discouraged worker effect' in the labour market (Unni and Rani, 2005). It is generally argued that women are engaged in low productive segments within non-farm activities and are relatively more circumscribed than men. In certain cases, women are better represented in this sector — mostly in trade that requires low capital and supposedly low-paying activities. Also, women are engaged in informal manufacturing activities on sub-contract or piece-rate basis operating from home, which are the hidden forms of employment and often vulnerable to exploitation.

Not only gender dimension, but also social-class dimension is so central in the rural areas that it prevents the access to the numerous non-farm activities. It has also been noted that the lower social class generally faces additional constraints in the labour market in accessing to non-farm employment, especially in high productivity activities, because of their low entitlement base as compared to other social classes (Lanjouw and Shariff, 2002; Ramachandran, *et al.,* 2002). Several field research results show that the upper castes tend to dominate local politics and social dynamics, and enjoy better asset endowments, more favourable access to education and information that helps them to avail better remunerative and productive non-farm employment opportunities. The types of economic activities pursued, in turn, influence the expenditure behaviour of the households. It has been observed that in the case of SCs, poverty ratio is higher both in farm and non-farm sectors and in activity-wise as well (Thorat, *et al.,* 2005).

In Uttarakhand too, various factors inhibit women to participate in the non-farm sector labour market, because of their pre-occupation in agriculture and allied activities, and other household activities. Labour market in the non-farm sector is distinctly segmented; women are overwhelmingly represented in agriculture sector and their share in non-farm sector is minuscule, while men dominate most of the activities in the non-farm sector. Barring public administration, manufacturing and construction; their share in other segments is virtually nil.

While the overall share of rural non-farm sector workers has increased during 1993-94 to 2004-05, yet there are perceptible variations across social groups. The share of STs declined sharply from 21 to 9 per cent and the share of males in particular saw a catastrophic fall of 24 percentage points (Table 4.21). Such an extremely sharp decline in the share of rural non-farm opportunities among STs raises serious concerns. The share of SCs has increased from 23 to 27 per cent; however, the share of females declined from 12 to 5 per cent. 'Others' group has registered a steady increase in the share of males but females saw a substantive increase (1.6 times) during the period.

Table 4.21 : Percentage of Rural Workers Engaged in Non-Farm Sector by Social Groups, 1993-94 to 1999-2005

Social group	*Male*		*Female*		*Person*	
	1993-94	*2004-05*	*1993-94*	*2004-05*	*1993-94*	*2004-05*
ST	39.63	15.50	2.00	0.91	21.09	8.57
SC	33.13	48.17	12.33	5.44	23.32	27.40
Others	26.65	33.67	1.90	3.07	13.17	18.30
Total	30.14	35.78	2.32	3.45	15.40	19.71

Note: Excludes Hardwar district.
Source: NSS, 50th and 61st rounds.

What are the reasons for relative fall and rise in the share of rural non-farm opportunities across different social groups? Why a steep fall in the share of non-farm opportunities among SCs has been noted and what are the possible reasons needs to be examined both within social structure perspective and household economy?

First, average size of landholding is the lowest among SCs and so also average household income is one of the lowest. Second, literacy rate and value of assets is the lowest among all the social groups (Chapter 5). Third, they enjoy the lowest social prestige in the caste hierarchies in the hill region and have been exploited over the years. When the education, income and asset holding capacity is very low, their backward-ness continues to perpetuate into social ladder. These factors constrict their entry into better paid non-farm employment.

Share in RNF among STs is reported to be the highest (31 per cent), male constituting 49 and females to about 8 per cent respectively. STs are primarily a trading community and have been engaged in traditional enterprises in particular in knitting, weaving and manufacturing of woollen products. However, there has been gradual obliteration of their traditional enterprises due to fierce competition from cheaper woollen products from the plain areas and difficulty in getting raw material and other technical support. This has impacted more particularly among females who combine household chores with household enterprises. Precisely, this is the reason for declining share of females in RNF activities over the period but presence of males is noted in diversified trading activities in the region. STs in the region are by and large economically well off (substantiated by our primary investigation as well in Chapter 5) and are well educated. They have also been benefited from reservation policy in education and employment compared to SCs.

4. Institutional Support

Lack of finance or access to credit is one of the major obstacles to the growth of various non-farm activities in the rural areas. Inadequate credit will not be fully overcome unless rural enterprises have access to modern financial institutions relying on social collateral than other form of collateral as guarantee. There are numerous examples of improved credit systems (micro-finances) created by NGOs and by governments in recent times through Self Help Groups (SHGs) that have proved highly facilitating in promoting non-farm activities. The outreach and impact of these efforts have expanded over the years either through bank-linked SHGs programme or bank acting as facilitating agency or NGOs act as facilitator and micro finance intermediaries to SHGs. Impact assessment studies at the micro level generally do indicate positive impact of these initiatives despite the fact that there are certain structural problems (Tankha, 2001; Kashyap, 2001; Upendranadh, 2005).

The other handicaps encountered in this sector are lack of capacity building and low demand of goods and services with poor market linkage effect and traditional technology. Education and training is the key to the increased employability and better income and earning possibilities. It is, therefore necessary to build capacity through training interventions, which is most critical input for delivery of micro-finance services (Rajsekhar, 2005). The RUDA (Rural non-farm Development Agency) training model is innovative and most successful scheme that imparts skill training to carpet weavers in Rajasthan that had enormous positive impact to the industry in terms of employment and incomes (Singh, 2001).

In view of the extremely low incomes and purchasing power of those who work and hire in this sector, this is an inadequate base for growth. In order to make non-farm activities viable, it is necessary to improve skills, upgrade technology and diversify products. In most cases the supply side instruments (access to credit, training, technology, market and the organizations) have been targeted to overcome various constraints than the demand side that includes the macro-economic policies and regulatory and institutional framework, which received scant attention.

There are other issues in the institutional and supportive mechanism that needs to be looked in an integrated manner within holistic framework of enabling environment, which are much larger issues in the context of market economy (Papola and Sharma, 2005; Mahajan and Raju, 2005).

In Uttarakhand, particularly in rural area that falls mostly in the hill districts does not have vibrant non-farm sector owing to many structural rigidities and hill specificities. The institutional support in terms of access to credit, training, technology and market also lacks in the rural areas of the state. There is a need for integrated input support for development of numerous non-farm activities particularly in niche sector.

5. Infrastructure

Infrastructure, both social and economic, has significantly positive relationship with the growth of non-farm activities. Better transportation linked to urban towns helps to generate employment through linkage effect, commuters find ample opportunities for employment and income in urban towns (Basant, 1993). Availability of power helps rural enterprises to take advantages of utilising locally available resources in manufacturing activities. However, sometimes better connectivity to urban towns has also adverse implication to the locally produced good that are found to be much cheaper. But there are studies, which show that urbanisation has net positive impact on the diversification of rural workforce (Dev, 1990; Unni, 1991, Papola and Sharma, 2005).

In rural Uttarakhand, state of infrastructure is generally poor due to hill specificities, road is the only means of transportation and it has limitation of outreach particularly in far-flung and remote areas. The region is rich in water resources with a niche for the generation of hydro-electricity. The estimated potential of power generation is about 20,000 MW of which 11.6 per cent has been harnessed presently. Urban centres are limited and the economic base being low, the employment and earning opportunities also become limited. There are no major industries in the hill region and most of the industrial units are small and tiny with limited market linkages. All these factors restrict the growth of sustainable non-farm activities.

VI. Conclusion

Labour Force Participation Rates (LFPR) for rural males and rural females in the state has been 53 and 47 per cent respectively in 2004-05. The corresponding figures at all-India have been 55 and 33 per cent.

Long-term trends of movement of LFPR in the state have marginally increased for rural males (1.0 per cent points) but registered huge fall for female (6.3 per cent points) during 1983 to 2004-05. The corresponding changes at all-India level have been negligible. It remained almost stable. Generally, LFPR has shown increasing trend from 1983 to 1993-94 both in rural and urban areas then it dipped in 1999-2000 and thereafter a clear up-trend is noticed in 2004-05.

Worker Population Ratio (WPR) in rural areas declined in the state as well as at all-India for both males and females from 1983 to 1999-2000; however 2004-05 saw a trend reversal and registered increase. Male WPR in the state registered substantive increase (8.3 percentage points) and female WPR increased by 5.8 percentage points. While at all-India, male and female WPR increased by about 2 and 2.7 percentage points respectively.

While at all-India level employment grew at about 0.98 per cent, in Uttarakhand there has been catastrophic fall in employment as it recorded negative growth (-1.44 per cent) and the fall was even more pronounced among females than males. Long-term rural employment growth during 1980s and 1990s (1999-2000 over 1983) in the state is very low (0.70 per cent per annum) as against 1.61 per cent per annum in all-India. Rural area in particular had recorded abysmally low employment growth. Recent results (2004-05) however show impressive performance in employment growth both in rural and urban areas in the state yet the long-term trends (1983 to 2004-05) show much lower growth of employment for males and females in the rural area compared to all-India. Even in urban area the growth for male employment has been lower than all-India.

Sectoral share of employment by and large correspond to the all-India pattern but there are huge dissimilarities in rural area. The relative gap between all-India and the state is largest and weakest too for females as there has been hardly any significant occupational diversification for females in the state. Their share in primary sector is disproportionately much higher (at 96 per cent) while in secondary and tertiary sector is pitifully lower (1.9 and 2.1 per cent respectively) compared to corresponding share of rural India in 2004-05. Such a structure of employment has serious implications for sectoral productivity.

The long-term shift in the structure of employment in rural areas shows that the self-employment base has eroded systematically both for males and females in the state. Casualisation among rural females has become most conspicuous phenomenon in terms of growth while regular employment shows improvement, more so among females.

Self-employment has been the principal mode of livelihoods for males as well as for females but for rural females it is indeed the sole source of employment as an overwhelmingly a large majority of workforce (94 per cent) is engaged in it, primarily in cultivation activities. Self-employment opportunities in the rural area showing improvement in 2004-05 over 1999-2000, yet such opportunities have generally shrunk compared to pre- 1999-2000 period both for males and females.

Regular employment for males as well as for females have generally declined, albeit marginally, during 1999-2000 to 2004-05. Share of casual employment also declined for males and females but decline is sharper for females compared to that of males. It clearly appears that restructuring process has halted and those who have moved on to non-agriculture sector earlier seems to have been reverted back to agriculture sector.

Another distinct feature noted is that an overwhelmingly large majority of rural females are working as subsidiary capacity (11.9 per cent in 2004-05) indicating their marginalization and vulnerability. The gap between the share of UPS and UPSS workers has increased from about 2.6 per cent in 1983 to about 6.1 per cent in 2004-05, while at all- India level this gap declined from 4.6 to 4.1 per cent.

There has been huge increase in rural subsidiary workers (4.49 lakh) of which female accounted for about 81 per cent in 2004-05. Agriculture is the most predominant activity for subsidiary employment both for males and females. For females, such a huge increase in subsidiary capacity employment was solely due to low productive sectors that are regarded lender of the last resort.

Work structure is highly gender biased in the rural areas of the state as women overwhelmingly work in agriculture related occupations while their male counterparts work in non-farm occupations. Such a low share of female employment in non-agriculture sector shows complete dichotomy and segmentation of labour market due to various socio-economic factors that inhibit females to participate in the labour market outside cultivation despite the fact that their literacy level has improved considerably over the years. Barring construction and public services their share is virtually nil in other segments of non-farm sector.

Majority of the sub-sectors in the rural economy consistently achieved lower performance both in terms of employment growth and Gross Value Added (GVA) per worker compared to the overall performance in the state. Even in certain sub-sectors where higher rate of employment growth was registered in rural area (namely, manufacture of cotton textile and land transport), the GVA per worker was lower than state average indicating proliferation of low productivity employment growth.

In rural Uttarakhand, maximum share of enterprises are in the trade segment followed by manufacturing and construction but the productivity in these segments is lower and in fact manufacturing has the lowest productivity among all the segments in the unorganised sector.

Sectoral GSDP growth in the state is consistently lower in every sector compared to all-India during 1994-2000. Overall GSDP growth is just half in the state than that of all-India. This pattern of productivity change in the state stands in marked contrast to the all-India in major segments of economy. Even per capita income in the state is lower by 28 per cent compared to all-India in 1999-2000. All this indicates a low level of development in the state.

However, there has been perceptible increase in sectoral growth in terms of per worker GSDP in the state during 2000-05. Barring primary sector every segment of economic activities saw substantive improvement in sectoral performance compared to all-India. Secondary sector has shown dramatic improvement in productivity and registered whopping growth in per worker GSDP (16 per cent per annum). In fact, every segment of secondary sector showed impressive performance. Sectoral performance in terms of per worker GSDP growth in the state has been far better than all-India. Overall GSDP growth per worker, per capita income and GDP growth in the state has doubled compared to all-India during the later period.

In spite of perceptible performance in the state during 2004-05 per worker GSDP (absolute terms) in primary and tertiary sectors and per capita income has been far lower throughout during 1993-94 to 2004-05 compared to all-India.

In the state, educational attainment has been highly facilitating factor for occupational shift towards non-farm activities, more so in the case of males. Gender, castes, land size and infrastructure seem to have been playing an important role in determining the growth of rural non-farm sector. It is important from the long-term policy perspectives to widen marketable skills base and strengthen infrastructure that have always had positive influence to the growth of non-farm sector, in which state even lacks basic social and economic infrastructure.

5

Socio-Economic and Demographic Characteristics of Sample Households

I. Introduction

This chapter provides the social, demographic and economic structures of population of the sample households across districts and development blocks. In addition, certain basic economic characteristics in terms of labour supply, work participation rate, educational attainments and migratory pattern have also been discussed. These features provide some indications of the status of well-being of the households and the local economy.

In all, 400 households have been chosen for detailed investigation which has been stratified in terms of administrative units (e.g districts and blocks), castes, land classes, and main occupation of the head of the household. These different categorisations of the household groups are necessary to understand the pattern of development among different social groups across different spatial units with their intersectoral linkages and interrelationships. The administrative unit at disaggregated levels reflects the extent of variations in different socio-economic indicators that may provide similarities or contrast within similar administrative units. Another important categorisation of socio-economic profile is the social class or caste that plays an important role in the social structure. Caste is an important social institution that largely determines the social fabric of any society. Also, occupation of the head of the household has also been juxtaposed across social caste in characterising the household features that indicate the livelihood patterns in the household economy in order to understand the nuances of regional differentiation in terms of development status.

Yet, another important classification of households is by their asset-holding capacity, mainly the land. Land is an important asset in rural setting that determines not only the means of livelihood but also the social status.

II. Social Features of the Sample Households

(i) Principal occupation of heads of the households

The occupational structure of the head of the household is indicative of the social status of the household and it also shows the linkages between the occupation and castes, if any, in the social structure of rural economy. In a typical mountain economy like Uttarakhand where employment opportunities are limited and most of the employment takes either the form of cultivation or regular jobs, mostly in government sector, and the other segments of economy are still in nascent stage primarily due to lack of general economic development that reinforces other development activities to hold back. It can be observed from Table 5.1 that principal occupation of majority of heads of the households are cultivation and animal husbandry (38%) followed by white collar workers (12.5%). Another major group of workers are shopkeepers and sales workers (8.0%). About 6.7 per cent heads of households are engaged in weaving and other production works, and 4.7 per cent heads of the households are reported as casual and other workers. Nearly, 30 per cent heads of the households report as non-workers (Figure 5.1).

Across caste, majority of heads of the households report cultivation and animal husbandry as their principal occupation; however, the intensity varies from a minimum of 25 per cent among Brahmins to 67 per cent in 'other castes' (constituted by Muslims). The other major occupational groups among Brahmins are white-collar jobs (15%) followed by labourers and other workers (5%) and shopkeepers (4%). For Kshatriyas, the other major occupations are white-collar jobs

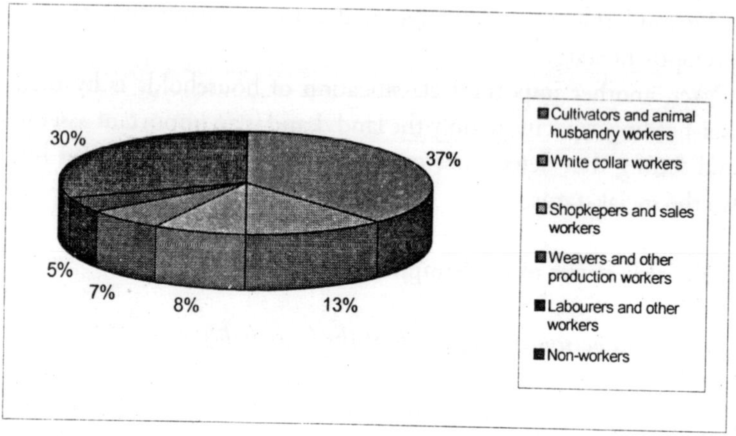

Fig. 5.1 : Principal Occupation of Head of the Households

(14%) and shopkeeping (7%). Among the Scheduled Caste heads of the households, the other major occupational workers are weavers and other production workers (19%), white-collar job holders (15%) and labourers (13%). In fact, labourers and other workers are highest among Scheduled Castes. Scheduled Tribes are mainly trading community and are engaged in weaving and manufacturing of woollen garments as household enterprise. Animal husbandry is an integrated activity for weaving and manufacturing of garments. About one-fifth heads of the households are engaged in weaving and related activities and another 16 per cent heads of the households are pursuing shopkeeping, etc. Majority of heads of the households in other castes are engaged in cultivation and related activities (67%) followed by white-collar jobs, weavers and shopkeepers.

The proportion of non-workers among heads of the households is higher among the upper castes (Brahmins and Kshatriyas) as compared to other castes, highest being among Brahmins (49%). Higher proportion of non-workers in these castes indicates relatively better resource endowments base of the households and in turn can afford to remain out of work, particularly at old age. On the other hand, 'other castes' and Scheduled Castes have lower proportion of non-workers as they might be forced to work due to poor economic conditions. In the case of Scheduled Tribes, the lower proportion of non-workers is primarily due to their engagements in household enterprises.

Table 5.1 : Principal Occupation of Head of the Household (%)

Principal occupation of the heads of households	*Social groups*					*Total*
	Brahmin	*Kshatriya*	*SC*	*ST*	*Others*	
Cultivator and animal husbandry workers	25.45	41.48	29.63	34.00	66.66	37.5
White-collar workers	14.54	13.97	14.81	2.00	8.33	12.5
Weavers and other production workers	1.82	2.19	18.52	20.00	8.33	6.75
Shopkeepers and sales workers	3.64	7.43	7.41	16.00	8.33	8.00
Labourers and other workers	5.46	3.06	12.96	4.00	0	4.75
Total workers	50.91	68.13	83.33	76.00	91.65	69.5
Non-workers	**49.09**	**31.88**	**16.67**	**24.00**	**8.33**	**30.5**
Total	100.00 (55)	100.00 (229)	100.00 (54)	100.00 (50)	100.00 (12)	100.00 (400)

Note : Figures in parentheses are absolute number of households.
Source : Field Survey, 2004-05.

(ii) Women-headed households

23 per cent of the households report themselves as women-headed households. This proportion is generally low in the households' demographic profile, but in the context of hill region this is not an unusual phenomenon primarily because of a high degree of male-specific out-migration to plane areas in search of jobs and livelihoods. The outflow of able-bodied males puts enormous burden on females in both farm and non-farm activities including the household chores. Relatively less developed blocks seem to have higher intensity of male-specific out-migration than the relatively developed ones. Also, in landless category, the proportion of women-headed households is

relatively smaller than that in marginal and small land size classes, but in medium land size class, no one is reported as female-headed household. The possible reasons for the low intensity of out-migration in landless category could be due to a high cost of out-migration, which is sometimes beyond their affordability of this category. In the medium land size class, the security of land probably restricts such an out-migration. The less developed blocks show a higher proportion of female-headed households than the developed ones (Table 5.2).

Table 5.2 : Female-Headed Households by Development Blocks and Land Class

District	*Block*	*% of female-headed households*
Almora	Hawalbagh	25.49
	Salt	25.49
Pithoragarh	Dharchula	24.00
	Berinag	32.69
T. Garhwal	Chamba	20.45
	Kirtinagar	30.00
Uttarkashi	Bhatwari	14.00
	Dunda	11.54
Land class	Landless	12.50
	Marginal	23.14
	Small	30.00
	Medium	00.00
Development status of blocks	Developed	21.03
	Less developed	24.88
Total		23.00

Source: Field Survey, 2004-05.

(iii) Casual labour households

Poor households tend to resort casual nature of work in order to supplement their livings and this is most common in rural areas. However, casual labour market in rural areas in the state is still at the nascent stage and generally such work is available for short spells. Occasional spurt of work generates the demand for casual works and that does not allow such labour market to develop and grow. It can be noted from Table 5.3 that 15 per cent households reported as casual workers and most of them belong to 'other castes' and SCs who are poor and from lower social class. Upper castes (Brahmins and

Kshatriyas) and ST households reported relatively low proportion of casual labour. Maximum number of casual work-reporting households belongs to landless category and these decline in higher land class sizes. In the medium landholding class, no one is reported as casual work-household. Less developed blocks showed higher intensity of casual work households than developed ones.

Table 5.3 : Casual Labour Reporting Households

Social category/ land class	*Casual labour households*	*Total households*	*Percentage of casual labour households*
Social category			
Brahmin	4	55	7.27
Kshatriya	35	229	15.28
SC	17	54	31.48
ST	1	50	2.00
Others	4	12	33.33
Land class			
Landless	4	16	25.00
Marginal	55	350	15.71
Small	2	30	6.67
Medium	0	4	00.00
Development status of blocks			
Developed	17	195	8.72
Less developed	44	205	21.46
Total	**61**	**400**	**15.25**

Source : Field Survey, 2004-05.

(iv) Literacy rates

As per 2001 Census, overall literacy in the state is 72 per cent (84% males and 60% females) with 71 per cent rural literacy. There has been a significant progress in the literacy rates over the years due to expansion of educational institutions and increasing awareness about the value of education in bettering the human life. Literacy rate in the sample population accounts for 79 per cent (5 years and above), male literacy constituted 91 per cent and female literacy 65 per cent. Across districts, literacy rate does not show a perceptible variation. In Uttarkashi where literacy is not only below average, both for males and females, but also the gender discrimination in literacy are highest.

Uttarkashi being located in the higher altitude and having tribal population in some parts of the district faces difficulty in accessing education due to harsh topographical conditions. Across blocks, female literacy is observed to be well below the average female literacy, particularly in Bhatwari, Chamba, Dunda and Salt. Gender inequity is higher in Dunda, Bhatwari and Salt blocks. General backwardness and inaccessibility due to harsh geographical conditions are the two main reasons that can be attributed to low female literacy. Such a gap in gender literacy is a matter of serious concern. Generally, less developed blocks have higher gender discrimination in literacy than the relatively developed ones. The upper caste households possess higher literacy both for males and females than the lower castes. Brahmins among upper castes have higher literacy rate, both for males and females as compared to other social categories. The SCs and STs among lower castes have low level of literacy, both for males and females as compared to upper castes and the overall literacy is well below the average literacy in the sample population. Lowest literacy is noted among 'other castes'. The literacy rate among STs is reported to be distinctly higher as compared to SCs and 'other castes'. Female literacy among SC population is lowest with highest gender discrimination followed by the 'other castes'. Age-specific literacy status among the sample population shows some interesting patterns. In the age group 5-14, literacy rate is cent per cent indicating an impressive attendance with no disparity between boys and girls. In 15-29 age group, literacy among youth is about 91 per cent with relatively higher proportion of male population (96%) and female literacy is recorded as 85 per cent. But in the higher age groups, not only literacy is low but also gender disparity increases. In 30-59 age group, male literacy is significantly higher (90%), but female literacy is abysmally low (42%), thereby widening the gender-disparity gap. Gender gap is still highest in the higher age group (59 and above) with male literacy at about 64 per cent and female literacy at 24 per cent. The land size class typically has a positive relationship with levels of literacy. In the lower land size class, literacy rate is low and it increases with higher land size classes. Females in landless category have lowest literacy levels with highest gender disparity (Table 5.4).

Table 5.4 : Male-Female Literacy Rates (Aged 5 and above)

District	*Block*	*Male*	*Female*	*Person*	*M/F gap*
Almora	Hawalbagh	96.43	73.91	86.27	76.65
	Salt	94.84	61.54	79.65	64.89
Pithoragarh	Dharchula	90.00	75.94	82.89	84.38
	Berinag	96.62	67.97	83.33	70.35
T. Garhwal	Chamba	87.10	61.82	75.21	70.97
	Kirtinagar	83.87	69.30	76.89	82.63
Uttarkashi	Bhatwari	86.21	54.90	71.56	63.68
	Dunda	90.07	54.10	73.38	60.06
Social category	Brahmin	98.13	74.81	87.46	76.24
	Kshatriya	93.42	67.37	81.16	72.12
	SC	85.43	50.40	69.57	59.00
	ST	83.90	61.82	73.25	73.68
	Others	69.23	62.50	65.82	90.28
Age group	5-14	100.00	100.00	100.00	100.00
	15-29	96.49	85.09	91.18	88.19
	30-59	89.80	42.36	66.29	47.17
	60+	64.17	24.32	45.02	37.91
Land class	Landless	86.36	46.43	70.83	53.76
	Marginal	90.99	65.69	79.02	72.20
	Small	95.56	67.95	82.74	71.11
	Medium	88.89	71.43	81.25	80.36
Development status	Less developed	91.73	63.16	78.44	68.85
	Developed	90.52	67.70	79.73	74.79
Total		**91.14**	**65.40**	**79.07**	**71.76**

Source : Field Survey, 2004-05.

III. Demographic Characteristics

Broad demographic aggregates and other related attributes show the average household size, average number of adults, population in the working age, proportion of children, old-age population, migrant households, etc. across districts and development blocks (Table 5.5).

(i) Average size of households

Average size of households is six with little or no variation across different districts and blocks. The ST households have relatively lower household size (5) than other social castes (6 to 7), and 'other castes' households have reported the highest household size (7) as compared to others (6). The average household size across land class shows a

Table 5.5 : Demographic Characteristics of Sample Households

District	*Block*	*Working age population (15-59 years) %*	*Percentage of adults*	*Av. HH Size*	*Percentage of children*	*Percentage of 60+ population*	*Migrant households %**
Almora	Hawalbagh	62.42	30.12	6	29.50	8.07	21.57
	Salt	60.33	30.82	6	29.18	10.49	43.14
Pithoragarh	Dharchula	60.00	29.47	5	30.18	9.82	38.00
	Berinag	57.42	27.42	6	29.03	13.55	42.31
T. Garhwal	Chamba	60.69	29.39	6	29.77	9.54	31.82
	Kirtinagar	57.79	26.42	5	32.70	9.51	52.00
Uttarkashi	Bhatwari	66.95	37.66	5	21.76	11.30	32.00
	Dunda	64.71	32.87	6	26.30	9.00	42.31
Development status of the blocks	Developed	62.36	31.41	6	28.07	9.57	30.77
	Less developed	60.07	29.48	6	29.22	10.71	44.88
Social category	Brahmin	58.31	28.21	6	26.96	14.73	32.73
	Kshatriya	61.07	31.02	6	29.38	9.56	36.68
	SC	61.56	29.64	6	32.90	5.54	29.63
	ST	63.60	30.13	5	21.34	15.06	50.00
	Others	65.85	32.93	7	29.27	4.88	75.00
Land class	Landless	68.83	33.77	5	25.97	5.19	31.25
	Marginal	61.48	30.41	6	28.73	9.68	38.57
	Small	56.25	29.17	6	27.60	16.15	30.00
	Medium	54.55	30.30	8	30.30	15.15	75.00
Total		**61.19**	**30.42**	**6**	**28.66**	**10.15**	**38.00**

*Excluding permanent out-migrating households.
Source : Field Survey, 2004-05.

positive relationship – lower the land sizes smaller is the average household size and the reverse is also true. Probably, higher land size in the rural context provides a sense of security that determines the demographic transition. Average adults in the households are three and maximum are five which indicates that half of the population is in the labour force. The proportion of children to the population is about 29 per cent and a relatively higher proportion of young age population leads to higher dependency burden. The increasing dependency ratio and declining working population affect the welfare of the population adversely due to declining growth of incomes per capita. Similarly, growth of working age population has strong and positive impact on the well-being of population through income growth.

(ii) Working age population

The working age population constitutes about 61 per cent of the sample population. Relatively developed blocks have higher proportion of the working population as compared to less developed blocks. Across land class, the proportion of working population is higher in the lower land class and lower proportion of working population in higher land class. Generally, higher proportion of working population in the lower land class helps them to provide additional hands to earn livelihood, as lower expenditures have to incur on education and health. However, it is apparent that in the lower land class relatively lower proportion of workers supports households possibly due to lack of land and other complementary resources.

(iii) Aged population

Population aged 60 and above constitutes 10 per cent of the sample population. The higher the proportion of the aged population, the higher will be the dependency ratio as the aged population depends on others for consumption needs including health. The less developed blocks entail higher burden of old aged population than the developed ones, and lower land class households share lower burden of aged population as compared to higher land class categories.

(iv) Migrants

Migration takes different forms ranging from purely seasonal or short-term phenomenon (less than 9 months) to long-term migration (9 months and more) to permanent migration. The intensity of different forms of migration varies in different regions and locations depending upon regional-specific characteristics. In the hill districts of the state, out-migration is a peculiar feature where the magnitude of out-migration is very high. Micro level studies indicate the magnitude of out-migration varying from 7 per cent (Pande, 1996) to 14 per cent (Mamgain, 2004) and 24 per cent (Bora, 1996). Employment opportunities are limited in the region due to low economic base. As a result, large proportion of households resort to multiple livelihood strategies and out-migration seems to be the most prominent livelihood option. In the present study, migrant population constitutes 10 per cent of the population (excluding permanently shifted). If permanently shifted population is included, it accounts for about 23 per cent. The permanently shifted migration seems to be emerging as an important phenomenon in which a significant number of household members out-migrate along with spouse and children permanently. This is a long drawn process in which the breadwinner migrates first and subsequently after getting a foothold in the labour market, the spouse and children also out-migrate leaving other members (including old and infirm) of the households in the place of origin. And, such permanently shifted migrants cease to become a part of the households. However, the permanent migrants maintain social transactions with the village through occasional visits and remittances. It can be seen from Table 5.5 that about 38 per cent households have reported at least one migrant from the family indicating the extent of out-migration. The magnitude of out-migration is higher in the relatively less developed blocks (45% households reporting out-migration) than the relatively developed blocks (31% household reporting out-migration). High out-migration is a peculiar phenomenon in the hill districts and is indicative of a low development base that forces people to move out for better options of livelihoods outside the region.

(v) Sex ratio

This phenomenon of male-specific out-migration makes the sex ratio in the hill areas favourable and stands at about 1005 females per thousand males excluding the migrant population. However, the sex ratio becomes highly unfavourable if the migrant population is included (866 females per thousand males). Age-wise sex ratio reveals that in the youth age group 15-29 and in the working age group 30-59, the sex ratio is significantly higher. The highest sex ratio (1238) is in the age group 30-59, which is the prime working age followed by youth age group (1178). In the higher age group (59+) the sex ratio declines. The higher sex ratio in these two groups indicates a higher propensity of male out-migration (Table 5.6 and Figure 5.2).

Table 5.6 : Sex Ratio of Sample Population

Age group	*Including migrants*	*Excluding migrants*
0-4	699	685
5-14	749	759
15-29	870	1178
30-59	983	1238
60+	925	925
Total	**866**	**1005**

Source : Field Survey, 2004-05 .

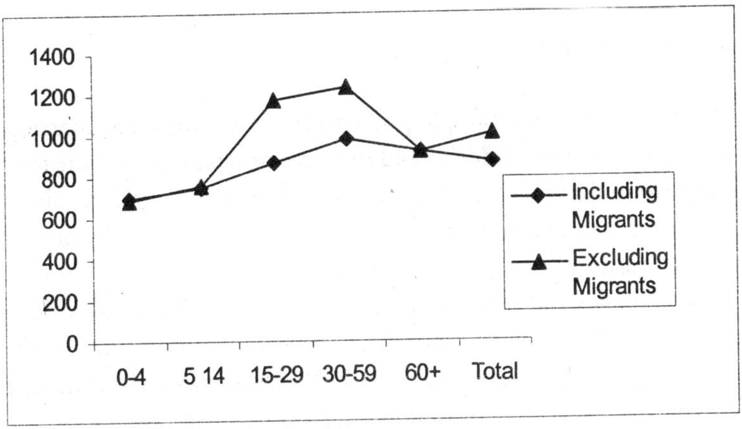

Fig. 5.2 : Sex Ratio.

(vi) Age structure of population

The age structure of population shows that young age population accounts for about 29 per cent. The youth population constitutes another 30 per cent and the old age population constitutes 10 per cent. The working age population (15-59) accounts for about 61 per cent in the total sample population. Sex-wise structure of population indicates that the proportion of female population is higher than that of males in 15-29, 30-59 and 60+ age groups while male proportion is higher in 0-14 age group (Table 5.7).

Table 5.7 : Age-Structure of Sample Population

Age group	*Male*	*Female*	*Person*
0-14	30.84	26.14	28.66
15-29	30.35	30.49	30.42
30-59	28.96	32.86	30.77
60+	9.84	10.51	10.15
Total	100.00 (1219)	100.00 (1056)	100.00 (2275)

Note : Figures in parenthesis show absolute numbers.
Source : Field Survey, 2004-05 .

(vii) Marital status

Marital status of the sample population is categorised as married, unmarried, widow/widower and divorcee or separated. Of the total sample population, 46 per cent of the population is married; about 48 per cent are unmarried, about 6 per cent are widows/widowers and a minuscule proportion (0.13%) is divorcee or separated. Between males and females, the proportion of married and widows is higher (59 per cent) among females, while among males, the percentage of unmarried is higher (53%) as compared to married population (43%). Widowers' population constitutes a relatively small proportion (3%) than the widows (9%) and most of the widow/widower and divorcee population is concentrated in 60 and above age group. Marital status by age group clearly indicates that there are no instances of child marriage in the region and improvement in education status and awareness has played a significant role in delaying the marriage age over a period of time (Table 5.8).

Table 5.8 : Marital Status among Sample Population

Population group	*Marital status*				
Sex	*Married*	*Unmarried*	*Widow/widower*	*Divorcee*	*Total*
Male	43.07	53.57	3.12	0.25	100.00 (1219)
Female	49.72	41.19	9.09	-	100.00 (1056)
Age-group					
0-14	-	100.00	-	-	100.00
15-29	38.44	56	-	-	100.00
30-59	91.57	1.43	6.86	0.14	100.00
60+	61.90	-	37.23	0.87	100.00
Total	46.15 (1050)	47.82 (1088)	5.90 (134)	0.13 (3)	100.00 (2275)

Note : Figures in parenthesis show absolute numbers.
Source : Field Survey, 2004-05.

IV. Economic Characteristics

(i) Assets holding

Land holdings: A good asset base is essential for improving the accessibility of employment and incomes. Asset has a very wide connotations – it includes all the physical and human capital that help enhance the livelihood opportunities and decent living. Land is the basic physical asset in rural setting that determines the access to livelihood and well-being of the household. Land includes all its attributes in terms of fertility, productivity and indestructibility with accessibility and affordability of inputs that helps in enhancing the livelihood opportunities. Although, agriculture is the main occupation of the people, but it suffers from several inherent handicaps. Cultivable land is not only scarce but also highly unfavourable for use of modern inputs. Irrigation facilities are very low and agriculture is mainly rainfed. The use of HYVs and other chemical fertilizers is very low (barring the *tarai* region). This has resulted in low productivity and low returns from agricultural crops.

Landholdings are small, fragmented and scattered. Preponderance of cultivators in tiny size of land parcels is most common. Majority of landholdings are marginal and the increasing population pressure leads to further fragmentation of holdings.

It can be observed from Table 5.9 that an overwhelmingly large majority of sample households (87%) belong to marginal landholdings and about one-tenth households belong to small and medium landholdings and none of the households have large landholding size. Also, 3.4 per cent households are reported as landless. Not only there is a preponderance of marginal holdings but also it is accompanied by iniquitous distribution of land across different land size class households. At the one end of the spectrum a small minority (8.5%) of the households in small and medium category owns 32 per cent area, while a large majority of marginal landholding households (87.5%) have 68 per cent area. The average size of holdings per household is about 1.05 acre and the distribution shows a highly uneven pattern in favour of small and medium land size classes than the marginal landholdings. The average land size in small and medium landholding classes is almost 7 and 9 times higher respectively as compared to marginal landholding class. Iniquitous distribution of land across different castes is also discernible. Landlessness is not that acute, as only 3.4 per cent households reported to be without land. But most importantly, the size of landholdings are not only tiny but the increasing process of fragmentation makes the land size highly uneconomical. Landlessness is observed as highest among ST households (17.0%) followed by SCs (8.0%), and to a small extent it is reported among the Kshatriyas (0.8%). The Scheduled Tribes have been traditionally a trading community engaged in animal rearing and household enterprises, such as weaving and manufacturing woollen garments with a distinct phenomenon of seasonal migration from high altitude to low altitude. The increasing competition of cheap products from plane areas has adversely affected their enterprises over time, and also their gradual settlement at lower altitude has put enormous pressure on them to look for alternative avenues of employment. Many of the tribal population has little land in such places and some of them are deprived of land resource. The Scheduled Castes have been the most disadvantaged section in the social class structure in the region and they have little land of their own as they have been providing services (*jajmani*) to the upper castes. Landlessness among SCs had been more acute but over the years government policy has helped them to own some land. Average size of landholding is still lowest among the SCs (0.56 acre) followed by STs (0.76 acre), and Brahmin households have the highest average size of land (1.60 acre). The most disturbing phenomenon is a fast fragmentation of already tiny sizes of holdings, which has not only become highly uneconomical but also leads to a near-landlessness situation for a large majority of households in marginal landholding size class. It can be seen from the Table 5.9 that 40 per cent of the marginal landholding class households have land size up to 0.50 acre with 10.2 per cent area indicating a near-landlessness situation (sub-marginal class) and the average size of land is minuscule (0.31 acre). Across social class, the situation becomes more serious as majority of households (73%) within 'other caste' fall in sub-marginal land class and 59 per cent households among SCs are in the threshold of near-landlessness situation.

Table 5.9 : Percentage Distribution of Households by Land Class Category

Social category	*Land size class*					*Total*	*Av. size of land (acre)*
	Land-less	*Sub-marginal (up to 0.50 acre)*	*Marginal (up to 2.50 acre)*	*Small (2.50-5 acre)*	*Medium (5-10 acre)*		
Brahmin	0.00	14.42	63.95	19.75	1.88	100.00	1.60
Kshatriya	0.83	28.69	61.52	8.06	0.90	100.00	1.10
SC	8.14	58.63	31.27	1.95	0.00	100.00	0.56
ST	17.15	26.78	49.37	6.69	0.00	100.00	0.76
Others	0.00	73.17	8.54	0.00	18.29	100.00	1.05
Total	3.38	32.13	54.59	8.44	1.45	100.00	-
Av. size of land (acre)	-	0.31	0.81*	5.51	7.55	-	1.05
% Area of land	-	10.18	57.57	25.06	7.19	100.00	-
Households (No.)	16	139	211	30	4	400	

*Including sub-marginal.
Source : Field Survey, 2004-05.

(ii) Other assets

In addition to land, there are other assets such as agricultural implements, livestock and other domestic assets that can be distributed between farm and non-farm assets. The farm assets include agricultural machineries & implements and livestock, etc. while non-farm assets include variety of durable household goods and other assets.*

Table 5.10 presents the average value of these assets and the average size of landholdings for different caste and land class households. The value of farm assets is very low in the mountain agriculture. Most of these implements are traditional, and modern implements are hardly used for cultivation. It can be observed from the table that the value of farm assets is positively related to land size owned per household and land size class; and this value is reported to be lowest among SCs, STs and landless households.

Cultivation and animal husbandry is an integrated activity in mountain agriculture that mutually supports each other and livestock population increases with land size class, primarily because of the requirement of animal traction for ploughing. Also, a larger land size can provide fodder to relatively large number of livestock.

This relationship holds good in the sample households – the larger the size of land the higher is the value of livestock. Across castes, STs have the highest value of livestock, while SCs have the lowest value.

In the case of STs, they have been traditionally depending on livestock for their livelihood, as it provided them wool for manufacturing woollen garments and also for carrying loads. However, over the years their dependence on livestock has greatly attenuated. Still some sample households have been observed to be depending on rearing large number of livestock for their livelihood.

It is observed that relatively developed blocks have higher value of livestock than the less developed ones, and it is highest in Bhatwari and Dharchula blocks, which also have higher proportion of ST households.

---

* Farm assets include all agricultural implements and machineries, such as wooden plough, spade, sickle, axe, shovel, etc., while non-farm assets include durable assets such as utensils, furniture, watch, radio, TV, refrigerator, fan, sewing machine, fodder cutter, knitting machine, welding machine, oil crusher, flour/rice/oil mill, motorcycle, jeep, bus, shops, PCO, photocopy machine, weaving machineries, etc.

Higher value of non-farm assets is a reflection of improved status of households and it is clear from the sample households that upper castes (Brahmins and Kshatriyas) own greater value of these assets while the lower castes have lower value of these assets. The total household asset value is highest among upper castes followed by STs and it is lowest among 'other castes'.

Table 5.10 : Asset Holding Characteristics

District	*Block*	*Farm assets per HH (Rs.)*			*Non-farm assets per HH (Rs.)*	*Total assets per HH (Rs.)*	*Land owned per HH (acre)*
		Farm implements	*Livestock*	*Total*			
Almora	Hawalbagh	2004	14139	16143	24658	40802	1.62
	Salt	1047	12688	13735	18466	32201	1.39
Pithoragarh	Dharchula	1250	17787	19037	19073	38109	1.21
	Berinag	1057	10033	11090	23109	34199	1.29
T. Garhwal	Chamba	1147	15423	16570	12689	29259	0.85
	Kirtinagar	959	7238	8197	10903	19100	0.60
Uttarkashi	Bhatwari	844	22905	23749	11005	34755	0.90
	Dunda	1124	7638	8762	19028	27789	0.50
Social category	Brahmin	1604	9580	11184	22731	33915	1.60
	Kshatriya	1226	12867	14093	19145	33238	1.10
	SC	862	6282	7144	10876	18020	0.56
	ST	899	28174	29073	13317	42390	0.76
	Others	970	11734	12704	9186	21890	1.05
Development status	Developed	1320	17612	18932	17024	35956	1.16
	Less developed	1048	13405	14453	17942	28393	0.95
Land class	Landless	253	5683	5936	13428	19365	0.00
	Marginal	1168	13527	14695	17129	31824	0.81
	Small	1616	14912	16528	23721	40249	3.51
	Medium	2675	22365	25040	19050	44090	7.55
Total		1180	13405	14585	17495	32080	1.05

Source : Field Survey, 2004-05.

Lack of productive assets among SCs not only reflects their poor situation but also explains the perpetuation of relative backwardness. Not only the holding of these assets is lowest but also the ratio of productive to non-productive assets is also lowest.

Scheduled Tribes in the state are not economically poor class as compared to other lower castes as majority of them are engag[illegible] household enterprises (weaving, for example) trading, and horticultural crops and other cash crops that provide them better incomes.

It can be observed that average value of assets per household is very low in the hill districts. The reason for such a low asset base is primarily due to a limited cultivable land and an widespread adoption of traditional agriculture practices that makes income base extremely narrow. Also, lack of general development in the region (infrastructure and industry, for example) does not allow the economic base to expand beyond a limited urban or semi-urban areas, where numerous activities tend to agglomerate and vast rural areas remain untouched from any significant development activities. This kind of development not only creates rural urban divide but also provides low prospects for either self-employment or regular employment opportunities resulting in a low income base for the majority of people.

(iii) Average annual household and per capita income

Collection of income data from rural households is difficult on account of the two reasons. Firstly, there are multiple sources of income such as cultivation, animal husbandry, transfer incomes (remittance, pension), regular wage incomes, income from self-employed non-farm enterprises, casual wage earnings, etc. from which the households receive incomes. Secondly, it is difficult to recall any income from these diverse sources particularly when there is no major and perennial source of incomes. It is therefore difficult to capture incomes from diverse sources, and as such underestimation of income is inevitable to certain extent. Despite these limitations, an attempt has been made to capture incomes from multiple sources from the rural households which we will discuss in the next chapter. The aggregate data is presented in Table 5.11.

It can be observed from the data that as in the case of assets, the average household income has also a skewed distribution among social [illegible]stes. The Brahmins and Scheduled Tribes have comparatively much [illegible]r household income than the other social groups. The inequity [illegible]r between these two social groups on the one hand and the [illegible] Caste and 'other caste' on the other. The inequity is also

Table 5.11 : Level of Household and Per Capita Income

District	*Block*	*Annual HH income (Mean)*	*Per capita income*
Almora	Hawalbagh	76200	12659
	Salt	48328	8995
Pithoragarh	Dharchula	69614	13491
	Berinag	49170	9035
T. Garhwal	Chamba	37775	6897
	Kirtinagar	40479	8800
Uttarkashi	Bhatwari	60347	15087
	Dunda	51918	10713
Social category	Brahmin	70880	13215
	Kshatriya	52982	9945
	SC	42179	8164
	ST	61615	16743
	Others	33489	5998
Land class	Landless	48303	11890
	Sub-marginal	37237	8000
	Marginal	61312	11479
	Small	85863	14390
	Medium	82495	12222
Development status of blocks	Developed	61776	11974
	Less developed	47538	9379
Total		54479	10656
CV		18.4	17.2

Source : Field Survey, 2004-05.

noticeable across different land size classes. Generally, higher land class households have higher household income than the lower ones, but sub-marginal land class households have the lowest income. The overall per capita income of the sample population (resident) comes out at Rs. 10,656 and the highest per capita income is recorded for Scheduled Tribes followed by the Brahmins. The other social groups have lower per capita income than the overall per capita income. The Scheduled Caste and the other social caste have the lowest per capita income.

The reason for the highest income among Scheduled Tribe is primarily because of their engagement in trading, household enterprises and cultivation of horticultural and commercial cr- The developed blocks show a higher per capita income thar developed ones with coefficient of variation 17.2 per cer

There are about 36 per cent households whose monthly per capita income is less than Rs 500. An overwhelmingly large majority (75%) of other caste households and over half (56%) of the Scheduled Caste households have monthly per capita income of less than Rs. 500 (Figure 5.3). Also, in upper caste households, this proportion ranges between 28 to 38 per cent. The lowest proportion is among Scheduled Tribe households (8%).

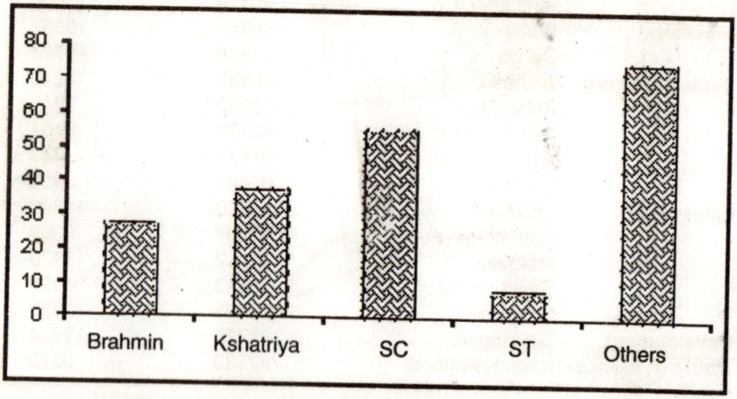

Fig. 5.3 : Per cent of Household with Monthly Per Capita Income below Rs. 500.

Low income is the direct manifestation of lack of employment opportunities available within the local economy, and as a result, a huge proportion of workforce either remains unemployed or underemployed for a significant part of the year. We will see in the next chapter that the workforce participation rate according to principal status is very low and a huge proportion of workforce is engaged in subsidiary capacity mainly in agriculture and allied activities. Though agriculture and allied activity is the main occupation for the majority of households but the income accruing from this source is only about one-third (32%) of the total household income. large part of income accrues from the non-farm source (48%) and fth part (20%) accrues from the transfer incomes.

The do

es of livelihood in the hill districts are agriculture

and allied activities, regular employment and other non-farm self-employment activities. Subsistence agriculture with an overwhelmingly large number of marginal holdings has made cultivation highly uneconomical and un-remunerative. Added to this, lack of development in general in rural areas has forced a significant proportion of the households to out-migrate from the state for earning livelihood. The significant improvement in literacy over the years has not helped in creating more employment, rather it accentuated the process of migration. Male-specific out-migration has put enormous burden on hill women in both cultivation and other household chores.

Households and per capita income for majority of households is low with marked inequity across castes and land classes. The lower castes particularly SCs and 'other castes' have very low per capita income. Also, the landless and marginal households have lower per capita income than the average household income exhibiting significant income differentials across land size classes. The low income obviously results in low asset holding capacity of the households with a significant differential across castes and land classes.

6

Employment and Livelihood Diversities

I. Introduction

Employment generation has been the central problem of development in the face of growing labour force and rightly so. However, employment growth has always lagged behind the growth of labour force that resulted in a huge backlog of unemployment across rural and urban areas. The problem is more serious in rural areas which are confronted with seasonal and intermittent nature of employment (as most of the workers are either engaged in low-paid agricultural activities as self-employed or as casual labour), and limited stable employment opportunities outside the agriculture sector on a sustainable basis. Over the years, the employment generating capacity in agricultural sector too has reached a near-saturation level in absorbing further workforce. All this has aggravated the unemployment situation more so in the rural areas.

It is widely known that in rural households, individuals derive their incomes from diverse and multiple sources of activities and often large official surveys provide little or no information about the informal nature of activities, in particular, secondary sources of employment and incomes. In the state, migration is a significant phenomenon and it has strong social and economic transactions with the local economy that are rarely captured in the usual surveys. Understanding this complexity is very much important to comprehend the heterogeneous character of the labour market.

In this chapter, we discuss the activity status of population, employment structure, status of employment, occupational structure, multiplicity of employment and diverse income sources based on primary survey results across different household characteristics. Analysis has been done both for migrants and non-migrants with a view to understanding the differentiated activity patterns.

II. Activity Status of Population

Total population can be broadly categorised into workforce, labour force and non-workers according to the activity status pursued during the specified reference period. Workforce is the economically active population participating in different economic activities for earnings, while the unemployed are those who are actively seeking jobs and available for job, and are thus included in the labour force. Non-workers are those who are neither available for work nor seeking work. The main constituents of this category are students, home workers, retired/pensioners, rentiers, too old or too young, beggars, etc. However, it is not easy to classify a person into a single category on the basis of his/her single occupation. Since a person may be involved in different (generally, more than one) types of economic activities, his or her occupational status may be determined by taking one or more occupations into consideration. Following broadly the above classification, sample population has been categorised into principal and principal & subsidiary status occupations.

Table 6.1 presents the activity status of the total population. Activity status of each individual has been determined on the basis of principal occupation as well as principal & subsidiary occupation of the population, and in doing so, time criterion has been considered. Activity status of the migrant population has also been considered along with resident population that gives an account of their differentiated activity patterns (Table 6.1A). Each component of population has been broadly grouped into few distinctly identifiable categories to have a broader view of population dynamics. The detailed classification of the workers and non-workers will be discussed at a later stage. Few important features emerge prominently from the activity status. It can be observed that only 42 per cent of the total population (including migrant population) is employed on the basis of principal occupation. The proportion rises steeply to 64 per cent if

Table 6.1 : Activity Status of Total Population

Occupation	*Principal occupation*			*Principal + subsidiary occupation*		
	Male	*Female*	*Person*	*Male*	*Female*	*Person*
1. Cultivators and animal husbandry workers	12.72	34.28	22.73	27.48	58.90	42.07
2. White-collar workers	14.44	0.66	8.04	14.52	0.66	8.09
3. Shopkeepers, sales workers and other self-employed workers	10.25	0.19	5.58	10.66	0.19	5.80
4. Weavers, tailors and other production workers	4.35	4.17	4.26	4.92	7.10	5.94
5. Labourers and other workers	2.13	1.04	1.63	2.54	1.14	1.88
Total workers	43.89	40.34	42.24	60.13	67.99	63.78
6. Unemployed	7.71	1.52	4.84	1.15	0.19	0.70
Labour force	51.60	41.86	47.08	61.28	68.18	64.48
7. Students	33.31	28.03	30.86	26.74	17.90	22.64
8. Pensioners	4.10	0.09	2.24	1.07	0.00	0.57
9. Other non-workers	10.99	30.02	19.82	10.91	13.92	12.31
Total non-workers	48.40	58.14	52.92	38.72	31.82	35.52
Total population	1219	1056	2275	1219	1056	2275

Source : Field Survey, 2004-05.

subsidiary workers are also considered. Majority of the workers are cultivators and animal husbandry workers followed by white-collar workers, shopkeepers and other production workers. Female workforce is predominantly engaged in cultivation and related activities followed by weaving. The unemployed constituted about 5 per cent as per principal status. The proportion of non-workers constituted about 53 per cent by principal status and it declines sharply to 36 per cent by principal & subsidiary capacity. Non-availability of durable employment forces the workers to engage in subsidiary capacity to such a large extent.

Activity status of the non-migrant population changes significantly if migrants are excluded. The proportion of workers declines to 38 per cent according to principal status and subsidiary

Table 6.1A : Activity Status of Resident Population

Occupation	*Principal occupation*			*Principal + subsidiary occupation*		
	Male	*Female*	*Person*	*Male*	*Female*	*Person*
1. Cultivators and animal husbandry workers	15.1	35.12	25.13	32.25	60.49	46.41
2. White-collar workers	5.88	0.68	3.28	5.98	0.68	3.33
3. Shopkeepers, sales workers and other self-employed workers	9.22	0.20	4.69	9.61	0.20	4.89
4. Weavers, tailors and other production workers	3.53	3.22	3.37	4.22	5.85	5.04
5. Labourers and other workers	2.35	0.98	1.66	2.75	1.07	1.91
Total workers	36.08	40.20	38.14	54.80	68.29	61.56
6. Unemployed	8.53	1.37	4.94	1.27	0.20	0.73
Labour force	44.61	41.57	43.08	56.07	68.49	62.29
7. Students	37.55	27.9	32.72	29.80	17.46	23.62
8. Pensioners	4.9	0.1	2.49	1.27	0.00	0.64
9. Other non-workers	12.94	30.43	21.71	12.84	14.05	13.45
Total non-workers	55.39	58.43	56.92	43.92	31.51	37.70
Total population	1020	1025	2045	1020	1025	2045

Source : Field Survey, 2004-05

employment rises to 62 per cent. The proportion of non-workers is substantially higher (53-57%) of which students' proportion is highest. Unemployment is low among females as compared to males resulting in a low supply of labour force. A distinct feature of segmented labour market is observed for males and females among resident workforce. While females are predominantly engaged in cultivation and animal husbandry activities, their male counterparts are engaged more in non-agricultural activities. Considering the migrant population alone, their work participation is as high as 79 per cent (84 and 45% respectively for males and females) and almost all are engaged in non-agricultural activities.

(i) Labour force characteristics among sample population

From the perspective of household unit analysis, it is necessary to discuss the labour force characteristics including the migrant population. Migrant population has strong social and economic transactions back to the place of origin and therefore forms an integral part of the household unit. However, from the perspective of local economy, migrant population needs a separate treatment in terms of its implications on the local economy. Labour Force Participation Rate (LFPR) of population in our sample stands out to be much higher in comparison to what has been generally reported in the large surveys such as NSS and Census. This variation is obvious, as large surveys often do not capture the population dynamics minutely as they are being captured in micro level studies, which are more of investigative and probing in nature. In the hill region of the state, where migration is a prominent phenomenon, often large surveys fail to capture this peculiar feature. Labour force in the sample population constitutes 47 per cent, males accounting for about 52 per cent and females 42 per cent. LFPR steeply rises to 64 per cent taking into consideration the principal & subsidiary workers. For females, the LFPR is much higher (68%) as compared to males (61%) (Table 6.2).

Table 6.2 : Labour Force and Workforce Participation Rates

Activity status	*Principal status workers*			*Principal status and subsidiary workers*		
	Male	*Female*	*Person*	*Male*	*Female*	*Person*
Including migrants and non-migrants						
Labour force	51.60	41.86	47.08	61.28	68.18	64.48
Workforce (All)	43.89	40.34	42.24	60.13	67.99	63.78
Unemployed*	14.94	3.62	10.27	1.87	0.28	1.09
Non-workers	48.40	58.14	52.92	38.72	31.82	35.52
Total	100.00	100.00	100.00	100.00	100.00	100.00
Population number	1219	1056	2275	1219	1056	2275

* Relates to unemployment rate (i.e. number of unemployed persons expressed as a percentage of the total labour force).

Source : Field Survey, 2004-05.

The age-specific labour force participation rates show that none of the children below 14 years has been observed to be participating in the labour force by principal status. However, in subsidiary capacity,

6.4 per cent children in this age group have been participating with a majority of female children (8.7%) as compared to male children (4.8%). Children assisting parents in agriculture and allied activities is a most common feature in poor families in the hill region. Participation rates gradually increases in the higher age groups, highest being in prime age group (30-59,) and then it starts falling significantly in the old age group (60 and above) (Table 6.3).

Table 6.3 : Age-specific Labour Force Participation Rate

Age-group	*Principal status*			*Principal plus subsidiary status*		
	Male	*Female*	*Person*	*Male*	*Female*	*Person*
0-4	0.00	0.00	0.00	0.00	0.00	0.00
5-14	0.00	0.00	0.00	4.79	8.70	6.44
15-29	61.08	39.44	51.01	77.84	94.10	85.40
30-59	95.75	82.13	89.00	99.72	97.12	98.43
60 and above	54.17	27.03	41.13	74.17	50.45	62.77
All age groups	51.60	41.86	47.08	61.28	68.18	64.48

Source : Field Survey, 2004-05

The workforce constitutes 42 per cent (male comprising 44% and female 40%), according to principal status. Workforce Participation Rates (WPR) increase significantly (64%) if subsidiary workers are also included and participation rate of males rises up to 60 per cent while for females it increases up to 68 per cent. The overall female WPR is higher than males by about 8 percentage points (Table 6.2).

The unemployment rate turns out to be 10.3 per cent in aggregate terms, which is very high. Male unemployment rate, in particular, is alarmingly high at 15.0 per cent, while female unemployment rate is comparatively much lower at 3.6 per cent (Table 6.2). Such a high rate of unemployment is an indicative of low economic base, in turn, resulting in a low absorption capacity of the labour force. The non-working population constitutes about 53 per cent and a large part of it includes students.

(ii) Labour force characteristics among non-migrants

From the viewpoint of local economy, the labour force characteristics show quite distinct patterns from that of household economy when migrant population is excluded. The overall labour force participation declines from about 47 to about 43 per cent by principal status and from 64 to 62 per cent by UPSS. Male LFPR in particular shows a declining trend while female LFPR does not show any change. Similarly, overall WPR by principal status declines sharply from 42 to 38 per cent and male WPR declines by 6 percentage points. Employment opportunities for the resident population are limited and a large part of workforce is engaged in subsidiary occupations. Unemployment rate also increases, and for males it goes up from 15 per cent to 19 per cent (Table 6.4).

The low rate of labour force participation (UPSS) among males is not a demographic phenomenon, rather it is purely an economic phenomenon where a large percentage of males do out-migrate for earning cash income; and females replace males' labour, thereby increasing their own overall participation. The high LFPRs among the sample population also show that in a subsistence economy like the mountain region in Uttarakhand, every able-bodied person has to engage himself to support the household income.

Table 6.4 : Labour Force and Workforce Participation Rates

	Residents (excluding migrants)					
Activity status	*Principal status workers*			*Principal and subsidiary status workers*		
	Male	*Female*	*Person*	*Male*	*Female*	*Person*
Labour force	44.61	41.56	43.08	56.08	68.49	62.30
Workforce	36.08	40.20	38.14	54.80	68.29	61.56
Unemployed*	19.12	3.29	11.46	2.27	0.28	1.18
Non-workers	55.39	58.44	56.92	43.92	31.51	37.70
Total	100.00	100.00	100.00	100.00	100.00	100.00
Population (number)	1020	1025	2045	1020	1025	2045

* Relates to unemployment rate (i.e. number of unemployed persons expressed as a percentage of the total labour force.

Source : Field Survey, 2004-05.

(iii) Labour force characteristics across spatial units and household levels

WPR (UPSS) across development blocks varies between 59 to 67 per cent with relatively developed blocks showing higher WPR as compared to less developed blocks, albeit marginally. Female WPR is reported to be higher than male WPR in all the blocks. It is primarily because females are often disproportionately engaged in agriculture and allied activities, because they are grossly underrepresented in the non-farm activities. An overwhelmingly large majority of female work force in agriculture and allied activities thus acts as sponge.

WPR varies significantly across caste groups, lowest being in the case of SCs (around 61%) and highest among STs (68%). Male WPR is highest among STs and lowest among Kshatriyas, while female WPR is highest for STs and lowest for SCs (Table 6.5).

The case of SCs where lowest WPR is reported can be explained on two counts. Firstly, lack of assets, particularly land assets, having lowest average size of land and lowest level of literacy have constricted their greater participation in the labour market. Secondly, many caste-based occupations in which males and females were engaged earlier have been gradually vanishing, which impacted their participation adversely. WPR tends to increase with higher age groups, much lower in the lowest age group (5-14), and then goes up consistently, highest being in 30 to 59 age group and then declines in the older age group (60 and above) (Figure 6.1).

It is also observed that medium land size class has the highest WPR followed by landless class. Male WPR is highest among medium land size class followed by landless. WPR among landless class has the lowest female WPR and very high male WPR (Table 6.5). The reason for high WPR in these two different land classes is altogether different. Landlessness forces male labour force to work for off-farm and non-farm jobs, while females, due to limited opportunity in the non-farm sector and also due to social inhibitions, have to remain idle for want of work outside very limited segments of labour market. In most of the agricultural and related activities, females tend to have greater participation than males barring limited farming operations like ploughing and terracing that are generally male-dominated operations.

Table 6.5 : Work Participation Rates (UPSS) Across Different Social Groups and Land Classes

District	*Block*	*Including migrants and non-migrants*		
		Male	*Female*	*Person*
Almora	Hawalbagh	63.48	70.83	66.77
	Salt	56.21	67.65	61.31
Pithoragarh	Dharchula	56.55	67.14	61.75
	Berinag	64.12	67.14	65.48
T. Garhwal	Chamba	61.59	66.94	64.12
	Kirtinagar	55.47	64.29	59.70
Uttarkashi	Bhatwari	59.84	75.89	67.36
	Dunda	61.94	64.93	63.32
Social category	Brahmin	60.00	71.53	65.20
	Kshatriya	59.52	67.92	63.40
	SC	60.71	59.71	60.26
	ST	62.30	73.50	67.78
	Others	62.50	69.05	65.85
Age group	5-14	4.79	8.70	6.44
	15-29	74.59	93.48	83.38
	30-59	99.15	97.12	98.14
	60+	74.17	50.45	62.77
Land class	Landless	70.21	63.33	67.53
	Marginal	59.37	68.33	63.56
	Small	60.19	66.29	63.02
	Medium	77.78	66.67	72.73
Development status of blocks	Developed	60.54	70.00	64.98
	Less developed	59.75	66.04	62.64
Total		60.13	67.99	63.78
Nos.		733	718	1451

Source : Field Survey, 2004-05.

There are significant differences in male and female participation rates across development blocks. Male participation is consistently throwing low rates as compared to their female counterparts. Developed blocks show higher WPR as compared to relatively less developed blocks and this is reflected both for males and for females (Table 6.6).

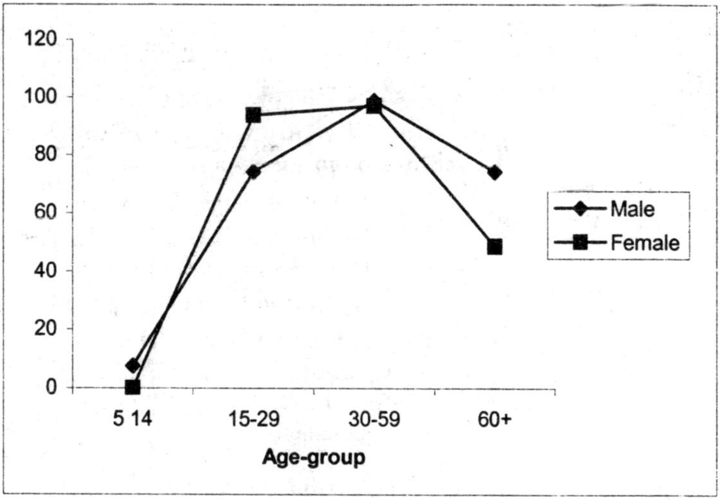

Fig. 6.1 : Work Participation Rate by Age-Groups.

Table 6.6 : Work Participation Rates (UPSS) across Development Blocks

District	*Block*	*Residents (excluding migrants)*		
		Male	*Female*	*Person*
Almora	Hawalbagh	60.12	70.83	65.15
	Salt	47.10	67.65	57.30
Pithoragarh	Dharchula	57.14	69.70	63.57
	Berinag	58.04	67.14	62.54
T. Garhwal	Chamba	54.70	66.94	61.00
	Kirtinagar	44.23	64.29	55.22
Uttarkashi	Bhatwari	58.82	79.59	69.00
	Dunda	55.91	62.40	59.13
Land class	Landless	69.44	62.07	66.15
	Marginal	53.98	68.79	61.44
	Small	55.43	65.52	60.34
	Medium	66.67	66.67	66.67
Development status of blocks	Developed	57.87	71.29	64.51
	Less developed	51.76	65.46	58.71
Total		54.80	68.29	61.56

Source : Field Survey, 2004-05.

(iv) Employment status of workers

Employment status of workers has been ascertained based on the principal and subsidiary status occupations and accordingly the workers have been categorised into self-employed, regular and casual status. It can be observed that self-employment is the principal mode of livelihood of the workforce as 82 per cent workers are engaged in numerous self-employment activities within agriculture and non-agricultural pursuits including migrants. About 13 per cent workforce is engaged in regular/salaried employment and another 6 per cent in casual works. The employment status of the workers is also distinctly different for males and females. Women are disproportionately engaged in self-employment activities (98%) with a negligible share in regular and casual employment (1% each respectively), while their male counterparts have 66 per cent share in self-employment, 24 per cent (about one-fourth) share in regular employment and one-tenth share in casual employment (Figure 6.2).

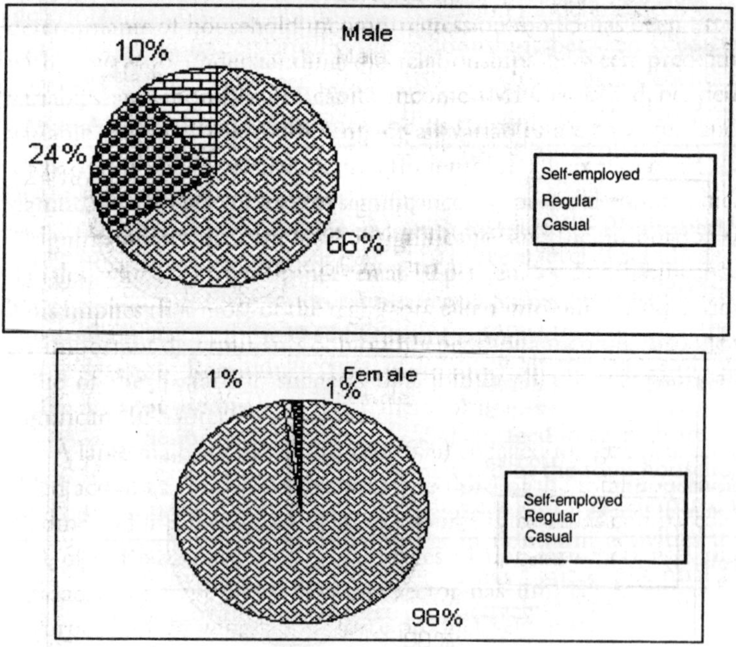

Fig. 6.2 : Status of Employment of All Workers (UPSS).

Status of employment changes significantly with the exclusion of migrant workers. The proportion of self-employed increases to about 91 per cent, while the share of regular employment declines to 6 per cent and that of casual employment to 3 per cent. The status of employment hardly changes in the case of female workers. However, for males the share in self-employment increases to 82 per cent, and regular employment declines to 13 per cent and casual employment to 5 per cent (Figure 6.3). About 15 per cent principal & subsidiary workers are migrants and almost all among them are regular employed; and with their inclusion, the status of employment of workforce changes significantly.

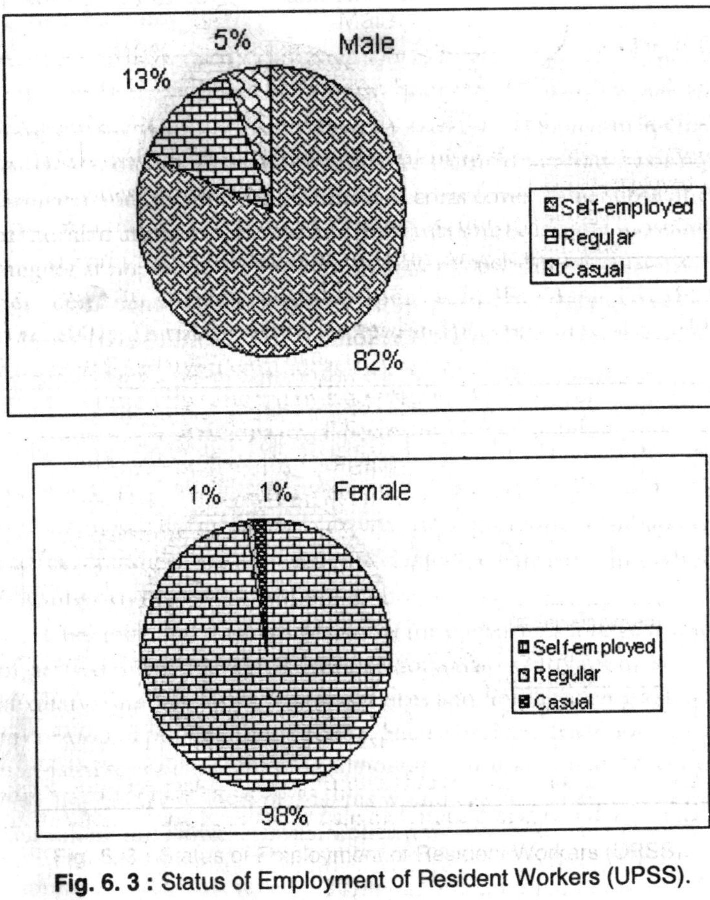

Fig. 6. 3 : Status of Employment of Resident Workers (UPSS).

III. Structure of Employment at Disaggregated Levels and by Household Groups

(i) Structure of employment

Structure of employment of the workforce can be analysed using standard occupational and industrial classifications. In this section, the structure of employment is analysed using industrial classification of workers, and in the later part of analysis we will use the occupational classifications. In order to maintain simplicity, the structure of employment by industrial classification is analysed according to principal status of workers and as such subsidiary status of workers has not been taken into account due to limitations in the primary data set. It has been observed that the analysis based on principal status gives a clearer picture of work activity and combining the subsidiary activity with principal status subsides the status of subsidiary worker. Also, those who are non-workers according to their principal status are mostly engaged in cultivation and animal husbandry activities in their subsidiary capacity.

Distribution of workers in the major sectors of economy shows that agriculture and allied segments is the dominant sector that employs nearly 55 per cent of the workforce including the migrant population. Women workforce, in particular, is disproportionately engaged (87%) in it that constitutes the backbone of the hill agriculture, while men workforce is comparatively much lower (29%). Within the agriculture sector, animal husbandry employs nearly 2.8 per cent with a higher female share (4.9%) than the males (1.1%), and it is one of the important and dependable sources of cash income for the poor households besides being an integral agricultural activity that provides main drought power and manure. While a great majority of women are engaged in agricultural and allied activities, men on the other hand tend to dominate the non-agricultural pursuits. The share of male workforce in the non-agriculture sector constitutes 71 per cent, while for women it is limited to only about 13 per cent indicating the distinctly segmented labour market for males and females (Table 6.7).

Table 6.7 : Distribution of Workers by Major Industry (UPS)

Industry	*Migrant and non-migrant workers*			*Non-migrant workers*		
	Male	*Female*	*Person*	*Male*	*Female*	*Person*
Agriculture and allied activities	29.21	86.62	54.69	42.12	89.08	66.92
Manufacturing	8.61	10.33	9.38	8.70	8.01	8.33
Electricity, water, gas etc.	2.06	0.00	1.15	1.90	0.00	0.90
Construction	5.81	0.23	3.33	7.61	0.24	3.72
Trade, hotel & restaurant	24.72	0.47	13.96	19.57	0.49	9.49
Transport & communication	8.24	0.00	4.58	7.88	0.00	3.72
Finance, business activities etc.	2.62	0.00	1.46	0.27	0.00	0.13
Public admin, education etc.	18.73	2.35	11.46	11.96	2.18	6.79
Total	100.00	100.00	100.00	100.00	100.00	100.00
Total workers	534	426	960	368	412	780

Source : Field Survey, 2004-05.

However, excluding migrants the share of farm employment rises steeply from about 55 to 67 per cent and that of non-agriculture share declines correspondingly from 45 per cent to 33 per cent. Female share in agriculture and allied activities increases to about 89 per cent with little occupational diversification to non-agricultural activities indicating their vulnerability to subsistence agriculture. Agriculture, therefore, assumes the predominant sector for employment for the large majority of labour force with little surplus-generating capacity, and by and large, this sector acts as labour sponge, in particular for females. Female workforce accounts for pitifully low share in all other segments of non-agricultural activities except in manufacturing that employs 8.0 per cent, which mainly consists of household-based activities.

The other important sectors are trade, hotel & restaurant (constituting petty trade and business), public administration, manufacturing and tra[illegible]mmunication accounting for about 39 per cent and 28 [illegible] respectively for migrant and non-migrant workers. Construction activities have been by and large male-dominated and females have a very low share in these activities.

Thus, accessibility to non-farm employment opportunities is mainly in the domain of males. This further accentuates the vulnerability of females. Although they are the main producers in agriculture, yet they have no direct access to income, howsoever little, accrues from agriculture. The hill economy thus presents a typical case of distinctively identifiable labour markets for males and females separately. While men are mostly engaged in non-agricultural activities, women seem to be largely concentrated in agricultural activities. Such a low mobility of women labour force is primarily attributed to the cultural factors that inhibit them to go beyond a limited segment of cultivation and related activities. This raises the issue of one kind of limited labour mobility of females and men assume the major source of cash needs working in non-agricultural activities. Another issue is structural rigidity in agricultural sector, in particular, the female labour force with high amount of drudgery that provides a little or no opportunity for upward mobility and skill formation, which is a matter of serious concern.

(ii) Employment structure at spatial levels

The distribution pattern of workers within local economy presents distinct variations across development blocks, social category and land class, and indeed, this makes sense to understand this diversity within the local economy. Agriculture and allied activities is the principal mode of sustenance in all the development blocks. This is primarily because the subsistence nature of agriculture that does not ensure better employment and income opportunities.

The disaggregated picture of industrial distribution of workers across development blocks show that the less developed blocks have higher share of workforce in agriculture and allied activities than the relatively more developed ones barring Dunda block, which shows a relatively lower share of workforce in agriculture and allied activities primarily due to its close proximity to the block and district headquarters that helps to provide more employment opportunities in non-farm activities (Table 6.8). This is partly attributed to a comparatively higher extent of commercial farming (as reflected in higher percentage of gross cultivated area under commercial crops) in these blocks that is able to retain the male workforce gainfully in agriculture.

Employment share in manufacturing is generally higher in developed blocks as compared to less developed blocks in the districts. Three blocks namely Dharchula, Bhatwari and Dunda have relatively higher share of workforce in manufacturing. This is primarily because of concentration of tribal population in some of the villages where almost every household seems to be engaged in manufacturing activity (e.g. weaving and manufacturing woollen garments). Electricity, water and gas constitutes very low share (less than 1%) in employment. Though construction activity provides employment to about 3.6 per cent workforce, yet it is an important activity for employment generation particularly for the poor and unskilled ones. This is particularly due to increase in the building of infrastructure like roads, school buildings, and drinking water under various government-funded development schemes in rural areas of Uttarakhand. At the same time, there has been a rapid increase in the building construction activity, both within the villages and nearby rural bazaars, which generated a demand for labour. The spurt in construction activity is mainly due to government support for building infrastructures like roads, culverts, bridges, buildings and also due to various wage employment programmes. However, it needs to be noted here that most of such rural non-farm jobs in the construction sector were not necessarily located within the boundaries of villages. A large proportion of these jobs were available through daily commuting to nearby towns/ rural bazaars. It is plausible that in these places people do not have other better opportunities, and construction works almost immediately provide a relief to them. Such wage employment opportunities are more in relatively less developed blocks as compared to developed blocks. Trade, hotel & restaurant is another important activity after agriculture, etc. that provides employment to a large number of people (9.5%), primarily because of low investment requirements and low risks associated in such types of activities. Most common activities are retail shops catering to the food and non-food needs, small tea stalls and restaurants (*dhabas*), which have sprung up in large numbers almost immediately in the villages nearby road-heads and nearer to market places and block headquarters. Most of the developed blocks have higher share in these activities. Transport and communication is emerging as yet another important activity employing a higher share of workforce in the relatively developed blocks than the relatively less developed ones. Employment in financial activities is abysmally low. As regards public administration, education, etc. no definite pattern is observed. Two relatively developed blocks have higher employment share, while another two relatively less developed blocks have lower employment share. The overall pattern of non-farm employment in developed blocks show a higher share than the less developed blocks (Table 6.8). By and large, it is observed that the villages nearer to block or district headquarters have more employment opportunities. The block and district centres being the hub of development activities for the adjoining villages, number of business activities get agglomerated near these centres, thus helping a market to spur. The block or district has numerous institutions such as schools, health centre, veterinary centre, training centre, demonstration farm centre, etc. All these establishments become the strong forces for springing up a market. The most common business activities observed around these villages are teashop, grocery shop, transport business (jeep transport), petty contractor, grain milling, STD booths, etc. These activities are common and wherever such growth points have occurred deliberately or otherwise, numerous such activities have sprung up almost immediately.

(iii) Employment structure by social class

Employment share across social classes shows that Brahmins, SCs and STs have relatively low share in agriculture and allied activities, while Kshatriyas and 'other castes' have high share. Employment in manufacturing is significantly higher among STs and SCs than other social groups. SCs are mostly engaged in repair related works, mainly caste-based occupations like basket weaving, blacksmithy, coppersmithy, etc. which are essentially low paying activities, while STs are engaged in weaving and manufacturing woollen garments. STs have distinctly higher share as their presence in household manufacturing is very high. Employment share in construction is highest among SCs followed by Kshatriyas. In trade, hotel & restaurant, all the social groups have fairly high share in employment for males, but females are grossly under-represented. In transport and communication too, all the social groups are represented barring 'other castes'. In public administration, education, etc. Brahmins have highest share followed by SCs and Kshatriyas. It can be observed that the upper castes and STs have relatively higher share in employment in every branch of activities, while the lower social classes have much lower share in employment barring construction (Table 6.8). Scheduled Tribes have highest share in non-agriculture employment (68%) followed by Scheduled Castes (40%). The Brahmins and Kshatriyas have 32 and 29 per cent share respectively, while the 'other castes' has the lowest share (12.5%). The reason for the highest share of non-agriculture employment among STs is primarily due to their engagement in traditional occupations like weaving, manufacturing of woollen garments and trading. Low average size of cultivable land among SCs forces some people (mostly illiterates and unskilled) into casual type of employment in construction sector on the one hand, and reservation in employment also seem to have helped others (better educated lot) to get regular/salaried employment on the other.

Brahmins are observed to have highest literacy, both among males and females in the present survey and also have traditionally been most forward class both in terms of education and employment in the region. Rightly so, their share in public administration, education, etc. constitutes the highest share (18%). The other dominant activity in which they are engaged is trading.

(iv) Employment structure by land size class

Apparently, the occupational structure of the workforce is determined to a large extent by the availability of productive asset like land. This is obvious, as land is the only asset which retains the workforce in the absence of other productive employment opportunities. As regards the relationship between land size class and share in rural non-agriculture employment is concerned, distinctly negative relationship between the land size class and the dependence on the non-agriculture employment is observed. It can be noted that the landless class depends to a significant extent on non-agriculture activities while the share considerably declines in higher land sizes. This is plausible in the context of rural setting where land is a prime asset and landlessness or lack of cultivable land forces people to find livelihoods in non-agricultural pursuits, whatsoever income or wages they receive. Interestingly, in the highest land size class, none of the household member is engaged in other non-agriculture activities except in public services (Table 6.8).

(v) Educational status of workers

Among the non-migrant workers, 33 per cent are illiterates (constituting 16% males and 49% females) while about 17 per cent are educated up to secondary school (14% up to primary and 18% up to middle). Another about 8 per cent workers are educated up to higher secondary and 7.0 per cent workers are graduates and above. A little over 1 per cent workers possess technical qualification. Educational attainment among females is very low as about 80 per cent workforce is educated up to middle level of education.

A cursory look at the educational status of the workers shows that the educational level attained by them is directly linked with their activities. The workers with higher levels of education are by and large concentrated more in public administration, education, etc; trade, hotel & restaurant and transport and communication; while those with lower levels of education are mainly engaged in agricultural and allied activities, manufacturing and construction (Table 6.9).

There are sharp dfferences in the levels of education and industry groups between males and females. Females are disproportionately represented in the agriculture and allied activities (89%) and almost half of them are illiterates. Similarly, in manufacturing, majority of

Table 6.8 : Structure of Employment by Industry Groups across Spatial Units and Household Groups

Block	*Agriculture and allied activities*	*Manufac-turing*	*Electricity water, gas etc.*	*Const-ruction*	*Trade, hotel & restaurant*	*Transport & communi-cation*	*Finance, Business activities etc.*	*Public admin., education etc.*	*Total*
Blocks									
Hawalbagh	63.06	2.70	0.00	6.31	10.81	3.60	0.90	12.61	100.00 (111)
Salt	71.13	1.03	3.09	5.15	12.37	2.06	0.00	5.15	100.00 (97)
Dharchula	51.43	15.24	0.00	4.76	11.43	10.48	0.00	6.67	100.00 (105)
Berinag	77.08	1.04	2.08	4.17	11.46	2.08	0.00	2.08	100.00 (96)
Chamba	78.13	4.17	1.04	0.00	11.46	4.17	0.00	1.04	100.00 (96)
Kirtinagar	81.25	1.25	0.00	5.00	2.50	1.25	0.00	8.75	100.00 (80)
Bhatwari	64.13	21.74	0.00	0.00	7.61	3.26	0.00	3.26	100.00 (92)
Dunda	54.37	18.45	0.97	3.88	6.80	1.94	0.00	13.59	100.00 (103)
Social category									
Brahmin	67.59	2.78	0.93	0.93	7.41	2.78	0.00	17.59	100.00 (108)
Kshatriya	73.91	0.87	1.09	3.91	10.87	4.13	0.00	5.22	100.00 (460)
SC	60.20	15.31	1.02	8.16	5.10	2.04	1.02	7.14	100.00 (98)
ST	32.22	46.67	0.00	2.22	10.00	5.56	0.00	3.33	100.00 (90)
Others	87.50	4.17	0.00	0.00	8.33	0.00	0.00	0.00	100.00 (24)
Land class									
Landless	23.33	53.33	3.33	3.33	3.33	3.33	0.00	10.00	100.00 (30)
Marginal	68.01	6.85	0.89	4.02	10.42	3.57	0.15	6.10	100.00 (672)
Small	72.06	4.41	0.00	1.47	4.41	5.88	0.00	11.76	100.00 (68)
Medium	90.00	0.00	0.00	0.00	0.00	0.00	0.00	10.00	100.00 (10)
Status of blocks									
Less developed	70.21	5.85	1.60	4.52	8.51	1.86	0.00	7.45	100.00 (376)
Developed	63.86	10.64	0.25	2.97	10.40	5.45	0.25	6.19	100.00 (404)
Total	66.92	8.33	0.90	3.72	9.49	3.72	0.13	6.79	100.00 (780)

Source : Fleid Survey, 2004-05.

Table 6.9 : Educational Status of Non-migrant Workers (UPS) by Industry and Education Levels

Industry	*Sex*	*Illiterate*	*Up to primary*	*Up to middle*	*Up to secondary*	*Up to higher secondary*	*Graduate and above*	*Technical*	*Total*
Agriculture and allied activities	Male	21.94	22.58	24.52	22.58	4.52	3.23	0.65	100.00(155)
	Female	49.32	15.26	15.80	11.17	5.45	3.00	0.00	100.00(367)
	Person	41.19	17.43	18.39	14.56	5.17	3.07	0.19	100.00(522)
Manufacturing	Male	31.25	15.63	12.50	31.25	6.25	0.00	3.12	100.00(32)
	Female	54.55	12.12	21.21	12.12	0.00	0.00	0.00	100.00(33)
	Person	43.08	13.85	16.92	21.54	3.08	0.00	1.54	100.00(65)
Electricity, water, gas, etc.	Male	0.00	14.29	28.57	14.29	28.57	0.00	14.29	100.00(7)
	Female	0.00	0.00	0.00	0.00	0.00	0.00	0.00	0.00
	Person	0.00	14.29	28.57	14.29	28.57	0.00	14.29	100.00(7)
Construction	Male	21.43	17.86	28.57	14.29	10.71	3.57	3.57	100.00(28)
	Female	100.00	0.00	0.00	0.00	0.00	0.00	0.00	100.00(1)
	Person	24.14	17.24	27.59	13.79	10.34	3.45	3.45	100.00(29)
Trade, hotel & restaurant	Male	9.72	5.56	22.22	23.61	20.83	16.67	1.39	100.00(72)
	Female	0.00	50.00	50.00	0.00	0.00	0.00	0.00	100.00(2)
	Person	9.46	6.76	22.97	22.97	20.27	16.22	1.35	100.00(74)
Transport & communication	Male	6.90	0.00	17.24	27.59	24.14	17.24	6.90	100.00(29)
	Female	0.00	0.00	0.00	100.00	0.00	0.00	0.00	0.00
	Person	6.90	0.00	17.24	27.59	24.14	17.24	6.90	100.00(29)
Finance, business activities, etc.	Male	0.00	0.00	0.00	100.00	0.00	0.00	0.00	100.00(1)
	Female	0.00	0.00	0.00	100.00	0.00	0.00	0.00	0.00
	Person	0.00	0.00	0.00	100.00	0.00	0.00	0.00	100.00 (1)
Public admin., education, etc.	Male	0.00	4.55	6.82	22.73	15.91	45.45	4.55	100.00(44)
	Female	11.11	0.00	0.00	11.11	33.33	44.44	0.00	100.00(9)
	Person	1.89	3.77	5.66	20.75	18.87	45.28	3.77	100.00(53)
Total	Male	16.03	14.13	20.65	23.37	11.68	11.68	2.45	100.00(368)
	Female	48.79	14.81	16.02	11.17	5.58	3.64	0.00	100.00(412)
	Person	33.33	14.49	18.21	16.92	8.46	7.44	1.15	100.00(780)

Source : Field Survey, 2004-05.

females are illiterates. This only shows the less importance attached to female education in a household, as they are forced to join agricultural activities and low-paid manufacturing activities even without basic schooling.

Almost 51 per cent workers in agriculture are educated only up to secondary level. The level of education in manufacturing is even more precarious. In construction sector, 10 per cent workforce is educated up to higher secondary levels. Understandably, the lack of employment opportunities forces many educated persons to take up such jobs under duress, particularly in public works, whatsoever wages are paid in lieu of their physical labour.

The level of technical education is almost negligible and illiteracy among female workers is also quite significant (49%) despite the fact that literacy rate stands out to be very high in the rural area of the state. From the policy perspective, low level of literacy among female worker has serious implications for their employability outside the agriculture. Their low educational and skill levels can hardly help them to secure employment outside agriculture. Therefore, efforts need to be made to improve their productivity in agriculture itself through imparting them knowledge and training of market-oriented farming. At present, hill women largely lack training in market-oriented farming and agro-processing. They have hardly been benefited with scientific agriculture, which could have otherwise reduced their drudgery.

(vi) Employment pattern among youth workers

Youth workers constitute around 27 per cent of the total workers according to principal activity. About 56 per cent workers are engaged in non-agricultural activities, but there are sharp differences in the relative share of male and female workers in the agriculture and non-agriculture activities (Table 6.10). While male youth workers have disproportionate share in the non-agriculture activities (92.5%), female workers on the other hand has minuscule share (7.2%) in this sector. Female workers' extraordinary engagement in agriculture and allied activities is the most conspicuous phenomenon that shows their vulnerability as well as drudgery. The share of male workers in trade, hotel & restaurant (36%); public admin., education, etc. (23%);

Table 6.10 : Employment Pattern among Youth Workers (Aged 15 to 29 years)

Industry	*Total workers (migrants and non-migrants)*			*Non-migrants workers*		
	Male	*Female*	*Person*	*Male*	*Female*	*Person*
Agriculture and allied activities	7.43	92.79	44.02	17.54	95.28	68.10
Manufacturing	7.43	5.41	6.56	7.02	2.83	4.29
Electricity, water, gas, etc.	2.03	0.00	1.16	0.00	0.00	0.00
Construction	2.70	0.00	1.54	5.26	0.00	1.84
Trade, hotel & restaurant	35.81	0.90	20.85	28.07	0.94	10.43
Transport & communication	16.89	0.00	9.65	31.58	0.00	11.04
Finance, business activities, etc.	4.73	0.00	2.70	0.00	0.00	0.00
Public admin., education, etc.	22.97	0.90	13.51	10.53	0.94	4.29
Total	100.00	100.00	100.00	100.00	100.00	100.00
Nos.	148	111	259	57	106	163

Source : Field Survey, 2004-05.

transport & communication (17%) is significantly higher. The proportion of youth workers declines to 21 per cent with a significant change in work pattern, if the migrant workers are excluded. The share in non-agriculture sector employment falls sharply from 56 per cent to 32 per cent, and that the share of agriculture and allied activities rises from about 44 to about 68 per cent, indicating a very high dependence on non-agriculture employment opportunities outside the region, mainly through out-migration. The corresponding share of male and female workers in the non-agriculture activities declines and that of agriculture and allied activities rises in almost every branches of activity. Majority of local employment opportunities (65%) in which male youth are engaged are low pay-off and petty activities like trade, hotel & restaurant; transport & communication, and construction activities. Only about 10 per cent male workers are engaged in regular employment in public administration and education, etc. The female youth have disproportionate share in agriculture and allied activities (95%) primarily because, they are grossly underrepresented in non-agriculture activities. Their share in non-agriculture activities is pitifully low and most of them are engaged in manufacturing (illiterate or less educated), and some are in regular/ salaried jobs in public administration and education, etc. (educated ones). It is obvious that almost all the agriculture and allied activities are primarily in the domain of females, while male have sole domination in non-agricultural activities. Such a clear-cut segmentation of work pattern in the labour market between males and females raises certain issues at the policy plane from long-term perspective that has a wider ramification on human resource development. Out of the total female workers engaged in agriculture and allied activities, 26 per cent are in the young age group (15-29) and 45 per cent have educational levels up to high school and above.

Such a huge educated workforce engaged in low productive activities which merely act as a sponge, and is indicative of lack of correspondence between the education system and needs of labour market. Education system with little content of marketable skills, produces a variety of obstacles in the labour market in terms of unemployment or underemployment. It is, therefore, of paramount importance to make the education system relevant to the market needs and to create a workforce that has the flexibility to acquire new skills for new jobs in the labour market.

IV. Occupational Structure of Workforce

(i) Occupational structure of migrant and nonmigrant workers

Detailed occupational structure for all the workers (including migrants) and for the non-migrant workers is presented in Tables 6.13 and 6.14, both by principal status and principal & subsidiary status. Cultivators form the major occupational group, both for males and females. According to principal status, the other major occupational groups are service workers followed by shopkeepers & sales workers, and weavers and related workers. Clerical and related workers, and teachers also account for about one-tenth of workforce. Majority of female workers (80%) are engaged as cultivators, and about one-tenth of them are also engaged in weaving and related occupations. Their share in non-agriculture occupational groups is very low (15%), while majority of male workforce are engaged in non-agriculture activities. Service workers account for about 17 per cent, shopkeepers & sales workers about 14 per cent, clerical workers about 10 per cent and teachers account for about 6 per cent in the occupational structure. The transport workers (drivers) also account for about 6 per cent. In the principal and subsidiary capacity, the overall agriculture and non-agriculture workers' share is about 66 and 34 per cent respectively. The share of female workers in non-farm activities hardly changes but in the case of male workers, the share of non-agriculture occupation declines from about 71 to 54 per cent. A large majority of male workers are engaged in agriculture and related activities in their subsidiary capacity (Table 6.11).

Table 6.11 : Occupational Structure of Migrant and Non-migrant Workers

Occupation	*Principal occupation*			*Principal + subsidiary occupation*		
	Male	*Female*	*Person*	*Male*	*Female*	*Person*
1. Cultivator	27.85	80.05	50.99	40.44	76.32	58.21
2. Animal husbandry worker	1.12	4.93	2.81	5.33	10.31	7.79
3. Technical and managerial worker	2.62	0.00	1.46	1.91	0.00	0.97
4. Teacher	5.98	1.64	4.06	4.37	0.97	2.69
5. Clerical and related worker	10.09	0.00	5.62	7.51	0.00	3.79
6. Shopkeeper and sales worker	14.02	0.47	8.01	10.52	0.28	5.45
7. Service worker*	17.20	0.00	9.57	12.84	0.00	6.48
8. Weaver and related worker	4.86	10.33	7.28	4.51	10.45	7.45
9. Other production worker**	5.05	0.00	2.81	3.69	0.00	1.86
10. Transport worker (drivers)	6.36	0.00	3.54	4.78	0.00	2.41
11. Labourer	4.11	1.88	3.12	3.55	1.25	2.41
12. Other worker***	0.75	0.70	0.73	0.55	0.42	0.48
Total workers	535	426	961	732	718	1450

Notes : * Service workers constitute hotel-room boys, cooks, domestic servants, security service workers, etc.

** Other production workers comprise grain miller, food preserver, bakery workers, brewers, dairy workers etc.

*** Other includes veterinary assistant, ANM, Dai and religious workers.

Source : Field Survey, 2004-05.

(ii) Occupational structure of non-migrant workers

The occupational structure gets significantly changed if only non-migrant workers are considered. The share of non-migrant workers in agricultural activities rises and that of share in non-agriculture activities declines to a substantial proportion. This is primarily because almost all the migrant workers are engaged in non-agriculture activities. It is important from the point of view of local economy to understand the occupational diversity of workforce. The occupational structure clearly shows the segmented labour market feature between male and female workforce. A little over 87 per cent female are primarily engaged in cultivation and animal husbandry activities according to principal status, while about 58% male workers are engaged in non-agriculture activities (Table 6.12). The occupational structure remains almost

Table 6.12 : Occupational Structure of Non-migrant Workers

Occupation	*Principal occupation*			*Principal + subsidiary occupation*		
	Male	*Female*	*Person*	*Male*	*Female*	*Person*
1. Cultivator	40.49	82.28	62.56	52.42	78.00	66.64
2. Animal husbandry worker	1.36	5.10	3.33	6.44	10.57	8.74
3. Technical and managerial worker	1.63	0.00	0.77	1.07	0.00	0.48
4. Teacher	6.79	1.70	4.10	4.47	1.00	2.54
5. Clerical and related workers	7.07	0.00	3.33	4.83	0.00	2.14
6. Shopkeeper and sales worker	15.49	0.49	7.56	10.55	0.29	4.85
7. Service worker*	4.35	0.00	2.05	3.04	0.00	1.35
8. Weaver and related worker	5.98	8.01	7.05	5.19	8.57	7.07
9. Other production worker**	3.80	0.00	1.79	2.50	0.00	1.11
10. Transport worker (driver)	6.52	0.00	3.08	4.47	0.00	1.99
11. Labourer	5.71	1.94	3.72	4.47	1.29	2.70
12. Other worker***	0.82	0.49	0.64	0.54	0.29	0.40
Total workers	368	412	780	559	700	1259

Notes : * Service workers constitute hotel-room boys, cooks, domestic servants, security service workers, etc.

** Other production workers comprise grain miller, food preserver, bakery workers, brewers, dairy workers etc.

*** Other includes veterinary assistant, ANM, Dai and religious workers.

Source : Field Survey, 2004-05.

same for females by principal and subsidiary status. Other than cultivation and allied activities; weaving, labouring and teaching are other occupations for female workers. For males, shopkeepers & sales workers account for the highest share (15%) followed by clerical and related workers and teachers (7% each). The other occupational groups are drivers, weavers and related workers, labourers and service workers constituting about 6 per cent each.

(iii) Occupational structure and household features

The occupational structure shows a distinct pattern of labour market segmentation in terms of castes, land classes, and income groups across development blocks (Table 6.13). In social category, there are huge variations in the share of non-agriculture occupational structure. Scheduled Castes and Scheduled Tribes have fairly high share in non-agriculture occupations (34 and 66% respectively) while the Brahmins (21%) and Kshatriyas (17%) have comparatively low share. The 'other caste' has the lowest share in non-agriculture occupations (8%). There are distinct patterns of non-agriculture occupations in each social group. Brahmins have comparatively higher share in teaching and technical & managerial occupations, while Kshatriyas have relatively high share in occupations like shopkeepers, clerical and related workers, transport workers (drivers) and service workers. Scheduled Castes have concentration in occupations like weavers, labourers and other production workers, and the Scheduled Tribes have concentration as weavers, shopkeepers and transport workers.

Land size classes and the structure of occupations in the non-farm sector have distinctly negative relationship throughout, and the proportion of cultivators increases with the increase in land size classes and rightly so. However, it is observed that in the landless and in the highest land size classes, the proportion of workers in animal husbandry is very high. The reasons seems to be different for both the classes; for the landless class, animal husbandry provides instant cash source of income particularly in rural setting; and in the highest land size class, animal husbandry becomes an integrated activity of cultivation and also it is one of the income-enhancing sources. In the landless category, majority of workers have concentration as weavers followed by animal husbandry workers, labourers and teachers. In

Table 6.13 : Occupational Structure of Non-migrant Workers across Household Features (UPSS)

Household features	*Cultivator*	*Animal husbandry worker*	*Technical and managerial*	*Teacher*	*Clerical*	*Shop - keeper and sales worker*	*Service worker*	*Weavers etc.*	*Other production worker*	*Transport worker (driver)*	*Labourers*	*Other worker*	*Total worker*
Social category													
Brahmin	68.65	10.81	1.08	5.95	2.16	3.78	0.54	1.08	1.08	1.62	1.62	1.62	(100.00) 185
Kshatriya	74.16	8.75	0.40	2.02	2.42	5.38	1.88	0.27	0.54	2.29	1.88	0.00	(100.00) 743
SC	57.23	8.81	0.63	3.14	1.26	2.52	0.63	10.53	4.40	1.26	8.81	0.63	(100.00) 159
ST	28.57	5.26	0.00	0.75	2.26	6.77	0.00	50.38	0.75	2.26	2.26	0.75	(100.00) 133
Others	82.05	10.26	0.00	0.00	0.00	2.56	2.56	2.56	0.00	0.00	0.00	0.00	(100.00) 39
Land class													
Landless	9.30	11.63	2.33	4.65	2.33	2.33	0.00	55.81	2.33	2.33	4.65	2.33	(100.00) 43
Marginal	67.80	9.08	0.37	2.11	2.02	5.32	1.47	5.41	1.19	2.02	2.84	0.37	(100.00) (109)
Small	75.00	3.70	0.93	5.56	3.70	1.85	0.93	5.56	0.00	1.85	0.93	0.00	(100.00) (108)
Medium	83.33	11.11	0.00	5.56	0.00	0.00	0.00	0.00	0.00	0.00	0.00	0.00	(100.00) (18)
Income group (MPCI)													
Up to Rs. 250	74.19	9.68	0.00	0.00	0.00	0.00	1.08	0.00	0.00	0.00	15.05	0.00	(100.00) (93)

Table 6.13 : (*Contd...*)

Rs. 250 to 500	74.15	9.09	0.00	0.57	0.57	3.41	1.70	4.26	1.99	0.00	3.98	0.28	(100.00) (352)
Rs. 500 to 1000	69.35	10.51	0.45	0.00	1.57	4.70	1.79	7.83	1.12	1.79	0.45	0.45	(100.00) (447)
Rs. 1000 to 2500	53.87	6.25	1.19	6.55	5.06	8.33	0.60	11.31	0.60	4.46	1.19	0.60	(100.00) (336)
More than Rs. 2500	58.06	3.23	0.00	25.81	3.23	0.00	0.00	3.23	0.00	6.45	0.00	0.00	(100.00) (31)
Development status of blocks													
Less developed	67.54	9.84	0.33	3.11	1.80	4.59	0.82	4.75	1.15	1.15	4.26	0.66	(100.00) (610)
Developed	65.79	7.70	0.62	2.00	2.47	5.08	1.85	9.24	1.08	2.77	1.23	0.15	(100.00) (649)
Total	66.64	8.74	0.48	2.54	2.14	4.85	1.35	7.07	1.11	1.99	2.70	0.40	(100.00) (1259)

Source : Field Survey, 2004-05.

the marginal landholding class, after cultivation majority of workers are engaged as animal husbandry workers, weavers and shopkeepers. In the small landholding class, weavers and teachers are major occupational categories in the non-agriculture occupations, and in the highest land size class cultivators, animal husbandry workers and teachers are the major occupational groups.

The higher the income groups the dependence on agriculture related occupations is lower and the opposite is also true. In the lowest income group, the major occupational groups are cultivators and animal husbandry workers in the agriculture based occupation, and labourers in the non-agriculture based occupation; while in the highest income groups, major non-agriculture occupations are teachers and transport workers. Generally, in the higher income groups, the dominant income groups are teachers, shopkeepers, clerical and related workers and weavers; while at the lower end, the concentration is more as weavers, shopkeepers and labourers.

(iv) Occupation and industrial distribution of workforce

The occupational distribution of workers by industry shows a very narrow base with little diversification across industry groups. Majority of workers are concentrated in a few industry groups. The cultivators, animal husbandry workers, teachers, shopkeepers & sales workers, weavers and transport workers are concentrated in a single industry; the remaining occupational groups are bunched into a few industry groups (Table 6.14). Such a narrow base of occupation across industry groups is an indicative of a less diversified base of the hill economy.

V. Employment Status of Workers

The structure of employment status of the workers also shows divergences across caste, landholding size and income groups among the non-migrants. Across caste groups, some differences in the share of self-employment are observed, but the variations are not that large. The Brahmins and Scheduled Castes have lower share as compared to other caste groups. The share is over 80 per cent in all the social

Table 6.14 : Occupation and Industrial Distribution of Workers (UPS)

Occupation group	*Agriculture and allied activities*	*Manu-facturing*	*Electricity, water, gas, etc.*	*Construction*	*Trade, hotel & restaurant*	*Transport & commu-nication etc.*	*Finance, business activities, etc.*	*Public admin., education,*	*All*
Cultivator	100.00	0.00	0.00	0.00	0.00	0.00	0.00	0.00	100.00 (488)
Animal husbandry worker	100.00	0.00	0.00	0.00	0.00	0.00	0.00	0.00	100.00 (26)
Technical and managerial worker	0.00	0.00	0.00	66.67	0.00	0.00	0.00	33.33	100.00 (6)
Teacher	0.00	0.00	0.00	0.00	0.00	0.00	0.00	100.00	100.00 (32)
Clerical and related worker	0.00	0.00	15.38	11.54	0.00	19.23	0.00	53.85	100.00 (26)
Shopkeeper & sales worker	0.00	0.00	0.00	0.00	100.00	0.00	0.00	0.00	100.00 (59)
Service worker	0.00	0.00	0.00	0.00	87.50	0.00	6.25	6.25	100.00 (16)
Weaver and related worker	0.00	100.00	0.00	0.00	0.00	0.00	0.00	0.00	100.00 (55)
Other production worker	0.00	71.43	21.43	0.00	7.14	0.00	0.00	0.00	100.00 (14)
Transport worker (drivers)	0.00	0.00	0.00	0.00	0.00	100.00	0.00	0.00	100.00 (24)
Labourer and other workers	26.67	0.00	0.00	73.33	0.00	0.00	0.00	0.00	100.00 (30)
Total	66.92 (522)	8.33 (65)	0.90 (7)	3.72 (29)	9.49 (74)	3.72 (29)	0.13 (1)	6.79 (53)	100.00 (780)

Note : Figures in parenthesis show absolute number.
Source : Field Survey, 2004-05.

groups, and the share of females is extraordinarily high, primarily because of their huge contribution in agriculture and allied activities.

Brahmins have the highest share in regular employment, both for males and females, and relatively low share in casual employment (Table 6.15). The Scheduled Castes have the highest share in casual employment (both for males and females), particularly for the illiterates and less educated. Interestingly, the reservation policy has also helped them (better educated ones) in regular employment, particularly in public employment. Scheduled Tribes have the lowest share in casual employment and a fairly high share in regular employment, next to Brahmins. The reason for the high share in regular employment is primarily due to the reservation policy that has helped them in getting regular employment, and in fact, literacy among Scheduled Tribes in the hill region is fairly high. While the 'other caste' is the most backward caste and their share in regular employment is the lowest, but in casual employment the share is high, next to Scheduled Castes.

By and large, the Scheduled Castes and the 'other caste' are socially and economically disadvantaged sections, primarily because of their low literacy levels as compared to other social groups.

It has been observed that the size of land class generally shows a positive relationship with the share of self-employment and a negative relationship with that of casual employment. The share of regular employment is highest in the small land- holding class, and lowest in the highest land size class; in other landholding classes, the variations are low.

In the higher income groups, the share of self-employment declines and that of regular employment increases, while casual employment shows a secular decline, both for males and females.

As regards employment status of educational levels, over one-fifth of illiterate workforce is engaged in self-employment activities and majority of them are females. A large majority of workforce (81%) has educational levels of high school and below. Conversely, in the regular employment status, a large majority of workforce (80%) has educational attainments of high school and above. A little over one-third (34%) male workforce and half (50%) of female workforce in the regular employment status has educational levels of graduate and above. None of the female worker has been reported in regular

Table 6.15 : Employment Status of Non-migrant Workers across Household Feature (UPSS)

Household features	*Self-employed*			*Regular*			*Casual*			*Total*		
	Male	*Female*	*Person*	*Male*	*Female*	*Person*	*Male*	*Female*	*Person*	*Male*	*Female*	*Person*
Social category												
Brahmin	76.83	97.09	88.11	20.73	1.94	10.27	2.44	0.97	1.62	100.00	100.00	100.00
Kshatriya	84.45	98.31	92.19	11.59	0.96	5.65	3.96	0.72	2.15	100.00	100.00	100.00
SC	74.70	92.11	83.02	10.84	1.32	6.29	14.46	6.58	10.69	100.00	100.00	100.00
ST	82.14	98.70	91.73	14.29	1.30	6.77	3.57	0.00	1.50	100.00	100.00	100.00
Others	80.00	100.00	94.87	10.00	0.00	2.56	10.00	0.00	2.56	100.00	100.00	100.00
Land class												
Landless	76.00	100.00	86.05	12.00	0.00	6.98	12.00	0.00	6.98	100.00	100.00	100.00
Marginal	81.89	97.56	90.73	12.63	0.98	6.06	5.47	1.46	3.21	100.00	100.00	100.00
Small	80.39	96.49	88.89	17.65	3.51	10.19	1.96	0.00	0.93	100.00	100.00	100.00
Medium	87.50	100.00	94.44	12.50	0.00	5.56	0.00	0.00	0.00	100.00	100.00	100.00
Income group (MPCI)												
Up to Rs. 250	79.07	88.00	83.87	0.00	0.00	0.00	20.93	12.00	16.13	100.00	100.00	100.00
Rs. 250 to 500	86.58	98.52	93.47	2.68	0.00	1.14	10.74	1.48	5.40	100.00	100.00	100.00
Rs. 500 to 1000	89.74	100.00	95.53	8.21	0.00	3.58	2.05	0.00	0.89	100.00	100.00	100.00
Rs. 1,000 to 2,500	69.62	97.19	84.23	29.75	2.81	15.48	0.63	0.00	0.30	100.00	100.00	100.00
More than Rs. 2,500	57.14	82.35	70.97	42.86	17.65	29.03	0.00	0.00	0.00	100.00	100.00	100.00
Educational levels												
Illiterates	12.50	38.95	28.36	2.74	0.00	2.47	23.33	77.78	35.90	100.00	100.00	100.00
Primary	12.28	12.45	12.38	8.22	0.00	7.41	10.00	22.22	12.82	100.00	100.00	100.00
Middle	19.96	19.18	19.49	10.96	0.00	9.88	36.67	0.00	28.21	100.00	100.00	100.00

Table 6.15 : (*Contd...*)

High school	28.29	15.37	20.54	26.03	12.50	24.69	16.67	0.00	12.82	100.00	100.00	100.00
Intermediate	16.45	9.52	12.29	15.07	37.50	17.28	13.33	0.00	10.26	100.00	100.00	100.00
Graduate and above	8.77	4.54	6.23	34.25	50.00	35.80	0.00	0.00	0.00	100.00	100.00	100.00
Technical	1.75	0.00	0.70	2.74	0.00	2.47	0.00	0.00	0.00	100.00	100.00	100.00
Development status of blocks												
Less developed	80.75	96.23	89.51	10.94	1.16	5.41	8.30	2.61	5.08	100.00	100.00	100.00
Developed	82.31	98.87	91.37	14.97	1.13	7.40	2.72	0.00	1.23	100.00	100.00	100.00
Total	81.57	97.57	90.47	13.06	1.14	6.43	5.37	1.29	3.10	100.00	100.00	100.00
	(456)	(683)	(1139)	(73)	(8)	(81)	(30)	(9)	(39)	(559)	(700)	(1259)

Note : Figures in parentheses show absolute figures.

Source : Field Survey, 2004-05.

employment status having educational level below high school. Over one-third (36%) illiterate workforce has casual employment status and a large majority of them (78%) are females. None of the casual workers has educational levels beyond graduate and above. The employment status by levels of education clearly indicates that a large proportion of those having regular employment status (80%) are educated up to high school and above levels, while majority of workers (77%) having casual employment status have educational levels of middle and below. Also, a large majority of self-employed status workers (81%) have educational levels below high school.

Across status of development blocks, relatively developed blocks have higher share of self-employment and regular employment, both for males and females; while the share of casual employment is lower as compared to the less developed blocks.

VI. Multiplicity of Employment

People deriving income from different sources are the most common features in poor regions, as single source of income is hardly sufficient to eke out a living. It is common to our understanding that poor regions are generally characterised by underdevelopment in terms of its resource base, both physical and human; and various factors reinforce it to remain at a low equilibrium trap in the development trajectory. This is more so in agrarian economies, which have abundance of labour supply that is manifested in terms of huge unemployment and underemployment of various forms. Lewisian development framework precisely deals with this kind of phenomenon, and it is argued that the industrialisation process would eventually help to graduate the backward economy into development process with a near-full employment. However, such development hypothesis has not proved correct and people in poor regions continue to have their dependence on multiple sources of income for living, despite the fact that there has been industrial development in other regions. Engagement in multiple sources of livelihoods is most common not only among poor, but also among relatively well-off households in order to augment their incomes. The two different processes seem to work simultaneously; first as a deliberate household strategy to enhance income as an involuntary response to crisis situation (Stark, 1991), and secondly, to seize opportunities as a means of accumulation (Davies, 1996). In poor regions, people depend on various sources of employment primarily because of sustenance in the absence of any sole option of employment. Multiple economic activities are most pervasive and widespread among different groups of population in the survey areas in Uttarakhand, manifesting symptoms of a backward economy.

It can be observed that about 26 per cent among all the workers have a single or sole activity, while a large majority of them (74%) resort to more than one activity (Table 6.16). It is most common feature in all the blocks and districts in the hill region of the state.

Table 6.16 : Multiplicity of Employment among All Workers

Household feature	*One employment*	*Two employments*	*Three employments*
Social category			
Land class (acre)			
Landless	67.44	23.26	9.30
Marginal	24.68	51.56	23.76
Small	19.63	52.34	28.04
Medium	27.78	50.00	22.22
Income group (MPCI)			
Up to Rs. 250	19.35	62.37	18.28
Rs.250 to 500	23.58	55.40	21.02
Rs.500 to 1,000	29.82	46.86	23.32
Rs.1,000 to 2,500	24.70	47.32	27.98
More than Rs.2,500	22.58	51.61	25.81
Educational levels			
Illiterate	25.44	52.96	21.60
Primary	19.08	50.00	30.92
Middle	24.48	50.21	25.31
High school	29.73	49.81	20.46
Intermediate	31.01	47.47	21.52
Graduate and above	22.00	54.00	24.00
Technical	20.00	30.00	50.00
Development status of blocks			
Less developed	27.70	52.62	19.67
Developed	23.92	48.77	27.31
Total	25.76	50.64	23.61
Number of workers	324	637	297

Source : Field Survey, 2004-05.

Apparently, there does not seem to be operating a single pattern of activities in different workers' group; rather different processes seem to work simultaneously that govern the pluri-activity of the work pattern. These processes are governed by the opportunities and options of livelihood available to the population that are operating in several labour markets. Interestingly, the landless workers seem to be depending primarily on a single activity (68%), probably because of the lack of opportunities and alternative options available to them due to entry barriers in the labour markets. This could precisely be the reason for the lowest household incomes in this group. In the case of marginal and small landholding classes, dependence on multiple activities increases in order to augment their household income. However, in the medium landholding classes, such dependence on multiple activities declines, probably because, these households have relatively higher incomes from agriculture and animal husbandry and other assured sources of incomes such as pension and other incomes. The income group (MPCI) shows an inverted U-shape curve – initially, dependence on a singular employment rises with the rise in income levels, but later tapers off as income levels rise. In the higher income group, dependence on a single employment declines and that of multiple employments rises. Educational levels also indicate somewhat similar pattern – initially, dependence on a single employment increases as we move to higher levels of education (up to intermediate), but then, such dependence gradually declines and multiplicity of employment rises.

Such a huge dependence on multiple activities seems to be a common feature in the mountain economy where cultivation is not only seasonal but the income from this activity is low (20%) which is not enough to provide livelihood beyond a few months in a year. Animal husbandry, though more or less a perennial activity, at best supplements the household incomes. Therefore, multiple engagements in activities form an important part of the household income strategy. Though there does not seem to be any perceptible variations in the activities pursued in the developed and less developed blocks, yet developed blocks show greater intensity of multiplicity of activities. This kind of phenomenon indicates that relatively better livelihood opportunities are available in the developed blocks.

This finding of the present study dispel the commonly derived hypothesis that poor households derive their incomes from multiple sources as part of their survival strategy, while the relatively better-off households and individuals depend on few and stable sources of incomes (Ellis, 2000; Gordon & Craig, 2001). It can be argued that in relatively less developed regions, lack of opportunities constrict the people to enter into the labour market, while in the relatively developed region, people seize the existing opportunities for better remunerated activities.

The extent of multiplicity of employment increases steeply among principal workers. About 92 per cent principal workers are such who are engaged in more than one type of employment. In the rural areas, such multiplicity of activities is not an unusual phenomenon and almost every principal worker is engaged either in cultivation or in animal husbandry activity. Even those who are in regular employment such as teachers and clerical & related workers, have also been working in agriculture and animal husbandry activities to a very large extent. In fact, all the principal workers in the category of the clerical & related workers, labourers and other production workers are also working as cultivators and animal husbandry workers in their subsidiary capacity. The extent of multiplicity of employment is relatively low among the transport workers (drivers), weavers, other workers and shopkeepers & sales workers (Table 6.17).

VII. Extent of Employment and Unemployment

(i) Average days of employment

Average annual days of employment available in agriculture and allied activities are indeed very low in the hill areas. This is primarily due to the nature of hill agriculture that poses insurmountable problems in terms of small, fragmented and scattered landholdings, where only limited traditional crops can be yielded in a year and there is little scope for any expansion either in terms of area or bringing about a radical technological transformation. Irrigation facilities are very low and agriculture is mainly rainfed; the use of HYVs and other chemical

Table 6.17 : Principal Workers pursuing Subsidiary Activities

Principal occupation	*Subsidiary occupation*							
	None	*Cultivator*	*Animal husbandry worker*	*Weaver and tailors*	*Labourers*	*Shop-keeper & sales worker*	*Other workers*	*Total*
Teacher	9.38	84.38	3.13	3.13	0.00	0.00	0.00	100.00
Clerical & related worker	0.00	96.15	0.00	3.85	0.00	0.00	0.00	100.00
Shopkeeper and sales worker	16.95	77.97	5.08	0.00	0.00	0.00	0.00	100.00
Service worker	6.25	81.25	0.00	0.00	0.00	6.25	6.25	100.00
Cultivator	3.48	15.98	68.24	0.82	7.99	0.61	2.87	100.00
Animal husbandry worker	15.38	65.38	0.00	7.69	11.54	0.00	0.00	100.00
Weaver and tailor	32.73	60.00	1.82	0.00	3.64	1.82	0.00	100.00
Other production worker	0.00	85.71	7.14	7.14	0.00	0.00	0.00	100.00
Transport worker (driver)	33.33	66.67	0.00	0.00	0.00	0.00	0.00	100.00
Labourers	0.00	75.86	20.69	0.00	3.45	0.00	0.00	100.00
Other workers	27.27	63.64	9.09	0.00	0.00	0.00	0.00	100.00
Total	8.21	37.95	44.36	1.15	5.77	0.64	1.92	100.00
No. of workers	64	296	346	9	45	5	15	780

Source : Field Survey, 2004-05.

fertilizers is also very low resulting in the low productivity and low returns from agricultural crops. All these factors lead to limited food availability and hence, food insecurity that is a common feature in many parts of the hill districts in the state. Although people seem to be working very hard in agriculture activities, yet it does not provide employment beyond few months in a year. On an average, agriculture and allied activities provide employment for about 56 days in a year for males, while for females, it provides employment for about 106 days (Table 6.18). Generally, in the context of hill agriculture, animal husbandry provides more days of employment than agriculture, particularly for females. This is principally due to the fact that agriculture is a seasonal activity, while animal husbandry is a perennial activity operated throughout the year. It is quite intriguing to observe that despite heavy engagement in agriculture and allied activities, it

Table 6.18 : Average Annual Person Days of Employment per Worker

District	*Block*	*Agriculture and allied activities (days)*	
		Male	*Female*
Almora	Hawalbagh	57	118
	Salt	53	108
Pithoragarh	Dharchula	56	114
	Berinag	55	102
T.Garhwal	Chamba	63	112
	Kirtinagar	51	99
Uttarkashi	Bhatwari	60	88
	Dunda	54	98
Social category	Brahmin	56	108
	Kshatriya	59	113
	SC	45	80
	ST	58	87
	Others	55	94
Land class	Landless	35	70
	Marginal	55	105
	Small	63	114
	Medium	74	118
Age-group	0-5	-	-
	6-14	25	40
	15-29	41	100
	30-59	70	121
	59+	62	93
Development status of blocks	Developed	59	109
	Less developed	54	102
Total		56	106

Source : Field Survey, 2004-05.

provides employment not beyond two months for males and three and half months for females. Across development blocks, one does not find any perceptible variation. However, it can be observed that the relatively developed blocks have generally higher person days' employment as compared to less developed blocks. The reasons for higher days of employment in the relatively developed blocks could be due to more areas under horticulture crops leading to commercialisation of agriculture (vegetables, fruits and other non-food crops) as compared to relatively less developed blocks (Table 6.19). This supports our hypothesis that diversification into high-value crops promotes more employment and incomes.

Table 6.19 : Areas under Horticultural Crops (Acres)

District	*Block*	*Gross cropped area*	*Area under horticulture*	*Per cent*
Almora	Hawalbagh	64.33	23.89	27.08
	Salt	85.85	0.00	0.00
Pithoragarh	Berinag	72.57	5.47	7.00
	Dharchula	61.10	12.50	16.98
T.Garhwal	Chamba	20.75	18.41	47.01
	Kirtinagar	46.63	2.66	5.39
Uttarkashi	Bhatwari	12.00	24.83	67.42
	Dunda	32.62	1.95	5.64
Total		395.85	89.71	22.66

Source : Field Survey, 2004-05.

Across caste category, Scheduled Castes have the lowest person days' employment available in agriculture and allied activities, both for males and females; the highest being for upper castes such as Kshatriyas and Brahmins. SCs have the lowest days of employment available in agriculture and allied activities primarily because of the lowest asset base (land, for example) that makes difficult to enhance their endowment base, hence it provides limited days of employment in agriculture and animal husbandry. STs have a relatively higher days of employment, available particularly for males, despite the fact that they have also lower per capita land available for cultivation. The reason for this is that STs are generally settled in higher altitude where agro-pastoralism is dominant and certain horticultural crops such as potato, radish, apple, *razma* (kidney beans) are grown in abundance along with animal husbandry (herd of sheep and goats) that provides raw wool for making woollen garments, which is the traditional occupation of the tribal community. Availability of days of employment and size of land class are positively correlated – higher the land size class the higher is the availability of man-days and rightly so. This clearly indicates that land endowment is the most important factor in determining the intensity of employment of a worker. Higher size of land obviously helps to employ more number of people, whatsoever the level of productivity of the people engaged in it.

Across age groups, days of employment increase gradually in the higher age-group, lowest being in the age-group 6-14 and highest in the age-group 30-59, but then drops in the highest age-group 59 and above, and rightly so. It is common in the hill districts that even school-going children (age-group 6-14) help their parents in agriculture and allied activities, particularly in harvesting season when the pressure of work increases. Female children are more conspicuously engaged than their male counterparts. While agriculture is a seasonal activity, animal husbandry is a perennial one that requires constant care and rearing. Children perform various activities such as taking animals for grazing, giving fodder and water, cutting fodder and bringing from the fields, cleaning the place of stay of these animals and sometimes milching the cows and buffaloes, etc. It is also observed that relatively developed blocks have higher intensity of employment than the less developed ones, albeit marginally. The intensity of employment therefore (per person annual person days of employment) is very low in the hill areas of Uttarakhand.

Average days of employment in casual works turns out to be about 51 days for males and 43 days for females per annum (Table 6.20). It is very low indeed and the nature of employment is such that people have to find multiple sources of employment to eke out their living. Casual employment is mostly available in construction activities both in private and public domain. Most common activities are construction of individual houses and construction of roads, culverts, bridges and buildings in public works. However, it needs to be mentioned here that such jobs in the construction sector are not necessarily available within the boundaries of villages. The fact is that some of these jobs are available through daily commuting to nearby towns and rural bazaars. However, the access to such jobs for females is somewhat limited owing to various socio-economic barriers. It is interesting to note that the days of employment in casual works is higher in relatively less developed blocks and female casual employment in particular is distinctly visible only in less developed blocks. For females, casual employment in construction activities is not much encouraged due to social and cultural inhibitions; however, casual works in agricultural activities is most common for landless and poor families. But, agriculture and allied activities does not ensure such employment beyond few days in weeding and harvesting season,

Table 6.20 : Average Annual Person Days of Employment per Worker

District	*Block*	*Casual employment (days)*	
		Male	*Female*
Almora	Hawalbagh	59	-
	Salt	42	30
Pithoragarh	Berinag	62	-
	Dharchula	43	-
T.Garhwal	Chamba	53	-
	Kirtinagar	54	45
Uttarkashi	Bhatwari	40	-
	Dunda	57	42
Social category	Brahmin	42	25
	Kshatriya	53	40
	SC	56	49
	ST	33	-
	Others	37	-
Land class	no land	48	35
	>0 <= .50	52	44
	>.50 <= 2.50	52	-
	>2.50 <= 5.0	45	-
Age-group	0-5	-	-
	6-14	-	-
	15-29	47	44
	30-59	51	43
	59+	56	34
Development status of blocks	Developed	49	-
	Less developed	53	43
Total		51	43

Source : Field Survey, 2004-05.

and casual employment in construction then becomes an economic necessity particularly for poor and landless families. It can be seen that females are employed in construction activities only in two blocks, which are relatively less developed varying from 30 to 45 days' employment. Across social category, dependence on casual employment is highest (in terms of days of employment available) among SCs (both males and females) followed by Kshatriyas and Brahmins in that order; and STs, on the other hand, have lowest days of employment available. One of the reasons for higher and lower dependence on casual type of employment is lack of assets (land, for example), low educational levels and non-availability of other regular sources of earnings that force people to go for casual type of jobs involving hard physical labour. Also, such opportunities are most likely available in rural bazaars and nearer to block and district headquarters. Proximity to such centres is perhaps the most important factor that generates variety of development activities and earning sources in construction and related activities. Dependence on casual works is higher among the sub-marginal, landless and marginal landholding classes and dependence on such employment gradually declines in the higher land size classes, and the fact is that none from the medium landholding class is available for casual type of employment. No one is reported to have engaged in casual employment up to 14 years and the days of casual employment for males increase with higher age groups while these decline for females.

(ii) Extent of unemployment

Unemployment rate among the principal workers works out to be about 11.5 per cent in the state, which is indeed very high by any measure. As usual, male unemployment rate is exorbitantly higher at about 19.1 per cent, while female unemployment is noted to be very low at 3.3 per cent.*

The reason for such a gap between unemployment rate among males and females is obvious in the context of hill region, where women do not seem to be either available or seek for work due to their heavy engagement in cultivation and household chores, and men on the other hand have rather limited involvement in agricultural activities that does not make them gainfully employed. Precisely, this is the reason that makes a huge gap between the unemployment rate among males and females. However, there are variations in the intensity of unemployment across blocks, caste groups, land class, age groups and across developed and less developed blocks (Table 6.21). Unemployment rate varies from minimum 7.0 per cent to maximum 21.3 per cent, and relatively less developed blocks within the districts

---

* The Planning Department, Government of Uttarakhand has estimated the rate of unemployment in the state to be 21.63 per cent in the terminal year of the Tenth Five Year Plan i.e. 2006-07, and the increment of unemployed persons to be 3.10 lakh (Directorate of Economics and Statistics, Uttarakhand, 2007).

are showing much higher rate of unemployment barring Hawalbagh block. Unemployment rates among males are much higher; and surprisingly in two less developed blocks, namely Berinag and Kirtinagar, unemployment rates are exceptionally higher – to the extent of 38.3 and 40.5 per cent respectively. One of the reasons for lower unemployment rates in the developed blocks is relatively higher share of cropped area under horticultural crops that probably have kept people gainfully employed.

Across social classes, the unemployment rate is highest among SCs (14.8%) and lowest among STs (3.2%) and 'others' (4%). Female unemployment rate is reportedly very low while male unemployment rate is disproportionately high. Male unemployment rate is high for upper classes as well (12-13%). Across land classes, landless category has the highest intensity of unemployment (14.3%) followed by small (12.8%) and marginal landholding classes (11.2%). Male unemployment is almost equal in these three categories (19-20%). Medium landholding class has comparatively lowest unemployment rate. Unemployment rate is positively correlated to the levels of education – higher the levels of education higher are the rates of unemployment and the opposite also seems to be true. Unemployment rate in the lower categories of education is indeed very low, particularly among illiterates and primary levels; and none of the females is reported as unemployed even up to high school level of education. The reason seems to be obvious as people with low educational and skill levels cannot afford to remain unemployed for any length of time and they have to necessarily find some source of livelihood for sustenance, whatsoever wages they get. Surprisingly, unemployment rates are very high among females in the graduate and post-graduate levels, and in fact, unemployment rate at post-graduate levels are extraordinarily higher. Understandably, there has been expansion and ease of access to higher educational institutions for girls through private examination system that has helped to acquire higher education even staying at home. But such education without employable and marketable skills has resulted in a huge unemployment, particularly among females. As usual, unemployment rate is highest among the young age group population (15-29), and the intensity of unemployment is higher in the less developed blocks than that of the developed ones (Table 6.21).

Table 6.21 : Unemployment Rate among Non-migrants (principal workers)

District	*Block*	*Unemployment rate*		
		Male	*Female*	*Total*
Almora	Hawalbagh	14.86	9.43	12.60
	Salt	13.46	0.00	6.73
Pithoragarh	Dharchula	10.00	3.77	7.08
	Berinag	38.33	4.84	21.31
T. Garhwal	Chamba	19.30	0.00	10.28
	Kirtinagar	40.54	1.69	16.67
Uttarkashi	Bhatwari	11.11	2.22	7.07
	Dunda	13.11	3.85	8.85
Social category	Brahmin	20.63	4.92	12.90
	Kshatriya	20.60	3.50	12.21
	SC	24.24	2.04	14.78
	ST	4.08	2.27	3.23
	Others	10.00	0.00	4.00
Land class	Landless	19.05	7.14	14.29
	Marginal	19.06	3.21	11.23
	Small	20.45	2.94	12.82
	Medium	14.29	0.00	9.09
Educational levels	Illiterate	3.23	0.00	0.76
	Primary	1.85	0.00	0.87
	Middle	16.67	0.00	9.62
	High school	22.02	0.00	15.48
	Intermediate	34.85	8.00	27.47
	Graduate	36.84	21.43	32.69
	Post-graduate	24.00	69.23	39.47
	Technical	18.18	0.00	18.18
Age-group	0-5	0.00	0.00	0.00
	6-14	0.00	0.00	0.00
	15-29	56.82	11.67	35.32
	30-59	4.65	0.00	2.25
	59+	0.00	0.00	0.00
Development status of blocks	Developed	13.88	3.98	9.42
	Less developed	25.24	2.67	13.56
All		**19.12**	**3.29**	**11.46**

Source : Field Survey, 2004-05.

The survey results clearly show that the problem of unemployment is huge in the hill districts of the state, and it is more pronounced among relatively less developed blocks than the relatively developed ones. Unemployment is concentrated more among lower social classes and among landless classes. The intensity of unemployment is visible among the higher educated categories.

VIII. Income and Earnings

Income is the outcome of diverse portfolio of activities perused by the rural households from cultivation, animal husbandry, casual wage works, regular wage works and other non-farm activities, etc. Income is accrued from these diverse activities as well as from transfer income such as pension and remittances. The sources of income are determined by various factors such as assets base of the households (farm and non-farm), level of education and skill attainment and employment opportunities available.

Cultivation and animal husbandry activities together contribute to about one-third (32%) of the total income. Regular employment is yet another important source of income that constitutes about 25 per cent followed by self-employment activities contributing to about 21 per cent income. Transfer income (pension) also contributes substantively (10%) and remittances account for about 9 per cent to the total household income. Uttarakhand hill economy has been postulated as a highly dependent economy on remittance income and often termed as money-order economy. However, this line of argument does not seem to bear much empirical evidences. Income from casual income (including government programmes) is minuscule contributing only 2 per cent in the share of household income (see Figure 6.4).

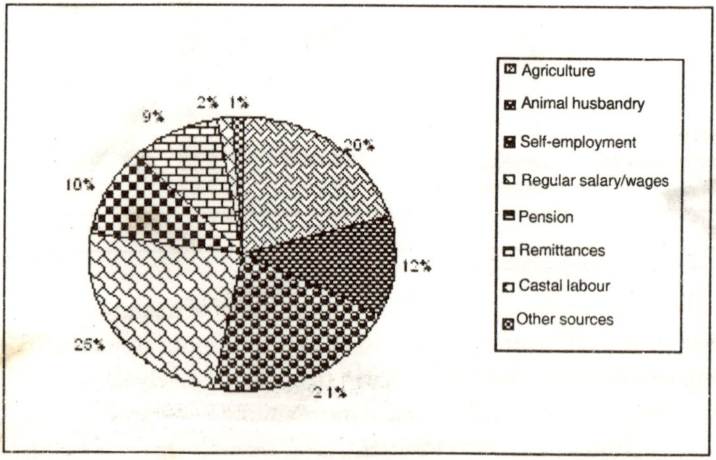

Fig. 6.4 : Proportion of Income from different Sources

The share of income varies across household features from different activities. It can be observed that the household income of Brahmins and STs is significantly higher as compared to other social categories. Average annual income of 'other caste' is lowest followed by SCs (see Figure 6.5).

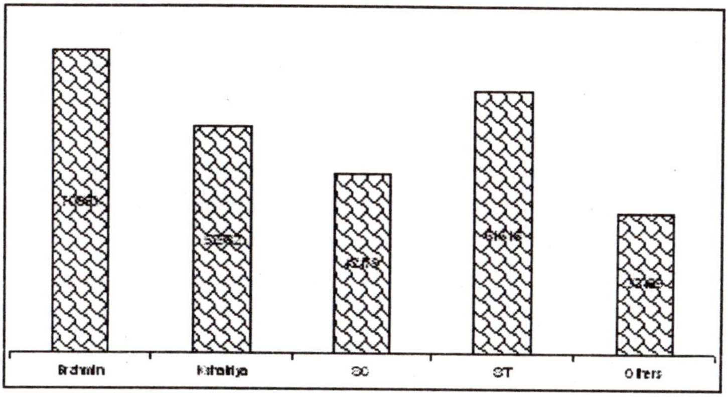

Fig. 6.5: Average Annual Income by Social Category

Majority of Brahmins and STs are associated with highest income quintiles, while the poorest social groups –SCs and 'other caste'– are concentrated in the lowest income quintiles, and Kshatriyas are in the middle quintiles (Table 6.22).

Table 6.22 : Distribution of Household Population by Social Category and Income Quintile Groups

Per capita income quintile group	*Brahmin*	*Kshatriya*	*SC*	*ST*	*Others*
Bottom	14.55	23.14	25.93	2.00	33.33
2nd	14.55	20.09	33.33	6.00	41.67
3rd	14.55	21.40	20.37	18.00	25.00
4th	21.82	20.09	9.26	34.00	0.00
Top	34.53	15.28	11.11	40.00	0.00
Total	**100.00**	**100.00**	**100.00**	**100.00**	**100.00**

Source : Field Survey, 2004-05.

The household income of the Brahmins comes from more stable

source of earnings such as regular jobs (41%) and pension (20%), which is an assured and a perennial source of income (Table 6.23). Major sources of income for the STs are self-employment (40%), agriculture and animal husbandry (31%) and regular salary income (18%). For Kshatriyas, agriculture and animal husbandry constitute the principal source of household income (35%) followed by regular salary income (22%); while in the case of SCs, the major sources of incomes are agriculture and animal husbandry (33%), self-employment (23%) and regular salary income (22%). Income from casual wages is highest for the Scheduled Castes as compared to other social groups (6.5%). For the 'other caste', the principal sources of incomes are agriculture and animal husbandry (contributing 47%) and remittances (27%). The main reasons for variations of income across castes are linked closely to the asset base of the households, and also educational and skill levels that have overarching influence on income generating capacity. As regards the land size classes, the share of income from agriculture increases with the land size class. For landless, the main sources of income are self-employment (49%), regular income (25%) and from remittances (15%). Though income accruing from casual employment is very low, yet the share is highest for landless category. In the higher land size classes, the share of income from self-employment declines and that of regular income rises. The income from animal husbandry forms an important source of income for marginal and small landholding size classes, contributing about 12 to 10 per cent of the total income respectively. In the lowest monthly per capita income group (up to Rs. 250), income from animal husbandry forms an important source of income, contributing 38 per cent of the total income and rightly so, as in the poorer family it is an instant source of cash income. The other important sources of income are casual wage income (22%) (including government programmes) and remittances (11%). Also, for the next income group (Rs. 250 to 500), animal husbandry, casual wage incomes and remittance contribute to 23, 7 and 18 per cent respectively. In the higher income groups (Rs. 500 to 1,000, 1,000 to 2,500 and more than Rs. 2,500), the share of income from agriculture and animal husbandry, casual wage incomes, remittances declines, and that the

Table 6.23 : Share of Income from Different Sources

Household features	*Sources of income*									
	Agriculture	*Animal husbandry*	*Self-employment*	*Regular salary/wage*	*Casual*	*Govt. programme*	*Pension*	*Remit-tances*	*Others*	*Total*
Social category										
Brahmin	10.77	9.07	11.77	41.37	0.49	0.18	20.10	5.64	0.60	100.00
Kshatriya	21.75	13.41	19.14	21.63	1.58	0.33	10.08	11.44	0.66	100.00
SC	22.64	10.16	22.92	21.86	6.50	1.02	6.72	6.63	1.56	100.00
ST	22.23	8.79	40.13	18.31	0.65	0.29	0.78	5.84	2.98	100.00
Others	29.56	17.24	13.69	7.47	1.02	0.66	0.00	26.63	3.73	100.00
Land class										
No land	0.69	4.88	49.34	24.84	2.40	0.25	0.00	15.27	2.33	100.00
Marginal	19.86	12.26	21.38	23.80	1.93	0.42	9.89	9.39	1.06	100.00
Small	24.89	10.20	13.22	27.39	0.60	0.12	15.19	7.59	0.80	100.00
Medium	40.30	9.27	0.00	36.37	0.00	0.12	0.00	9.39	4.55	100.00
Income group (MPCI)										
Up to Rs. 250	22.29	38.39	2.34	0.00	18.03	3.64	3.00	10.56	1.76	100.00
Rs. 250 to 500	26.16	22.78	15.81	3.62	6.16	1.02	5.19	18.22	1.05	100.00
Rs.500 to 1,000	25.35	13.56	23.33	9.34	1.53	0.40	13.14	12.21	1.14	100.00
Rs.1,000 to 2,500	16.33	6.91	23.91	36.95	0.06	0.07	9.02	5.55	1.20	100.00
More than Rs.2,500	7.59	3.71	10.61	61.58	0.00	0.00	13.37	2.51	0.63	100.00
Educational levels										
Illiterates	21.60	14.36	20.58	20.41	2.41	0.37	7.33	11.62	1.33	100.00
Primary	26.55	12.60	18.45	17.65	1.88	0.60	9.91	11.32	1.04	100.00

Table 6.23 : (contd...)

Middle	24.07	12.37	23.89	18.19	2.91	0.50	9.19	8.20	0.67	100.00
High school	17.67	11.01	25.40	25.18	1.05	0.31	9.47	8.53	1.37	100.00
Intermediate	19.92	10.87	22.35	18.82	0.82	0.23	19.20	6.43	1.36	100.00
Graduate and above	6.67	3.98	12.92	57.60	0.00	0.10	11.66	6.09	0.98	100.00
Technical	5.61	15.34	43.84	5.72	0.00	0.41	17.15	11.91	0.00	100.00
Status of development blocks										
Less developed	8.20	12.43	19.38	26.11	2.48	0.38	16.76	13.54	0.72	100.00
Developed	29.70	11.12	22.46	23.12	1.18	0.38	4.56	6.03	1.46	100.00
Total	20.09	11.71	21.08	24.45	1.76	0.38	10.02	9.39	1.13	100.00

Source : Field Survey, 2004-05.

share from regular incomes and pension increases. As regards the levels of education and share of incomes from different sources, the share from cultivation, animal husbandry, casual income and remittances declines and that of the share from regular income and pension rises. The income from self-employment generally declines with higher level of education barring technical education, where the share of income from self-employment is very high; and from regular source the share is low which is plausible. Relatively less developed blocks show comparatively low share of income from cultivation and self-employment, but higher proportion of income from regular income, casual income, pension and remittances as compared to developed blocks. The major sources of income in the developed blocks are agriculture and animal husbandry (41%), regular income (23%) and self-employment (22%).

(i) Household income

It can be observed that a large number of households (78%) in the less developed blocks have concentration in the monthly income group below Rs.1,000 while in the relatively developed blocks (77%) have concentration in the monthly per capita income of Rs.1,000 and above barring Chamba block, which is showing similar case of less developed block. Overall, 36 per cent households have monthly per capita income less than Rs. 500, which is closer to the poverty line threshold (Table 6.24). Across social category, SCs and 'other caste' have fairly large proportion (ranging from 56 to 75%) of their household population falling in the income groups of less than Rs. 500. The STs and Brahmins, on the other hand, have high concentration in the higher income groups (Rs.1,000-2,500 and Rs. 2,500 and above). In the lower land size classes, the concentration of households is more at the lower ends of income, while in the higher land size classes the opposite is true. It can be observed that the relatively developed blocks are showing a low proportion of their households in the low income groups and less developed blocks are showing a relatively higher proportion of households in the lower income groups.

Maximum disparities across income groups measured as co-

Table 6.24 : Household Incomes Across the Blocks, Social Class and Land Class

Household feature	*Monthly per capita income group (Rs.)*					
	Up to Rs.250	*Rs.250 to 500*	*Rs.500 to 1,000*	*Rs.1,000 to 2,500*	*More than Rs.2,500*	*CV*
Development Blocks						
Berinag	7.69	23.08	51.92	13.46	3.85	96.30
Bhatwari	0.00	6.00	50.00	42.00	2.00	120.00
Chamba	2.27	47.73	47.73	2.27	0.00	126.65
Dharchula	0.00	12.00	32.00	54.00	2.00	114.24
Dunda	11.54	30.77	36.54	21.15	0.00	73.42
Hawalbagh	1.96	25.49	33.33	35.29	3.92	80.07
Kirtinagar	24.00	40.00	18.00	12.00	6.00	65.19
Salt	19.61	37.25	11.76	23.53	7.84	57.33
Social category						
Brahmin	5.45	21.82	32.73	32.73	7.27	66.19
Kshatriya	10.48	27.07	37.12	21.83	3.49	66.59
SC	11.11	44.44	29.63	14.81	0.00	86.47
ST	0.00	8.00	36.00	54.00	2.00	119.37
Others	8.33	66.67	25.00	0.00	0.00	140.07
Land class						
No land	6.25	31.25	37.50	25.00	0.00	80.89
>0 <= .50	14.39	34.53	36.69	14.39	0.00	77.16
>.50 <= 2.50	6.16	24.17	34.12	31.28	4.27	69.97
>2.50 <= 5.0	0.00	13.33	36.67	36.67	13.33	80.79
>5.0 <= 10.0	0.00	50.00	0.00	50.00	0.00	136.93
Status of blocks						
Less developed	15.61	32.68	29.76	17.56	4.39	57.28
Developed	1.03	22.05	40.51	34.36	2.05	90.59
Total	8.50	27.50	35.00	25.75	3.25	67.41

Source : Field Survey, 2004-05.

efficient of variation occur in case of Chamba (126.65), Bhatwari (120.00) and Dharchula (114.24), and the lowest in Salt (57.33) and Kirtinagar (65.19) blocks. The widest disparity across social category is noted among the 'other caste' and STs with the coefficient of variations of 140.07 and 119.37 respectively. Medium landholding classes appear to have the highest degree of variability with a co-efficient of variation of 136.93. The variability between developed and less developed blocks also appears to be significant.

There are various factors that determine the income levels of the household in a typical hill economy like Uttarakhand. These factors are asset base (primarily, land), educational and skill levels, proportion of non-farm employment, social groups, infrastructure index of villages and out-migration, etc. In order to ascertain causality, a regression model has been fitted with a view to understanding the relationships between predictor variables and dependent variable. Results of the regression are presented in the next chapter. The regression results show that the per capita income of the household is positively and significantly affected by the proportion of farm employment, area under horticulture, educational attainments, per capita land owned, migrant status of the worker (shifted) and development index of the villages. While the proportion of dependents, households belonging to social groups, casual labour households and migrant households (short- and long-term) have negative impacts on per capita income of household with a statistically significant sign of the coefficients of all the variables are in accordance with our *a priori* intuition.

(ii) Wages

There are variations in wages across different occupations and locations, and also within occupations and locations. Variability in wages is widespread in the hill region and wages are typically governed by different factors that have causal relationships with a number of socio-economic variables. Not only the demand for and supply of labour that govern the wage rate in the hill areas, but also caste-class composition of the village, interpersonal relationship, locational advantages and barriers, geographical mobility of the labour, etc. play their roles in deciding the wage structure and wage rates. Owing to hill specificities, the labour market is not developed and imperfections often create rigidity in the labour market.

As may be noted from Table 6.25 that mean earnings per day varies widely across blocks and occupations. The returns to labour input for rural households are very low in agriculture and allied activities. It can be observed that the mean earnings per day from this activity is Rs.56, which is the lowest; while for self-employed in the non-farm activities it is the highest at Rs.145 per day, which is higher by over two and half times as compared to those engaged in agriculture

Table 6.25 : Per Person Day Mean Earnings for Self-employed and Casual Wage Works

Household features	*Agriculture and allied activities*			*Self-employed in non-farm activities*			*Casual wage*		
	Male	*Female*	*Person*	*Male*	*Female*	*Person*	*Male*	*Female*	*Person*
Blocks									
Berinag	26.13	27.73	26.67	173.19	110.00	170.74	83.35	66.52	73.84
Bhatwari	182.47	232.88	187.21	111.02	70.12	104.62	81.33	85.91	81.71
Chamba	75.22	82.61	76.63	152.86	250.00	157.74	80.66	73.71	79.34
Dharchula	61.63	50.60	59.42	158.55	92.22	149.26	58.23	74.42	61.48
Dunda	49.27	47.49	49.05	130.71	119.35	129.55	85.27	59.84	82.50
Hawalbagh	61.97	53.72	60.02	195.71	170.00	191.34	76.92	74.40	76.50
Kirtinagar	36.69	37.93	37.03	291.84	129.31	231.41	64.78	68.76	65.43
Salt	26.90	32.55	28.43	156.38	228.57	172.71	80.11	88.97	82.21
Social cotegory	Brahmin	37.62	33.20	36.91	200.45	110.00	196.57	79.93	76.00
79.34	Kshatriya	57.57	43.12	53.60	184.09	192.15	185.32	77.10	65.44
74.37	SC	60.74	105.09	66.99	135.32	79.76	129.53	76.69	79.21
77.02	ST	110.22	76.20	103.52	103.54	71.06	98.53	72.50	87.28
75.98	Others	76.85	55.79	70.74	229.17	0.00	229.17	58.00	92.28
81.54	**Land class**								
No land	43.35	35.21	40.57	108.82	112.50	108.94	78.02	80.19	78.80
>0 <= .50	59.20	54.37	57.87	128.39	98.55	122.76	74.36	72.13	73.92
>.50 <= 2.50	56.41	43.80	53.80	169.75	138.03	166.78	80.49	70.69	78.80
>2.50 <= 5.0	70.28	50.26	63.09	155.51	178.95	164.10	66.15	69.41	67.15
>5.0 <= 10.0	74.52	0.00	74.52	0.00	0.00	0.00	58.00	0.00	58.00
Status of blocks									
Less developed	31.50	32.19	31.69	153.36	162.50	154.58	76.65	70.34	75.21
Developed	84.52	70.72	81.81	144.76	103.67	139.00	76.84	75.83	76.68
Total	58.70	47.66	56.08	148.09	125.77	145.01	76.73	72.04	75.80
CV	77.83	95.72	79.40	32.08	44.14	23.56	12.61	13.01	10.62

Source : Field Survey, 2004-05 .

and allied activities. Even per person-day earnings are much higher for labour input engaged in casual wage works (Rs.76 per day) as compared to agriculture and allied activities. It can be observed that 75 per cent workforce engaged in agriculture and allied activities contributes to about 32 per cent income and the per capita mean earnings from this source is the lowest, which validates our hypothesis that this sector has limited potential for absorption of growing labour force productively.

One of the reasons for the lowest mean earnings in agriculture and allied activities is the subsistence nature of agriculture that does not produce any surplus for the market and hence generates no demand for labour. Agriculture labour market is by and large absent or dormant in the hill area and mostly family labour is used, or sometimes exchange labour is also practised. However, in the case of shortage of family labour, hired labour is used particularly in ploughing, weeding and harvesting seasons, but the practice of hired labour is not widely prevalent. Such work is generally undertaken by the uneducated and unskilled labour and often one has to work at low or depressed wages. But it is also observed that despite low overall mean earnings per day, developed blocks (namely, Bhatwari, Chamba, Dharchula and Hawalbagh) have higher average mean earnings per day as compared to less developed blocks. Bhatwari block is showing exceptionally high mean earnings at Rs.187 per day. The reason for the high mean earnings in the developed blocks is primarily due to relatively large area under horticulture crops (see Table 6.19) that has high cash income values and requires more labour inputs per unit of output. Across social category, Scheduled Tribes have the highest mean earnings followed by 'other caste' and SCs. The land size class and earnings are positively correlated; the higher the size of landholding higher is the mean earnings per worker. Average mean earnings for males are higher by about one-fifth than females indicating a disparity in mean earnings. The developed blocks have about two and half times higher mean earning per day than the less developed blocks.

Mean earnings per day in the case of self-employed in non-farm activities are observed to be much higher than agriculture and allied activities (61% higher). Earnings are slightly higher (10%) in relatively less developed blocks than the developed ones. Across social category, 'other caste' has the highest mean earnings, while STs have the lowest. The reason for the highest mean earnings for the 'other caste' is primarily due to low average man-days' employment as compared to other caste groups. Mean earnings generally rise as the size of the land class increases but in the highest land size class, there is no earnings from this source, probably because the land assets engage family labour in cultivation.

In the case of casual wage labour in non-farm activities, there are some variations in the mean earnings across blocks, social category, land size class and between males and females, but the overall wage variations between males and females are not that large. The average mean earnings per day are noted to be higher than the minimum prescribed wages for unskilled workers. The coefficient of variation is highest in agriculture and allied activities followed by self-employed in non-farm activities, and least in the case of casual wage labour in non-farm activities (Table 6.25).

IX. Conclusion

Typically, the hill economy of Uttarakhand is showing a higher female LFPR than that of males, which has distinctly come out from the field data and also corroborates with the Census and NSS data. Survey data also show that there is a highly gender biased work structure in the rural areas of the state, as women overwhelmingly work in agriculture-related occupations while their male counterparts work in non-farm occupations. This is primarily because of the subsistence farming economy with a precarious industrial base. Agriculture assumes the predominant sector for employment for a large majority of labour force with little surplus generating capacity, and by and large, this sector acts as a labour sponge, in particular for the females. Non-farm activities constituting petty trade and business, wage/ salaried employment and casual employment, particularly in construction activities have been mostly male dominated activities and females have a very low share in these activities. Generally, developed blocks show a higher share in non-farm activities than the less developed ones, primarily because of the diversification from cereal crops to horticulture crops and better infrastructure, and proximity to block and district headquarters.

Agriculture is increasingly becoming an uneconomic family enterprise, and employment opportunities outside agriculture are extremely limited, particularly for females. Within the farm sector there is a huge incidence of underemployment in terms of unutilised labour time, and majority of rural households are forced to diversify their activities as a part of their survival strategy to cope with seasonality and uncertainty of production. Unemployment rate turns out to be 11.5 per cent in aggregate terms, which is indeed very high. Male unemployment rate, in particular, is alarmingly high at 19 per cent, while the female unemployment rate is comparatively much lower at 3 per cent. The survey results clearly show that the problem of unemployment is huge in the hill districts of the state, and it is more pronounced among relatively less developed blocks than the relatively developed blocks. Unemployment is concentrated more among lower social classes and among landless class. The intensity of unemployment is visible among the higher educated categories.

Females are disproportionately represented in the agriculture and allied activities (90%) with low levels of education and a very high proportion of them are illiterates. Generally, low levels of education of a large majority of workers in rural areas of Uttarakhand, particularly of females, have implications from the policy perspective for their employability outside agriculture. Their low educational levels can hardly help them to secure employment outside agriculture.

Average annual days of employment available in agriculture and allied activities are indeed very low in the hill areas. Although people seem to be working very hard in agriculture activities, yet it does not provide them employment beyond few months in a year. On an average, agriculture and allied activities provide employment to about 56 days in a year for males, while for females it provides for about 106 days' employment.

However, it can be observed that the relatively developed blocks have generally higher person days' employment as compared to less developed blocks. The reasons for higher days of employment in the relatively developed blocks could be due to more areas under horticulture crops leading to commercialisation of agriculture (vegetables, fruits and other non-food crops) as compared to relatively less developed blocks. Availability of casual employment is less than two months (50 days) in a year, providing on an average 51 days' employment for males and 43 days' for females.

Multiple economic activities are most pervasive and widespread among different groups of population in the survey areas in Uttarakhand, manifesting symptoms of a backward economy. The average annual income of the households is estimated to be low with significant variations across different castes and land size classes. The principal reasons for variations of income across the castes are linked closely to the asset base of the households and also educational and skill levels that have overarching influence on income generating capacity. It can be observed that the relatively developed blocks are showing low proportion of their population in low income groups and less developed blocks are showing relatively higher proportion of population in the lower income groups. In order to know the determinants of household income, regression model has been fitted with a view to understanding the relationships between predictor variables and monthly per capita income (MPCI) as a dependent variable. Signs of the coefficients of all variables are in accordance with our *a priori* intuition. Coefficients of all explanatory are significant at 1 per cent level of significance except social group, which is significant at 5 per cent level of significance and the proportion of females, which is insignificant even at 10 per cent level of significance. This implies that most of the regressors taken into our consideration are important determinants of monthly per capita income. Also the p value of the F statistic suggests that jointly all the regressors are significant (Chapter 7).

A large majority of workforce (75%) engaged in agriculture and allied activities contribute to about one-third of the total household income and mean earnings from this source is lowest as compared to that of self-employed and casual wages in non-farm activities that validates our hypothesis that this sector has limited potential for absorption of growing labour force productively.

7

Pattern of Non-farm Employment and Rural Enterprises

I. Non-farm Employment and Incomes: The Size and Share

Rural non-farm sector has generated a lot of interests among the policy-makers and practitioners, both from the point of view of generating employment and a way out of poverty removal. The recent research has shown that the rural households are engaged in a variety of non-farm activities to generate income as a complement and supplement of the farm incomes. The income from this source is quite substantial ranging from about 40 per cent in Latin American countries to 45 per cent in Africa and 35 per cent in Asia (Reardon *et al.*, 2001). Pluriactivity is widespread and pervasive in rural economy with heterogeneity in terms of activities and incomes from numerous non-farm pursuits. The overriding emphasis on the non-farm sector is obvious in the wake of a low labour absorption capacity in the farm sector, and income from the non-farm sources has been higher than that of the farm sector (For detailed review, see Chapter 3). The research questions invoke us to explore the diversities, heterogeneity, and the access to and determinants of diversification in order to formulate strategies and aid policies.

Conceptually, rural non-farm sector constitutes a large number of activities outside agriculture sector (crop cultivation) such as auxiliary, rural industrial sector, services and non-agricultural labour in creation of public infrastructure. Such a broader definition of rural non-farm sector encompassing all non-agricultural activities excluding crop husbandry is desirable, as this would capture all aspects of rural diversification. However, for simplicity, we have taken all the activities in the non-farm sector excluding agriculture sector (crop cultivation) and allied activities, broadly conforming a standard definition of non-farm sector. We have endeavoured to capture all the non-farm activities within household enquiry frame disaggregated across spatial units, social category, land size class, and income groups classified by industry groups. Also, the non-farm sector has been grouped broadly into three segments – casual wage earners, regular/salaried workers and self-employed in rural enterprises with a view to capturing the heterogeneity and inequities across different segments of the non-farm sector.

It has been noted that the households reporting non-farm employment is quite pervasive across all blocks and social groups, and it forms a major source of livelihood in the hill economy. One of the principal reasons for such a huge participation by the households in non-farm activities is that the hill agriculture is by and large traditional and cannot be expected to provide sustainable employment and earning opportunities. Precisely, this is the reason why the intensity and incidence of participation in non-farm activities at household level is extraordinarily high. This is true across all development blocks, social classes and land classes. Some variations across land size class and social category is distinctly noted. Households belonging to landless and marginal land classes are relatively disadvantaged in terms of household assets and incomes, and are reporting a higher dependence on non-farm pursuits. The share of income from the non-farm source forms a significant proportion of the household income. It can be observed that overall 66 per cent households depend on non-farm activities for livelihood that accrues 68 per cent of the household income* (Table 7.1). It can be seen that the relatively less developed blocks have much higher dependence on the non-farm employment and incomes than the developed ones. Nearly 78 per cent households in the less developed blocks depend on non-farm employment contributing 79 per cent of their household incomes. Conversely, in relatively developed blocks, 54 per cent households depend on non-farm employment contributing 59 per cent of the household incomes. Relatively developed blocks like Bhatwari,

* Similar kind of study conducted in the North-East and Eastern Himalayas shows that non-farm activities generate on an average 60 per cent of the rural households' income and 73 per cent of the households are engaged in non-farm activities (Micevska and Rahut, ICRIER, 2008).

Chamba, Hawalbagh and Dharchula have a relatively high share (67, 47, 27 and 17% area respectively) under horticulture out of the gross cropped area (Chapter 6, Table 6.19). Horticulture crops (fruits and vegetables) are grown for the market and contribute significantly to the household income. The household income in these blocks is much

Table 7.1 : Household Shares in Non-farm Employment and Incomes

Household feature	*Farm HHs*	*Non-farm HHs*	*Share of non-farm income*
Blocks			
Berinag	17.31	82.69	77.14
Bhatwari	60.00	40.00	44.57
Chamba	47.73	52.27	48.84
Dharchula	32.00	68.00	69.74
Dunda	19.23	80.77	85.89
Hawalbagh	45.10	54.90	65.48
Kirtinagar	18.00	82.00	81.84
Salt	35.29	64.71	72.48
Social Category			
Brahmin	21.82	78.18	80.16
Kshatriya	35.37	64.63	64.85
SC	37.04	62.96	67.21
ST	34.00	66.00	68.98
Others	50.00	50.00	53.19
Land class (acre)			
No land	12.50	87.50	94.43
>0 <= 0.50	33.09	66.91	68.02
>.50 <= 2.50	34.60	65.40	67.82
>2.50 <= 5.0	40.00	60.00	64.91
>5.0 <= 10.0	75.00	25.00	50.43
Income group (MPCI)			
Up to Rs. 250	64.71	35.29	41.29
Rs. 250 to 500	50.00	50.00	50.77
Rs. 500 to 1,000	29. 29	70.71	61.72
Rs. 1000 to 2,500	17.48	82.52	76.25
More than Rs. 2,500	0.00	100.00	88.70
Development status of blocks			
Less developed	22.44	77.56	79.36
Developed	46.15	53.85	59.17
All	34.00	66.00	68.20
	(136)	(264)	

Notes : (i) Figures in brackets show number of HHs.
(ii) Non-farm household is defined as the household whose main source of income from non-farm pursuits is 50 per cent or more.

Source : Field Survey, 2004-05.

higher than the less developed blocks barring Chamba, where household income dips primarily because of the concentration of 'other caste' who are the poorest and whose household and per capita incomes are the lowest. Across social category, dependence of Brahmin households in the non-farm employment and incomes is highest, while the 'other caste' has least dependence on this source and consequently the average household income is highest for the former case and lowest for the later category. Land size classes are consistently showing a negative relationship with non-farm employment and incomes – the higher the landholding sizes the lower is the dependence of the households on non-farm employment and incomes. Income classes show a positive relationship – the higher the levels of household incomes the higher is the dependence on the non-farm employment. Regression results corroborate the findings and are found to be statistically significant.

II. Pattern of Non-farm Employment

Non-farm employment constitutes about one-third (33%) share in total employment (UPS), male workforce accounting for about 58 per cent and female workforce about 11 per cent. Non-farm employment pattern shows a distinct pattern across household features. Four development blocks (namely, Hawalbagh, Dharchula, Bhatwari and Dunda) show a relatively higher share of non-farm employment as compared to the overall average share in non-farm employment (Table 7.2). The reasons for the relatively higher share of non-farm employment in four blocks are different in some ways.

Dharchula block accounts for the highest share (48.6%) in non-farm employment. Out of five villages selected, two are tribal villages, which are far-off from the block and tehsil, and their primary occupation is cultivation of crops (like paddy, Himalayan wheat, *fagopyrum tataricuem*, Tibetan barley, maize, potato and radish) and animal husbandry. Along with these, they are engaged in traditional occupation of weaving/knitting as household enterprise. The other villages are normal villages (non-tribal) and located near the block headquarters. The two different processes seem to work simultaneously for the substantively higher share in the non-farm employment. First, in tribal villages, the share of non-farm employment is higher primarily

Table 7.2 : Employment Share in Non-farm Sectors by Industry

Household features	*UPS*		
	Male	*Female*	*Person*
Blocks			
Berinag	56.76	1.69	22.92
Bhatwari	37.50	34.09	35.87
Chamba	45.65	0.00	21.88
Dharchula	66.67	29.41	48.57
Dunda	71.70	18.00	45.63
Hawalbagh	63.49	2.08	36.94
Kirtinagar	54.55	5.17	18.75
Salt	60.00	1.92	28.87
Social category			
Brahmin	66.00	3.45	32.41
Kshatriya	53.30	2.82	26.09
SC	66.00	12.50	39.80
ST	65.96	69.77	67.78
Others	33.33	0.00	12.50
Land size class (acre)			
No land	82.35	69.23	76.67
>0 <= .50	62.26	9.22	31.98
>.50 <= 2.50	57.35	8.60	32.00
>2.50 <= 5.0	42.86	12.12	27.94
>5.0 <= 10.0	16.67	0.00	10.00
Educational level			
Illiterate	42.37	9.95	17.31
Primary	32.69	8.20	19.47
Middle	50.00	12.12	32.39
High School	59.30	10.87	42.42
Intermediate/ Sr. Secondary	83.72	13.04	59.09
Graduate and above	88.37	26.67	72.41
Technical	88.89	0.00	88.89
Income group (MPCI)			
Up to Rs. 250	30.43	2.94	14.04
Rs. 250 to 500	43.14	4.07	21.78
Rs. 500 to 1,000	53.04	8.33	28.19
Rs. 1,000 to 2,500	78.15	24.00	53.42
More than Rs. 2,500	88.89	27.27	55.00
Development status of blocks			
Less developed	62.42	6.40	29.79
Developed	54.50	16.05	36.15
Total	57.88	10.92	33.08

Source : Field Survey, 2004-05.

because of their engagement in household manufacturing enterprises. Second, in normal villages, the locational advantages play an important role in providing wage and self-employment opportunities. In addition, some villages grow off-season vegetables that find a ready market at Dharchula, which is the block and tehsil headquarters. Female share in the non-farm employment is also high (29%), primarily because of the engagement of Scheduled Tribe females in weaving and manufacturing of woollen garments as household enterprise.

The other block with a higher share in non-farm employment (45.6 %) is Dunda. The primary reason for such a higher share in Dunda block is due to the locational advantage – the sample villages fall closer to the block and district headquarters (Uttarkashi) that has helped village economies to find some ready markets for their products (viz. vegetables and milk); and closer linkages to these market centres (through commuting) has spurt certain self-employment opportunities for the local economy. Since the block and district are the nodal centres for developmental activities, proximity to such centres creates better opportunities for employment and income for the local population. The other reason is that one sample village, (Dunda) has a relatively higher proportion of tribal population, and most of the male as well as female workforce is engaged in manufacturing of woollen garments as household enterprise.

The other block is Hawalbagh that has nearly 37 per cent share in non-farm employment. The sample villages fall in the three different locations in each block; two villages were drawn each from middle distance and very far-off locations from the block headquarters, while one village was chosen nearer to the block headquarters in order to have representativeness. The distant villages are mainly depending on crop cultivation, fruit cultivation and animal husbandry. The other occupations are small trading and public employment. The two villages, which are closer to the block headquarters, have a relatively higher share in trading, public employment and self-employment. These two villages also grow off-season vegetables that find a ready market at the district headquarters (Almora), which is 10 to 12 km from the block. The proximity to block and district centres has created better opportunities for self-employment, transport business and petty trade as well. The middle-distance villages show a combination of activities that have been observed in the long-distance and closer to block villages.

Bhatwari is yet another block in Uttarkashi district that has 36 per cent share in the non-farm employment. The two villages chosen in the block are located at a higher altitude, are relatively far-off from the market centres (block and district headquarters), and are inhabited by tribal population. Traditional cereal-based crops have limited scope due to high altitude and therefore fruits (apple, for example), vegetables (potato) and kidney beans (*razma*) are grown which have a good market, though there are transport bottlenecks, particularly in long winters when the area is cut-off from the rest of the state due to heavy snowfall. Also, tribal population (both males as well as females) are mostly engaged in traditional household enterprises (weaving) that provide them a perennial source of employment and income. While male workforce is engaged in trading as well as in household enterprises, the females are mostly engaged in household manufacturing enterprises. This is the reason that makes the share of females in non-farm activities very high which is almost equal to that of males (34%).

In other blocks, the share of non-farm employment is low ranging from 19 to 29 per cent and female share is abysmally low. The labour market is highly segmented for both the sexes, particularly in less developed blocks, where males do have a fairly large share in non-farm activities while females have a minuscule share in most of the non-farm activities.

Across social category, the Scheduled Tribes have the highest share in non-farm employment followed by the Scheduled Castes, Brahmins and Kshatriyas, while the 'other caste' has the lowest share. Scheduled Tribes have the highest share primarily because of their high dependence on household manufacturing and trading, owing to typical physiographic conditions that do not allow a diversified cropping pattern, and resultantly limited crops can be grown in a year. Precisely, this is the reason why the share in the non-farm employment is very high both for males and females; while in the case of Scheduled Castes, low landholding size compels them to pursue non-farm employment.

The 'other caste' has the lowest share in non-farm employment due to their low asset base and low educational levels. However, the share of non-farm employment across males and females shows a divergent situation – the males have a relatively higher share while their female counterparts have a low share, barring the Scheduled Tribes. Male share is about two-thirds in the case of Brahmins, Scheduled Castes and Scheduled Tribes, a little over half for Kshatriyas and about one-third in the case of 'other caste'. The share of females is very low, nil in the case of 'other caste' and a little over one-tenth in the case of Scheduled Castes.

The land size classes and the share of non-farm employment clearly show a negative relationship, while the educational levels and income levels are positively correlated with that of non-farm employment.

The developed blocks generally show a higher share in non-farm employment than the relatively less developed blocks. The share of females in non-farm employment shows a higher degree of variability in the less developed blocks as compared to the relatively developed blocks. A distinct pattern of segmented labour market is noted wherein male workforce is increasingly tend to dominate in the non-farm employment pursuits, while their female counterparts are overwhelmingly represented in cultivation activities.

III. Sectoral Composition of Non-farm Employment by Industry

Table 7.3 has been reproduced from Chapter 6 (Table 6.8) to analyse the sectoral share more from the gender perspective. The disaggregated picture of non-farm employment by industry group clearly shows that the access of females to most of the non-farm employment is extremely limited barring in certain cases. Such a clear segmentation is noted throughout the discussion on the employment structure. There is diversity in the share of non-farm employment across spatial units, social groups, activities and sexes. Why there is an abysmally low share of females in most of the non-farm activities and also why there is a fairly high share in some of the non-farm activity in certain social category? The reasons for such a wide diversity primarily lie with locational, socio-economic and cultural factors. It is observed from Table 7.3 that only about 11 per cent of female workforce is

Table 7.3 : Structure of Employment by Industry Groups across Blocks

Block	*Sex*	*Agriculture and allied activities*	*Manufacturing*	*Electricity, water, gas etc.*	*Construction*	*Trade, hotel & restaurant*	*Transport & Communication*	*Finance, business activities etc.*	*Pub. admin., education etc.*	*Total non-farm employment*	*Total*
Hawalbagh	Male	36.51	4.76	0.00	11.11	19.05	6.35	1.59	20.63	63.49	100.00 (63)
	Female	97.92	0.00	0.00	0.00	0.00	0.00	0.00	2.08	2.08	100.00 (48)
	Person	63.06	2.70	0.00	6.31	10.81	3.60	0.90	12.61	36.93	100.00 (111)
Salt	Male	40.00	2.22	6.67	8.89	26.67	4.44	0.00	11.11	60	100.00 (45)
	Female	98.08	0.00	0.00	1.92	0.00	0.00	0.00	0.00	1.92	100.00 (52)
	Person	71.13	1.03	3.09	5.15	12.37	2.06	0.00	5.15	28.85	100.00 (97)
Dharchula	Male	33.33	5.56	0.00	9.26	20.37	20.37	0.00	11.11	66.67	100.00 (54)
	Female	70.59	25.49	0.00	0.00	1.96	0.00	0.00	1.96	29.41	100.00 (51)
	Person	51.43	15.24	0.00	4.76	11.43	10.48	0.00	6.67	48.58	100.00 (105)
Berinag	Male	43.24	2.70	5.41	10.81	27.03	5.41	0.00	5.41	56.77	100.00 (37)
	Female	98.31	0.00	0.00	0.00	1.69	0.00	0.00	0.00	1.69	100.00 (59)

Table 7.3 : (contd...)

	Person	77.08	1.04	2.08	4.17	11.46	2.08	0.00	2.08	22.91	100.00 (96)
Chamba	Male	54.35	8.70	2.17	0.00	23.91	8.70	0.00	2.17	45.65	100.00 (46)
	Female	100.00	0.00	0.00	0.00	0.00	0.00	0.00	0.00	0	100.00 (50)
	Person	78.13	4.17	1.04	0.00	11.46	4.17	0.00	1.04	21.88	100.00 (96)
Kirtinagar	Male	45.45	4.55	0.00	18.18	9.09	4.55	0.00	18.18	54.55	100.00 (22)
	Female	94.83	0.00	0.00	0.00	0.00	0.00	0.00	5.17	5.17	100.00 (58)
	Person	81.25	1.25	0.00	5.00	2.50	1.25	0.00	8.75	18.75	100.00 (80)
Bhatwari	Male	62.50	14.58	0.00	0.00	14.58	6.25	0.00	2.08	37.49	100.00 (48)
	Female	65.91	29.55	0.00	0.00	0.00	0.00	0.00	4.55	34.1	100.00 (44)
	Person	64.13	21.74	0.00	0.00	7.61	3.26	0.00	3.26	35.87	100.00 (92)
Dunda	Male	28.30	22.64	1.89	7.55	13.21	3.77	0.00	22.64	71.7	100.00 (53)
	Female	82.00	14.00	0.00	0.00	0.00	0.00	0.00	4.00	18	100.00 (50)
	Person	54.37	18.45	0.97	3.88	6.80	1.94	0.00	13.59	45.63	100.00 (103)
Developed	Male	45.50	8.06	0.47	5.69	19.43	10.43	0.47	9.95	54.5	100.00 (211)

Table 7.3 : (contd...)

	Female	83.94	13.47	0.00	0.00	0.52	0.00	0.00	2.07	16.06	100.00 (193)
	Person	63.86	10.64	0.25	2.97	10.40	5.45	0.25	6.19	36.15	100.00 (404)
Less developed	Male	37.58	9.55	3.82	10.19	19.75	4.46	0.00	14.65	62.42	100.00 (157)
	Female	93.61	3.20	0.00	0.46	0.46	0.00	0.00	2.28	6.4	100.00 (219)
	Person	70.21	5.85	1.60	4.52	8.51	1.86	0.00	7.45	29.79	100.00 (376)
Total	Male	42.12	8.70	1.90	7.61	19.57	7.88	0.27	11.96	57.89	100.00 (368)
	Female	89.08	8.01	0.00	0.24	0.49	0.00	0.00	2.18	10.92	100.00 (412)
	Person	66.92	8.33	0.90	3.72	9.49	3.72	0.13	6.79	33.08	100.00 (780)

engaged in non-farm activities mainly because of their overwhelming presence in agriculture and allied activities (89%), while the share of male workforce in non-agricultural pursuits is very high (58%). The share of female workforce in most of the non-farm activities is almost negligible barring manufacturing and public services.

In manufacturing, the share of females is reported as fairly high (8%) and is almost equal to that of males (8.7%). Most of the manufacturing employment is concentrated in three blocks (namely, Dharchula, Bhatwari and Dunda), and the share of females is much higher than males in former two blocks. The sample villages selected in these blocks have tribal population who are mostly engaged in household manufacturing enterprises. Manufacturing woollen garments has been the traditional occupation of the tribal population and most of the family members are engaged in family enterprises; while in other blocks, the share in manufacturing employment is very low. In electricity, gas and water; the overall share is negligible (less than 1%) and females have virtually no share in it. In construction, the overall share is about 4 per cent and females have an abysmally low share (0.24%). Most of such employ-ment opportunities are male dominated in the hill region primarily because of cultural factors that inhibit females to participate in such labour markets. The relatively less developed blocks have much higher share in most of the construction employment than the relatively developed blocks.

Trade, hotel and restaurant is an important segment that provides employment for almost one-tenth of the workforce. This segment consists of variety of activities constituting largely small retail shops dealing both in food and non-food items, small tea stalls and restaurants (*dhabas*). Males dominate in such activities and the share of female employment is very low (less than a half per cent). The less developed blocks show a higher proportion of trade related employment (10.40%) than the developed blocks (8.50%). Transport and communication account for about 4 per cent employment, which is virtually dominated by males. Finance, business activities, etc. has a negligible employment share (0.13%), primarily because this segment is by and large inactive and dormant in rural economy of the state. Yet another important segment is public administration, education services, etc. that accounts for about 8 per cent employment. Male employment constitutes about 12 per cent and female employment accounts for 2 per cent. The relatively less developed blocks have a higher share of male and female employment in public services.

(i) Non-farm employment by social category

Diversities in the share of non-farm employment exist not only across spatial units but across social category also. As noted, the share of males in non-farm employment is over five times higher than that of females, and within social category there is a huge divergence between the relative shares of males and females. Scheduled Tribes have the highest share in non-farm employment (68%) with little or no divergence between male and female workforce, while the 'other caste' has the lowest share (12.50%) with an extreme form of divergence across sexes. In other social groups, the gender gap in terms of share in non-farm employment is significantly higher (Table 7.4).

In the case of Scheduled Tribes, the share of females in non-farm employment is higher (70%) than the males (66%). As argued earlier, the main reason for such a high share in non-farm employment among Scheduled Tribes is primarily due to their substantive share in manufacturing and trade. The STs have mostly been trading community, weaving and manufacturing of woollen garments being their traditional occupation. While male workforce has a substantially high share in manufacturing (27%) followed by trade (19%), and transport & communication (11%); the female workforce is almost entirely engaged in household manufacturing activities (67%). The share in public administration, education etc. is about 3.3 per cent (male accounting for 4 and female for 2%, respectively) and construction provides employment to 2 per cent – entirely to the male workforce.

While on the other extreme, the 'other caste' who are the most disadvantaged section, have the lowest overall share in non-farm employment (12.5%) with no share of females. The share in trade is 8.3 per cent followed by manufacturing (4.2%). Males are engaged in low remunerative types of trading and manufacturing activities that fetch low incomes. Most of the manufacturing activities pertain to metal related works, while trading activities relate to petty shops etc.

Scheduled Castes have a fairly high share in non-farm employment

Table 7.4 : Structure of Employment by Industry Groups across Social Groups

Industry	*Brahmin*			*Kshatriya*			*SC*			*ST*			*Others*		
	Male	*Female*	*Person*	*Male*	*Female*	*Person*	*Male*	*Female*	*Person*	*Male*	*Female*	*Person*	*Male*	*Female*	*Person*
Agriculture and allied activities	34.00	96.55	67.59	46.70	97.18	73.91	34.00	87.50	60.20	34.04	30.23	32.22	66.67	100	87.50
Farm	34.00	96.55	67.59	46.70	97.18	73.91	34.00	87.50	60.20	34.04	30.23	32.22	66.67	100	87.50
Manufacturing	6.00	0.00	2.78	1.89	0.00	0.87	22.00	8.33	15.31	27.66	67.44	46.67	11.11	0	4.17
Electricity, water, gas etc.	2.00	0.00	0.93	2.36	0.00	1.09	2.00	0.00	1.02	0.00	0.00	0.00	0.00	0	0.00
Construction	2.00	0.00	0.93	8.02	0.40	3.91	16.00	0.00	8.16	4.26	0.00	2.22	0.00	0	0.00
Trade, hotel & restaurant	16.00	0.00	7.41	22.64	0.81	10.87	10.00	0.00	5.10	19.15	0.00	10.00	22.22	0	8.33
Transport & communication	6.00	0.00	2.78	8.96	0.00	4.13	4.00	0.00	2.04	10.64	0.00	5.56	0.00	0	0.00
Finance, business activities etc.	0.00	0.00	0.00	0.00	0.00	0.00	2.00	0.00	1.02	0.00	0.00	0.00	0.00	0	0.00
Public admin., education etc.	34.00	3.45	17.59	9.43	1.61	5.22	10.00	4.17	7.14	4.26	2.33	3.33	0.00	0	0.00
Non-Farm	66.00	3.45	32.41	53.30	2.82	26.09	66.00	12.50	39.80	65.96	69.77	67.78	33.33	0.00	12.50
Total	100.00	100.00	100.00	100.00	100.00	100.00	100.00	100.00	100.00	100.00	100.00	100.00	100.00	100	100.00
Nos.	50	58	108	212	248	460	50	48	98	47	43	90	9	15	24

Source : Field Survey, 2004-05.

(40%), males accounting for about 66 per cent and females 12.5 per cent. Males are mostly engaged in manufacturing (22%), in particular; manufacturing of agriculture implements and machineries, and construction activities (16%), trade & hotels (10%) and public services (10%). In fact, they have the highest share in construction activities across all social groups. Their share in public administration and education is fairly high primarily due to reservation in public employment. However, access of females to non-farm employment opportunities are limited to manufacturing (8%) and public administration, education etc. (4%). Reservation in public employment is also visible in the case of Scheduled Caste females.

Brahmins and Kshatriyas have 32 and 24 per cent share respectively in non-farm employment. Male share is much higher (66%) than female share (53%), with a broader participation base in almost every segment of activity, while the share of females is very low (3 to 4%) with a limited access to only a few types of activities. Brahmins have been the most forward and educated class in the hill areas of Uttarakhand and participation of males is noted in every branch of non-farm activities. Male share in pubic administration, education etc. is highest (34%) among all social categories, primarily because of their high educational status. The other important activities are trade, hotel & restaurant (16%), manufacturing, transport & communication (accounting for 6% each). Female share in non-farm activity is extremely low (3.4%) and all of them are engaged in public administration, education etc. Kshatriyas have the highest share in trade, hotel & restaurant (11%) followed by public administration, education etc. (5%); transport & communication (4%) and construction (4%). Predominant activities for male workers are trade, hotel & restaurant (23%); public administration, education etc.; transport & communication (9% each) and construction (8%); while for females the access is limited to public administration, education etc; trade, hotel & restaurant; and construction activities to an awfully low extent.

IV. Non-farm Employment by Occupation

Here, we analyse the non-farm employment by occupation, both principal and principal & subsidiary statuses. According to principal status, the share of non-farm employment is at 34.10 per cent,* while according to principal & subsidiary status, the share turns out to be about 24.63 per cent (Table 7.5).

According to principal status, 58 per cent males and about 13 per cent females are engaged in various non-farm occupations. Males' presence is conspicuous as shopkeepers & sales workers (15.5%); clerical & related workers (7.0%); teachers (6.8%); transport workers (6.5%); weavers & related workers (6.0%) and labourers (5.7%). Service workers and other production workers constitute 4.3 and 3.8 per cent respectively. The share of technical and managerial workers is indeed very low (1.6%). Females' absence is conspicuous in most of the non-farm activities primarily because of their pre-dominant engagement in agriculture and allied activities. Weavers & related workers is the major group that constitutes 8 per cent, the other occupation groups are labourers (2%), teachers (1.9%), shopkeepers and other workers (about a half per cent each). Barring weaving & related activities, females' share in other non-farm activities is very low. For males, white-collar jobs (such as teachers, clerical and managerial workers) and shopkeepers & salesmen form the dominant share in non-farm activities. The other emerging non-farm activity is transport segment which is gaining importance primarily due to accessibility of credit for purchasing vehicles. The educated youth who could not get foothold in the regular employment prefer self-employment in transport sector.

The share of non-farm workers declines from 34 per cent (UPS) to about 25 per cent according to principal and principal & subsidiary status (UPSS), male share falls sharply to about 17 percentage points, while female share declines marginally to a little over 1 percentage point. All males, who are non-workers by their principal occupation, are engaged in agriculture and allied activities in their subsidiary

* A minor difference between the share of non-farm employment by industry and occupation divisions (UPS) occurs primarily because agriculture labourers, which are in small numbers (8), have been combined with agriculture and allied activities in the former case, while these have been combined with that of labourers in the later case. However, such minor re-classification does not affect the analysis.

capacity, as reflected by steep and corresponding rise in the share of cultivators and animal husbandry workers. For females, the decline in cultivators has been fully offset by the increase in animal husbandry workers. Such a huge subsidiary engagement acts, by and large, as sponge to agriculture and allied activities that merely engage them for want of any other non-farm activity in the rural area.

Table 7.5 : Occupational Structure of Non-migrant Workers

Occupation	*Principal occupation*			*Principal + subsidiary occupation*		
	Male	*Female*	*Person*	*Male*	*Female*	*Person*
1. Cultivator	40.49	82.28	62.56	52.42	78.00	66.64
2. Animal husbandry worker	1.36	5.10	3.33	6.44	10.57	8.74
Farm sector	**41.85**	**87.38**	**65.89**	**58.86**	**88.57**	**75.38**
3. Technical and managerial worker	1.63	0.00	0.77	1.07	0.00	0.48
4. Teacher	6.79	1.70	4.10	4.47	1.00	2.54
5. Clerical and related worker	7.07	0.00	3.33	4.83	0.00	2.14
6. Shopkeeper and sales worker	15.49	0.49	7.56	10.55	0.29	4.85
7. Service worker*	4.35	0.00	2.05	3.04	0.00	1.35
8. Weavers and related worker	5.98	8.01	7.05	5.19	8.57	7.07
9. Other production** worker	3.80	0.00	1.79	2.50	0.00	1.11
10. Transport worker (driver)	6.52	0.00	3.08	4.47	0.00	1.99
11. Labourer	5.71	1.94	3.72	4.47	1.29	2.70
12. Other worker***	0.82	0.49	0.64	0.54	0.29	0.40
Non-farm sector	**58.15**	**12.62**	**34.10**	**41.14**	**11.43**	**24.62**
Total workers (Nos.)	**368**	**412**	**780**	**559**	**700**	**1259**

* Service workers constitute hotel-room boy, cook, domestic servant, security service worker etc.

** Other production workers comprise grain miller, food preserver, bakery worker, brewer, dairy worker etc.

*** Other workers include veterinary assistant, ANM, Dai and religious worker etc.

Source : Field Survey, 2004-05.

V. Non-farm Employment by Household Features

Looking at the occupational structure of workforce (UPSS) across blocks, only three blocks stand out clearly with a higher share in non-farm employment than the average share in the rural economy of the state (25%). These three blocks are Bhatwari, Dharchula and Dunda, while other five blocks having lower proportion than the average share (Table 7.6). The three blocks having distinctly higher share of non-farm employment have some commonalities in the sense that these blocks have a higher proportion of weavers and related workers, primarily because the tribal population resides in some of the villages of these blocks and they are engaged in weaving and manufacturing of woollen garments etc. The share of weavers & related workers constitute 24 per cent in Bhatwari, 15 per cent in Dharchula and 17 per cent in Dunda. The other important segment of non-farm workers in Bhatwari is shopkeepers (4%), but in other activities the share of workers is very low. Bhatwari being located at a higher altitude and far-off from the block and district headquarters faces the lack of transport and market. In Dharchula, shopkeepers (7%) and transport workers (5%) constitute the other major chunk of non-farm workers. Dharchula being the block and tehsil headquarters provides better opportunities for trading that spur the transport activities. While in Dunda, teachers (5%), clerical workers (3%) and labourers (4%) constitute the other major segments of non-farm workers. Dunda being closer to the block and district centres provides better opportunities for white-collar jobs (viz., teachers, clerical and related workers) and for wage labourers.

There is an uneven pattern of non-farm occupations across other development blocks. Shopkeeping is the most common activity in the rural area which can be started almost immediately, as it does not require a huge capital investment and also entails minimum risk. The other activity is white-collar jobs (viz., teachers, clerical & related workers and other technical & managerial workers), which are most preferred activities. Dependence on public employment is still very high in the hill areas. In some development blocks, transport workers constitute an important occupational category (Chamba), while in some other relatively less developed blocks, the wage labourers constitute an important category of workers (Kirtinagar and Salt).

Various non-farm segments have come up across space largely by the centripetal forces of market centres and development centres such as block and district headquarters that generate demand for various

Table 7.6 : Employment Share in Non-farm Occupations

Household features	*Culti-vator*	*Animal husbandry worker*	*Technical and managerial worker*	*Teacher*	*Clerical and related worker*	*Shop-keeper and sales worker*	*Service worker*	*Weaver and related worker*	*Other Production worker*	*Transport worker (driver)*	*Labourer*	*Other workers*	*Total non-farm workers*	
Development blocks														
Berinag	76.27	9.04	0.00	1.13	2.26	6.21	1.13	0.56	0.00	1.13	1.69	0.56	14.67	100.00 (177)
Bhatwari	57.25	7.97	0.00	1.45	1.45	3.62	1.45	23.91	0.72	1.45	0.72	0	34.77	100.00 (138)
Chamba	80.27	5.44	0.00	0.68	0	5.44	2.04	1.36	2.04	2.72	0.00	0	14.28	100.00 (147)
Dharchula	58.54	4.88	0.61	2.44	3.66	7.32	0	15.24	0.00	4.88	1.83	0.61	35.98	100.00 (164)
Dunda	54.36	4.70	0.67	4.70	3.36	3.36	1.34	17.45	2.68	1.34	4.70	1.34	40.27	100.00 (149)
Hawalbagh	67.00	11.5	1.50	3.00	4.00	4.00	3.50	0.00	1.50	2.00	2	0.00	20.00	100.00 (200)
Kirtinagar	67.72	14.96	0.79	3.94	0.79	1.57	0.00	0.79	0.00	0.79	7.87	0.79	16.54	100.00 (127)
Salt	70.06	11.46	0.00	3.18	0.64	6.37	0.64	0.64	1.91	1.27	3.82	0.00	18.47	100.00 (157)
Social category														
Brahmin	68.65	10.81	1.08	5.95	2.16	3.78	0.54	1.08	1.08	1.62	1.62	1.62	20.53	100.00 (185)
Kshatriya	74.16	8.75	0.4	2.02	2.42	5.38	1.88	0.27	0.54	2.29	1.88	0	17.08	100.00 (743)
SC	57.23	8.81	0.63	3.14	1.26	2.52	0.63	10.69	4.40	1.26	8.81	0.63	33.97	100.00 (159)
ST	28.57	5.26	0.00	0.75	2.26	6.77	0	50.38	0.75	2.26	2.26	0.75	66.18	100.00 (133)
Others	82.05	10.26	0.00	0.00	0.00	2.56	2.56	2.56	0.00	0.00	0.00	0.00	7.68	100.00 (39)

(Contd...)

Table 7.6 : (Contd...)

Land class (acre)														
No land	9.30	11.63	2.33	4.65	2.33	2.33	0.00	55.81	2.33	2.33	4.65	2.33	79.09	100.00 (43)
>0 <= .50	60.42	12.5	0.26	0.52	1.82	4.69	1.56	9.11	1.82	1.56	5.21	0.52	27.07	100.00 (384)
>.50 <= 2.50	71.81	7.22	0.42	2.97	2.12	5.67	1.42	3.4	0.85	2.27	1.56	0.28	20.96	100.00 (706)
>2.50 <= 5.0	75.00	3.70	0.93	5.56	3.7	1.85	0.93	5.56	0.00	1.85	0.93	0.00	21.31	100.00 (108)
>5.0 <= 10.0	83.33	11.11	0.00	5.56	0.00	0.00	0.00	0.00	0.00	0.00	0.00	0.00	5.56	100.00 (18)
Income group (MPCI)														
Up to Rs. 250	74.19	9.68	0.00	0.00	0.00	0.00	1.08	0.00	0.00	0.00	15.05	0.00	16.13	100.00 (93)
Rs. 250 to 500	74.15	9.09	0.00	0.57	0.57	3.41	1.7	4.26	1.99	0.00	3.98	0.28	11.08	100.00 (352)
Rs. 500 to 1,000	69.35	10.51	0.45	0.00	1.57	4.7	1.79	7.83	1.12	1.79	0.45	0.45	17.91	100.00 (447)
Rs. 1,000 to 2,500	53.87	6.25	1.19	6.55	5.06	8.33	0.6	11.31	0.60	4.46	1.19	0.6	38.1	100.00 (336)
More than Rs. 2,500	58.06	3.23	0.00	25.81	3.23	0.00	0.00	3.23	0.00	6.45	0.00	0.00	38.72	100.00 (31)
Less developed	67.54	9.84	0.33	3.11	1.8	4.59	0.82	4.75	1.15	1.15	4.26	0.66	22.62	100.00 (610)
Developed	65.79	7.70	0.62	2.00	2.47	5.08	1.85	9.24	1.08	2.77	1.23	0.15	26.49	100.00 (649)
Total	**66.64**	**8.74**	**0.48**	**2.54**	**2.14**	**4.85**	**1.35**	**7.07**	**1.11**	**1.99**	**2.70**	**0.40**	**24.63**	**100.00 (1259)**

Source: Field Survey, 2004-05.

types of goods and services. Though weaving activity has been a traditional occupation, especially for tribal population, yet the market centres have helped enhance demand for such products.

Across social category, Scheduled Castes (34%) and Scheduled Tribes (66%) have a very high proportion of workers in non-farm occupations. In other social categories, the proportion is lower than the average share. Among the Scheduled Castes, the most conspicuous workers' categories are weavers & related workers (11%) and labourers (9%). Labourers constitute the highest proportion among all the caste groups. The other occupation group is teacher which accounts for a little over 3 per cent, which is next to Brahmins. The relatively better-educated lot gets employment in public services, primarily because of reservation policy; while illiterates and less educated ones resort to labourers' in different forms. For Scheduled Tribes, weavers & related workers (50%) and shopkeepers & sales workers (7%) are the major occupational groups. Brahmins account for about 21 per cent share in non-farm occupations, with a dominant share of white-collar workers (9%) comprising teachers, clerical & related workers and technical & managerial workers followed by shopkeepers (4%). Brahmins are regarded as a highly educated social group in the hill districts and their proportion in white-collar jobs also turn out to be the highest and rightly so. The major occupational categories for Kshatriyas are shopkeepers (5%), white-collar workers (5%), and transport workers (2%). The 'other caste' category has the lowest share in non-farm employment (8%) and they are engaged in occupations such as shopkeepers, weavers and service workers.

Land size classes and the share of non-farm employment are negatively correlated; lower the land size class the higher is the share of non-farm sector and *vice versa*. In the landless category, a sizeable proportion of workers are weavers & related workers (56%), followed by wage labourers (5%) and teachers (5%). In the marginal land size class (up to 2.50 acre), weavers and shopkeepers constitute the highest share (5% each) followed by wage labourers (3%), while in the small and medium size land classes (>2.50 <= 5.0 and >5.0 <= 10.0 acre) the white-collar workers constitute the highest proportion. It is clear that in the lower land size classes, the dependence on self-employment and wage labour is substantially higher while in higher land size classes, the dependence on better-remunerated white-collar jobs is higher. Also, at the lower end of land size classes, dependence on animal husbandry is very high.

Proportion of non-farm workers are positively correlated with that of income groups (monthly per capita income). In the lower income classes (up to Rs. 500), wage labourers constitute a major occupational group; and in the next income group (Rs. 500 to 1,000), weavers and shopkeepers have the highest share (8 and 5% respectively). In the next higher income bracket (Rs. 1,000 to 2,500); weavers, shopkeepers, teachers & clerical workers constitute the major occupational groups in that order, while in the highest income group (Rs. 2,500 and above), teachers constitute the major group (26%) followed by transport workers (6%). By and large, in the lower income groups, a large proportion of workers constitute the wage labourers and weavers; in the middle-income groups, the weavers and shopkeepers constitute the major groups; while in the highest income group majority of them are white-collar workers (teachers, clerical & related workers and technical & managerial workers). In the highest income group (Rs. 2,500 and above), teachers & clerical workers constitute about 29 per cent.

There does not seem to be a substantive difference in the share of non-farm workers in the relatively less developed and relatively developed blocks. In both cases, the weavers and shopkeepers dominate. However, in the former case, wage labourers seem to have a distinct presence while in the later case, it is the transport workers.

VI. Non-farm Employment by Educational Levels

Almost 27 per cent workers are illiterate (males constituting 12% and females 39%), 12 per cent have schooling up to primary, 19 per cent are educated up to middle level, 42 per cent are educated up to secondary and above levels of which 8 per cent are graduates and above (Table 7.7). The level of technical education is abysmally low (less than 1%) and none of the female workers possess technical education. The educational status is lower for females in each level of education as compared to males. Most of the illiterates are concentrated

Table 7.7 : Occupational Distribution of Workers by Levels of Education

Occupation	*Sex*	*Illiterate*	*Up to primary*	*Up to middle*	*Up to secondary*	*Up to senior secondary*	*Graduate and above*	*Technical*	*Total*
Cultivator	Male	11.60	14.33	21.50	28.67	14.33	8.87	0.68	100.00 (293)
	Female	37.91	13.00	19.60	15.02	9.34	5.13	0.00	100.00 (546)
	Person	28.72	13.47	20.26	19.79	11.08	6.44	0.24	100 (839)
Animal husbandry worker	Male	16.67	16.67	25.00	22.22	16.67	2.78	0.00	100.00 (36)
	Female	36.49	9.46	17.57	21.62	13.51	1.35	0.00	100.00 (74)
	Person	30.00	11.82	20.00	21.82	14.55	1.82	0.00	100.00 (110)
Technical and managerial worker	Male	0.00	0.00	16.67	16.67	33.33	0.00	33.33	100.00 (6)
	Female	0.00	0.00	0.00	0.00	0.00	0.00	0.00	0.00 (0)
	Person	0.00	0.00	16.67	16.67	33.33	0.00	33.33	100.00 (6)
Teachers	Male	0.00	0.00	0.00	8.00	12.00	76.00	4.00	100.00 (25)
	Female	0.00	0.00	0.00	14.29	28.57	57.14	0.00	100.00 (7)
	Person	0.00	0.00	0.00	9.38	15.63	71.88	3.13	100.00 (32)

(Contd...)

Table 7.7 : (Contd...)

Clerical & related worker	Male	0.00	14.81	18.52	37.04	14.81	14.81	0.00	100.00 (27)
	Female	0.00	0.00	0.00	0.00	0.00	0.00	0.00	0.00 (0)
	Person	0.00	14.81	18.52	37.04	14.81	14.81	0.00	100.00 (27)
Shopkeeper & sales worker	Male	8.47	5.08	18.64	22.03	27.12	18.64	0.00	100.00 (59)
	Female	0.00	50.00	50.00	0.00	0.00	0.00	0.00	100.00 (2)
	Person	8.20	6.56	19.67	21.31	26.23	18.03	0.00	100.00 (61)
Service worker	Male	11.76	5.88	29.41	41.18	0.00	11.76	0.00	100.00 (17)
	Female	0.00	0.00	0.00	0.00	0.00	0.00	0.00	0.00 (0)
	Person	11.76	5.88	29.41	41.18	0.00	11.76	0.00	100.00 (17)
Weaver and related worker	Male	27.59	10.34	10.34	37.93	10.34	0.00	3.45	100.00 (29)
	Female	51.67	10.00	16.67	11.67	6.67	3.33	0.00	100.00 (60)
	Person	43.82	10.11	14.61	20.22	7.87	2.25	1.12	100.00 (89)
Other production worker	Male	14.29	14.29	14.29	28.57	14.29	0.00	14.29	100.00 (14)
	Female	0.00	0.00	0.00	0.00	0.00	0.00	0.00	0.00 (0)

(Contd...)

Table 7.7 : *(Contd...)*

	Person	14.29	14.29	14.29	28.57	14.29	0.00	14.29	100.00 (14)
Transport worker (driver)	Male	8.00	0.00	12.00	32.00	32.00	8.00	8.00	100.00 (25)
	Female	0.00	0.00	0.00	0.00	0.00	0.00	0.00	0.00 (0)
	Person	8.00	0.00	12.00	32.00	32.00	8.00	8.00	100.00 (25)
Labourer	Male	28.00	16.00	28.00	16.00	12.00	0.00	0.00	100.00 (25)
	Female	77.78	22.22	0.00	0.00	0.00	0.00	0.00	100.00 (9)
	Person	41.18	17.65	20.59	11.76	8.82	0.00	0.00	100.00 (34)
Other workers	Male	0.00	0.00	33.33	33.33	33.33	0.00	0.00	100.00 (3)
	Female	50.00	0.00	0.00	0.00	50.00	0.00	0.00	100.00 (2)
	Person	20.00	0.00	20.00	20.00	40.00	0.00	0.00	100.00 (5)
Total workers	Male	11.81	11.63	19.68	27.37	16.10	11.63	1.79	100.00 (559)
	Female	39.00	12.43	18.71	15.14	9.71	5.00	0.00	100.00 (700)
	Person	26.93	12.07	19.14	20.57	12.55	7.94	0.79	100.00 (1259)

Note : Figures in parentheses show numbers.
Source : Field Survey, 2004-05.

among cultivators, animal husbandry workers, weavers and labourers, and the proportion of female illiterates is higher than that of males across the board. Majority of cultivators and animal husbandry workers have education between primary and secondary levels (54%). Teachers have the highest level of education – nearly 72 per cent of them are graduate and above (male accounts for about 76% and female 57%). A majority of clerical & related workers and shopkeepers (66 to 67%) are educated between secondary and graduates levels. Service workers, weavers and labourers are mostly educated between primary and secondary levels. Technical & managerial workers, other production workers, transport workers and other workers are mostly educated between secondary and senior secondary school. One can therefore broadly observe a five-tier educational structure of the workforce. Teachers are conspicuous at the highest educational level (graduate and above), while clerical & related workers and shopkeepers are in the next ladder of educational structure (secondary to graduate). Technical & managerial workers, other production workers, transport workers and other workers are bunched at the secondary and senior secondary level education. Service workers are between middle to secondary levels; and cultivators, animal husbandry workers, weavers and labourers are at the lowest level of educational structure – between illiterates and middle level education.

The above analysis clearly supports the hypothesis that the low level of education among female workforce is one of the principal reasons that has created disparities in employment opportunities in the non-farm sector, as their share in non-farm sector is low (11%) as compared to their male counterparts (41%).

VII. Determinants of Non-farm Employment

(i) The Logit Model

In order to ascertain the factors that affect the probability of a person seeking non-farm employment, logistic regression model is fitted, which is as follows:

$$Y\,(P) = \frac{1}{1 + e^{-z}}$$

$$z = \beta_0 + \beta_1 x_1 + \beta_2 x_2 + \beta_3 x_3 + \beta_4 x_4 + \beta_5 x_5 + \beta_6 x_6 + \beta_7 x_7 + \beta_8 x_8 + \beta_9 x_9 + \beta_{10} x_{10} + \mu$$

Where :

Y= Probability of person seeking non-farm employment
P =1, when engaged in non-farm employment
P =0, when not engaged in non-farm employment
e = Base of natural logarithms
x_1= Log of household size (*lnhhsz*)
x_2= Per capita land in acre (*pc_land*)
x_3= Caste of the worker (dummy, if SC, ST and others = 1, otherwise = 0) (*dcaste*)
x_4= Area under horticulture in acre (*ar_hort*)
x_5 = Educated (dummy, if educated higher secondary and above =1 non-educated = 0) *(educated)*
x_6= Skilled worker (dummy, if skilled = 1 otherwise = 0)(*skilled*)
x_7 = Age in completed years (*age*)
x_8 = Age square (*age2*)
x_9 = Male (dummy, if male =1 otherwise = 0)(*male*)
x_{10} = Development index of villages (*devindx*)
μ = Stochastic error term

P indicates the probability of p occurring (i.e. the probability that a case belongs to a certain category). As such, the resulting value from the equation is a probability value that varies between 0 and 1. A value close to zero means that p is very unlikely to have occurred and a value close to one means that p is very likely to have occurred. For this model, only workers have been considered and therefore results are based on 961 observations. The results of logistic regression are given in Table 7.7A.

Table 7.7A : Results of Logistic Regression

nfemem	*Odds ratio*	*Std. error.*	*Z*	*P>lzl*
lnhhsz	.8135#	0.2023	-0.83	0.407
pc_land	.2775**	0.1446	-2.46	0.014
dcaste	1.8747**	0.4784	2.46	0.014
ar_hort	.2014***	0.0879	-3.67	0.000
educated	6.2095***	1.7113	6.63	0.000
skilled	90.1916***	40.9068	9.93	0.000
age	.8792***	0.0415	-2.73	0.006
age2	1.0009*	0.0005	1.74	0.082
male	59.5522***	17.6136	13.82	0.000
devindx	17.0581*	29.3365	1.65	0.099

*** Significant at 1 per cent level of significance.
** Significant at 5 per cent level of significance.
* Significant at 10 per cent level of significance.
\# Insignificant at 10 per cent level of significance.

Notes : Dependent variable is probability of person seeking non-farm employment.

N= 961
Pseudo R^2=0.5081

Odds is the ratio of the probability of the occurrence of an event divided by the probability of the corresponding non-event. In the context of log-linear analysis, odds refers to the probability of a case being in a particular cell of a table divided by the probability of its not being in that cell.

We find that odds ratio reported above is in accordance with our *a priori* expectations. Moreover, most of the odds ratios are significant at 1 per cent level of significance except that of per capita land (pc_land), and caste of worker (dcaste), which is significant at 5 per cent level of significance and age2, development index of villages (devindx) turns out to be significant only at 10 per cent level of significance. However, log of household size (lnhhsz) is insignificant at 10 per cent level of significance.

Table 7.7A shows that odds of being engaged in non-farm employment gets reduced as household size goes up. This is more so particularly in poorer households where education and skill levels are low; which constrict the access to non-farm employment. The increase in one unit of per capita land (in acre) reduces the odds of non-farm employment by 72.25 per cent. It can be deduced that if a household owns sufficient per capita land, probability of a person seeking non-farm employment tends to decline. From the policy perspective, it is important to address the institutional aspects that aim at distribution of land to landless or those having very low land per capita (sub-marginal category). For SC, ST and 'other caste' workers, odds of being engaged in non-farm employment are 87 per cent greater as compared to upper caste workers. This is quite plausible as SCs and STs have comparatively lower per capita availability of land that often forces them to search employment opportunities in off-farm and non-farm sector.

One acre increase in land area under horticulture reduces the odds of employment in non-farm sector by 79.86 per cent. Increasing area under commercial crop, such as fruits, vegetable and other non-food crops significantly improve income levels. This helps in increasing the productive engagement of people in such remunerative activities that dissuade them from seeking employment in non-farm activities. Odds of being in the non-farm employment for an educated worker is 6.21 times greater as compared to an uneducated worker. For skilled workers, odds of being engaged in non-farm employment is 90.19 times greater as compared to an unskilled worker. What emerges strongly from the logistic regression model is that improvement in educational levels has a significant positive impact on their diversification from farm to non-farm occupations. Similarly, enhancement of skill level has considerable positive impact on the workforce in shifting from farm to non-farm sector activities. This has a clear policy message. Improving educational and skill level of workforce would significantly improve chances of employability in the non-farm sector with better income opportunities. This becomes clear from the values of odds ratios.

Probability of seeking non-farm employment at younger age is higher and it gets attenuated as the age increases but after certain age, people gradually withdraw from agriculture and pursue non-farm employment, which is supposedly less arduous than crop cultivation activities. This is evident from the coefficients of age and age2 that initially increases as age increases by one year, odds of being in non-farm employment goes down by 12.08 per cent, but after achieving a certain age (generally at higher age), odds of employment in non-farm sector goes up (albeit, marginally). For males, odds of being engaged in non-farm employment are 59.55 times greater as compared to female workers. Also, we note that as village development index (constituting social and economic infrastructure) goes up by one unit, odds of being employed in non-farm employment increases by 17.06 times. Clearly, village development index has a profound impact on increasing the non-farm employment opportunities.

Number of observations taken into consideration are 2,275 for all the individuals. Mean value of some key independent variables such as per capita land (in acres), age, area under horticulture (in acres) and development index are 0.18, 28.56, 0.20 and 0.50 respectively. Standard deviations for the same variables are 0.22, 19.83, 0.25 and 0.065 respectively (Annexure VI.1A). The number of observations taken into account are 961, considering only principal status workers. Mean value of some key independent variables such as per capita land (in acres), age, area under horticulture (in acres) and development index are 0.19, 39.43, 0.21 and 0.51 respectively. Standard deviations for the same variables are 0.22, 13.01, 0.26 and 0.065 respectively (Annexure VI.1B).

VIII. Sources of Income

One of the important manifestations of non-farm sector is considerable heterogeneity in terms of numerous activities and occupations. We have seen in an earlier section that there exits a wide diversity of occupational groups across different spatial units, caste and land size classes. Such diversity exists not only in terms of share of employment but also in terms of sources of income.

Table 7.7B provides income quintile groups of population and average percentage share of income derived from different sources. Various sources of income have differing importance and relevance for different income groups. For instance, the poorest quintile group derives the highest share of income (56%) from agriculture & animal husbandry. Animal husbandry (305) alone contributes the highest

Table 7.7B : Sources of Income

Per capita income quintile group	*Cultivation*	*Animal husbandry*	*Self-employment*	*Regular wage income*	*Casual wage income*	*Pension*	*Remittance*	*Others**	*Total*
Bottom	25.39	30.20	10.38	1.20	12.50	1.94	17.52	0.87	100
2nd	26.08	19.92	16.26	4.22	5.82	10.14	16.54	1.02	100
3rd	25.87	14.07	24.23	3.62	2.61	14.70	13.23	1.67	100
4th	21.04	10.46	23.48	24.94	0.41	9.98	9.13	0.57	100
Top	14.26	5.70	21.64	43.32	0.05	9.44	4.27	1.32	100
Total	20.09	11.71	21.08	24.45	2.14	10.02	9.39	1.13	100

* Includes income from rent, brew making, religious performance and other minor irregular incomes.

Source : Field Survey, 2004-05.

share of income. Dependence on this source is critical for the poorest people for meeting the cash income needs. Within non-farm sector, remittance and casual income are the most important sources of income that contribute the highest share for the bottom quintile group. Remittance and casual income account nearly 18 and 12.5 per cent incomes respectively. The income from regular source and pension is the lowest for the poorest quintile. While for the highest quintile group, regular/salaried income forms the major and the most important source of income contributing 43 per cent income and the contribution from the casual income and remittance is the lowest. In the middle-income quintiles, income from self-employment, pension and remittance forms important sources of non-farm income.

(i) Sources of income by social category and status of blocks

Income sources of different social classes help to understand the principal source of their earning and relative access to different activities that broadly determines their welfare. By and large, the trend shows that at the lower end of quintile groups, cultivation and animal husbandry are important sources of income in the agriculture and allied activities, while casual income and remittance forms the important source of income in the non-farm sector for the poorest quintiles; and regular/salaried income is the principal source of income for the richest quintiles in all the social groups. Self-employment and pension appear as important sources of income for the middle quintiles. Scheduled Tribes, however, show some aberration from this trend particularly in remittance, self-employment, pension and casual wage income sources (Table 7.8). There are no perceptible variations across two sets of blocks in terms of their relative importance in the sources of incomes from the broad trend noted above, barring self-employment and pension incomes which is associated with the middle quintiles in less developed blocks, while in developed blocks these sources are associated more with the top quintile group.

(ii) Determinants of household income

There are various factors that determine the income levels of the household. These factors are asset base (primarily, land), educational

Table 7.8 : Sources of Income by Social Category and Status of Blocks

Per capita income quintile group	*Cultivation*	*Animal husbandry*	*Self-employment*	*Regular wage income*	*Casual wage income*	*Pension*	*Remittance*	*Others*	*Total*
Brahmins									
Bottom	34.98	31.39	17.42	0.00	8.01	4.00	4.19	0.00	100.00
2nd	10.81	14.20	14.51	0.00	3.17	34.72	19.45	3.15	100.00
3rd	17.41	13.30	6.16	0.00	0.56	52.00	10.59	0.00	100.00
4th	14.50	12.06	23.46	31.43	0.18	7.82	9.77	0.78	100.00
Top	6.63	5.00	8.01	61.07	0.00	17.53	1.45	0.32	100.00
Total	10.77	9.07	11.77	41.37	0.68	20.10	5.64	0.60	100.00
Kshatriyas									
Bottom	25.05	30.74	8.76	1.79	10.46	2.27	20.51	0.42	100.00
2nd	25.78	22.15	19.37	3.58	4.07	7.80	17.25	0.00	100.00
3rd	25.64	16.03	23.26	3.47	2.45	11.68	17.30	0.17	100.00
4th	22.05	11.05	20.88	22.95	0.35	13.66	8.74	0.30	100.00
Top	17.28	6.58	18.07	41.20	0.00	9.25	6.15	1.46	100.00
Total	21.75	13.41	19.14	21.63	1.91	10.08	11.44	0.66	100.00
Scheduled castes									
Bottom	20.51	23.62	14.71	0.00	30.23	0.00	7.02	3.91	100.00
2nd	31.63	17.01	10.43	5.22	13.56	7.56	14.17	0.42	100.00
3rd	35.43	5.73	27.34	10.74	4.03	12.23	3.98	0.54	100.00
4th	21.77	7.01	30.03	21.10	0.47	12.99	5.68	0.95	100.00
Top	4.69	4.15	29.90	55.81	0.39	0.00	2.08	2.99	100.00
Total	22.64	10.16	22.92	21.86	7.52	6.72	6.63	1.56	100.00
Scheduled tribes									
Bottom	0.00	56.25	43.75	0.00	0.00	0.00	0.00	0.00	100.00
2nd	27.98	31.32	38.67	0.00	2.03	0.00	0.00	0.00	100.00

(Contd...)

Table 7.8 : (*Contd...*)

3rd	25.99	16.21	38.59	0.00	4.62	0.00	0.00	14.59	100.00
4th	22.49	8.85	28.65	27.33	0.71	0.00	10.93	1.05	100.00
Top	20.95	4.84	49.01	17.68	0.14	1.61	4.02	1.75	100.00
Total	22.23	8.79	40.13	18.31	0.94	0.78	5.84	2.98	100.00
Others									
Bottom	29.29	33.84	0.00	0.00	1.04	0.00	35.84	0.00	100.00
2nd	36.67	14.49	0.00	15.83	2.93	0.00	22.17	7.92	100.00
3rd	18.33	8.30	46.80	0.00	0.20	0.00	26.38	0.00	100.00
4th	0.00	0.00	0.00	0.00	0.00	0.00	0.00	0.00	100.00
Top	0.00	0.00	0.00	0.00	0.00	0.00	0.00	0.00	100.00
Total	29.56	17.24	13.69	7.47	1.68	0.00	26.63	3.73	100.00
Less developed blocks									
Bottom	19.24	33.87	4.99	0.00	17.31	3.01	20.22	1.36	100.00
2nd	12.14	19.23	22.45	4.34	5.07	14.97	21.03	0.76	100.00
3rd	11.52	13.29	24.09	0.00	1.44	27.77	21.90	0.00	100.00
4th	5.08	8.81	28.18	21.71	0.05	18.19	17.22	0.77	100.00
Top	3.48	5.04	15.17	57.47	0.07	15.38	2.55	0.85	100.00
Total	8.20	12.43	19.38	26.11	2.85	16.76	13.54	0.72	100.00
Developed blocks									
Bottom	36.43	23.60	20.05	3.36	3.87	0.00	12.68	0.00	100.00
2nd	48.24	21.00	6.43	4.03	7.02	2.45	9.40	1.44	100.00
3rd	38.39	14.74	24.36	6.78	3.63	3.31	5.67	3.12	100.00
4th	29.28	11.32	21.05	26.60	0.60	5.74	4.95	0.47	100.00
Top	22.05	6.17	26.32	33.10	0.04	5.14	5.51	1.67	100.00
Total	29.70	11.12	22.46	23.12	1.56	4.56	6.03	1.46	100.00

Source : Field Survey, 2004-05.

levels, proportion of non-farm employment, type of social groups, proportion of dependents, diversification of crops, infrastructural index of villages and out-migration etc. Here, regression model has been fitted with a view to understanding the relationship between predictor variables and Monthly Per Capita Income (MPCI) as dependent variable.

Regression Results

The model used gives function

$$y = \beta_0 + \beta_1 x_1 + \beta_2 x_2 + \beta_3 x_3 + \beta_4 x_4 + \beta_5 x_5 + \beta_6 x_6 + \beta_7 x_7 + \beta_8 x_{8} + \beta_9 x_{9} + \beta_{10} x_{10} + \beta_{11} x_{11} + \mu$$

where:

y = Monthly per capita income of household in rupees (*MPCI*);

x_1 =Proportion of total household members engaged in non-farm employment as their primary occupation (*prop_nfe*);

x_2 = Percentage area under horticulture (*pr_hort*);

x_3 = Proportion of females in the households (*pr_fem*);

x_4 = Proportion of dependents (below age 15 years and above 59 years) (*pr_depnd*);

x_5 = Percentage of member of household educated higher secondary and above (*d_hh_edu*);

x_6 = Social group (dummy, if household belongs to SC and 'others' =1, otherwise= 0) (*d_s_grp*);

x_7 = Per capita land in acre (*pc_land*);

x_8 = Household mainly depending on casual labour income (dummy, if belongs to casual labour household =1, otherwise = 0) (*caslab_hh*);

x_9 = HH reporting migration at least one member of the family (dummy, if short and long term migration =1 otherwise = 0) (*migr_hh*);

x_{10} = HH reporting migration at least one member of the family (dummy, if household reporting permanent migration (shifted) =1 otherwise = 0) (*shft_hh*);

x_{11} = Development index of villages (*dev_index*);

μ = Stochastic error term.

$\beta_1, \beta_{2,\ldots} \beta_k$ are the corresponding regression coefficients and β_0 is the constant term. Values of β coefficients of multiple regression models show the extent of impact of predictor variables on criterion variable.

Based on the above model, the results are presented in Table 7.8A.

The regression results show that the monthly per capita income of the household is positively and significantly affected by proportion of non-farm employment, area under horticulture, educational attainments, per capita land owned, migrant status of worker (shifted) and development index of villages. While proportion of dependents, households belonging to disadvan-tage social groups, casual labour households and migrant households (migrating out for short- and long-term) have negative impact on per capita income of the household with statistically significant sign*.

Table 7.8A : Result of Multiple Regressions

	Unstandardized Coefficients		*Standardized Coefficients*	*t- value*	*Sig. (p-value)*
	β	*Std. Error*	*β*		
(Constant)	5.4278	0.2567		21.1465	0.0000
prop_nfe	1.2713	0.1473	0.3401***	8.6301	0.0000
pr_hort	0.4293	0.1114	0.1530***	3.8539	0.0001
pr_fem	-0.1204	0.1681	-0.0264#	-0.7160	0.4744
pr_depnd	-0.4197	0.1193	-0.1392***	-3.5172	0.0005
d_hh_edu	0.1714	0.0589	0.1154***	2.9088	0.0038
d_s_grp	-0.1622	0.0754	-0.0816**	-2.1527	0.0320
pc_land	0.6988	0.1077	0.2624***	6.4876	0.0000
caslb _hh	-0.3929	0.0811	-0.1914***	-4.8453	0.0000
migr_hh	-0.2187	0.0581	-0.1438***	-3.7640	0.0002
shft_ hh	0.2557	0.0813	0.1270***	3.1461	0.0018
dev_index	1.6359	0.4693	0.1459***	3.4859	0.0005

*** Significant at 1 per cent level of significance;
** significant at 5 per cent level of significance;
# Insignificant at 10 per cent level of significance.
Note : Dependent variable monthly per capita income.

* While analysing the impact of any independent variable on the dependent variable, we keep the impact of the remaining variables on the dependent variables constant.

N	R^2	F	Sig.
400	0.5089	36.5522	0

Standardised coefficients have only been considered and since it makes the scale of the regressors irrelevant, all explanatory variables are put on equal footing. Hence, the coefficients can be compared directly. Signs of the coefficients of all the variables are in accordance with our *a priori* intuition. Coefficients of all explanatory variables are significant at 1 per cent level of significance, except social group (d_s_grp), which is significant at 5 per cent level of significance and proportion of females (pr_fem), which is insignificant even at 10 per cent level of significance. This implies that most of the regressors taken into our consideration are important determinants of monthly per capita income. Also, the p value of the F statistic suggests that jointly all the regressors are significant.

The interpretation of the coefficient of prop_nfe is that one standard deviation increase in the proportion of non-farm employment increases the per capita income by .34 standard deviation. It is observed that the proportion of non-farm employment variable has the largest standardised effect i.e. it contributes the most in the explanation of the regress and (MPCI). Regression results supports our hypothesis that the higher share of the workforce in non-farm sector translates into higher income at household and region levels. This is followed by per capita land owned (pc_land) which implies that one standard deviation increase in per capita land owned (acre) increases the per capita income by .26 standard deviation. This variable has second largest standardised effect. This indicates that per capita availability of cultivated land is a critical asset for enhancing the incomes of the households. These are followed by casual labour households (caslab_hh), percentage area under horticulture (pr_hort), development index of villages (dev_index),short- and long-term migrating households (migr_hh), proportion of dependents (pr_depnd), households reporting permanent migration (shft_hh), percentage of member of households educated higher secondary and above (d_hh_edu), and social groups (d_s_grp) arranged in decreasing order of their contribution in explaining the variation in MPCI.

The results show that (i) Most of the variables are significant, (ii) Proportion of non-farm employment and per capita land owned are the most important variables in explaining the regress, (iii) Percentage area under horticulture, development index of villages, permanently shifted migrants and education of households (higher secondary and above) impact positively on the household monthly per capita income, and (iv) Casual labour households, migrant households (short- and long-term), proportion of dependents in the households (aged below 15 and above 59 years), disadvantaged social groups (SCs and 'others') and proportion of females in the households negatively affect the monthly per capita household incomes.

Relative importance of the other regressors in explaining the variation in the regress and can be gauged by comparing their standardised coefficients.

For knowing the effects of each independent variable on the monthly per capita income, we can use unstandardised variables.

IX. The Heterogeneity in Non-farm Sector

The non-farm sector has been grouped broadly into three segments – the casual wage earners, the regular/salaried workers and the self-employed in rural enterprises. Within each segment, there are divergent activities and occupational groups with considerable heterogeneity and inequities across different segments of non-farm sector in terms of days of work, average earnings and capital requirements etc. Below, we will discuss each segment in some details.

(i) Casual wage workers

Table 7.9 shows the proportion of casual workers by different measures. Casual workers in the hill districts of the state do not constitute a dominant occupational group. It comprises a small proportion (3%) of the total workforce (UPSS), male constituting 5 per cent and female 1 per cent. This proportion increases up to 4 per cent by UPS, males accounting for 7 per cent and females 4 per cent. It is demonstrated that a substantial proportion of casual workers, who are either engaged as self-employed or regular workers by principal status, and are also engaged intermittently or part-time basis in casual works, are often not captured by the usual measurement statuses either by principal or principal & subsidiary status, which are substantially in large numbers (Bhalla *et al.*, 2004). It is also noted in the following table that a large number of workers who are self-employed in their principal status are also working as casual workers for varying length of time in their subsidiary capacity, but somehow they do not get reported in either status. This phenomenon is most common in agriculture sector, which is by and large a seasonal activity and characterised by huge underemployment in terms of labour time; and people resort to casual employment in order to meet their cash income needs. This is so particularly in poorer households with little or no means of durable income source. Almost one and half times, casual workers do not get reported by the usual measurement methods and inclusion of such workers pushes up the casual workers by two and half times to the total workforce.

Table 7.9 : Casual Workers by Different Measures of Work Status

Status	*Casual workers*			*Total workers*
	Male	*Female*	*Person*	
UPS	26 (7.07)	8 (1.94)	34(4.36)	780
UPSS	30 (5.37)	9(1.29)	39(3.10)	1259
Self-employed by principal status but casual worker by subsidiary status	50	7	57	
Total casual workers	80	16	96	

Note : Figures in brackets show per cent to total workers.
Source : Field Survey, 2004-05.

Casual workers constitute one-third by principal status, while two-thirds of them work in a subsidiary capacity and male members dominate in the casual works (83%). Construction workers are the major occupational group accounting for 70 per cent, while agricultural labourers and 'others' constitute 15 per cent each (Table 7.9A). Females are mostly engaged as agriculture labourers, while their male counterparts are engaged in construction works. In the hill districts of the state, females have social inhibitions that constrict their entry into the construction activity and they prefer to work as agriculture labourers, despite the fact that wages are lower in the agricultural works than construction activity.

Table 7.9A : Casual Workers by Major Activity

Activity	*Principal*		*Subsidiary*		*All*		
	Male	*Female*	*Male*	*Female*	*Male*	*Female*	*Person*
Construction labourers	23.44	66.67	76.56	33.33	95.52 (64)	4.48 (3)	100.00 (67)
Agriculture labourers	0.00	46.15	100.00	53.85	13.33 (2)	86.67 (13)	100.00 (15)
Others*	71.43	0.00	28.57	0.00	100.00 (14)	0.00 (0)	100.00 (14)
Total	31.25 (25)	50.00 (8)	68.75 (55)	50.00 (8)	83.33 (80)	16.67 (16)	100.00 (96)

Note : Figures in brackets show absolute numbers.
* 'Others' include helpers, loaders (other than construction), dairy workers, carpenters etc.

Source : Field Survey, 2004-05 .

Casual workers seem to be increasingly concentrated among Kshatriyas and Scheduled Castes, both by principal and principal & subsidiary statuses, while other social groups tend to have a lesser dependence on casual works. Understandably, Brahmins and Scheduled Tribes are relatively better-off social groups in terms of household and per capita income and their dependence on casual employment is lower as compared to other social groups. But it is not clear why 'other caste' which is one of the most disadvantaged groups in terms of income and asset base, have the lowest dependence on casual employment. The reason seems to be an outright preference of able-bodied persons for out-migrating for better work opportunities elsewhere, as their dependence on remittance is found to be very high (27%), and those who do not migrate prefer to engage in self-employment occupations rather than in casual works.

Majority of casual workers belong to sub-marginal and marginal landholding size classes and none of them is from highest land size class. Although, the number of casual workers is small in the landless category, yet it is highest in terms of proportion to total workers. Most of the casual workers belong to illiterate category, and to those who have completed middle level education. Majority of female casual workers are illiterates, while males dominate in the middle level education. Beyond the intermediate level of education, no one seems to be attracted for casual employment, probably because they can afford to remain either unemployed or to stay in educational institutions for a much longer time. Most of the casual workers are driven desperately from the lower income groups and such intensity gets attenuated in higher income groups. Clearly, the less developed blocks show a greater demand for such sporadic nature of employment than the developed ones (Table 7.10).

Table 7.10 : Casual Workers by Household Features

Household features	*Male*	*Female*	*Person*
Activity			
Construction labourers	80.00	18.75	69.79
Agriculture labourers	2.50	81.25	15.63
Others	17.50	0.00	14.58
Social category			
Brahmins	5.00	12.50	6.25
Kshatriyas	53.75	31.25	50.00
SCs	31.25	56.25	35.42
STs	8.75	0.00	7.29
Others	1.25	0.00	1.04
Land size class (acre)			
No land	5.00	6.25	5.21
>0 <= .50	42.50	93.75	51.04
>.50 <= 2.50	46.25	0.00	38.54
>2.50 <= 5.0	6.25	0.00	5.21
>5.0 <= 10.0	0.00	0.00	0.00
Educational levels			
Illiterate	20.00	68.75	28.13
Primary	20.00	12.50	18.75
Middle	31.25	6.25	27.08
High School	21.25	6.25	18.75
Intermediate/Sr. secondary	7.50	6.25	7.29
Income group (MPCI)			
Up to Rs. 250	18.75	50.00	23.96
Rs. 250 to 500	47.50	50.00	47.92
Rs. 500 to 1,000	31.25	0.00	26.04
Rs. 1,000 to 2,500	2.50	0.00	2.08
More than Rs. 2,500	0.00	0.00	0.00
Development status of blocks			
Less developed	56.25	100.00	63.54
Developed	43.75	0.00	36.46
Total	100.00 (80)	100.00 (16)	100.00 (96)

Note : Figures in brackets show absolute numbers.
Source : Field Survey, 2004-05.

On an average, casual works provide employment for about 50 days in a year (Table 7.11). Males get most of the employment in non-agriculture activities, while females have limited access to such opportunities. Cultivation, particularly weeding, transplanting and harvesting activities provide them major source of casual employment. The days of employment do not differ considerably for males and

Table 7.11 : Average Days of Employment

Household features	*Average days worked*		
	Male	*Female*	*Person*
Activity			
Construction labourers	48	25	47
Agriculture labourers	39	47	46
Others	69	0	69
Social category			
Brahmins	42	25	36
Kshatriyas	53	40	51
SCs	56	49	54
STs	33	0	33
Others	37	0	37
Land size class (acre)			
No land	48	35	45
>0 <= 0.50	52	44	49
>.50 <= 2.50	52	0	52
>2.50 <= 5.0	45	0	45
>5.0 <= 10.0	0	0	0
Educational levels			
Illiterate	58	46	53
Primary	46	44	46
Middle	57	35	56
High School	47	50	47
Intermediate/Sr. secondary	37	15	34
Income group (MPCI)			
Up to Rs. 250	54	44	50
Rs. 250 to 500	54	42	52
Rs. 500 to 1,000	47	0	47
Rs. 1,000 to 2,500	28	0	28
More than Rs. 2,500	0	0	0
Development status of blocks			
Less developed	53	43	50
Developed	49	0	49
Total	51	43	50

Source : Field Survey, 2004-05.

females. Although construction is the major activity in casual works, yet the average days of employment is highest in other activities consisting of carpentry, dairying, loading & unloading and other sporadic activities. On an average, Scheduled Castes get maximum days of employment (54 days), followed by Kshatriyas (51 days) and it is lowest among Brahmins (36 days) and Scheduled Tribes (33 days). Barring the highest land size class, everyone works for casual employment. It has often been noted that in government programmes, villagers avail such opportunities irrespective of their caste and land size class for whatever days it is available. Illiterates and those who have completed middle level education, and who are at the lower end of income groups get maximum days of casual employment.

Average wage works out at Rs.80 per day and females get one-third (36%) lower wages than their male counterparts. Highest wage is recorded in construction works (Rs.86) followed by others (Rs.77) and agriculture works (Rs.57). Average wages in agriculture is also lower by one-third as compared to construction activity, but there is no variation of male wages between these two activities (Table 7.12).

Table 7.12 : Mean Wages per Day

Activity	*Average wages/day (Rs.)*		
	Male	*Female*	*All*
Construction labourers	87.07	61.67	85.94
Agriculture labourers	86.60	52.69	57.21
Others	76.87	0.00	76.87
Total	85.28	54.38	80.13

Source : Field Survey, 2004-05.

(ii) Regular wage/salaried workers

Regular salaried workers constitute 6.4 per cent of the total workforce (UPSS), males accounting for about 13 per cent and females 1.3 per cent. Majority of regular wage/salaried workers are in teaching profession (39.5%) followed by clerical (25%) and transportation activities (25%). Females are mostly associated with teaching activity (78%) (Table 7.13). Kshatriyas account for over half of the total such workers followed by Brahmins (23%), Scheduled Castes (12%), and Scheduled Tribes (11%) in that order, while 'others' have the lowest proportion (1%). Marginal landholding class dominates in regular workers and landless; and the highest land size class has the lowest access to such employment. Those who are graduates and above have better chances for wage employment and such prospects are low for those who are illiterates or have lower level of education. Improving the levels of education is, therefore, necessary in order to promote better-paid regular/salaried employment. Levels of income and proportion of regular workers are by and large positively correlated barring in the highest income category, which is showing somewhat of an erratic pattern due to low sample size. In the less developed blocks, dependence on regular wage employment appears to be lower than the developed ones, possibly because of the lack of general development in less developed blocks.

Mean earnings for regular/salaried workers turns out to be Rs. 5,482 per month (pm) and for females it is slightly higher (Rs. 5,739) than males (Rs. 5,450) (Table 7.14). Teaching profession attracts the highest salary (Rs. 7,369), while transportation activity the lowest (Rs. 2,485). Teachers, clerks and postal departmental workers are mostly on the government rolls and their mean earnings tend to be higher than the other occupational groups. Even construction workers have a temporary status and they work more or less on regular basis in public works department, and are governed by the minimum wages. Mean earnings for transportation workers turns out to be the lowest, primarily because these workers are mostly in the private sector where the earnings are decided by the market prices. Across social category, mean earnings are highest for Brahmins (Rs. 7,074) and lowest for 'others' (Rs. 2,500). By and large, earnings are determined by the levels of education – higher the level of education higher are the earnings and *vice versa*. Land size classes, educational levels and per capita income groups are positively correlated to the levels of earnings. The less developed blocks are showing a higher mean earnings than the developed blocks but in the case of females, developed blocks are showing a much higher average earnings.

The third most important segment of the non-farm employment is rural enterprises which we will discuss in the next section.

Table 7.13 : Regular/Salaried Workers by Household Features

Household features	*Male*	*Female*	*Person*
Activity			
Teaching	34.72	77.78	39.51
Clerical	27.78	0.00	24.69
Postal services	4.17	0.00	3.70
Construction	4.17	0.00	3.70
Transportation	18.06	0.00	16.05
Others*	11.11	22.22	12.35
Social category			
Brahmin	23.61	22.22	23.46
Kshatriya	51.39	55.56	51.85
SC	12.50	11.11	12.35
ST	11.11	11.11	11.11
Others	1.39	0.00	1.23
Land size class (acre)			
No land	4.17	0.00	3.70
>0 <= .50	23.61	11.11	22.22
>.50 <= 2.50	59.72	66.67	60.49
>2.50 <= 5.0	11.11	22.22	12.35
>5.0 <= 10.0	1.39	0.00	1.23
Educational levels			
Illiterate	2.78	11.11	3.70
Primary	8.33	0.00	7.41
Middle	11.11	0.00	9.88
High School	25.00	11.11	23.46
Intermediate/Sr. Secondary	13.89	33.33	16.05
Graduate and above	34.72	44.44	35.80
Technical	4.17	0.00	3.70
Income group (MPCI)			
Up to Rs. 250	0.00	0.00	0.00
Rs. 250 to 500	6.94	0.00	6.17
Rs. 500 to 1,000	20.83	11.11	19.75
Rs. 1,000 to 2,500	63.89	55.56	62.96
More than Rs. 2,500	8.33	33.33	11.11
Development status of blocks			
Less developed	40.28	44.44	40.74
Developed	59.72	55.56	59.26
Total	100.00	100.00	100.00
	(72)	(9)	(81)

* Others include laboratory asstt., veterinary asstt., ANM, security services, food preservers and tailors working as regular/salaried workers etc.

Note : Figures in brackets show absolute numbers.

Source : Field Survey, 2004-05.

Table 7.14 : Mean Earnings of Regular/Salaried Workers by Household Features

Household features	*Mean earnings per month (Rs.)*		
	Male	*Female*	*Person*
Activity			
Teaching	7664	6314	7369
Clerical	5430	0	5430
Postal services	5333	0	5333
Construction	4667	0	4667
Transportation	2485	0	2485
Others	3771	3725	3761
Social category			
Brahmin	7112	6750	7074
Kshatriya	5181	5390	5206
SC	4144	4200	4150
ST	5000	7000	5222
Others	2500	0	2500
Land size class (acre)			
No land	5333	0	5333
>0 <= .50	4312	450	4097
>.50 <= 2.50	5740	6450	5827
>2.50 <= 5.0	5788	6250	5880
>5.0 <= 10.0	10000	0	10000
Educational levels			
Illiterate	3750	450	2650
Primary	5250	0	5250
Middle	4125	0	4125
High school	4056	4200	4063
Intermediate/Sr. Secondary	5230	7667	5792
Graduate	6780	8000	6891
Post-graduate	8153	5333	7683
Technical	1667	0	1667
Income group (MPCI)			
Up to Rs. 250	0	0	0
Rs. 250 to 500	1900	0	1900
Rs. 500 to 1,000	3613	450	3416
Rs. 1,000 to 2,500	5591	6940	5724
More than Rs. 2,500	11917	5500	9778
Development status of blocks			
Less developed	6579	5300	6424
Developed	4688	6090	4834
Total	**5450**	**5739**	**5482**

Source: Field Survey, 2004-05.

X. Rural Enterprises

Enterprise development is closely related to the economic base of a region in question. Entrepreneurial activities typically occur selectively in a few regions or centres, which have locational or comparative advantages in certain products or services. Certain regions are endowed with natural resources or locational advantages that stimulate enterprise-based activities to spring up. There is a strong motivation to agglomerate numerous entrepreneurial activities around these centres due to comparative advantages or external economies of a higher scale.

Hill economies are characterised by the subsistence agriculture and any drastic transformation within cereal-based agriculture has obvious limitations to provide employment and income opportunities due to the problems associated with hill agriculture. In any case, traditional agriculture with its low productive base and increasing pressure of population on limited cultivable land do not seem to be viable and a sustainable option for providing employment and livelihood any longer. Also, the industrial base is precarious in the hill economies and large-scale industrial activity is neither possible nor desirable in view of ecological and environmental considerations. Enterprise-based activities utilising local resources is critical for a sustainable employment generation and for enhancing the income levels, which in turn can help in improving the living standards of the people.

Traditionally, hill economies have developed numerous tiny and household-based enterprises utilising locally available resources and skills, mostly for sub-serving the needs of local economy through trade and exchange under mutual obligation system, but very little is meant for external trade. This kind of enterprise-based activities had, however, limited product lines, carried out on a small scale with little surplus for reinvestment. Entrepreneurial activities, however, continued within numerous internal and external constraints. But over the years, these enterprises are languishing and operating at a low equilibrium trap with little product diversification and surplus. The major reasons for sickness of these enterprises can be attributed to both the supply and demand side aspects. Supply side constraints are related to lack of credit, training, market support, availability of appropriate technology, power, shrinking local resource base, and other structural bottlenecks. While demand side constraints are typically related to lack of product competitiveness (hence low internal and external demand), increasing competition in the product market from the plain areas, limited linkages and integration to other directly productive segments of the economy etc. Various demand and supply side constraints therefore put the enterprises at a disadvantaged position. Notwithstanding, the region offers a comparative advantage in certain lines that have potentials for enterprise development activities (Papola *et al.*, 2005).

(i) Composition of enterprises

In the self-employed category, there are three distinct sub-categories, namely, own account workers, unpaid family workers and employers. Own account workers are those who work on their own and have not engaged any employees to work on a continuous basis. Unpaid family workers are those who contribute to the family enterprise and do not get an independent remuneration for their labour inputs. Employer is the person who hire wage worker – at least one but less than ten workers during the reference period. This classification helps understand the linkages between workers and enterprises in the unorganised sector, which is necessary in order to formulate policies for this heterogeneous sector (NCEUS, 2007).

In the rural area of the state, almost all of enterprises are tiny in nature and it becomes extremely difficult to differentiate them in clearly identifiable categories due to fuzziness. An overwhelmingly large number of enterprises fall in own account enterprises as the owner operators are using unpaid family labour. The sole motive of such tiny enterprises is to maximise earnings through using their labour inputs, and skills without making any distinction between wages and profit. Average capital use is low with the small scale of operation resulting in low returns. This makes these tiny enterprises vulnerable, as they operate in low margin of subsistence rather than carrying out business for profit.

The present survey results bring some of these issues at fore and amply corroborate the broad contours indicated above. In all, 179 non-agricultural enterprises were surveyed capturing all kinds of activities in rural set-up. It can be observed that retail trading dominates in all the enterprises (34%) followed by weaving (30%), small restaurants (9%) and transportation activities (7%) (Table 7.15).

Table 7.15 : Compositions of Enterprises by Household Features

Household features	*Per cent of enterprises*
Contractor services	2.79
Communication service	1.12
Retail trading	34.08
Selling agent	2.23
Restaurant	8.94
Weaving	30.17
Grain milling	2.23
Tailoring	4.47
Electric services	1.12
Transport services	7.26
Animal traction services	2.79
Others*	2.79
Social category	
Brahmin	8.38
Kshatriya	45.81
SC	11.17
ST	33.52
Others	1.12
Land size class (acre)	
No land	7.26
>0 <= .50	31.84
>.50 <= 2.50	54.75
>2.50 <= 5.0	6.15
>5.0 <= 10.0	0.00
Educational levels	
Illiterate	23.46
Primary	8.94
Middle	17.32
High school	22.35
Intermediate/Sr. Secondary	15.08
Graduate and above	10.06
Technical	2.79
Income group (MPCI)	
Up to Rs. 250	0.56
Rs. 250 to 500	15.64
Rs. 500 to 1,000	38.55
Rs. 1,000 to 2,500	43.02
More than Rs. 2,500	2.23
Development status of blocks	
Less developed	36.87
Developed	63.13
Total	100.00 (179)

* Others include dairy workers, carpenter and blacksmith etc.

Note : Figure in bracket shows absolute number.

Source : Field Survey, 2004-05.

In other activities, their proportion is low. Kshatriyas and Scheduled Tribes are the dominant social groups who run these enterprises and most of these entrepreneurs belong to sub-marginal and marginal landholding classes. Level of education among the entrepreneurs is low; almost three-fourths are educated below secondary level and about one-fourth among them are illiterates. A large majority of entrepreneurs belong to middle-income brackets and participation from the lowest and highest income groups is very low. Developed blocks show more concentration of entrepreneurial activities than the less developed ones.

(ii) Nature of operation

Majority of enterprises (68%) are permanent in nature, a little over one-fifth (22%) are operating seasonally and about one-tenth units (9.5%) are such which are running occasionally. Communication service, retail trading, small restaurants, weaving, electric services and transport services are observed to be more or less perennial activity in the rural area; while contractor services, selling agents, grain milling, tailoring and animal transportation are seasonal in nature (Table 7.16).

Table 7.16 : Nature of Enterprises

Block	*Occasional*	*Seasonal*	*Permanent*	*Total*
Contractor services	20.00	80.00	0.00	100.00
Communication service	0.00	0.00	100.00	100.00
Retail trading	1.64	11.48	86.89	100.00
Selling agent	0.00	50.00	50.00	100.00
Restaurant	0.00	37.50	62.50	100.00
Weaving	25.93	12.96	61.11	100.00
Grain mill	0.00	50.00	50.00	100.00
Tailoring	0.00	62.50	37.50	100.00
Electrical services	0.00	0.00	100.00	100.00
Transport services	7.69	0.00	92.31	100.00
Animal traction services	0.00	100.00	0.00	100.00
Others	0.00	40.00	60.00	100.00
Total	9.50 (17)	22.35 (40)	68.16 (122)	100.00 (179)

Note : Figures in brackets show absolute numbers.
Source : Field Survey, 2004-05.

(iii) Location of enterprises

Over two-thirds of enterprises (78%) are located within villages and nearby villages. Majority of such enterprises are communication services (PCO, STD booths), retail trading (grocery shops), seasonal agricultural produce agents (grains, fruits and vegetables), small restaurants (tea shops and eatables etc.), weaving, grain milling, tailoring, electrical servicing, animal transportation etc. A large majority of weaving enterprises carry out their operations within the household premises. Contractor service activities (construction of roads, culverts, buildings etc.) are largely concentrated within block and nearby villages, while transportation (jeep services) services are mostly carried out in the district, block and nearby villages (Table 7.17).

Table 7.17 : Location of Enterprises

Type of enterprise	*Within village*	*Nearby village*	*Block town*	*District town*	*Total*
Contractor services	0.00	40.00	60.00	0.00	100.00
Communication service	50.00	50.00	0.00	0.00	100.00
Retail trading	26.23	49.18	24.59	0.00	100.00
Selling agent	25.00	50.00	25.00	0.00	100.00
Restaurant	25.00	50.00	25.00	0.00	100.00
Weaving	94.44	0.00	5.56	0.00	100.00
Grain milling	100.00	0.00	0.00	0.00	100.00
Tailoring	62.50	25.00	12.50	0.00	100.00
Electrical services	50.00	50.00	0.00	0.00	100.00
Transport services	0.00	7.69	38.46	53.85	100.00
Animal traction services	100.00	0.00	0.00	0.00	100.00
Others	40.00	40.00	0.00	20.00	100.00
Total	50.28 (90)	27.37 (49)	17.88 (32)	4.47 (8)	100.00 (179)

Note : Figures in brackets show absolute numbers.
Source : Field Survey, 2004-05.

The conclusion seems to be straightforward. Majority of the enterprises appear to be dominated by trading and service activities with limited profile of activities. Education levels of entrepreneurs are low and nearly one-fourth are illiterates and nearly half of the entrepreneurs have schooling up to high school level only. Those who are in the highest and lowest income groups, scarcely participate in such activities. Probably, those in the lowest income group do not have requisite start-up capital and skills to pursue for entrepreneurial activities, and those in the highest income group have preference for regular wage/salaried jobs than self-employment in rural enterprises. Majority of enterprises are observed to be permanent in nature and operating within and nearby villages, which act as main market centres for the villagers for meeting their daily needs.

(iv) Employment

Family labour is more prominent in rural enterprises, nearly three-fourths of employment (74%) constitute family labour and one-fourth (26%) hired labour (Table 7.18). On an average, each enterprise provides employment to two persons. Contractor service provides the highest employment (12 persons) followed by weaving (2.3 persons), transport services (2.1 persons) and restaurants (1.7 persons). Most of the enterprises are very small in nature and largely depend on family labour and skills barring contractor services, restaurants and transport services; which use hired labour. Other enterprises either do not use hired labour at all or hire occasionally depending on the needs. Weaving enterprises utilise family labour more intensively and per unit employment tend to be the highest for the family labour. It has been generally seen that family members in such enterprises do not get independent remuneration, but they contribute to family income which are referred to as 'contributing family member' (NCEUS, 2007).

On an average, these enterprises provide employment for about 3.7 months in a year, four months to family labour and three months to hired labour. People generally undertake multiple activities and often combine entrepreneurial activities with cultivation and animal husbandry, which is a major occupation for many people in the rural areas. Certain activities provide employment for a relatively longer duration, while some other activities provide employment for a few months in a year. For instance, transport services, retail trading, grain milling and animal traction services provide employment for about

Table 7.18 : Family and Hired Labour by Type of Enterprise

Type of enterprise	*Enterprise (Nos.)*	*Employment (Nos)*			*Employment per enterprise*
		Family worker	*Hired worker*	*Total*	
Contractor services	5	5	55	60	12
Communication service	2	3	0	3	1.5
Retail trading	61	75	8	83	1.4
Selling agent	4	4	2	6	1.5
Restaurant	16	16	11	27	1.7
Weaving	54	125	0	125	2.3
Grain milling	4	4	1	5	1.2
Tailoring	8	8	3	11	1.4
Electrical services	2	2	0	2	1.0
Transport services	13	15	13	28	2.1
Animal traction services	5	5	0	5	1.0
Others	5	5	2	7	1.4
Total	179	267	95	362	2.0

Source : Field Survey, 2004-05.

five months, while communication and contractor services provide employment for a couple of months. Most of other enterprises provide employment between three to four months in a year. Communication service, weaving, electric services and animal transportation service depend fully on family labour and do not engage any hired labour; while transport services, grain milling, and retail trading engage hired labour for about five months in a year (Table 7.19). It would therefore be imperative from the policy point of view to promote these activities that have potential for employing hired labour. There are certain emerging activities that have better prospects for engaging hired labour such as transportation and grain milling.

(v) Education and skill levels

Education and skills are most critical factors for increasing productivity and promoting remunerative employment in the non-farm sector. Education tends to be closely correlated with higher levels of income. Education directly increases workers' productivity and helps enhance their skill levels. Numerous studies document the existence of positive links between education and earnings on the one hand and increased productivity of workforce on the other (cited from Islam, 1997; Gordon and Craig, 2001).

Table 7.19 : Average Days of Employment by Type of Enterprise

Type of enterprise	*Average days of employment*		
	Family workers	*Hired workers*	*Total Mandays*
Contractor services	62	68	68
Communication service	38	0	38
Retail trading	145	143	145
Selling agent	98	60	85
Restaurant	129	103	118
Weaving	102	0	102
Grain milling	140	150	142
Tailoring	113	67	100
Electric services	123	0	123
Transport services	149	156	153
Animal traction services	142	0	142
Others	110	135	117
Total	119	92	112

Source : Field Survey, 2004-05.

Table 7.20 reveals that about one-third (31%) family workers are illiterate and one-tenth have schooling up to primary level. A large majority of the educated workers have education up to senior secondary level. The proportion of graduates and above is small (9%) and the level of technical education is even much lower (2%). The level of education among hired workers is much higher than the family workers. One-fifth of the workers are graduate and above, and nearly 17 per cent workers are having technical education. The level of illiteracy is also very low (3%) among hired workers as compared to family workers.

Most of the entrepreneurial activities in the rural area require some degree of skills which are acquired through informal means rather than through a formal system. Such training is supposed to be flexible, adaptable and appropriate for the rural entrepreneurship. For instance, tailoring, weaving, blacksmithing, carpentry are all skilled activities and in the rural set-up, these skills reflect largely as cognitive skills rather than credential skills.

Table 7.20 : Levels of Education in the Enterprise

Educational level	*Family workers*	*Hired workers*
Illiterate	31.09	3.16
Primary	10.49	3.16
Middle	17.23	16.84
High School	19.85	24.21
Intermediate/Sr. Secondary	10.86	15.79
Graduate and above	8.61	20.00
Technical	1.87	16.84
Total	100.00 (267)	100.00 (95)

Note : Figures in brackets show absolute numbers.
Source : Field Survey, 2004-05.

Interestingly, skills levels among the family workers are observed to be much higher (55%) than the hired workers (17%), which counter the conventional wisdom that hired workers are endowed with better skills profiles. It can be noted that among the family workers, weavers possess the highest percentage of skilled workers (80%) followed by motor drivers (10%), other skilled workers such as blacksmith, carpenters and mechanics (5%) and tailors (5%) (Table 7.21). Among the hired workers, motor drivers are most prominent followed by tailors and others. In the rural area, the route to skill acquisition for most of the activities is through informal means barring motor driving, which requires some formal training. Motor vehicle is gaining importance as an alternative means of public transport system in the hill districts that has been attracting educated unemployed youth in transport enterprise.

Table 7.21 : Skill Profiles in the Enterprise

Skill category	*Family worker*	*Hired worker*
Tailoring	4.79	18.75
Weaving	80.15	0.00
Motor driving	9.59	75.00
Others*	5.47	6.25
Skilled	100.0 (146)	100.00 (16)
No skill	(121)	(79)
Total workers	(267)	(95)

* Others include blacksmithing, carpentry and mechanics.
Note : Figures in brackets show absolute numbers.
Source : Field Survey, 2004-05.

(vi) Access to credit

One of the obstacles to growth of enterprises is the lack of access to credit from banking system. A small minority of small enterprises is able to obtain credit from banks as banking institutions insist on some form of collateral as security. As a result, a large majority of enterprises have to depend on their own sources, often from informal institutions at high interest rate. It can be observed from Table 7.22 that out of 179 sample enterprises, only 46 enterprises (26%) have availed credit from formal banking institutions. Transport services are the most conspicuous activity that has availed credit (87%) from banks followed by retail trading (44%), restaurant (19%), others (18%), tailoring (13%) and weaving (25).

When a large number of enterprises do not have access to formal credit market, it becomes impossible for these enterprises to expand their initial endowment base resulting in low productivity and depressed level of earnings.

Table 7.22 : Sources of Finance

Type of enterprise	*Sources of credit*		
	Own	*Bank*	*Total*
Contractor services	100.00	0.00	100.00 (5)
Retail trading	55.74	44.26	100.00 (61)
Restaurant	81.25	18.75	100.00 (16)
Weaving	98.15	1.85	100.00 (54)
Tailoring	87.50	12.50	100.00 (8)
Transport services	15.38	84.62	100.00 (13)
Animal traction services	100.00	0.00	100.00 (5)
Others	82.35	17.65	100.00 (17)
Total	74.30	25.70	100.00 (179)

Note : Figures in brackets show number of enterprises.
Source : Field Survey, 2004-05.

(vii) Linkages

Enterprises in the hill region of the state are tiny in size and dominated mostly by petty trade, services and household manufacturing with limited product lines and product diversification. Most of the enterprises are operating at a low margin of subsistence, subserving the food and non-food needs of local population and local market, rather than being linked to the wider markets. Though majority of enterprises are reported to be permanent (68%) in nature, yet average days of employment are no more than even four months in a year, primarily because enterprise activity is, by and large, undertaken as secondary to main occupation (cultivation and animal husbandry). The agriculture base is low due to subsistence nature of farming and industrial base is precarious as there is no major and medium industry. Majority of small and tiny enterprises are facing a variety of constraints and handicaps that hinder their efficient operation. Apart from the low economic base, various constraints reinforce these enterprises to operate at a low margin of subsistence. These constraints relate to accessibility due to typical geo-physical conditions, underdeveloped infrastructure (transport and communication, market, technology etc.) and lack of product competitiveness. All these factors result in an extremely poor linkage effect of enterprise-based activities to the local economy.

(a) Input linkages

Various possible sources of inputs for different enterprises have been presented in Table 7.23 in order to understand the linkage effects to the local economy. It can be observed that there is an extremely limited input linkage to the local economy, and some of the products have only seasonal linkages. Barring vegetables; milk (catering to tea stall and restaurants); milling (village grinding units); dairying, carpentry; agriculture produce, majority of enterprises have little or no input linkages to the local economy. Most of the input linkages are observed to be outside the local economy. A significant part of input linkages (80%) fall outside the local economy. Contractor services, retail trading, tailoring and transport services wholly depend on outside the local economy (e.g.; block town, district town and outside the district town) for procurement of inputs. Weaving enterprises are even increasingly relying on raw wool produced from the plain areas (76%) than the local economy for manufacturing woollen products, which

Table 7.23 : Sources of Input Linkages

Type of enterprise	*Input linkages*												
	Within village	*Within village and nearby village*	*Within villages and block town*	*Within village and district town*	*Nearby village*	*Nearby village and block town*	*Nearby village and district town*	*Block town*	*Block and district town*	*District*	*District and outside district town*	*Outside district town*	*Total*
Contractor services	0.00	0.00	0.00	0.00	0.00	0.00	0.00	20.00	20.00	40.00	20.00	0.00	100.00 (5)
Retail trading	0.00	0.00	0.00	0.00	0.00	0.00	0.00	3.28	3.28	62.30	19.67	11.48	100.00 (61)
Restaurant	0.00	0.00	18.75	0.00	0.00	31.25	12.50	25.00	12.50	0.00	0.00	0.00	100.00 (16)
Weaving	16.67	0.00	1.85	1.85	1.85	0.00	0.00	40.74	11.11	24.07	0.00	1.85	100.00 (54)
Tailoring	0.00	0.00	0.00	0.00	0.00	0.00	0.00	75.00	0.00	25.00	0.00	0.00	100.00 (8)
Transport services	0.00	0.00	0.00	0.00	0.00	0.00	0.00	0.00	38.46	61.54	0.00	0.00	100.00 (13)
Animal traction services	0.00	100.00	0.00	0.00	0.00	0.00	0.00	0.00	0.00	0.00	0.00	0.00	100.00 (5)
Others*	5.88	35.29	0.00	0.00	0.00	11.76	0.00	11.76	5.88	11.76	0.00	17.65	100.00 (17)
Total	5.59	6.15	2.23	0.56	0.56	3.91	1.12	20.67	9.50	36.31	7.26	6.15	100.00 (179)

* Others include PCO booths, agriculture produce selling agents, grain millers, electrician, dairy workers, carpenter and blacksmith etc.

Note : Figures in brackets show absolute numbers.

Source : Field Survey, 2004-05 .

used to be locally available earlier. Other activities have some linkages to the village economy. All these enterprises have weak linkage effects to stimulate entrepreneurial activities in the rural economy. Many traditional enterprises (basket making, rope making, metal works, carpentry, blacksmithing etc.), which used to have a strong presence in the rural area have either vanished or attenuated due to cheap and better products available from plane areas. Even weaving enterprises have languished over the years, which used to be the main occupation of the tribal people.

(b) Output linkages

While input linkages are weak in the local economy, output linkages appear to be much stronger. Nearly 62 per cent output is used within the local economy. A large part of output from retail trading (84%), restaurant (76%), tailoring (90%), animal transportation (100%), other enterprises (70%) and transportation (60%) is consumed by the local population (Table 7.24). Weaving enterprises have the weakest linkage with the local economy as the major part of the output (woollen garments) is sold at the block town, which is one of the important marketing centres in rural area. It is clear that almost all the output is meant for final consumption than being used as an input for other enterprises that is critical for value addition and increasing productivity of enterprises.

Table 7.24 : Sources of Output Linkages

Type of enterprise	*Output linkages*					
	Within villages	*Nearby villages*	*Block town*	*District town*	*Outside district*	*Total*
Contractor services	0.00	40.00	60.00	0.00	0.00	100.00
Retail trading	51.97	31.80	15.57	0.00	0.66	100.00
Restaurant	41.88	33.75	21.88	2.50	0.00	100.00
Weaving	23.15	5.00	58.15	9.44	4.26	100.00
Tailoring	67.50	22.50	10.00	0.00	0.00	100.00
Transport services	13.85	46.15	13.85	26.15	0.00	100.00
Animal traction services	26.00	74.00	0.00	0.00	0.00	100.00
Others*	46.10	23.90	7.00	14.00	9.00	100.00
Total	37.04	24.92	28.77	6.65	2.63	100.00

* Others include PCO booths, agriculture produce selling agents, grain millers, electrician, dairy workers, carpenter and blacksmith etc.

Source : Field Survey, 2004-05.

The conclusion seems to be straightforward. When an overwhelmingly large number of enterprises have no input linkages with the local economy and output is singularly used as final consumption with a negligible value addition, the enterprises are bound to generate little or no surplus; which is necessary for sustained growth of enterprises. Most of the manufacturing enterprises (weaving, milling, metal works etc.) use traditional technology and manual skills without any product diversification. Barring the household demand, there does not seem to be any intermediate and export demand of these products. Woollen garments, which are niche products, can reach the wider markets provided this segment receives adequate promotional policy support to address its constraints.

Productivity of these enterprises is so low that unless these are restructured through variety of measures to upgrade technology, improve skill base and product diversification to meet the demand of emerging market, these enterprises would either disappear sooner or later or continue to subsist at a low productivity trap.

(viii) Capital use

The capital generally includes machinery, tools, factory buildings, raw material, partly finished goods, means of transportation, and unsold stocks of goods etc. However, 'capital' has been used here in somewhat a limited sense and includes value of machinery and raw material, partly finished goods, unsold stocks of goods including furniture and other assets, but does not include the value of land and buildings, as it was difficult to segregate and estimate value separately; particularly in rural area where enterprise activity is also carried out within the household chores.

The average capital employed per enterprise works out to be a little over one lakh Rupees (Rs. 1,04,970). Variability of capital use across enterprises is very high. It ranges from as high as Rs.3,02,000 in contractor services to lowest at Rs.11,946 in weaving enterprises (Table 7.25). Transport services, retail trading and grain milling enterprises have relatively high capital use per enterprise. Contractor service includes petty construction and repair works of roads, culverts and buildings etc., and it requires relatively high capital in procurement of raw material and for wage component. Likewise, transport service also requires huge capital, mainly in purchasing jeeps and small cars that have become most popular means of transport in the hill districts. Capital use in retail trading is observed to be Rs 1.73 lakh per enterprise. In rural set-up, trading enterprises often include retail shops that do not specialise in particular goods but include all sorts of goods like groceries, clothes, utensils and other food & non-food items. Selling agents who deal in agricultural produce employ capital to the tune of Rs. 1.47 lakh mainly in procuring seasonal agricultural produce (fruits, vegetables and pulses), and these agents work on commission basis. Average investment in grain milling (grinding units) is also reported to be high at Rs. 1.30 lakh that includes rice, wheat, spice grinding and oil extracting units. This has become a common activity in rural areas as grinding through water milling has almost become obsolete. Animal transport also requires high capital investment in buying the pony that is used in carrying heavy loads in the hill areas. Restaurants, tailoring units, electrical services require relatively low investment per unit.

Table 7.25 : Use of Capital in the Enterprise

Type of enterprise	*Average capital employed (Rs.)*	*Rank*
Contractor services	302000	1
Communication service	23750	11
Retail trading	172951	3
Selling agent	147500	4
Restaurant	51500	8
Weaving	11946	12
Grain milling	130000	5
Tailoring	28750	10
Electrical services	50000	9
Transport services	225000	2
Animal traction services	90000	6
Others*	79600	7
Total	104970	

* 'Others' include PCO booths, agriculture produce selling agents, grain millers, electricians, dairy workers, carpenter and blacksmith etc.

Source : Field Survey, 2004-05.

Net value of output (mean) has been arrived after deducting all the input costs. Input cost includes the cost of raw material, establishment cost (rent, electricity bill, interest on loans, taxes and other operating expenses) and wage payment. It can be observed that the overall capital output ratio works out to be 4.1. Contractor service appears to have the highest capital output ratio, or in other words, capital requirement in contractor service is highest per unit of output (6.8) followed by retail trading (5.7), while in weaving enterprises the capital requirement is lowest (Table 7.26). The reason for the lowest capital requirement in weaving enterprises is due to the use of traditional technology which is operated manually and requires very little capital. Also, tailoring, other enterprises, animal transportation require relatively low capital per unit of output. It, therefore, becomes important from policy point of view to promote those enterprises that conserve scarce resource (capital) and utilises local resources including the labour. But to make employment productive and efficient, it would also be worthwhile to see that mean earnings from these enterprises should be enough to attract people into self-employment.

Table 7.26 : Net Value of Output and Use of Capital

Type of enterprise	*Net value of output (Rs.)*	*Average capital employed (Rs.)*	*Capital output ratio*
Contractor services	44600	302000	6.8
Communication service	7250	23750	3.3
Retail trading	30107	172951	5.7
Selling agent	37500	147500	3.9
Restaurant	14781	51500	3.5
Weaving	16200	11946	0.7
Grain milling	32500	130000	4.0
Tailoring	12875	28750	2.2
Electrical services	14000	50000	3.6
Transport services	53154	225000	4.2
Animal traction services	32000	90000	2.8
Others	29400	79600	2.7
Total	25666	104970	4.1

Source : Field Survey, 2004-05.

Overall mean earnings (per man-day) in the enterprise work out to be Rs. 145. The variation in mean earnings is significantly higher across rural enterprises. The highest being Rs.719 in contractor services and the lowest at Rs. 69 in weaving enterprise (Table 7.27). Mean earnings for selling agents and transport owners is substantively higher at Rs. 385 and Rs. 308 respectively. Self-employed in grain milling, 'other enterprises' (PCO operators, dairying, carpentry and blacksmithing) and animal transportation earn between Rs. 225 and Rs. 267 per day, while retail traders, restaurant owners and those self-employed in tailoring and electrical services earn between Rs. 114 and Rs. 169 per day. The lowest mean earning is noted for the weavers (Rs.69 per day), which provides highest man-days of family employment. In fact, their earnings are observed to be below than casual wage earners. It is necessary to rejuvenate the weaving home-based enterprise through variety of promotional measures which has potential for generating strong forward and backward linkages to the local economy.

Table 7.27 : Mean Earnings per Day by Type of Enterprise

Type of enterprise	*Net value of output (Rs.)*	*Family man-days*	*Per man-day earnings (Rs.)*
Contractor services	223000	310	719
Communication service	14500	115	126
Retail trading	1836500	10870	169
Selling agent	150000	390	385
Restaurant	236500	2065	115
Weaving	874800	12722	69
Grain milling	130000	560	232
Tailoring	103000	905	114
Electrical services	28000	245	114
Transport services	691000	2240	308
Animal traction services	160000	710	225
Others	147000	550	267
Total	4594300	31682	145

Source : Field Survey, 2004-05.

XI. What Ails these Enterprises?

In addition to the collection of quantitative information about enterprises, qualitative information was also sought from the entrepreneurs with a view to understanding the problems being faced by them in running enterprises. These problems can be broadly grouped into the following headings:

(i) Structural constraints
(ii) Supply related constraints
(iii) Demand related constraints

(i) Structural constraints

Structural constraints relate to geo-physical and topographical conditions that severely constrict the enterprises due to inaccessibility, fragile resource base, harsh physical conditions, difficulty in accessing market and information etc. Precisely, this makes the large and medium entrepreneurs shy away from setting up enterprises in such difficult regions. However, numerous small and tiny enterprises have either come up spontaneously or have been promoted based on local resources and skills. But many of these enterprises suffer from numerous constraints and handicaps and as a result, some of them have either discontinued and some others are languishing in low efficiency trap. A large majority of enterprises have therefore sprung up in trade and service related activities rather than manufacturing based on local resources and skills. Such enterprises have weak linkage effects and they largely cater to the needs of final demands of population instead of being linked as intermediate inputs to the other enterprises.

(ii) Supply side related constraints

Supply side constraints relate to credit, training, market, technology and institutions; which are often interrelated. Credit has often been seen one of the most important factors restricting entrepreneurial activities. Few enterprises avail credit from banking institutions primarily because collateral requirement often poses serious bottlenecks in availing credit. Also, many of the activities for which credit is required are not regarded as bankable projects. In the rural set-up where banking coverage is extremely poor and is not often aimed at promoting entrepreneurial activity, further add to the woes of enterprises.

In the existing set-up, commercial and cooperative banks have not been able to meet the credit needs of micro-enterprises primarily because of insistence on bankable projects and collateral needs which often discourage entrepreneurs to start their activities. Existing financial institutions, therefore, need to be increasingly sensitised about the role of micro-enterprises in the area development; and they need to act as catalysts of development rather than thwart the development activities by their rigid and targeted approach. There is hardly any micro-financial institution in the Non-Governmental Organisation (NGO) sector in the region that could take care of the financial needs of entrepreneurial activities. To overcome the problem, it is also suggested that a specialised agency, in the line of existing Venture Capital Fund, can be set-up which can exclusively facilitate the diverse credit needs of entrepreneurs in the non-farm sector (Papola and Sharma, 2005).

Imparting skill training through formal institutions is abysmally low and most of the skills acquired are through informal means (weaving, tailoring, basket making, metal works, for example). The Technical Institutions (ITIs) that impart training are often located at distant places and nearer to towns, thereby having little relevance of such training for rural enterprises.

The skill training is mostly traditional type which is suitable to low productive enterprises and have little relevance in an increasing competitive environment. It is, therefore, important to upgrade the skill training to make the enterprises efficient and compete with the products and services that are available from the plane areas. Existing institutional mechanisms of training needs to be strengthened and revitalized with proper integration and coordination to make them more relevant to the needs of competitive environment. Location- and sector-specific training needs to be organized with a decentralised framework on a continuous basis. There are certain activities where skills levels are changing fast due to changes in technology. This is the area where training and skills upgradation is a crucial factor.

Technology is an important factor in a bid to improve the productivity of rural non-farm enterprises. In most cases, technology used is traditional and outdated with little or no surplus creating capacity which is must for the efficiency of enterprises. Introduction of new and improved technology is necessary in order to raise productivity and incomes of non-farm enterprises. There is a need for a wider application of information technology that would not only bring about efficiency but also open up significant employment and income opportunities. There is also a need for replication of innovative and viable technologies suiting to the hill region with similar bio-physical conditions.

Some of the appropriate technologies are available for certain products and service groups elsewhere, yet it is difficult to disseminate such technologies in remote hill areas due to lack of institutional mechanism. There is therefore the need for creating a proper institutional mechanism which is relevant to meet the local needs, and which would not only link up the existing institutions and revitalise them but also create new institutions in a dynamic framework.

(iii) Demand side related constraints

Trade and service related activities dominate the product structure, and manufacturing has narrow product lines. A large part of demands for goods and services comes from the local population whose income is low and, therefore, it becomes an inadequate base for growth unless the demand is linked to wider markets. The lack of product diversification and price competitiveness makes these enterprises highly inefficient and often they have to face stiff competition from the cheap and better products from the plane areas.

Demand constraint is therefore closely related to the quality of products. Introduction of new and upgraded products is important in an effort to widen the markets and raising productivity. Linking local markets to wider markets at regional and national levels is necessary with a view to strengthening the rural-urban linkages and establishing channels of information which would help local entrepreneurs to get fair prices of their products.

This would, however, require multifaceted interventions from the supply side on an integrated manner and a strong policy thrust to trigger off large-scale enterprise development. For this purpose there is a need to set-up business development services that would provide all the relevant services (information about market, demand and supply situation, product specification and development, benchmarking, technology outsourcing, critical raw material, entrepreneurial development programmes etc.) in an integrated manner.

Hill areas suffer from inherent internal and external constraints that severely restrict the development of enterprises, many of which emanate from the nature of mountain specificities. The question arises here as to how to trigger off enterprise development in these economies.

Not only have the infrastructure in general, but also the lack of power, communication credit and technology severely constricted the growth of enterprise. Provision of basic infrastructure like roads, power and communication are critical for general development, and these facilities should receive priority in any development agenda. A number of studies document the fact that in spite of institutional mechanism in place, the ease of access to these inputs is limited to a small proportion of entrepreneurs, and often at a high transaction cost which is beyond the affordability of a large number of entrepreneurs. Precisely, this is the reason why most of the entrepreneurs resort to informal financial institutions for their credit needs.

There is, therefore, need for accessibility of these inputs in an integrated manner and at an affordable cost with a view to promoting enterprise activities. The present support system is not only inadequate but also inappropriate for enterprise development. There is, also need for evolving special policies and support mechanism to promote the micro and small enterprises taking into account the diversity and constraints in the regions.

It is also argued that mountain areas should primarily focus on niche products in which the region has a comparative advantage rather than producing those products that do not have any distinct advantage in terms of product and price competitiveness (Papola *et al.*, 2005). Such enterprise-based activities would provide higher income through processing and value addition and help develop the upstream and downstream linkages necessary to generate internal momentum of growth. Some of the enterprise-based activities have been developed in certain parts of hilly region in the Hindu Kush Himalayan region based on niche products. The most widely known example is Western Sichuan (China), where over two-dozen products have been developed based on mountain-specific resources. The other areas where specific products (rather limited one) have been developed are apple cultivation in Himachal Pradesh, vegetable farming in Garampani area in Nainital district, ginger and pineapple in Meghalaya and other parts of North-Eastern states, tea plantation and processing in Ilam district in Nepal, livestock and dairy development in the areas closer to Kathmandu and apple cultivation in Arunachal Pradesh. The other important mountain product is tourism that has been promoted in a number of countries (e.g. Nepal, Central Himalayan region in India, NWFP in Pakistan). The hill region of Uttarakhand has also immense potential for developing such enterprises particularly in horticulture, minor forest products, forest-based products, wool processing and woollen products, micro hydel plants and tourism, and other amenity services.

XII. Conclusion

Dependence on the non-farm sources of employment and income is pervasive at the household level. A significant part of household income constitutes from non-farm sources (68%). The better-off and more educated lot takes the advantages of more remunerative opportunities (regular/salaried employ-ment) in the non-farm sector, while poor depends more on unskilled wage employment and transfer incomes (remittance). Despite the numerous constraints, a significantly large number of households depend on non-farm source of employment (66%) that contributes 68 per cent income from this source. There exists a wide diversity of occupational groups across different spatial units, caste and land size classes. Such diversity exists not only in terms of share of employment but also in terms of sources of income. This is true for all the social groups across different development blocks and the finding of our study supports our hypothesis that higher share of workforce in non-farm sector translates into higher income at household and region levels.

Field level data amply show a highly gender biased work structure in rural areas of the state as women overwhelmingly work in agriculture-related occupations, while their male counterparts work in non-farm occupations. About 27 per cent of non-farm workers are illiterates (males accounting for 12 per cent and female 39 per cent) and about 1 per cent possesses technical education (none female). Educational status is lower for females in each level of education as compared to males. Most of the illiterates are concentrated in weavers, labourers, shopkeepers, service workers. This has resulted in an entry barrier of females in the non-farm sector. This finding also supports our hypothesis that low level of education among females has created disparities in employment opportunities in the non-farm sector as their share in the non-farm sector is about 11 per cent, while the share of males accounts for about 41 per cent.

Field data help to understand the diversities across different occupational groups within non-farm segments – the casual wage earners, the regular/salaried workers and the non-agricultural rural enterprises. Within each segment, there are divergent activities and occupational groups with considerable heterogeneity and inequities across different segments of non-farm sector in terms of days of work, average earnings and capital requirements etc.

Majority of casual workers belong to sub-marginal and marginal landholding size classes. Most of the casual workers belong to illiterate category and those, who have completed middle level schooling. Most of the casual workers are driven desperately from the lower income groups and such intensity gets attenuated in higher income groups. Clearly, the less developed blocks show a greater demand for such sporadic nature of employment than the developed ones. On an average, casual works provide employment of less than two months in a year. Males get most of the employment in non-agriculture activities while females have limited access to such opportunities. Female get almost one-third lower wages than their male counterparts.

Those who possess higher level of education have also better prospects of getting regular/salaried employment. Improving the levels of education is, therefore, necessary in order to promote better-paid regular/salaried employment. Land size classes, educational levels and per capita income groups are positively correlated to the levels of earnings.

Majority of enterprises appear to be dominated by service activities with a narrow profile of activities. This kind of enterprise-based activities had, however, limited product lines, carried out on a small scale with little surplus for reinvestment. Entrepreneurial activities, however, continued within numerous internal and external constraints. But over the years, these enterprises are languishing and operating at a low equilibrium trap with little product diversification and surplus. The major reasons for sickness of these enterprises can be attributed to both supply and demand side aspects.

Education levels of entrepreneurs are low and nearly one-fourth are illiterates, and nearly half of the entrepreneurs have schooling up to high school level only. Those who are in the highest and lowest income groups scarcely participate in such activities.

Family labour is more prominent in rural enterprises, nearly three-fourths of employment constitute family labour and one-fourth hired labour. On an average, these enterprises provide employment for about four months in a year. Access to credit, technology and market is low and most of the output of these enterprises is meant for the local markets. Input linkages are extremely weak and generate little or no value addition to the enterprises. Mean earnings per man-day works out to be Rs.145 with large variations across enterprises. The lowest mean earnings is noted for weavers, which provides highest man-days of family employment but earnings are observed to be below the casual wage earners. It is necessary to rejuvenate the weaving home-based enterprise through variety of promotional measures, which has the potential for generating strong forward and backward linkages to the local economy.

It can be observed that a significantly large number of households depend on the non-farm source of employment (66%) that contributes to about 68 per cent of incomes. Regression results also show that the monthly per capita income of the household is positively and significantly affected by the higher share of non-farm employment and higher area under horticulture, which contribute the most in explaining the regression. The logistic model clearly shows that one unit increase in land area under horticulture reduces the odds of employment in non-farm sector significantly, thus helping in productive engagement of people in remunerative activities. This supports our hypothesis that diversification process promotes more employment and incomes at household and region levels.

8

Migration Patterns and Linkages

I. Introduction

Extensive research has been done on the different aspects of migration – its nature, causes, patterns and consequences – within different theoretical constructs. On the one extreme, there are individualistic approaches to migration that emphasises that migration is primarily stimulated by rational choice of individual; and the decision to migration depends upon the expected wage differentials rather than the actual wage differentials. A notable articulation of this model is associated with Todaro (1969). The other variant of this approach is push-pull model of Lee (1966) that identifies the push and pull related factors of spatial movement, built on Ravenstein law of migration (1885). At the other end, there is structuralist formulation to migration, which argues that labour migration is inevitable in the process of capitalistic production structure, and capitalistic system exploits the labour for its own advantages. Labour mobility for poor is, therefore, not a choice but the only option available for survival. The strand of thoughts is credited to scholars like Safa, Mc Gee, Standing and Breman, who have analysed labour mobility within the Marxian framework (cited from de Haan, 1999). In between these two extreme approaches, there is yet another strand of analysis which is basically an extension of Todaro Model, which views the migration process within the framework of households in which households' decisions are central to migration rather than individuals' as the rational actors (Stark; 1980, 1991). Both the individual and household-based decisions consider migration as an essential economic phenomenon which has positive consequences; while the structural school views labour mobility as an exploitative mechanism of capitalistic framework, which have negative consequences, both at destination and source areas.

In Uttarakhand, migration outflows can be traced within a broad framework of underdevelopment theory and in the structuralist postulation that has influenced the decisions to migrate. Both the theoretical strands reinforced one another and have been closely related to each other having a great underpinning to the cause of out-migration from the region.

Migration has been a common phenomenon in the hill region of Uttarakhand and is closely related to its socio-economic and cultural patterns. Most of the earliest works on migration in the Uttarakhand hill areas have focused on the seasonal nature of migration, which was prominent among tribal population (cited from Bora, 1996). Scheduled Tribes (*Bhotia*) had a long tradition of migration, both due to cultural and economic reasons, which was primarily motivated by trading activities with Tibet and their mobility was guided by the trade interests. The complete ban on trade with Tibet in 1962 had however adversely affected their economy and hence mobility.

Earliest literature on migration is therefore essentially related to a temporary or seasonal nature of migration of one community and it sheds very little light on the differing nature and pattern of migration in the region. There has been no comprehensive study on migration that deals with different aspects of population movement from the region, barring some micro level and village level studies. Notwithstanding the limitations of these studies in terms of sample size and coverage, all these micro level studies do indicate that male-specific out-migration from the region is huge and has been increasing over the years (Sharma, 1980; Khanka, 1984; Bora, 1986). The main reason for out-migration is closely related to the economic backwardness of the region, which is regarded as a most common feature of backward regions. In fact, in the region, out-migration and economic underdevelopment reinforce each other and produces a vicious circle that further accentuates the process of underdevelopment (Joshi, 1980). Some of the field studies also corroborate the increasing mobility of population from different parts of the underdeveloped region (Breman, 1978, 1985; Ghosh and Sharma 1995; Bora, 1996; de Haan, 1999).

The hill region of Uttarakhand is by and large characterised as a subsistence economy. Agriculture is predominantly a low pay-off activity and no dramatic improvement can be brought about in the existing situation due to typical biophysical constraints. Also, there has been an extremely limited diversification of agriculture crops into high value horticultural crops that is regarded as an important policy option for the hill agriculture. Growing population and declining land-man ratio has made cultivation of traditional cereal crops highly uneconomical. As a result, foodgrain production has not been sufficient to meet the growing demand, thus resulting in an increasing dependence on importing foodgrains outside the region. Further, increasing resource scarcity and degradation of natural resources have posed a serious challenge to environment and livelihood sustainability. Industrial base is precariously small and most of the industrial activities fall outside the hill districts. Therefore, the region is bereft of any major industrial activity, barring some household and tiny enterprises.

It has generally been argued that one of the main reasons for underdevelopment of the region is the complete neglect of mountain perspective while designing and implementing various development plans, which have peculiar specificities (Jodha, 2000). Hill areas are vastly different from plane areas in terms of setting, resources, accessibility to infrastructure, technology, and knowledge and opportunities. The development interventions also needs to be entirely different in the case of mountain economy which requires a special treatment; but unfortunately most often mountain frame has been found missing in all the developmental interventions. In spite of low development, the region has certain potentials in which it has comparative advantages such as forest resources, hydro-power, minerals and tourism. However, these niche opportunities did not help the region either; rather these resources have been extracted to the advantage of urban areas. These resources have thus limited linkages to the local population and the economy, and most of the benefits (value addition) have been accrued to the urban centres. Such exploitative relations acted as suction pumps, pulling in the resources from the highland (hill) for the benefits to the low land (urban areas) for the advantage of later with little or no value additions to the former (Jodha, 1997, 2000). Such an unequal highland and low-land relationship has resulted in a low economic base for the former that has resulted in limited employment and livelihood opportunities for the growing labour force. When the economic base is low, livelihood opportunities outside agriculture is bound to be limited, and most often out-migration is looked as an important livelihood diversification strategy. Even a relatively higher literacy rate and higher educational attainments have not helped either to restrict the flow of out-migration, rather these have further accentuated the process due to lack of opportunities in the region. Out-migration is therefore not an unusual event but a constant response to a fragile resource base (land and forest), environmental degradation and hence livelihood insecurity.

II. Typology of Migration

Here, we have considered three types of migrants – short-term migrants, long-term migrants and permanently shifted migrants. All persons migrating for less than nine months during the last one year has been considered as short-term migrant. Persons migrating for a total period of nine months and more during the last one year have been considered as a long-term migrant. Permanently migrated persons are those who have been earlier a member of the household, but has permanently settled elsewhere along with other family members and maintain some sort of social and economic transactions back to the place of origin through remittance and occasional visits. Migrating households has been defined as those households from where at least one family member reported to be migrated and those who do not report any migration from the household has been defined as non-migrating households.

III. Migrating Households and Household Features

Some of the micro level studies conducted in the Uttarakhand hill area indicate that 42 to 57 per cent households report at least one out-migrant (Sharma, 1980; Khanka, 1984; Bora, 1986, 1996). Our results show that 48 per cent household report out-migration (Awasthi, 2010). There are 34 per cent households, which report long-term migration and 16 per cent households report permanent migration whereas 4 per cent households are such that report short-term migration (Table 8.1). Some of the households report more than one type of migration. Propensity to out-migrate is generally reported as higher in less developed blocks (Berinag, Kirtinagar, Salt and Dunda) than relatively developed blocks, barring Dharchula which is showing a considerably higher propensity of out-migration. Short-term migration is prominent in two blocks (Bhatwari and Dunda) in Uttarkashi district from where households move from Bhatwari (higher altitude) to Dunda (lower altitude) during the winter season for about 3-4 months. This has been part of a long tradition of tribal culture when they used to move from higher altitude to lower one and *vice versa* along with herd of sheep, but gradually this practice of seasonal migration has attenuated due to declining traditional household manufacturing base. Extreme cold and inclement weather conditions in these villages also force other social groups (Kshatriyas and Scheduled Castes) to move to lower altitude area. In any case, seasonal migration is reported to be very low and by and large motivated by other than economic reasons. The other two blocks also report short-term migration but the intensity is very low (4%) and this migration takes place to nearby urban towns (Mussoorie and Ramnagar) in search of some manual or casual work (Rickshaw pulling in Mussoorie and hotel-room servicing in Ramnagar, for instance). Intensity of long-term and permanent out-migrating households is also higher in relatively less developed blocks than the developed blocks with an exception at Dharchula. We have noted earlier in Chapter 7 that Bhatwari, Chamba and Hawalbagh, which are relatively developed blocks, have higher area under horticulture and other non-food crops and also report lower intensity of migration. This is one of the distinct findings of the migrating households and supports our hypothesis that if horticulture base is developed, it can productively engage its male workforce in horticulture and eventually help restrict out-migration. Badhani (1998) also comes out with similar findings in a study of Garampani in Nainital district.

As regards the intensity of migration among social groups, Scheduled Tribes and 'other caste' are showing very high intensity of out-migration, while the upper castes and Scheduled Castes are reporting lower out-migration. In fact, the intensity is lowest among the Scheduled Castes. The relationship between the social category and intensity of out-migration among all migrating households appears to be less clear but more complex. Earlier findings on migration had consistently shown that out-migration is highest among the upper castes and least among the Scheduled Castes, and backward castes (Bora, 1996). However, our results prohibit such simplistic generalisation and show that migration now tends to be more complex and diversified. For instance, the present result shows that out-migration is highest among the 'other caste' with lowest household incomes, and a very high out-migration is reported among Scheduled Tribes, which are better-off households. It is clear that migration is not necessarily conspicuous among the poorer households; rather two different processes seem to work at a time. People move out with different motivations – some people are forced to move out in order to eke out their livings as earning opportunities at the place of origin are extremely limited, while some people do out-migrate in order to seize better employment and income opportunities. Migration is most widespread across all social groups, even in the case of Scheduled Castes that report the lowest out-migration, have an out-migrant at every third house. However, the intensity of permanent out-migration is much higher among Brahmins and Scheduled Tribes and rightly so. Permanent out-migration is a long drawn process; people generally out-migrate for a considerable length of time either as short or long-term migrants and eventually get footholds (livelihood opportunities) in the urban centres/towns that help them to settle permanently. Permanent migration is probably the terminus point in this process, when the out-migrants have some perennial source of income and social security. These two social groups have the highest household incomes that precisely help them to seize better employment and earning opportunities outside, and eventually settle down there permanently. Higher educational attainments and social network have also helped people to get some foothold and ultimately settle permanently. For instance, Brahmins having highest educational levels and a fairly high share in regular wage/salaried employment have got permanent footholds at the place of destination, while Scheduled Tribes form a closely knit society. A large number of tribal households have moved out from their place of residence to commercial and trading centres where business opportunities are better, and some who are highly educated have also settled outside. The 'other caste' and the Scheduled Castes which are economically disadvantaged classes have rather limited opportunities of such types; hence, the rate of permanent migration among them is low.

It has been noted that the rate of migration increases with the increase in the size of landholdings and the trend appears to be clear and consistent throughout. But certain aberrations are clearly observed from this pattern, when other forms of out-migration are analysed. Short-term out-migrating households, for instance, show a negative relationship with landholding sizes; highest propensity is reported among the landless followed by the sub-marginal landholding class. In the case of permanent out-migrating households, the propensity dips in the case of highest land-owning class, probably because the highland asset acts as a discouraging factor for such sort of movement.

The propensity to migrate generally increases with the increase of per capita income, with some erratic trend in between. Flow of migration gradually increases with the increase in per capita income at the lower end and then falls in the middle, and finally rises steeply. Probably, the trend indicates that at the lower end of incomes, people are forced to driven out due to extremely low incomes; and then migration stream gets stabilised as some minimum threshold level of income is reached, which discourages out-migration; but at the higher end of income levels, people are pulled up or tempted to out-migrate as better opportunities are available there for them. However, the trend seems to be clearer in the case of long-term and permanent migration. The trends of long-term and permanent migration are observed to be working in an opposite direction with respect to the levels of per capita income. Long-term migration increases relatively

Table 8.1 : Percentage of Households Reporting Different Types of Migration according to Household Features

Household feature	*Short-term migrating HHs*	*Long-term migrating HHs*	*Permanently migrating HHs*	*All migrating HHs*
Blocks				
Berinag	0.00	42.31	21.15	55.77
Bhatwari	20.00	14.00	12.00	38.00
Chamba	0.00	31.82	4.55	31.82
Dharchula	0.00	38.00	22.00	56.00
Dunda	9.62	34.62	1.92	44.23
Hawalbagh	0.00	21.57	11.76	27.45
Kirtinagar	2.00	50.00	18.00	60.00
Salt	1.96	41.18	35.29	70.59
Social Category				
Brahmins	0.00	32.73	30.91	54.55
Kshatriyas	1.31	35.37	11.79	43.67
SCs	9.26	22.22	7.41	35.19
STs	18.00	34.00	30.00	70.00
Others	0.00	75.00	8.33	75.00
Land class (acre)				
No land	12.50	25.00	0.00	31.25
>0 <= 0.50	7.19	34.53	7.91	45.32
>0.50 <= 2.50	1.90	35.07	18.96	49.76
>2.50 <= 5.0	3.33	26.67	40.00	56.67
>5.0 <= 10.0	0.00	75.00	25.00	75.00
Income group (MPCI)				
Up to Rs. 250	5.88	23.53	5.88	32.35
Rs. 250 to 500	2.73	41.82	9.09	50.00
Rs. 500 to 1,000	5.00	34.29	10.71	44.29
Rs. 1,000 to 2,500	4.85	31.07	27.18	53.40
More than Rs. 2,500	0.00	23.08	69.23	76.92
Development status of blocks				
Less developed	3.41	41.95	19.02	57.56
Developed	5.13	26.15	12.82	38.46
All	4.25 (17)	34.25 (137)	16.00 (64)	48.25 (193)

Note: Figures in parentheses indicate number of migrating households out of total 400 sample households.

Source: Field Survey, 2004-05.

faster at the lower end of per capita income, and then starts declining at the middle level, albeit slowly, then falls at the higher end of income group; while in the case of permanent migration, the intensity of migration increases with the income levels and both appear to be positively correlated. This trend clearly indicates that long-term migration and income levels are, by and large, negatively correlated and higher intensity of migration is primarily motivated by low levels of income. However, in the case of permanent migration, the opposite is the case and this clearly shows that permanent migration is closely related to higher levels of income.

IV. Magnitude of Out-migration

Village level studies in the Uttarakhand hill area indicate that 27 to 74 per cent male workers were absent and worked outside from their villages (cited from Bora, 1996). Some of the other micro level studies indicate that the magnitude of out-migration varied between 7 per cent and 24 per cent (Pande, 1996; Bora, 1996; Mamgain, 2004). The variations in the intensity of migration basically arise due to differing treatment to the concept of migration. Some of the studies did not consider permanent migrants in the frame of migration, which is taking place in an unprecedented scale in the hill region. We have tried to capture all types of out-migrants from the household survey. It can be observed from Table 8.2 that out of the total sample population, 23 per cent is recorded as migrants, who out-migrate for different durations according to the types of migration. About 29 per cent males and 17 per cent females are reported as migrants. Looking at the types of migration it can be noted that permanent migrants constitute the highest proportion (14%), followed by long-term migrants (8%), and least in the case of short term-migrants (2%). Female share is very low particularly among long-term migrants, but among permanently shifted out-migrants, they share almost equal proportion.

The intensity of migration varies among social groups by types of migration. We have noted earlier that short-term migration is more

Table 8.2 : Magnitude of Out-migrants

Type of migrants	*Male*	*Female*	*Person*
Short-term migrants	2.21 (27)	1.80 (19)	2.02 (46)
Long-term migrants	14.10 (172)	1.14 (12)	8.08 (184)
Sample population (excluding permanently shifted)	(1219)	(1056)	(2275)
Permanently shifted migrants	14.76 (211)	14.01 (172)	14.41 (383)
Sample population (including permanently shifted)	(1430)	(1228)	(2658)
Total migrants (including permanently shifted)	(410)	(203)	(613)
Per cent of total migrants (including permanently shifted)	28.67	16.53	23.06

Note : Figures in parentheses show absolute numbers.
Source : Field Survey, 2004-05.

prominent in two blocks, which is primarily motivated by non-economic reasons rather than economic reasoning. Earlier, such migration was associated to only Scheduled Tribes and their movement was induced by both economic (trade) and socio-cultural reasons; but now other social groups also move due to extreme cold and harsh conditions during winters. Scheduled Tribes and Scheduled Castes are the major social groups in the surveyed villages that have been moving seasonally every year constituting 12 per cent of tribal population and 4 per cent of Scheduled Caste population (Table 8.3). By and large, seasonal migration is not much in prevalence in Uttarakhand, which is primarily an economic phenomenon of movement of population in other parts of the country during crop harvesting season and in construction projects.

Long-term migration from the region for livelihood has been the most common feature since a long time, and over the years this process has accentuated and gradually culminated into permanent out-migration as migrants got some footholds in the urban centres. In the surveyed sample households, it was observed that a large number of migrants were reported as permanently shifted (14%), which is much higher than those reported as long-term migrants (8%). There has been a radical shift in the nature of out-migration over the years.

Earlier, people used to move only for long duration (usually for more than 9 months) and maintained strong linkages to the place of origin through regular visits and remittances, but gradually people preferred to migrate out permanently along with spouse and children, as urban centres provided better educational facilities and livelihood opportunities.

We have analysed the stream of out-migrants from the perspective of household composition. It can be noted that the intensity of out-migration is higher among Brahmins and Scheduled Tribes as compared to other social groups. This is true in case of overall migrating persons and permanent migrants. The incidence of long-term migration is, however, higher among the 'other caste' and Scheduled Tribes, and it is much lower among other social groups. As argued, permanent migration is a long drawn process and selective to those who have higher level of educational status and higher income levels. In our sample, Brahmins and Scheduled Tribes are the prominent social groups having higher number of households and per capita incomes than the other social groups. Brahmins are regarded as one of the high social groups in the region with a high social status and higher educational attainments. Their share in regular employment is also observed to be much higher than the other social groups and this precisely helped them to out-migrate permanently. Scheduled Tribes, on the other hand, have been a trading community and most of the tribals have shifted away from their abode nearer to urban centres and market places (district/block headquarters) due to loss of their traditional trade, which forced them to shift elsewhere permanently.

Long-term migration has been reported as highest among the 'other caste' followed by Scheduled Tribes. Here, two distinct processes seem to work together. First, the 'other caste', which is the poorest group, shows highest intensity of long-term out-migration and they are driven out primarily due to their poor economic conditions, as this group is the most disadvantaged one (constituting Muslims) in terms of educational status and income levels. Second, the Scheduled Tribes, who are better-off in terms of income levels, do also report a higher intensity of out-migration, which is induced not by their poor economic conditions but to seize better livelihood opportunities. Reservation in employment has also helped them to migrate for long duration. The conventional wisdom that argues that, most of the out-migration from this region is selective and associated to upper castes seems to be loosing ground in the changing context (Bora, 1996).

The relationship between the intensity of migration and land-ownership seems to be less clear and inconclusive. Some of the village studies found inverse relationship between the landholding and migration (Connell *et al.*, 1976), while some other observed that both are positively correlated (Yadava *et al.*, 1996-97). Some of the migration studies do suggest that the poorest and landless are more prone to out-migrate (Sharma, 1997; Deshingkar *et al.*, 2004). Yet, some other study shows different patterns with different streams of migration (Dayal and Karan, 2003).

Our results also do not point towards any definite pattern. The short-term migration seems to be conspicuous among those who are either landless or own a very little land; while long-term migration is highest among those who have the highest land ownership followed by the landless class. It is clear that migration does not have a single set of patterns; rather it shows different patterns in different land size classes. People do out-migrate with different motivations – landless do out-migrate for earning some livelihood as part of survival strategy, while the landed class out-migrate probably for availing better livelihood opportunities or what is termed as stabilisation strategy (Stark, 1991; Unni, 2001). Such clustering at the lower and higher ends (bimodal relationship) is also noted in micro level investigations (Connell *et al.*, 1976). The intensity of long-term out-migrants is higher in lower income groups of households, while the shifted out-migrants seem to be concentrated in two highest income groups.

However, permanent out-migration is showing some positive relationship with that of land size classes up to a point; but then in the highest land size class, the intensity declines sharply probably indicating that the highest land-owning class discourages permanent out-migration. One can therefore notice that there is a significant diversity in migration streams both in terms of incidence and intensity across social category; land size classes and across region; and within regions. Such diversity has been noted in other regions as well (Srivastava, 1999, 2005).

Table 8.3 : Percentages of Migrating Persons according to Types of Migration

Household feature	*Short-term migrants*	*Long-term migrants*	*Permanent migrants*	*All migrants*
Social Category				
Brahmins	0.00	7.52	26.50	32.03
Kshatriyas	0.45	7.68	8.92	16.32
SCs	3.91	5.21	9.44	17.70
STs	11.72	11.30	30.52	46.51
Others	0.00	18.29	1.20	19.28
Land class (acre)				
No land	6.49	9.09	0.00	15.58
>0 <= 0.50	3.97	7.52	9.64	20.02
>0.50 <= 2.50	0.72	8.53	15.45	23.28
>2.50 <= 5.0	1.56	5.21	28.62	33.46
>5.0 <= 10.0	0.00	18.18	2.94	20.59
Income group (MPCI)				
Up to Rs. 250	1.02	5.61	7.85	13.68
Rs. 250 to 500	1.60	9.30	7.83	17.88
Rs. 500 to 1,000	2.21	8.09	9.60	18.90
Rs. 1,000 to 2,500	2.80	7.48	24.46	32.30
More than Rs. 2,500	0.00	7.50	54.55	57.96
Development status of blocks				
Less developed	1.46	9.51	16.40	25.57
Developed	2.62	6.59	12.20	20.29
All	2.02	8.09	14.41	23.06
Migrants (Nos.)	46	184	383	613

Source: Field Survey, 2004-05.

(i) The Logit Model

In order to ascertain the factors which affect the probability of a person to out-migrate from a household, logistic regression model is fitted, which is as follows:

$$y(P) = \frac{1}{1 + e^{-z}}$$

$$z = \beta_0 + \beta_1 x_1 + \beta_2 x_2 + \beta_! x_! + \beta_4 x_4 + \beta_5 x_5 \quad \beta_6 x_6 + \beta_\forall x_\forall + \beta_8 x_8 + \beta_9 x_9 + \beta_{10} x_{10} + \mu$$

Where :

x_1 = Household Income (*y*)
x_2 = Log of household size (*lnhhsz*)
$x_!$ = Log of per capita land in acre (*lnpcland*)
x_4 = Caste of a worker (dummy, if SC, ST and others=1, otherwise=0) (*dcaste*)
x_5 = Casual labour (dummy, if household belongs to casual labour household=1, otherwise=0) (*caslab*)
x_6 = Male (dummy, if male=1 otherwise=0) (*male*)
$x_"$= Age in completed years (*age*)
x_8= Age square (*age2*)
x_9= Educated (dummy, if educated higher secondary and above =1 non-educated=0)(*educated*)
x_{10}= Skilled worker (dummy, if skilled=1 otherwise=0) (*skilled*)
x_{11}= Status of blocks (dummy, if status of block developed=1 otherwise=0) (*bloksta*)
μ= Stochastic error term

However, using simple logistic model may lead biased estimates of explanatory variable viz., income, because of endogeneity between the income and probability of migration. This essentially implies that the said two variables are mutually determined by each other in the shape of simultaneous equation model.

The exact functional form takes the form of simultaneous equation as follows:

$$P(M) = \beta_0 + \beta_1 x + \beta_2 x_1 + \beta_3 x_2 + \beta_4 x_3 + \_\_\_ + \mu \quad (1)$$

$$Y = \alpha_0 + \alpha_1 M + \alpha_2 x_1 + \alpha_! x_2 + \alpha_4 x_3 + \_\_\_ + \Omega \quad (2)$$

In order to correct the endogeneity problem, 2-stage least square (2SLS) model has been used. Under the 2SLS, income (Y) variable is first regressed upon exogenous variable viz., non-labour income and asset-holding and other control variables.*

y = f (nlab in, asset, control)

The predicted value of y has been used in the logistic model. Hence, the logistic model becomes $P(M) = \beta_0 + \beta\ \hat{y}\ \beta_1 x_1 + \beta_2 x_2 + \beta_! x_! + \beta_4 x_4\ \_\ \beta_n x_n$

where y is predicted value of y (income of households) and $x_{1,}$ x_2 __x_n are control variables.

Results of logistic regressions are presented in Table 8.3A.

Table 8.3A : Results of Logistic Regression

Variables	*All migrants*		*Excluding permanently shifted migrants*		*Long-term migrants*	
migst	*Odds ratio*	*Std. error*	*Odds ratio*	*Std. error*	*Odds ratio*	*Std. error*
$\hat{y}$	1.0014***	0.0005	1.0049***	0.0007	1.0057***	0.0007
lnhhsz	1.2144#	0.2992	5.2107***	1.7771	7.0307***	2.6560
lnpcland	0.8889#	0.1140	0.3964***	0.0659	0.4063***	0.0741
dcaste	3.2518***	0.7721	2.8178***	0.8394	1.0269#	0.3522
caslab	1.0651#	0.2910	12.5450***	4.9862	23.5050***	10.5583
male	17.8040***	4.7856	16.4874***	5.7809	78.8641***	54.3914
age	0.8531***	0.0374	0.9111#	0.0633	0.8324**	0.0634
age2	1.0009*	0.0005	0.9998#	0.0009	1.0009#	0.0010
educated	1.4568#	0.3756	0.2598***	0.0948	0.1951***	0.0765
skilled	1.0417#	0.3012	0.5416*	0.1946	0.15057***	0.0657
bloksta	0.2648***	0.0567	0.1425***	0.0413	0.1298***	0.0413
Pseudo R^2	0.3565		0.4485		0.5134	

*** Significant at 1 per cent level of significance;
**Significant at 5 per cent level of significance;
* Significant at 10 per cent level of significance;
# Insignificant at 10 per cent level of significance.
Note : Dependent variable is probability of migration among household members;

* Non-labour income has been used as an alternate instrumental variable which is well recognized in the literature (Duraiswamy, 2000).

As we have noted earlier, people out-migrate with different motivations according to types of migration that has significant implications on people and on local economy. Here, we analyse all types of out-migration separately and the factors that affect the probability of a person to out-migrate. We notice that there is significant diversity in different types of migration which signifies in terms of the values of coefficients.

It is noted that the coefficients of all independent variables which represent the odds ratio are in accordance with our *a priori* expectations, barring non-labour household income ($\hat{y}$) which is not as per expectation.

In the case of all migrants taken together, the coefficients of non-labour household income ($\hat{y}$), disadvantaged social group workers (dcaste), male workers (male), age (age), and block status (bloksta) are significant at 1 per cent level of significance. While coefficients of log of household size (lnhhsz), log of per capita land (lnpcland), casual labour workers (caslabhh), skilled workers (skilled), educated person (educated) turns out to be insignificant even at 10 per cent level of significance. However, age2 is significant at 10 per cent level of significance.

For permanently excluding the shifted migrants (short- and long-term together) and long-term migrants, most of the variables are significant at 1 per cent level of significance, barring age and age2 for short and long-term migrants taken together and disadvantaged social group workers (dcaste) and age2 for long-term migrants which are insignificant even at 10 per cent level of significance.

It is important to note that odds ratio for non-labour household income ($\hat{y}$) is close to 1 suggesting very small impact on the probability of person to out-migrate.

It is noted that the odds of migration considerably goes up as household size increases. This is quite plausible in the poor households with higher dependency ratio that in turn pushes the able-bodied male members to out-migrate in search of jobs and livelihoods. This is more in the case of long-term migrants who are the most vulnerable lots. Short-term migration is not that conspicuous in the region as it occurs largely as temporary movements of people as part of the tradition which is motivated by certain socio-economic reasons. Such movements take place from higher altitude to lower one in the winter season and back to higher altitude during the summer season. This has been a long tradition of tribals in the region and such migration largely takes place within the sub-regions (block).

Also we notice that as per capita land increases, odds of migration goes down. It can be inferred that if a household owns sufficient per capita land, probability of migration of its members tends to decline. This has policy implications, particularly for those migrants who own very little land or are landless. Odds of migration in the case of disadvantaged social group workers (dcaste) is higher than non-SC and ST workers. For casual-work households, probability of out-migration is significantly higher for all types of migrants. For long-term migrants, it is indeed 23 times greater as compared to non-casual labour households. Similarly, odds of migration for male workers are much higher as compared to female workers. For long-term migrants, it is almost 79 times greater than females.

As age of an individual worker increases by one year, odds of migration declines, meaning thereby that migration is more conspicuous among younger age groups than the older age groups. This is evident from the coefficients of age and age2 that, initially, as age increases by one year, odds of migration goes down but after achieving certain age (generally at higher age) odds of migration goes up (albeit, marginally). Such out-migration is primarily motivated by a greater need for social security including health and care at older age.

Odds of migration for an educated person (higher secondary and above) is 45.7 per cent more than an uneducated worker, for all migrants taken together. But when we look at the coefficients of excluding permanently shifted migrants and long-term migrants, then we notice that odds of migration is 74.0 and 80.5 per cent lower respectively as compared to non-educated ones. Long-term migrants are relatively more vulnerable as compared to other forms of migrants. Permanently shifted migrants are much better in terms of education status than short- and long-term migrants. Similarly, probability of out-migration for skilled workers is 45.8 and 84.9 per cent lower for excluding permanently shifted migrants and long-term migrants respectively. An overwhelmingly large number of long-term migrants are without skills.

It is important to note that without requisite education and relevant marketable skills, it becomes extremely difficult for the long-term migrants to compete in the skilled urban labour market, which obviously result in low income at the place of destination.

Also, out-migration is taking place from relatively less developed blocks than the developed ones. Overall, probability of migration is reduced by 73.5 per cent in the case of developed block status as compared to the less-developed one and this intensity is highest in the case of long-term migrants (87%). This has important policy implications. As region is developed, it restricts out-migration substantively.

It is clear from the above analysis that out-migration is one of the important livelihood strategies in the hill districts, and such outflow is more conspicuous in the less developed blocks, which are relatively less endowed in terms of resources. Such outflow of people is concentrated more among the disadvantaged social groups (SCs, STs and 'other caste') and from among the casual labour households. Without requisite education levels and marketable skills, an overwhelmingly large number of long-term migrant workers have low incomes which add to their vulnerability at the place of destination. Lack of opportunities in the local economy pushes them out to find jobs under duress conditions.

V. Characteristics of Migrant Workers

We analyse the migrant characteristics within certain limitations that are usually associated with the household surveys. First, information about the migrants has been collected from the migrating household members and not necessarily from the migrants. However, every care has been taken to elicit migrant's information as accurately as possible from the household member who have some detailed information about the migrants. In certain cases, we have authenticated the migrants' information from other knowledgeable person in the village community.

Second, we shall focus our analysis on long-term and permanently shifted migrants and exclude the short-term migrants from the analysis, primarily because an overwhel-mingly large majority of short-term migrants (96%) move on account of non-economic reasons, while our basic interest lies on understanding the migratory pattern from the economic angle.

Within this limitation, we discuss the characteristics of out-migrants in what follows :

(i) Age-profile

Majority of migrant workers had moved out at their prime age (between 15 to 24 years) (Table 8.4). Results are consistent for both types of migrants. Mean average at the time of migration comes to be

Table 8.4 : Age Profiles of Migrant Workers

Age-group	*Long-term migrants*		*Permanently shifted*		*All*	
	At the time of migration	*At the time of survey*	*At the time of migration*	*At the time of survey*	*At the time of migration*	*At the time of survey*
Up to 14	2.60	0.00	3.77	0.00	3.08	0.00
15-19	7.14	6.49	24.53	12.26	14.23	8.87
20-24	61.69	24.03	40.57	56.60	53.08	36.29
25-29	20.78	25.97	17.92	20.75	19.62	24.19
30-34	7.79	18.18	13.21	6.60	10.00	14.11
35-39	0.00	10.39	0.00	2.83	0.00	6.45
40-59	0.00	14.94	0.00	0.94	0.00	9.68
60 and above	0.00	0.00	0.00	0.00	0.00	100.00
Total	100.00 (154)	100.00 (154)	100.00 (106)	100.00 (106)	100.00 (260)	100.00 (260)

Note : Figures in parentheses show absolute number of workers.
Source : Field Survey, 2004-05.

22 years, while at the time of survey it is estimated to be 34 years. Most of the field studies support this type of findings, primarily because the returns from migration are supposedly to be higher at younger age than at matured age. Nearly one-fourth permanently shifted workers seem to be having moved at a much younger age (15-19 years) than the long-term out-migrants. Probably, it takes longer time for them to get permanent footholds in the urban labour market.

(ii) Educational status

Generally, illiterates and less educated tend to migrate for short duration (seasonal migrants), and better educated out-migrate for longer duration. This is one of the consistent findings of most of the migration studies (cited from de Haan, 1999; Deshingakar *et al.*, 2004). Also, those workers who migrate for long duration generally posses higher educational and skill levels than those who are resident workers, as the migrants have to compete with others in the urban labour market. Our field level data also corroborate this broad finding. If we compare the educational levels of migrant workers with that of resident workers, then it becomes clear that migrant workers have much better educational status than the resident workers (Tables 8.5). A little over one-fourth to one-third resident workers are illiterate, both by UPS and UPSS statuses respectively; while illiteracy among migrant worker is very low (3-4%). About 28 per cent migrant workers are graduates and above and 5 per cent possess technical education, while the respective figures for resident workers are 7-8 per cent and 1 per cent. It is also noted that different migration streams have different educational levels. For instance, permanently shifted migrants seem to have much better levels of educational status than the long-term migrants. Almost half of the permanently shifted migrants possess graduate and above levels of education.

(iii) Present activity status of migrants

Workers constitute about 46 per cent of the total migrant population and the remaining are non-workers (54%) with little unemployment

Table 8.5 : Educational Levels of Migrant and Non-migrant Workers

Educational level	*Migrants*			*Non-migrants*	
	Long-term	*Permanently Shifted*	*All*	*UPS*	*UPSS*
Illiterate	3.90	2.83	3.46	33.33	26.93
Primary	3.90	1.89	3.08	14.49	12.07
Middle	14.94	5.66	11.15	18.21	19.14
High School	34.42	20.75	28.85	16.92	20.57
Intermediate	21.43	19.81	20.77	8.46	12.55
Graduate and above	12.99	49.06	27.69	7.44	7.94
Technical education	8.44	0.00	5.00	1.15	0.79
Total	100.00 (154)	100.00 (106)	100.00 (260)	100.00 (780)	100.00 (1259)

Note : Figures in parentheses show absolute number of workers.
Source : Field Survey, 2004-05.

among them. But there is a significant difference in activity status between the long-term and permanently shifted migrants (Table 8.6). In the case of long-term migrants, proportion of workers is very high (84%) and non-working population is very low; while in the case of permanently shifted migrants the opposite is true – workers constitute 28 per cent and the remaining are non-workers; students constitute 38 per cent and 'others' 34 per cent comprising mainly housewives. This divergence in activity status is primarily due to the nature of migration streams. Long-term migrants are the unsettled lot at destination and they have to face numerous handicaps in the labour market in terms of job search, duration of employment, employment status, wages, and conditions of work. Sometimes in-migrants also suffer discriminatory treatment in the labour market from the resident migrants. Many a times they have to accept the employment under duress and it takes considerable time for them to get foothold in the labour market and be able to choose between the jobs. This is the reason why work participation rate among them is extraordinarily high. Contrary to long-term migrants, the permanent migrants are better placed in the labour market; work participation rate is low indicating a positive outcome in terms of status and quality of employment. Elderly persons withdraw from the labour market primarily due to improved economic condition and they tend to invest more in children's education. Divergence is also noted from gender perspective – females constitute 45 per cent among permanently shifted population, while in the case of long-term migrants it is around 7 per cent, indicating an overwhelmingly male-specific out-migration.

Table 8.6 : Activity Statuses of Out-migrants

Activity status	*Long-term migrants*			*Permanently shifted*			*All*		
	Male	*Female*	*Person*	*Male*	*Female*	*Person*	*Male*	*Female*	*Person*
Worker	88.95	8.33	83.69	45.03	6.40	27.68	64.75	6.52	45.86
Unemployed	0.58	0.00	0.54	0.47	0.58	0.52	0.52	0.54	0.53
Student	10.47	75.00	14.67	39.81	36.05	38.12	26.63	38.59	30.51
Others*	0.00	16.66	1.08	14.69	56.98	33.68	8.09	54.35	23.10
Total	172	12	184	211	172	383	383	184	567

* Includes housewives, pensioners, too old and too young.
Source : Field Survey, 2004-05.

(iv) Status of employment and occupation of migrants

Table 8.7 presents the status of employment of migrant workers. It can be observed that there is a significant difference in the status of employment between long-term migrants and permanently shifted migrants. The share of regular employment among permanently

Table 8.7 : Status of Employment

Status of employment	*Long-term migrants*			*Permanently shifted migrants*		
	Male	*Female*	*Person*	*Male*	*Female*	*Person*
Self-employed[1]	7.84	0.00	7.79	16.84	45.45	19.81
Regular	38.56	100.00	38.96	65.26	54.55	64.15
Temporary	25.49	0.00	25.32	13.68	0.00	12.26
Casual	28.10	0.00	27.92	4.21	0.00	3.77
Total	100.00 (153)	100.00 (1)	100.00 (154)	100.00 (95)	100.00 (11)	100.00 (106)

Note : Figures in parentheses show absolute number of workers.
Source : Field Survey, 2004-05.

shifted migrant workers is much higher (64%) and casual employment is very low (4%) as compared to long-term migrant workers (39 and 28% respectively). Also, the proportion of temporary employment among permanently shifted migrant workers is lower (12%) than the long-term migrant workers (25%).

The occupational profile of the migrant workers also shows variations between the two different migrant streams. Proportion of technical & managerial personnel; teachers, and clerical & related workers are higher among the permanently shifted workers than the long-term migrant workers, which can be regarded as a better quality of employment. In the case of long-term migrants, service workers constitute the major chunk, of which many have casual and temporary employment status. Female workers constitute about 10 per cent among the permanently shifted workers, while only one female worker has been reported among long-term migrant workers (Table 8.8).

(v) Mean earnings

Monthly mean earnings of migrant workers also tend to show a wide

Table 8.8 : Occupational Profiles of Migrant Workers

Occupation category	*Long-term migrants*			*Permanently shifted migrants*		
	Male	*Female*	*Person*	*Male*	*Female*	*Person*
Technical & managerial worker	5.23	0.00	5.19	22.11	9.09	20.75
Teacher	3.92	100.00	4.55	5.26	36.36	8.49
Clerical & related worker	17.65	0.00	17.53	32.63	9.09	30.19
Shopkeeper & sales worker	8.50	0.00	8.44	14.74	0.00	13.21
Service worker	49.02	0.00	48.70	17.89	0.00	16.04
Other production worker	9.80	0.00	9.74	7.37	45.45	11.32
Transport worker (driver)	5.88	0.00	5.84	0.00	0.00	0.00
Total	100.00 (153)	100.00 (1)	100.00 (154)	100.00 (95)	100.00 (11)	100.00 (106)

Note : Figures in parentheses show absolute number of workers.
Source : Field Survey, 2004-05.

divergence between the two types of migrant workers. Monthly income of permanently shifted workers is nearly 3.3 times higher than the long-term migrants (Table 8.9). Each and every occupation shows a much higher mean income for permanently shifted migrant workers than the long-term migrants, barring weaving and tailoring. The difference is indeed huge for shopkeepers and sales workers (4.5 times), technical & managerial personnel (3.3 times), service workers (2.6 times) and other production workers (2.2 times). Mean earnings is reported to be highest for technical & managerial personnel followed by teachers. Educational status and mean income are positively correlated – the higher is the educational status higher is the mean

Table 8.9 : Mean Monthly Income of Migrant Workers

Particulars	*Long-term migrants (Rs.)*	*Permanently Shifted migrants (Rs.)*
Occupation		
Technical & managerial worker	9750	32045
Teacher	8143	13944
Clerical & related worker	4796	10625
Shopkeeper and sales worker	2792	12500
Service worker	3843	10029
Weavers and tailors	8000	5167
Other production worker	3208	7100
Transport worker (driver)	5722	-
Other workers	9500	11000
Educational Status		
Illiterate	1900	3667
Primary	4283	5500
Middle	3352	7833
High School	3849	10091
Intermediate	4358	12929
Graduate and above	7828	18279
Technical	6423	-
Employment status		
Self-employed	5500	10762
Regular/salaried	6775	18324
Temporary salaried	3718	8000
Casual	2023	6300
Total	4584	15023

Source : Field Survey, 2004-05.

earnings. Highest mean income is associated with regular/salaried employment status followed by self-employment and temporary salaried workers. The lowest income is recorded for casual workers.

The above analysis provides much credence to our hypothesis that permanently shifted workers are better-off than the long-term migrant workers in the long drawn process of out-migration, both in terms of status of employment and earnings. Recent migration story, particularly in 1990s, also tells that much of out-migration flows comprise of permanently shifted migrants than the long-term migrants that have often not discussed much in migration literature in the context of Uttarakhand region.

(vi) Remittance

Remittances play an important role in the individual household as well as village economy at the place of origin. Remittance forms an important source of income, if not major, particularly for poorer households that depend considerably on such transfer income. It also helps stimulate the development of village economy by investing the remittance income on various farm and non-farm activities, which ultimately provide insurance against loss of entitlement (crop failure or other calamity or job loss, for example). But the migration studies on both aspects – the volume of remittance and its impact on the village economy – do not provide any conclusive evidence (Stark, 1980, 1982; Lipton, 1980). Nevertheless, the literature on migration argues that remittance is an important means for poor households, which helps to diversify their incomes and ensure survival (Harris 2004, Ellis and Harris 2004).

We have noted earlier that remittance constitutes 9.4 per cent of the total household income and for the bottom quintile income group; it comprises 17.5 per cent, which is quite substantial. Nearly 37 per cent households (either long-term or permanently shifted) reported having received remittance during last year, of which 29 per cent long-term migrants households and 10 per cent permanently shifted households received such transfer income (Table 8.10). Dependence on remittance of 'other caste' household is the highest from long-term migrants. The 'other caste' is the poorest social group and their share in household income is also observed to be much higher (27%) next to agriculture (30%). Nearly, one-third households among Kshatriyas and Brahmins report having received remittance from long-term migrants, which is much lower for Schedule Caste and Schedules Tribe households. However, a higher proportion of Brahmin and Scheduled Tribe households appear to be receiving remittance from permanent migrants. Most of the households receiving remittance from long-term migrants belong to lower income groups, while those receiving remittance from permanently shifted migrants belong to highest income group. The intensity of households receiving remittance is higher in the less developed blocks than the developed ones.

Table 8.10 : Households Receiving Remittance

Particulars	*Long-term migrant HHs*	*Permanently shifted migrant HHs*	*Any migrant HHs*
Social category			
Brahmins	29.09	18.18	43.64
Kshatriyas	32.31	7.86	38.43
SCs	18.52	7.41	24.07
STs	12.00	12.00	24.00
Others	75.00	8.33	75.00
Income group (MPCI)			
Up to Rs. 250	17.65	5.88	23.53
Rs. 250 to 500	40.00	6.36	43.64
Rs. 500 to 1,000	27.86	6.43	32.14
Rs.1,000 to 2,500	23.30	17.48	38.83
More than Rs. 2,500	15.38	23.08	38.46
Status of blocks			
Less developed	37.56	11.22	47.32
Developed	19.49	8.21	25.13
Total	28.75 (115)	9.75 (39)	36.50 (146)

Source : Field Survey, 2004-05.

Average remittance from long-term migrants is about Rs. 12,235 and from permanently shifted *migrants,* it is Rs. 4,602 per annum that forms 22 per cent and 2.5 per cent of annual income respectively (Table 8.11). It is evident that the flow of remittance is

Table 8.11 : Mean Remittance per Year

Particulars	*Long-term migrants (Rs.)*	*Permanently Shifted migrants (Rs.)*
Social category		
Brahmins	9500	2143
Kshatriyas	13423	6648
SCs	10462	2143
STs	17250	4200
Others	7286	5000
Educational Status		
Illiterate	10000	-
Primary	13917	-
Middle	9910	2600
High School	12569	4273
Intermediate	12710	2600
Graduate and above	16117	5992
Technical	9773	-
Land class (acre)		
No land	19667	-
>0 <= 0.50	12110	3889
>.50 <= 2.50	12267	4026
>2.50 <= 5.0	11200	6958
>5.0 <= 10.0	6200	-
Employment status		
Self-employed	8714	3667
Regular/Salaried	17227	5250
Temporary salaried	11386	2143
Casual	6405	1333
Development status of blocks		
Less developed	12362	3636
Developed	11979	5827
Total	12235	4602

Source : Field Survey, 2004-05.

much lower in the case of permanently shifted out-migrants and the remittance from long-term migrants constitutes an important component for the households, which helps to understand the remittance behaviour and its implications on the local economy. Across social category, Scheduled Tribes and Kshatriyas are remitting a much higher amount among long-term migrants, and the 'others' is remitting the lowest amount. This pattern seems to be consistent with the per capita income behaviour of the households. Educational levels and behaviour of remittance show that those possessing the highest and lowest educational status tend to have a higher remitting intensity than others. Land size classes and the remittance pattern show a negative relationship among the long-term migrants, but for permanently shifted migrants, it shows somewhat positive trends. It is quite plausible that long-term migrants maintain strong linkages to the place of origin and remittance becomes one of the important sources of income for the household members; while in the later case, such linkages do not appear to be stronger and remittance is often occasional. Propensity to remit is closely related to the status of employment. Regular wage/salaried workers have highest average remittance and casual workers have the lowest average remittance. Less developed blocks receive higher average remittance from long-term migrants as compared to the developed blocks, albeit marginally, but the remittance from the permanent migrants flow more to the developed blocks.

(vii) Frequency of remittance

Apart from the volume of remittance, frequency of remittance is also one of the important links at the source area. Both of these would largely depend on the average size of income and relative compulsion and priorities, both at source and destination areas of migrants. Evidence on frequency of remittance is rather scarce. Our field data show that frequency of remittance is very high despite the fact that the average earnings are small (Table 8.12). This in fact is indicative of compulsion at the source area, particularly for poor households. The data show that monthly remittance is the most common feature in both types of migrants. Long-term migrant households depend more on monthly remittance than permanent migrant households. This kind of remittance behaviour indicates that the migrants do maintain closer links to the source area irrespective of duration of migration.

Table 8.12 : Frequency of Remittance

Migration stream	*Once in a month*	*Once in 3 months*	*Once in 6 months*	*Others*	*Total*
Long-term	75.69 (109)	15.97 (23)	6.94 (10)	1.39 (2)	100.00 (144)
Shifted	65.52 (38)	18.97 (11)	8.62 (5)	6.90 (4)	100.00 (58)
Total	72.77 (147)	16.83 (34)	7.43 (15)	2.97 (6)	100.00 (202)

Note : Figures in brackets indicates number of remitters.
Source : Field Survey, 2004-05.

(viii) Contribution to household income

Overall contribution of remittance to the household income is about 9 per cent which is not very significant, yet it is a vital source of income particularly for poor households and low income groups. For instance, it can be noted from Table 8.13 that 'others', constituting Muslims, is the most disadvantaged group whose household income is lowest and their dependence on this source of income is reported to be highest (27%). Also, landless and sub-marginal land size class households have a higher dependence on this source of income. At the lower end of income groups, contribution from remittance is higher as compared to higher per capita income groups. It is clearly revealed by the data set that contribution of remittance to the household income is crucial and an important livelihood strategy particularly for poor households.

Occupation of the heads of households and contribution from the remittance to the household income do not show a very clear relationship. Yet it can be seen that remittance contributes more to the households having occupations like service worker and animal husbandry worker whose household income is relatively very low. Also, remittance contribution to household income in case of teachers is very low, whose household income is highest. In less developed blocks, contribution of remittance to the household income is much higher (2.2 times) than developed blocks.

Table 8.13 : Mean Annual Remittance and its Contribution to Household Income

Household features	*Household income (Rs.)*	*Household income without remittance (Rs.)*	*Net increase due to remittance (Rs.)*	*% increase*
Social category				
Brahmins	70880	66880	4000	5.64 (55)
Kshatriyas	52982	46923	6059	11.44 (229)
SCs	42179	39382	2796	6.63 (54)
STs	61615	58015	3600	5.84 (50)
Others	33489	24573	8917	26.63 (12)
Land class (acre)				
No land	48303	40928	7375	15.27 (16)
>0 <= 0.50	37237	32542	4695	12.61 (139)
>.50 <= 2.50	61312	56343	4969	8.10 (211)
>2.50 <= 5.0	85863	79346	6517	7.59 (30)
>5.0 <= 10.0	82495	74745	7750	9.39 (4)
Occupation of head of household				
Technical & managerial worker	67207	55407	11800	17.56 (5)
Teachers	159229	155062	4167	2.62 (12)
Clerical & related worker	84478	70645	13833	16.38 (18)
Shopkeeper and sales worker	56980	54702	2278	4.00 (27)
Service worker	31758	22318	9440	29.72 (15)
Cultivator	44207	40878	3330	7.53 (141)
Animal husbandry worker	36312	26201	10111	27.85 (9)
Weaver and tailor	50080	47845	2235	4.46 (17)
Other production worker	37870	34870	3000	7.92 (10)
Transport worker (driver)	51741	39741	12000	23.19 (5)
Labourer	29884	28227	1656	5.54 (16)
Housewife	52036	47003	5032	9.67 (31)
Pensioner	74815	68012	6802	9.09 (43)
Not able to work (too old)	54700	47567	7133	13.04 (45)
Others	24113	24113	0	0.00 (6)
Income group (MPCI)				
Up to Rs.250	12558	11232	1326	10.56 (34)
Rs.250 to 500	28612	23398	5214	18.22 (110)
Rs.500 to 1,000	50158	44033	6125	12.21 (140)
Rs.1,000 to 2,500	92043	86931	5112	5.55 (103)
More than Rs.2,500	131908	128600	3308	2.51 (13)
Development status of blocks				
Less developed	47538	41103	6435	13.54 (205)
Developed	61776	58050	3726	6.03 (195)
Total	54479	49365	5114	9.39 (400)

Note : Figures in brackets show number of households.
Source : Field Survey, 2004-05.

(ix) Year of migration

Information was also sought for the year of migration from the migrating households with a view to knowing the pattern of out-migration over the period. The trend of long-term migration for work seems to be increasingly abated over the years and majority of long-term migrants among the sample households seems to have out-migrated during 2000 to 2005. In terms of growth, 1990s saw a fastest growth of out-migration. For permanently shifted migrant workers, the decade of 1970s recorded highest growth. Outflow of permanently shifted migrants was at its peak during 1990-1999, and the trend appears to have somewhat halted in recent years (Table 8.14). It is probably because of high cost of living in urban areas which might have discouraged such process to continue.

Table 8.14 : Year of Out-migration

Type of migrant	*Before 1970s*	*1970-1979*	*1980-1989*	*1990-1999*	*2000-2005*	*All*
Long-term	–	5.84 (9)	11.69 (18)	37.66 (58)	44.81 (69)	100.00 (154)
Permanently shifted	3.77 (4)	11.32 (12)	22.64 (24)	55.66 (59)	6.60 (7)	100.00 (106)

Note : Figures in parentheses indicate number of workers.
Source : Field Survey, 2004-05.

(x) Frequency of visit

Remittance and frequency of visit are important links that have far-reaching implications on the household economy at the source area. Such transactions are important not only in terms of transfer of income and bettering livelihood source but have profound cultural values (sense of collective identity, for example) in itself. Such links are the constant sources of channelling information, communication, sharing knowledge and strengthening ties in a two-way process. However, the strength of such links depends, to a considerable extent, on the duration and nature of migration. Our field data show that frequency of visit to the place of origin is significantly higher among the migrants.

A little above one-tenth long-term migrants visit their native places in less than six months and 59 per cent visit their native places in every six months. There are 27 per cent migrants who visit once in every year. A large majority of long-term migrants (70%), therefore make regular visit to their native place in less than six months, 27 per cent visit once in a year and the percentage of migrants visiting once in two years and occasional visitors are low (3%). In the case of permanently shifted migrants, the frequency of visit is lower as compared to long-term migrants, but 52 per cent migrants make regular visit every year, 30 per cent visit occasionally (social ceremony, performing *puja* etc.) and 18 per cent visit once in two years (Table 8.15).

Table 8.15 : Frequency of Visit by the Migrant Workers

Type of migrant	*Less than 6 months*	*Once in 6 months*	*Once in 1 year*	*Once in 2 years*	*Occasional*	*All*
Long-term	11.04 (17)	58.44 (90)	27.27 (42)	2.60 (4)	0.64 (1)	100.00 (154)
Permanently shifted	–	–	51.89 (55)	17.92 (19)	30.19 (32)	100.00 (106)

Note : Figures in parentheses indicate number of workers.
Source : Field Survey, 2004-05.

VI. Reasons for Migration

Various socio-economic and cultural factors govern the process of out-migration at the place of origin, which may be general or location specific. The most common reasons identified are low income and unemployment at the source area that push out the migrants to the destination which promises better opportunities of livelihood (Oberai and Singh, 1983). Some of the studies show that out-migration is caused principally by the distress reasons at the source area that could be either due to crop failure or drought conditions (cited from Deshingkar *et al.*, 2004) or mass poverty and lack of employment opportunities (Sharma, 1997; Karan 2003; Dayal and Karan 2003), or combination of these and other reasons as well (Deshingkar *et al.*, 2004). However, migration is not always motivated by push factors, people do also out-migrate to enhance their income opportunities and to seize better opportunities at the destination area (Deshingkar and Start, 2003; Deshingkar *et al.*, 2004). The push and pull factors of migration are not coterminus but they are linked to each other and may occur simultaneously due to enormous diversity in migration pattern across different regions (Srivastava, 2005).

In Uttarakhand, the reasons for out-migration are primarily attributed to subsistence agriculture base, economic backwardness and fast depletion of natural resource that have pushed out people from the region since long time. Increasing population pressure on the limited cultivable land made agriculture highly uneconomical for marginal and sub-marginal landholdings. Hill area became gradually food-deficient and dependence on food import increased. Natural resources (forests, mineral and water resources, for example) have been over-exploited with utter neglect of ecological and environment considerations, and most of the benefits of these resources accrued to the plane areas with little or no benefit for the local population and economy. Such exploitative relationship that existed between the producer (hill areas) and the user areas (plane areas) made the former marginalised in the development process. Even special development efforts for the hill region has hardly made any perceptible impact on the increase of employment and earning opportunities, primarily because of utter neglect of the development perspective of the region. All these factors accentuated the process of out-migration from the region and it became the most common livelihood strategy across all the social groups.

We have tried to ascertain the possible reasons for out-migration from both the migrant streams separately, which is presented in Tables 8.16 and 8.17.

Table 8.16 presents the reasons for long-term migrants. It can be observed that unemployment is one of the prime reasons for out-migration across social category and land class. Some aberrations are noted particularly among Scheduled Tribes and landless class where new employment or getting a job is reported to be the main reason for out-migration. This is primarily due to reservation in jobs and majority of landless in this category belong to Scheduled Tribes.

Table 8.16 : Reasons for Migration (Long-term)

Particulars	*Low Income*	*Unem-ployment*	*Better Prospects*	*Got a job/ new employment*	*Others*	*Total*
Social category						
Brahmins	0.00	82.61	4.35	13.04	0.00	100.00 (23)
Kshatriyas	5.38	51.61	0.00	40.86	2.15	100.00 (93)
SCs	7.14	50.00	0.00	28.57	14.29	100.00 (14)
STs	0.00	20.00	20.00	50.00	10.00	100.00 (10)
Others	13.33	86.67	0.00	0.00	0.00	100.00 (14)
Land class (acre)						
No land	0.00	33.33	0.00	66.67	0.00	100.00 (6)
>0 <= 0.50	11.54	59.62	0.00	25.00	3.85	100.00 (52)
>.50 <= 2.50	2.47	55.56	3.70	35.80	2.47	100.00 (81)
>2.50 <= 5.0	0.00	60.00	0.00	30.00	10.00	100.00 (10)
>5.0 <= 10.0	0.00	83.33	0.00	16.67	0.00	100.00 (5)
Educational level						
Illiterate	16.67	83.33	0.00	0.00	0.00	100.00 (6)
Primary	16.67	83.33	0.00	0.00	0.00	100.00 (6)
Middle	12.50	66.67	4.17	16.67	0.00	100.00 (24)
High School	5.66	49.06	1.89	39.62	3.77	100.00 (53)
Intermediate	0.00	53.13	0.00	43.75	3.13	100.00 (32)
Graduate	0.00	50.00	6.25	37.50	6.25	100.00 (16)
Post-graduate	0.00	50.00	0.00	50.00	0.00	100.00 (4)
Technical	0.00	69.23	0.00	23.08	7.69	100.00 (13)
Occupation of head of household						
Teacher	0.00	80.00	0.00	20.00	0.00	100.00 (5)
Clerical & related worker	0.00	46.67	0.00	46.67	6.67	100.00 (15)
Shopkeeper and sales worker	0.00	50.00	0.00	33.33	16.67	100.00 (6)
Service worker	0.00	30.00	0.00	60.00	10.00	100.00 (10)
Transport worker (driver)	66.67	0.00	0.00	33.33	0.00	100.00 (3)
Other workers	0.00	75.00	0.00	25.00	0.00	100.00 (8)
Cultivator	2.38	69.05	7.14	19.05	2.38	100.00 (42)
Animal husbandry worker	0.00	50.00	0.00	50.00	0.00	100.00 (6)
Labourer	0.00	100.00	0.00	0.00	0.00	100.00 (4)
Pensioner	4.17	54.17	0.00	41.67	0.00	100.00(24)
Not able to work (too old)	9.52	52.38	0.00	38.10	0.00	100.00(21)
Housewife	20.00	50.00	0.00	20.00	10.00	100.00(10)

(Contd...)

Table 8.16 : *(Contd...)*

Income group (MPCI)						
Up to Rs.250	33.33	66.67	0.00	0.00	0.00	100.00(9)
Rs.250 to 500	3.23	77.42	1.61	14.52	3.23	100.00(62)
Rs.500 to 1,000	3.85	44.23	3.85	46.15	1.92	100.00(52)
Rs.1,000 to 2,500	3.45	34.48	0.00	55.17	6.90	100.00(28)
More than Rs.2,500	0.00	66.67	0.00	33.33	0.00	100.00(3)
Development status						
Less developed	5.77	59.62	0.96	29.81	3.85	100.00(103)
Developed	3.92	52.94	3.92	37.25	1.96	100.00(51)
Total	5.16(8)	57.42 (89)	1.94(3)	32.26(50)	3.23(5)	100.00 (154)

* Others include unspecified and personal reasons.
Note : Figures in parentheses indicate number of workers.
Source : Field Survey, 2004-05.

Unemployment also dominates as the reason for out-migration across educational status of migrants and more so at lower levels of education. At the lower levels of education, unemployment and low income together are the main motivating forces that unleash the migration process; while at the higher levels of education, new employment plays a significant role. Unemployment and low income, by and large, seems to be the major reason for out-migration irrespective of the occupation of the households, barring in certain cases where the head of the household is having clerical and service occupations. As regards the household income groups, unemployment and low income dominate the lower income groups and highest income groups. However at the middle income groups, new employment is the major reason for out-migration. The two sets of development blocks do not show any significant divergence in terms of decision to migrate; both are dominated by unemployment and low income. Unemployment and low income have thus emerged as the major reason for out-migration for long-term out-migrants.

Low income has emerged as the single major reason for migration among the permanent migrants across social category, in particular, among the Scheduled Castes and the 'others' who are the most disadvantaged sections of the society. Better economic prospects and education at the destination also have an influence, to a significant extent, among the Brahmins, Kshatriyas and Scheduled Tribes. At the lower end of land classes, low income forms the dominant reason for migration, while at the upper end, better economic prospects and education figure more prominently (Table 8.17). Interestingly, none of the permanent migrant workers is reported from the landless and highest land classes (>5.0 <= 10.0 acre). The reason for migration is also related to educational status of the workers. It can be noted that at lower levels of education, low incomes is the major reason and at higher levels, better prospects and education are dominant reasons for migration. Occupation of head of the households also indicates that low income tends to be a dominant factor for majority of migrants. Household income groups and reasons for migration, however do not present a clear trend. At the lowest income group, low income emerges as a dominant reason for out-migration while at the highest income group, education is the prime reason. In the middle income group, better economic prospects and education influence the decision to migrate. Interestingly, low income emerged as the principal reason exerting the decision to out-migrate in the less developed blocks, while in the developed blocks the better economic prospects influence the decision to out-migrate.

Table 8.17 : Reasons for Migration (Permanently Shifted)

Particulars	*Low income*	*Unem-ployment*	*Better economic prospects*	*Education*	*Others*	*Total*
Social category						
Brahmins	43.75	0.00	21.88	31.25	3.13	100.00 (32)
Kshatriyas	51.28	2.56	43.59	0.00	2.56	100.00 (39)
SCs	71.43	0.00	28.57	0.00	0.00	100.00 (7)
STs	33.33	7.41	29.63	14.81	14.81	100.00 (27)
Others	100.00	0.00	0.00	0.00	0.00	100.00 (1)
Land class (acre)						
>0 <= 0.50	62.50	0.00	31.25	6.25	0.00	100.00 (16)
>0.50 <= 2.50	49.23	4.62	30.77	7.69	7.69	100.00 (65)
>2.50 <= 5.0	28.00	0.00	36.00	32.00	4.00	100.00 (25)
Educational level						
Illiterate	66.67	33.33	0.00	0.00	0.00	100.00 (3)
Primary	50.00	50.00	0.00	0.00	0.00	100.00 (2)

(Contd...)

Table 8.17 : *(Contd...)*

Middle	66.67	0.00	33.33	0.00	0.00	100.00 (6)
High School	68.18	0.00	27.27	0.00	4.55	100.00 (22)
Intermediate	47.62	0.00	33.33	4.76	14.29	100.00 (21)
Graduate	36.11	2.78	36.11	22.22	2.78	100.00 (36)
Post-graduate	25.00	0.00	37.50	31.25	6.25	100.00 (16)
Occupation of head of the household						
Teacher	66.67	0.00	0.00	33.33	0.00	100.00 (3)
Shopkeeper and sales worker	83.33	0.00	16.67	0.00	0.00	100.00 (6)
Weaver and tailor	0.00	0.00	100.00	0.00	0.00	100.00 (3)
Cultivator	50.00	3.57	25.00	7.14	14.29	100.00 (28)
Animal husbandry worker	66.67	0.00	33.33	0.00	0.00	100.00 (3)
Housewife	30.00	0.00	30.00	20.00	20.00	100.00 (10)
Not able to work (too old)	23.81	4.76	66.67	4.76	0.00	100.00 (21)
Pensioner	55.56	3.70	14.81	25.93	0.00	100.00 (27)
Other workers	60.00	20.00	0.00	20.00	0.00	100.00 (5)
Income group (MPCI)						
Up to Rs.250	66.67	0.00	33.33	0.00	0.00	100.00 (3)
Rs.250 to 500	50.00	0.00	50.00	0.00	0.00	100.00 (14)
Rs.500 to 1,000	32.00	0.00	32.00	20.00	16.00	100.00 (25)
Rs.1,000 to 2,500	52.08	6.25	35.42	2.08	4.17	100.00 (48)
More than Rs.2,500	43.75	0.00	6.25	50.00	0.00	100.00 (16)
Development status						
Less developed	54.84	1.61	24.19	16.13	3.23	100.00 (62)
Developed	34.09	4.55	43.18	9.09	9.09	100.00 (44)
Total	46.23 (49)	2.83 (3)	32.08 (34)	13.21 (14)	5.66 (6)	100.00 (106)

* Others include unspecified and personal reasons.
Note : Figures in parentheses indicate number of workers.
Source : Field Survey, 2004-05.

These reasons have been broadly categorised into push and pull factors in Lee's framework. Push factors refer to the state of unemployment and low income at the source area while pull factors are indicative of better economic prospects, better educational facilities and availability of jobs at the destination. It is not to our surprise that push factors appear to have dominated more both the migrant streams than the pull factors, though one can observe certain aberrations in some occupational groups. But, by and large, the trend appears to be clear and straightforward and our hypothesis has not been proved erroneous either. It also provides empirical support from other studies in the region (Khanka, 1988; Bora, 1996).

Table 8.18 presents the push and pull factors of out-migration. The occupation of the head of households is juxtaposed in order to understand the relative strength of these forces in different occupation groups. Push factor seems to be more dominating among long-term migrants than among the permanently shifted migrants. Almost 63 per cent long-term migrants were driven out by push foctors and 34 per cent were attracted or pulled up by better opportunities at destination, while the respective figures for permanently shifted migrants is 49 and 45 per cent. Education is reported to be one of the important motivating factors for out-migration among permanently

Table 8.18 : Push and Pull Factors of Out-migration

Occupation of the head of the households	*Long-term migrants*			*Permanently shifted migrants*		
	Push	*Pull*	*Others**	*Push*	*Pull*	*Others**
Teacher	80.00	20.00	0.00	66.67	33.33	0.00
Clerical & related worker	46.67	46.75	6.67	—	—	—
Shopkeeper and sales worker	50.00	33.33	16.67	83.33	16.67	0.00
Service worker	30.00	60.00	10.00	—	—	—
Cultivator	71.43	26.19	2.38	53.57	32.14	14.29
Animal husbandry worker	50.00	50.00	0.00	66.67	33.33	0.00
Labourer	100.00	0.00	0.00	—	—	—
Pensioner	58.34	41.66	0.00	59.26	40.74	0.00
Not able to work (too old)	61.9	38.1	0.00	28.57	71.43	0.00
Housewife	70.00	20.00	10.00	30.00	50.00	20.00
Other production worker	75.00	25.00	0.00	—	—	—
Transport worker (driver)	66.67	33.33	0.00	—	—	—
Weaver	—	—	—	0.00	100.00	0.00
Other workers	75.00	25.00	0.00	80.00	20.00	0.00
Total	62.58 (97)	34.20 (53)	3.23 (5)	49.05 (52)	45.29 (48)	5.66 (6)

* Others include unspecified and personal reasons.

Note : Figures in parentheses indicate number of workers.

Source : Tables 8.16 and 8.17.

shifted migrants. Certain occupational categories like 'not able to work (too old)' and 'housewife', however, show divergent strengths of these forces.

VII. Uses of Remittances

Households make use of remittance income in different ways depending on the income of the household and their relative compulsions, priorities and options that determine to a large extent the use of such incomes. The households may use the remittance incomes either in consumption or for investment purposes or as a combination of both. Normally, a rational household is expected to spread this income in different uses so that maximum benefits can be derived out of it. Uses of remittance income provide an idea of the relative preference of the households between consumption and investment requirements. We have elicited the information from the households about the primary use of remittance income, which is presented in Tables 8.19 and 8.20. Table 8.19 gives the uses of remittance income among the long-term migrating households, while Table 8.20 presents data for the permanently shifted households. We can observe from these tables that there is a significant difference in the uses of remittance incomes across both the migrant streams.

A large part of remittance income (51%) from the long-term migrants is primarily being used for consumption purposes followed by investment (26%) and education (13%). Repayment of loan and other uses constitute about 5 per cent. This is true in most of the features that have been juxtaposed across primary uses of remittance incomes. Some divergences are also noted particularly in certain social category, occupation of heads of households, and income group. For instance, Brahmins use a major part of remittance incomes for educating their children and Scheduled Tribes use for investment purposes. This is quite reasonable as Brahmins has the highest literacy and they are the most forward social group whereas Scheduled Tribes being trading community make use of such incomes in their trade related activities. It is also noted that relatively poorer social classes (viz. Scheduled Castes and 'other' caste) also spend a good part of

Table 8.19 : Uses of Remittance (Long-term migrant)

Particulars	*Use of remittance*						
	Repayment of loan	*Consumption**	*Investment***	*Education*	*Social ceremory*	*Others#*	*Total*
Social category							
Brahmins	5.00	35.00	20.00	40.00	0.00	0.00	100.00(20)
Kshatriyas	2.25	50.56	28.09	12.36	4.49	2.25	100.00(89)
SCs	0.00	69.23	23.08	0.00	7.69	0.00	100.00(13)
STs	25.00	37.50	37.50	0.00	0.00	0.00	100.00(8)
Others	0.00	64.29	21.43	0.00	14.29	0.00	100.00(14)
Land class (acre)							
No land	33.33	33.33	16.67	16.67	0.00	0.00	100.00(6)
>0 <= .50	0.00	46.00	30.00	14.00	10.00	0.00	100.00(50)
>.50 <= 2.50	4.11	56.16	23.29	12.33	1.37	2.74	100.00(73)
>2.50 <= 5.0	0.00	50.00	40.00	10.00	0.00	0.00	100.00(10)
>5.0 <= 10.0	0.00	40.00	20.00	20.00	20.00	0.00	100.00(5)
Occupation of head of household							
Technical and managerial	0.00	75.00	25.00	0.00	0.00	0.00	100.00(4)
Teacher	0.00	50.00	0.00	50.00	0.00	0.00	100.00(4)
Clerical and related worker	0.00	57.14	28.57	7.14	7.14	0.00	100.00(14)
Shopkeepers	0.00	60.00	40.00	0.00	0.00	0.00	100.00(5)
Service workers	0.00	60.00	30.00	0.00	10.00	0.00	100.00(10)
Cultivator	2.63	52.63	13.16	21.05	7.89	2.63	100.00(38)
Animal husbandry worker	33.33	16.67	33.33	0.00	0.00	16.67	100.00(6)
Labourer	0.00	75.00	25.00	0.00	0.00	0.00	100.00(4)
Housewife	0.00	40.00	40.00	10.00	10.00	0.00	100.00(10)
Pensioner	4.55	50.00	18.18	22.73	4.55	0.00	100.00(22)
Not able to work (too old)	0.00	52.38	38.10	9.52	0.00	0.00	100.00(21)
Other workers	16.67	16.67	66.67	0.00	0.00	0.00	100.00(6)
Income group (MPCI)							
Up to Rs.250	0.00	75.00	12.50	0.00	12.50	0.00	100.00(8)
Rs.250 to 500	0.00	49.15	25.42	18.64	6.78	0.00	100.00(59)
Rs.500 to 1,000	8.51	42.55	29.79	12.77	2.13	4.26	100.00(47)
Rs.1,000 to 2,500	0.00	64.29	28.57	3.57	3.57	0.00	100.00(28)
More than Rs.2,500	50.00	0.00	0.00	50.00	0.00	0.00	100.00(2)
Development status							
Less developed	5.21	52.08	23.96	12.50	4.17	2.08	100.00(96)
Developed	0.00	47.92	31.25	14.58	6.25	0.00	100.00(48)
Total	3.47 (5)	50.69 (73)	26.39 (38)	13.19 (19)	4.86 (7)	1.39 (2)	100.00 (144)

* Consumption includes expenses on food and clothing;
** Investment includes purchase of land, construction of houses, purchase of bullocks, milch animals or expenditure on business;
\# 'others' include unspecified reasons.
Note : Figures in brackets indicate number of remitters.
Source : Field Survey, 2004-05.

remittance incomes on social ceremony as compared to other social classes. One-third of landless class utilises the remittance income on repayment of loan, and as the size of land classes increases, productive use (investment and education) also tends to increase. One-tenth of remittance income is also used on social ceremony by the highest land-owning class. Majority of heads of households spend remittance income on consumption irrespective of their occupation pattern barring 'other workers' (constituting transport workers, weavers and other production workers) who have been spending larger portion of remittance incomes on investment and rightly so. Housewives, shopkeepers and animal husbandry workers also use a significant part of remittance income on investment. Teachers, pensioners and cultivators do utilise a good part of remittance income on educating their children. In majority of income groups, consumption on food and clothing dominates followed by investment with exception in the highest income class, where repayment of loan and education appear to be the preferences of households. In the lowest income groups, households do spend a larger proportion of remittance income on social ceremony as compared to higher income groups. Across status of development blocks, the developed blocks seem to be spending a higher share of remittance income on investment and education as compared to less developed blocks.

In the case of permanent migrants too, the consumption on food and clothing emerges as the major item (48%) in which households utilise the remittance income. Social ceremony is yet another important activity in which households spend a significant portion (29%) of remittance income. However, households spend a small fraction (7 to 9%) of remitted income on education and investment (Table 8.20). The frequency of remittance is irregular and the amount of money remitted is generally small as compared to the pattern observed in the case of long-term migrants. Nevertheless, it has been noted that

Table 8.20 : Uses of Remittance (Permanent Migrants)

Particulars	*Use of remittance*						
	Repayment of loan	*Consumption**	*Investment***	*Education*	*Social ceremony*	*Others#*	*Total*
Social category							
Brahmins	0.00	50.00	0.00	7.14	28.57	14.29	100.00(14)
Kshatriyas	3.70	37.04	14.81	7.41	37.04	0.00	100.00(27)
SCs	0.00	71.43	0.00	14.29	14.29	0.00	100.00(7)
STs	0.00	55.56	11.11	0.00	22.22	11.11	100.00(9)
Others	0.00	100.00	0.00	0.00	0.00	0.00	100.00(1)
Land class (acre)							
>0 <= 0.50	0.00	55.56	11.11	0.00	33.33	0.00	100.00(9)
>0.50 <=2.50	0.00	47.37	7.89	7.89	28.95	7.89	100.00(38)
>2.50 <= 5.0	9.09	45.45	9.09	9.09	27.27	0.00	100.00(11)
Occupation of head of household							
Shopkeeper	0.00	66.67	0.00	0.00	33.33	0.00	100.00(3)
Cultivator	0.00	52.94	11.76	11.76	17.65	5.88	100.00(17)
Weaver and tailor	0.00	33.33	0.00	0.00	66.67	0.00	100.00(3)
Housewife	0.00	42.86	14.29	0.00	28.57	14.29	100.00(7)
Pensioner	0.00	50.00	0.00	10.00	40.00	0.00	100.00(10)
Not able to work (too old)	7.14	42.86	14.29	0.00	28.57	7.14	100.00(14)
Other workers	0.00	50.00	0.00	25.00	25.00	0.00	100.00(4)
Income group (MPCI)							
Up to Rs.250	0.00	100.00	0.00	0.00	0.00	0.00	100.00(3)
Rs.250 to 500	0.00	50.00	20.00	0.00	30.00	0.00	100.00(10)
Rs.500 to 1,000	0.00	33.33	16.67	16.67	16.67	16.67	100.00(12)
Rs.1,000 to 2,500	3.45	48.28	3.45	6.90	34.48	3.45	100.00(29)
More than Rs.2,500	0.00	50.00	0.00	0.00	50.00	0.00	100.00(4)
Development status							
Less developed	0.00	48.48	6.06	3.03	36.36	6.06	100.00(33)
Developed	4.00	48.00	12.00	12.00	20.00	4.00	10000(25)
Total	1.72 (1)	48.28 (28)	8.62 (5)	6.90 (4)	29.31 (17)	5.17 (3)	100 (58)

* Consumption includes expenses on food and clothing;

** Investment includes purchase of land, construction of houses, purchase of bullocks, milch animals or expenditure on business;

\# 'others' include unspecified reasons.

Note : Figures in brackets indicate number of remitters.

Source: Field Survey, 2004-05.

permanent migrants do remit money on every occasion of social ceremony at the place of origin.

It can be observed that consumption and social ceremony are the two most important activities in which migrating households spend the remittance income and this is common across social categories, land classes, household groups and income classes. The disadvantaged social groups (Scheduled Caste and 'others'), lowest land size class and lowest income class spend a larger proportion of remittance income on consumption. Expenditure on social ceremony tends to increase with the increase in income levels. Less developed blocks spend a larger proportion (36%) of remittance income on social ceremony and less on productive uses (investment and education), while the developed blocks show a somewhat opposite trend by spending more on productive uses than on social ceremony.

In the migration literature, there is less clear evidence about the remittance income and its impact on development activities at the source area. There are two contrasting theme that emerges in the migration discourse; one view, rather a dominant one, is that the income from migration is not only meagre but highly unstable and a very large part of it is used for meeting consumption needs with little or no surplus left for investment, either in farm or non-farm activities. The other view, rather a scarce one, is that it helps stimulate development at the place of origin through productive investment. The former view is generally associated with the distress type of migration while later one is referred to as accumulative type of migration (Deshingakar *et al.,* 2004; Deshingakar and Start, 2003). Many of these evidences are context specific, hence difficult to make any generalisation. Nevertheless, it is generally agreed that remittance income helps to increase the welfare of people, alleviate poverty and also increases inequality.

The field data indicate that a large part of remittance income (from long-term and permanent migrants together) is used for consumption purposes (62%), one-fifth on investment purposes (21%) and one-tenth on supporting education (11%). Consumption includes expenditure both on food and clothing, and on social ceremony as well, while major part of investment goes on repair and construction of houses. In fact, a little amount of remittance is used for purchasing milch animals and nothing really is reinvested either on improved machinery or high yielding inputs. This remittance use behaviour does not invalidate our basic premise that out-migration is largely a survival strategy rather than an accumulation process in the hill region of the state. Our field data also do not support that remittance income spurs development. As is argued, remittances do not automatically lead to accelerate development. Development is a complex and sordid process, which is governed by a variety of factors in the way development proceeds. Frequency and size of remittance are important but transforming it into investment is more important. In the hill region, the volume of remittance is small, primarily owing to a low mean income, and a large part of it is used for meeting daily needs. Hence, very little is left for investment that helps to enhance the income generating source for the migrating households. Not only this, out-migration affects agriculture productivity adversely. Out-migration of young and able-bodied male members results in shortage of hands for cultivation of crops, which is solely a labour-intensive enterprise, and it has an immediate fall out on women and children who have to share the added responsibility (Cited from Srivastava *et al.*, 2003). Some of the activities that are done only by male members (ploughing and hoeing, for instance) cannot be easily replaced with family members. This has two possible implications on the farming family and local labour market. First, either to hire male member as a ploughman and second, to utilise the services of school-going male children in the family to do the job, which is not uncommon in some of the poor families. In the former case, which is most common, the local labour market gets tightened and almost immediately it results in pushing up the local wage rates thereby making cultivation less profitable; and in the later case, using male children for ploughing disrupts their continuous schooling. These kinds of implications have been supported by our field data in terms of very high female participation rate and involvement of children in cultivation activity and relatively much higher average wage per day (Chapter 6).

It is sometimes argued that the development process spur not necessarily through spending on investment goods, but it can stimulate through spending on consumption goods as well – probably farming provides the best example for food related stuffs. But in the case of fragile economies like hill region of Uttarakhand, such linkage effect in the local economy are weak, primarily because consumption goods are imported from urban centres.

This kind of remittance behaviour can, thus, be seen largely as contractual agreement between the migrants and family members back home as an insurance against livelihood insecurity rather than an instrument for capital creation, more so on Rosenzweig frame rather than Stark's construction (cited from Haan & De, 1999). Remittance behaviour in Nepal, with similar conditions of hill economy, is also evident that remittance has virtually little contribution to capital investment (Regmi and Tisdell, 2002).

VIII. Linkages

When people move from the source area, either voluntarily or being forced to the destination area, they do maintain linkages with the family members left behind as part of an implicit understanding between them. This kind of movement generates a variety of linkages with both the source area and the destination of migrants, what can be called as social and economic transactions. How strong and weak links such transactions would generate depends on factors such as nature and patterns of migration, distance, emotional attachment to kith and kin, personal networks, societal norms and relations, labour market conditions at destination, etc. In the literature, various metaphors have been used for such interconnections as threads, chains, anchors, umbilical links and different forms of communication links (Werbner 1990, cited from Christopher and Haan, 1997).

Our field enquiry shows the existence of such links between the source area and at destination, within a broad framework of social and economic process of migratory pattern. Such links have been identified in the form of labour market linkage, remittance and communication linkages that we shall dwell upon based on the evidences thrown by the primary investigation.

(i) Labour market links

Out-migration has obvious labour market implication on both the source area as well as destination area. The implications have to be construed within labour market conditions in both the areas. Labour movement can take place in both the situations when source area experience excess supply or shortage of labour, and this could also be true at destination. When people move from catchment area, whatsoever be the reason, it has immediate implications on labour markets at source area and at destination. In the case of hill region of Uttarakhand, out-migration results in high sex ratio, tightening of local labour market that eventually leads to high female drudgery, involvement of children in cultivation and livestock rearing. The drain of young people has cascading socio-economic effects on the migrating family and local labour market conditions. Socio-economic implications take the form of a drain of human resource, impact on reproductive behaviour, long separation from family adding to family insecurity, etc. To some extent, shortage of labour gets replaced by women who put long hours of work, thereby increasing their drudgery and by children who help in cultivation and animal care activities. Shortage of labour affects adversely the agriculture productivity and is manifested in the labour market through increased wage rates, which is generally higher than market determined wage rate. The overall wage per day for agriculture male worker comes out to Rs. 87 (Chapter 7), while wages paid in public works is around Rs.58. Though remittance increases cash income of the migrating households, which is a positive feature, yet high wage rate has snowballing effects on the local economy and this makes agriculture sector highly cost-ineffective. In any case, productivity of hill agriculture is very low with a foodgrain producing capacity of not beyond few months in a year. Thus, it further increases the reliance on imports of foodgrains from outside the region.

(ii) Remittance links

Remittance income enhances the welfare of migrating households through increased disposable income in hand that can either be used in meeting daily consumption needs or/and on investment goods. We have observed that the average amount of remittance is generally low and most of such income is used primarily for meeting the consumption needs, rather than on creating capital. The impact of remittance income on the local economy seems to be insignificant.

Nevertheless, the frequency of remittance has been consistently very high indicating strong links at the source area.

(iii) Communication links

Communication is an important channel for strengthening such links at the source area and it can take different forms depending on the available means (writing letters, telephoning, sending messages in person and personal visits). We have relied on the information on personal visits of migrants that supports our hypothesis, that the migrants do maintain strong links with the source area. A large majority of migrant workers do visit their home town regularly, thus strengthening such links.

Our enquiry fairly supports that the migrants have strong linkages with the source area through employment, remittance and personal visits. Such links generate both positive and negative consequences at the source area but negative consequences seem to outstrip the positive impacts (Bora, 1987).

IX. Conclusion

Out-migration from the hill region is a most conspicuous phenomenon resulting primarily due to low economic base, which in turn, results in low employment and earning opportunities in the region. Almost half of the surveyed households report out-migration (out-migrating at least one family member). The intensity of out-migration is high and it is the most common household strategy for supplementing the consumption needs at the source area. Long-term migration from the hill region has been an old tradition primarily to eke out livings in towns and cities. Although income earned has been low, yet it provided some sort of security to the family at the source area. Of late, permanent migration has emerged as an important phenomenon with a view to bettering life and investing on children's education. Our enquiry has revealed this phenomenon clearly. By and large, push factors dominate the pull factors, and the implications of remittances on the source area have been negligible for promoting and accelerating development. However, it has at the best supplemented the consumption requirements of the people. Regression results show that short- and long-term out-migration do not affect household income positively and significantly. Nevertheless, migrants do maintain strong linkages with the source area through employment, remittance and regular visits.

The survey results support our hypothesis that, if horticulture base is developed in which the region has comparative advantage, it can productively engage its work- force in horticulture and eventually help restrict out-migration. It is important to note that odds ratio for non-labour household income ($\hat{y}$) is close to 1, suggesting a very little impact on the probability of the person to out-migrate. Logistic regression results clearly lend credence to our postulations that a large proportion of out-migrants are primarily motivated by push factors. Such outflow of people is concentrated more among the disadvantaged social groups and from among the casual labour households. Relatively less developed blocks show higher intensity of out-migration than the developed blocks. An overwhelmingly large number of the long-term migrant workers are without requisite education levels and marketable skills, resulting in low incomes which add vulnerability at the place of destination. Lack of opportunities in the local economy pushes them out to find jobs under duress conditions.

9

Summary and Conclusions and Policy Imperatives

This chapter summarises the major findings of the study undertaken through field work in the hill region of Uttarakhand focusing mainly on rural non-farm employment and its implication on employment and incomes. Based on theoretical postulations and empirical evidences thrown by the field enquiry, some policy options have been put forward which might be helpful in drawing an appropriate development strategy that would eventually take the economy into a higher trajectory of growth.

I. Diversity in Mountain Economies

The mountain habitat shares certain similar bio-climatic features and concerns across the world, whether these are the Alps mountain regions of European countries or Andean mountain ranges in the South America or Hindu Kush Himalayan (HKH) region in the South Asia. These countries are characterised by certain common features or specificities. The important specificities are inaccessibility, fragility, marginality, diversity or heterogeneity, and niche and human adaptive mechanisms. These specificities may differ across different situations and locations or countries, and also may have different implications (positive as well as negative) on the resources and activities.

There are concerns for the changing mountain environment due to degradation of resources as a result of excessive exploitation. This has resulted in a reduction in biomass production, marginalisation and low human welfare. Many of these mountain regions are prone to natural hazards (landslides, earthquakes, avalanches, diseases etc.) and human conflict and wars are also concentrated in many of the poor regions making the mountain people more vulnerable. The minority of inhabitants in certain mountain regions suffered not only from the resources exploitation but also from ethnic conflict, violence and wars. But then, there are major differences in the mountain economies of the developed countries of Europe and that of Andean regions and HKH regions in respect of their development trajectories.

European mountain regions developed fast primarily because of their strong external linkages with the developed regions, experiencing industrial revolution, and in this process, mountain regions benefited significantly from the strong linkage effect. For instance, the major growth drivers of industrialisation in Alps has been the hydropower-based industries and tourism. This was possible to a significant extent by the state protection and institutional mechanisms put in place with a considerable political will that helped ameliorate the in-built inequalities in the mountain economies.

In the least developed mountain regions, the most common economic activities include subsistence land-based activities (crop production combined with animal husbandry, horticulture, forestry), traditional enterprises drawing upon local raw material, resources, use of rudimentary technology, limited use of external inputs and resources. Low productivity of resources including land, human drudgery, infrastructural bottlenecks and emigration are the other features of such economies. This system exhibited a closed system that resulted in limited trade, exchange and surplus. By and large, such a subsistence nature of economic activities provided the base for sustenance of the people.

Despite the increasing interventions brought about in the mountain regions through various programmes and project approaches by the national governments, donor agencies; and increasing environmental and sustainability concerns expressed by the international agencies, the mountain regions have, by and large, remained at the lowest ebb of the development trajectory barring a few stray cases. Primary reason for this failure has been attributed to inappropriate development strategy in which the mountain perspectives were entirely missing, and most often, development has been undertaken from the outside flatlanders or mainstream institutions. The problems of sustainable development in the poor countries are much more severe than the mountain regions of industrialised countries. The major challenges and concerns in the former countries have been subsistence agriculture and food deficits, persistent human poverty, adverse terms of trade and exploitative linkage relations, gender inequity, drudgery and environmental degradation.

The Himalayan region of India covers 10 states namely, Jammu & Kashmir, Himachal Pradesh, Uttarakhand, Sikkim, Arunachal Pradesh, Nagaland, Manipur, Mizoram, Tripura, Meghalaya and Darjeeling district of West Bengal, and Karbi Anglong and North Cachar districts of Assam. In spite of similar biophysical attributes, the development patterns vary across the hill states in terms of various development indicators.

Among all the hill states, Himachal Pradesh is one of the fastest growing and socially progressive hill states in the country. The case of Himachal Pradesh provides a unique example among all the hill states – the transformation from subsistence agriculture to one of the lead horticulture-producing region is worth emulating. The development strategy gave primacy to development of transport network (mainly, roads), communication and hydroelectric projects. The government provided institutional support for diversifying from traditional cereal crops to horticulture crops along with dairy development. The state also adopted an appropriate land use pattern with a view to optimising the returns. This has significantly improved the livelihood options and income levels of the people.

Most of the North-eastern hill states have low economic performance, high unemployment and reportedly high rural poverty. Primary sector still constitutes the bulk of the labour force in all the hill states of the region, and secondary sector has remained stagnant. In some cases, hill economies are experiencing some sort of de-industrialisation. In Sikkim, despite its impressive performance in economic and social indicators, poverty levels and unemployment rates continue to be significantly higher.

Jammu & Kashmir state has recorded a relatively higher decadal population growth and lowest overall and female literacy rates, and highest gender disparity among all the hill states. Though poverty level is lowest in the state, yet per capita NSDP is low, and it is lower than the national average. Infant Mortality Rate (IMR) is estimated to be high. In spite of a large natural and human resource base, the state lags behind in industrial development.

Uttarakhand has achieved impressive literacy rates with a relatively lower gender gap, but poverty has been the highest among all the hill states. In terms of NSDP (Net State Domestic Product) growth, it has recorded a very low growth as compared to All-India average. Employment growth is abysmally low in the state and rural areas in particular recorded a negative growth rate during 1993-94 to 1999-2000. NSS results (2004-05) however show an impressive performance in employment growth, both in rural and urban areas in the state. Yet, the long-term trends (1983 to 2004-05) show a much lower growth of employment in rural area as compared to all-India. In spite of a perceptible performance in GSDP (Gross State Domestic Product) growth in the state during 2004-05, per worker GSDP (absolute terms) in primary and tertiary sectors and per capita income have been far lower throughout during 1993-94 to 2004-05 as compared to all-India.

Most of the hill states supposedly have advantage in terms of hydroelectricity, forest resources, horticulture, tourism & amenities and other hill-specific products. However, many of these activities could not be developed primarily due to lack of appropriate development strategy. In spite of a reportedly good resource base, most of the hill states have low industrial development and a very high dependence on central assistance; and very little efforts have gone into mobilising their own resources and accelerating the pace of capital formation.

II. Uttarakhand Hill Region : A Case of Underdeveloped Region

(i) Employment, labour market features, and economy

Uttarakhand hill region is characterised by subsistence agriculture and any drastic transformation within the cereal-based agriculture on terraced type cultivation has obvious limitations on expansion of its land-based activities. The industrial base, in any case, is precariously small and large-scale industrial activity is neither possible nor desirable in view of ecological and environmental considerations. From the long term perspective, traditional agriculture with its low productive base and rudimentary industrial activities do not seem to be viable and a sustainable option for providing employment and income opportunities to the burgeoning labour force. This precisely makes a strong case for diversification within agriculture sector according to its potential land capability and also for promoting other non-farm pursuits.

One of the noticeable features of LFPR (Labour Force Participation Rate) in the rural areas is a very high LFPR among females. The main reason for such a high LFPR among females is the subsistence nature of agriculture economy that provides the only source of employment. Also, there are limited opportunities of employment outside agriculture.

The LFPRs for rural males and rural females in the state has been 53 and 47 per cent respectively in 2004-05. The corresponding figures at the All-India level have been 55 and 33 per cent.

Long-term trends of movement of LFPR in the state have marginally increased for rural males (1.0% points) but registered a huge fall for females (6.3% points) during 1983 to 2004-05. The corresponding changes at all-India level have been negligible. It remained almost stable. Generally, LFPR has shown an increasing trend from 1983 to 1993-94, both in rural and urban areas; then it dipped in 1999-2000 and thereafter a clear up-trend is noticed in 2004-05.

The Worker Population Ratio (WPR) in rural areas declined in the state as well as at all-India for both males and females from 1983 to 1999-2000; however, 2004-05 saw a trend reversal and registered a significant increase. Male WPR in the state registered a substantive increase (8.3% points) and female WPR increased by 5.8 percentage points. While at all-India, male and female WPR increased by about 2 and 2.7 percentage points respectively.

While at all-India level, employment grew at about 0.98 per cent; in Uttarakhand, there has been a catastrophic fall in employment as it recorded a negative growth (-1.44%) and the fall was even more pronounced among females than males during 1994-2000. Long-term rural employment growth during 1980s and 1990s (1999-2000 over 1983) in the state is very low (0.70% per annum) as against 1.61 per cent per annum in all-India. Rural area in particular has recorded an abysmally low employment growth. NSS results (2004-05) however show an impressive performance in employment growth, both in rural and urban areas in the state; yet the long-term trends (1983 to 2004-05) show a much lower growth of employment for males and females in the rural area as compared to all-India. Even in urban areas, the growth for male employment has been lower than all-India.

The sectoral share of employment, by and large, corresponds to the all-India pattern but there are huge dissimilarities in rural area. The relative gap between all-India and the state is largest and weakest too for females as there has been hardly any significant occupational diversification for females in the state. Their share in primary sector is disproportionately much higher (at 96%), while in secondary and tertiary sector it is pitifully lower (1.9 and 2.1% respectively) as compared to the corresponding share of rural India in 2004-05. Such a structure of employment is bound to have serious implications for sectoral productivity.

The long-term shift in the structure of employment in rural areas shows that the self-employment base has eroded systematically, both for males and females in the state. Casualisation among rural females has become a most conspicuous phenomenon in terms of growth; while regular employment shows an improvement, more so among females.

Self-employment has been the principal mode of livelihoods for males as well as for females; but for rural females it is indeed the sole source of employment as an overwhelmingly large majority of workforce (94%) is engaged in it, primarily in cultivation activities. Self-employment opportunities in the rural area are showing an improvement in 2004-05 over 1999-2000, yet such opportunities have generally shrunk as compared to pre-1999/2000 period, both for males and females. Regular employment for males as well as females have generally declined, albeit marginally, during 1999-2000 to 2004-

05. The share of casual employment also declined for males and females but the decline is sharper for females as compared to that of males. It clearly appears that restructuring process has halted and those who have moved on to non-agriculture sector earlier seems to have been reverted back to agriculture sector.

Another distinct feature noted is that an overwhelmingly large majority of rural females are working as subsidiary capacity (11.9% in 2004-05) indicating their marginalisation and vulnerability. The gap between the share of UPS and UPSS workers has increased from about 2.6 per cent in 1983 to about 6.1 per cent in 2004-05, while at all-India level this gap declined from 4.6 to 4.1 per cent.

There has been a huge increase in rural subsidiary workers (4.49 lakh) of which females accounted for about 81 per cent in 2004-05. Agriculture is the most predominant activity for subsidiary employment, both for males and females. For females, such a huge increase in subsidiary capacity employment was solely due to the low productive sectors that are regarded lenders of the last resort.

The work structure is highly gender biased in the rural areas of the state as women overwhelmingly work in agriculture related occupations (96%), while their male counterparts work in non-farm occupations (37%). Such a low share of female employment in non-agriculture sector (4%) shows a complete dichotomy and segmentation of work activity due to various socio-economic factors that inhibit females to participate in the labour market outside cultivation, despite the fact that their literacy level has improved considerably over the years. Barring manufacturing, construction and public services, their share is virtually nil in other segments of non-farm sector.

Growing majority of the sub-sectors in the rural economy consistently achieved lower performance both in terms of employment growth and Gross Value Added (GVA) per worker as compared to the overall performance in the state. Even in certain sub-sectors where higher rate of employment growth was registered in rural area (namely, manufacture of cotton textile and land transport), the GVA per worker was lower than the state average indicating a proliferation of low productivity employment growth.

In rural Uttarakhand, the maximum share of enterprises is in trade segment followed by manufacturing and construction, but the productivity in these segments is lower; in fact, manufacturing has the lowest productivity among all the segments in the unorganised sector.

The sectoral GSDP growth in the state is consistently lower in every sector as compared to all-India during 1994-2000. The overall GSDP growth is just half in the state than that of all-India. This pattern of productivity change in the state stands in marked contrast to the all-India in major segments of the economy. Even per capita income in the state is lower by 28 per cent as compared to all-India in 1999-2000. All this indicates a low level of development in the state.

However, there has been a perceptible improvement in sectoral growth in terms of per worker GSDP in the state during 2000-05. Barring primary sector, every segment of economic activities saw a substantive improvement in sectoral performance as compared to all-India. Secondary sector has shown a dramatic improvement in productivity and registered a whopping growth in per worker GSDP (16% per annum). In fact, every segment of secondary sector showed an impressive performance. Sectoral performance in terms of per worker GSDP growth in the state has been far better than all-India. The overall GSDP growth per worker, per capita income and GDP growth in the state have doubled as compared to all-India during the later period.

In spite of a perceptible performance in the state during 2004-05, per worker GSDP (absolute terms) in primary and tertiary sectors have been far lower throughout during 1993-94 to 2004-05 as compared to all-India.

In the state, educational attainment has been a hignly facilitating factor for occupational shift towards non-farm activities, more so in the case of males. Gender, castes, land size and infrastructure seem to have been playing important roles in determining the growth of rural non-farm sector. It is important from the long-term policy perspectives to widen the marketable skills base and strengthen the social and economic infrastructure that the state lacks in, which always have a positive influence on the growth of non-farm sector.

Our review has shown that the context of analysis in most of the studies on rural non-farm has been restricted to the non-hill economy. The constraints posed by the terraced type cultivation do not lend much support to the Mellorian type of linkages for the growth of non-farm sector. Not only this, the lack of development in general, raises the issues of the productivity and income of numerous types of non-farm activities mushrooming with little linkages to local economy. It is, therefore argued that non-farm based activities and enterprises ought to be promoted; particularly in the activities in which the region enjoys certain comparative advantages.

In this context, the enterprise based activity needs to be construed in a much wider sense and it can take different forms – diversification from cereal based products to high value horticultural products to simple processing, and other enterprise based activities such as based on livestock, forest (non-timber), artisan and tourism, and amenity services.

(ii) Household characteristics – field enquiry

Our field enquiry based on household survey shows that agriculture and allied activities are the dominant activities of livelihood in the region. Subsistence agriculture with overwhelmingly large number of marginal holdings has made cultivation highly uneconomical and unremunerative. Added to this, lack of development in general in rural areas has forced a significant proportion of households to out-migrate outside the state for earning livelihood. Nearly 23 per cent households report to be women-headed households, and 15 per cent households has reported as casual workers, most of whom belong to 'other caste' and SCs who are poor and from lower social class. Maximum number of casual-work-reporting household belongs to landless category. Less developed blocks show a higher intensity of female-headed households and casual-work-households than the developed ones. Literacy rate in the sample population accounts for about 79 per cent (5 years and above), male literacy constitutes 91 per cent and female literacy 65 per cent. Generally, less developed blocks have higher gender gaps in literacy than the relatively developed ones. Social group-wise literacy among the households shows that the upper caste households possess higher literacy, both for males and females than the social groups.

Significant improvement in literacy over the years has not helped to make room for more employment, rather it accentuated the process of out-migration. Male-specific out-migration has put an enormous burden on hill women, both in cultivation and other household chores.

Migrant population constitutes 10 per cent (excluding permanent migrants), and nearly 38 per cent households report at least one migrant indicating the extent of out-migration.

An overwhelmingly large majority of sample households (87%) belong to marginal landholdings and about one-tenth households belong to small and medium landholdings. None of the households have large landholding size. The most disturbing phenomenon is the fast fragmentation of already tiny sizes of holdings, which has not only become highly uneconomical but also leading to near-landlessness situation for a large majority of households in sub-marginal and marginal landholding size classes.

Value of farm assets is very low in hill agriculture since most of these implements are traditional and modern implements are hardly used for cultivation. Value of farm assets is positively correlated to land size owned per household and land size class. Farm asset value is reported to be lowest among SCs and STs, and among landless households.

Households and per capita income for majority of households are low with marked inequity across castes and land classes. Overall per capita income of the sample population (resident) comes out at Rs.10,656. The lower social groups particularly SCs, and 'other caste' has very low per capita income. Also, landless and marginal households have lower per capita income than the average household income exhibiting significant income differentials across land size classes. Low income obviously results in low asset-holding capacity of the households with significant differential across castes and land classes.

Overall, 36 per cent households have monthly per capita income of less than Rs.500, which is closer to the poverty line threshold. An overwhelmingly large majority (75%) of 'other caste' households and over half (56%) of the Scheduled Caste households have monthly per capita income of less than Rs. 500. The Scheduled Tribes and Brahmins, on the other hand, have a high concentration in the higher income groups (Rs. 1,000-2,500 and Rs. 2,500 and above). The principal reasons for variations of income across castes are linked closely to the asset base of the households and also to the educational and skill levels that have overarching influence on income generating capacity. It can be observed that the relatively developed blocks are showing low proportion of their population in low income groups and less developed blocks are showing a relatively higher proportion of population in the lower income groups.

(iii) Employment, unemployment and earnings

Typically, the hill economy of Uttarakhand shows a higher female LFPR than males. This has distinctly come out from the field data and this also corroborates with the Census and NSS data. Survey data also show that there is a highly gender biased work structure in the rural areas of the state, as women overwhelmingly work in agriculture-related occupations while their male counterparts work in non-farm occupations. This is primarily because of the subsistence farming economy with precarious industrial base. Agriculture is the predominant sector for employment for a large majority of labour force with little surplus generating capacity, and by and large, this sector acts as a labour sponge, especially for females. Non-farm activities constituting petty trade and business, wage/salaried employment and casual employment particularly in construction activities, have been mostly male dominated activities and females have a very low share in these activities. Generally, developed blocks show a higher share in non-farm activities than the less developed ones, primarily because of diversification from cereal crops to horticulture crops and better infrastructure and proximity to block and district headquarters.

Agriculture is increasingly becoming an uneconomic family enterprise, and employment opportunities outside agriculture are extremely limited. Within farm sector, there is a huge incidence of underemployment in terms of unutilised labour time and majority of rural households are forced to diversify their activities as a part of their survival strategy to cope with seasonality and uncertainty of production. Unemployment rate turns out to be 11.5 per cent in aggregate terms, which is indeed very high. Male unemployment rate, in particular, is alarmingly high at 19 per cent; while female unemployment rate is comparatively much lower at 3 per cent. The survey results clearly show that the problem of unemployment is a huge one in the hill districts of the state, and it is more pronounced among relatively less developed blocks than the relatively developed blocks. Unemployment is concentrated more among the lower social classes and among landless class. Intensity of unemployment is visible among the higher educated categories.

Females are disproportionately represented in the agriculture and allied activities (90%) with low levels of education and a very high proportion of them are illiterates. Generally, low levels of education of a large majority of workers in rural areas of Uttarakhand, particularly of females, have implications from the policy perspective for their employability outside agriculture. Their low educational levels can hardly help them secure employment outside agriculture.

Average annual days of employment available in agriculture and allied activities are indeed very low in the hill areas. Although, people seem to be working very hard in agriculture activities, yet it does not provide employment beyond a few months in a year. On an average, agriculture and allied activities provide employment to about 56 days in a year for males; while for females it provides for about 106 days of employment.

However, it can be observed that the relatively developed blocks have generally higher person days of employment as compared to less developed blocks. The reasons for higher days of employment in the relatively developed blocks is due to more areas under horticulture crops leading to commercialisation of agriculture (vegetables, fruits and other non-food crops) as compared to relatively less developed blocks. More area under horticulture also fetches a higher share of income from agriculture as compared to relatively less developed blocks. This also supports our hypothesis that diversification into high value crops promotes more employment and incomes.

Availability of casual employment is less than two months (50 days) in a year, providing on an average 51 days of employment for males and 43 days for females.

Multiple economic activities are most pervasive and widespread among different groups of population in the survey areas in Uttarakhand, manifesting symptoms of a backward economy. About 26 per cent among all the workers have single or sole activity, while a large majority of them (74%) resort to more than one activity. Even the dependence of highest income group in more than one activity is 51 per cent. Clearly, two different processes seem to be at work together. First, there is a deliberate household strategy to enhance income as an involuntary response to crisis situation, and second, to seize opportunities as a means of accumulation.

The finding of the present study dispel the commonly derived hypothesis that poor households derive their income from multiple sources as part of their survival strategy, while the relatively better-off households and individuals depend on few and stable sources of incomes. It can be argued that in relatively less developed regions, lack of opportunities constrict the people to enter into the labour market; while in the relatively developed region, people seize the existing opportunities for better remunerated activities.

Mean earnings per day varies widely across blocks and occupations. Returns to labour input for rural households are very low in agriculture and allied activities, as can be observed that the mean earnings per day from this activity is Rs. 56; which is the lowest, while for non-farm activities it is the highest at Rs. 145 per day which is higher by over two and a half times as compared to those engaged in agriculture and allied activities. Even per person-day earnings are much higher for labour input engaged in casual wage works (Rs.76 per day) as compared to agriculture and allied activities.

(iv) Non-farm employment and rural enterprises

The dependence on non-farm sources of employment and income is pervasive at the household level. A significant part of the household income constitutes from non-farm sources (68%). The better-off and more educated lot takes the advantages of more remunerative opportunities (regular/salaried employment) in the non-farm sector, while the poor depend more on unskilled wage employment and transfer incomes (remittance). Field level data amply show a highly gender biased work structure in the rural areas of the state, as women overwhelmingly work in agriculture-related occupations; while their male counterparts work in non-farm occupations. There exists a wide diversity of occupational groups across different spatial units, castes and land size classes. Such diversity exists not only in terms of share of employment but also in terms of sources of income.

In order to know the determinants of household income, regression model has been fitted with a view to understanding the relationships between predictor variables and dependent variable (MPCI). The results show that: (i) Most of the variables are significant, (ii) Proportion of non-farm employment and per capita land owned are the most important variables in explaining the regress and, (iii) Percentage area under horticulture, development index of villages and education levels of households (higher secondary and above) impact positively on the household's monthly per capita income.

Field data help to understand the diversities across different occupational groups within non-farm segments – casual wage earners, regular/salaried workers and non-agricultural rural enterprises. Within each segment, there are divergent activities and occupational groups with considerable heterogeneity and inequities across different segments of non-farm sector in terms of days of work, average earnings and capital requirements etc. Majority of casual workers belong to sub-marginal and marginal landholding size classes. Most of the casual workers belong to illiterate category and to those who have completed middle level schooling. Most of the casual workers are driven desperately from the lower income groups and such intensity gets attenuated in higher income groups. Clearly, the less developed blocks show a greater demand for such sporadic nature of employment than the developed ones. On an average, casual works provide employment of less than two months in a year. Males get most of employment in non-agriculture activities, while females have limited access to such opportunities. Females get almost one-third lower wages than their male counterparts. Those who possess higher level of education have also better prospects of getting regular/salaried employment. Improving the levels of education is, therefore, necessary in order to promote better-paid regular/salaried employment. Land size classes, educational levels and per capita income groups are positively correlated to the levels of earnings.

In order to ascertain the factors that affect the probability of a person seeking non-farm employment, logistic regression model is run. What emerges strongly from the logistic regression model is that improvement in educational levels has a significant positive impact on a person's diversification from farm to non-farm occupations. Similarly, enhancement of skill level has considerable positive impact on the workforce for a shift from farm to non-farm sector activities. This has a clear policy message. Improving educational and skill levels of the workforce would significantly improve the chances of employability in the non-farm sector with better income opportunities. This becomes clear from the values of odds ratios.

Majority of enterprises appear to be dominated by service and manufacturing activities with a narrow profile of activities. This kind of enterprise-based activities had limited product lines carried out in small scale with little surplus for reinvestment. Entrepreneurial activities, however, continued within numerous internal and external constraints. But over the years, these enterprises are languishing and operating at a low equilibrium trap with little product diversification and surplus. The major reasons for sickness of these enterprises can be attributed to both the supply and demand side aspects.

Education levels of entrepreneurs are low – nearly one-fourth is illiterates and nearly half of the entrepreneurs have schooling up to high school level only. Those who are in the highest and lowest income groups scarcely participate in such activities.

Family labour is more prominent in the rural enterprises –nearly three-fourths employment constitutes family labour and one-fourth hired labour. On an average, these enterprises provide employment for about four months in a year. Access to credit, technology and market is low and most of the output of these enterprises is meant for the local markets. Input linkages are extremely weak for the local economy and generate little or no value addition to the enterprises. Mean earnings per man-day works out to be at Rs.145 with large variations across enterprises. The lowest mean earnings is noted for the weavers, which provides highest man-days of family employment but earnings are observed to be below than casual wage earners. It is necessary to rejuvenate weaving as a home-based enterprise through variety of promotional measures that has potential to generate strong forward and backward linkages to the local economy. About 27 per cent non-farm workers are illiterate (males accounting for 12 per cent and females 39 per cent), and about 1 per cent possess technical education (none is female). Educational status is lower for females in each level of education as compared to males. Most of the illiterates are concentrated in weavers, labourers, shopkeepers, and service workers. This has acted as an entry barrier for females in the non-farm sector. This finding also supports our hypothesis that low level of education among females has created disparities in employment opportunities in the non-farm sector as their share in non-farm sector is about 11 per cent, while the share of males accounts for about 41 per cent.

(v) Migration patterns and linkages

Migration has been a common phenomenon in the hill region of Uttarakhand and is closely related to the economic backwardness of the region. In fact, out-migration and economic underdevelopment reinforce one another and produce a vicious circle that further accentuates the process of underdevelopment.

Out-migration is not an unusual event but a constant response to uneconomical agriculture enterprise, fragile resource base (land and forest), environmental degradation, limited employment opportunities, and hence, livelihood insecurity. Micro-level studies indicate that male-specific out-migration from the region is huge and has been increasing over the years.

Our survey results also show that almost half of the surveyed households report out-migration (at least one family member out-migrating) and 23 per cent of sample population is recorded as migrants who out-migrate for different durations according to types of migration. Migration is most widespread among all the social groups and land classes, and there is a significant diversity in migration streams both in terms of incidence and intensity across social category, land size classes and across region and within the regions.

Long-term migration from the hill region has been a long tradition primarily to eke out livings in towns and cities, but of late permanent migration has emerged as an important phenomenon with a view to bettering life and investing on children's education. Our enquiry has revealed this phenomenon clearly.

Permanent migrants are observed to be the better-off lots than the long-term out-migrants in terms of educational profile, employment and income levels. Remittance forms an important source of income, particularly for poorer households that depend considerably on such transfer income. Average remittance from the long-term migrants constitutes about 22 per cent and from permanent migrants 2.5 per cent of their annual income respectively. Low incomes and unemployment emerged as the principal reasons exerting the decision to out-migrate, and push factors dominated over the pull factors.

Implications of remittances to the source area in terms of promoting and accelerating development have been negligible. However, it has helped in supplementing the consumption requirements of the people. It has been noted that migrants do maintain strong linkages to the source area through remittance and regular visits.

The survey results support our hypothesis that if horticulture base, in which the region has comparative advantage, is developed it can productively engage its workforce in horticulture and eventually help restrict out-migration. Logistic regression results clearly lend credence to our postulations that a large proportion of out-migrants are primarily motivated by push factors. Such outflow of people is concentrated more among disadvantaged social groups and from among casual labour households. Relatively less developed blocks show a higher intensity of out-migration than the developed blocks. An overwhelmingly large number of long-term migrant workers are without requisite education levels and marketable skills resulting in low incomes and add vulnerability at the place of destination. Lack of opportunities in the local economy pushes them out to find jobs under duress conditions.

III. Policy Implications

The present study brings out following major issues that have wider ramifications for policy formulation and implementation with a view to improving the livelihoods in the region. Some of the results have direct implications for policy and programmes based on evidences drawn from household survey that have great underpinning to evolve a long-term policy for sustainable livelihood security and for raising the living standards.

(i) Diversification strategy

Traditional hill agricultural practices have become increasingly uneconomical, and therefore, there is a need for diversifications from field crops to horticulture and non-food crops that have enormous potential for improvement in livelihood and income generation. Focus Group Discussion (FGD) results clearly bring out area-wise potential of resources. Regression results corroborate the findings that horticulture base has profound positive impact on household incomes. Area studies have also indicated that there has been a substantial transfer of area from cereal production to vegetable production with greater advantages to the farmers in terms of income and employment (Badhani, 1998). From the long-term perspective, this shift from low value field crops to high value added horticultural crops seems to be the most obvious and strategic option in the region. However, lack of proper institutional mechanisms such as credit, processing, storage, post-harvesting technologies and marketing network have severely hampered the systemic growth of this sector in Uttarakhand. If all these services are efficiently organised with necessary institutional back-up, horticulture can generate significant employment and earning opportunities in the region. In certain parts of the region, particularly lower and middle Himalayas, it offers significant scope for development and could even become a lead sector. Establishment of linkages from growers to local processing and to large plants (within and outside region) is most crucial for sustainable growth of horticulture. Enterprise-based activities based on local resources is critical for sustainable employment generation and enhancing income levels, which in turn, can help improving the living standard of the people. With appropriate policy interventions, it is possible to develop enterprise-based activities that would provide higher income through processing and value addition and help develop upstream and downstream linkages necessary to generate internal momentum of growth. Such enterprise-based activities have been developed in certain parts of the hilly region in the Hindu Kuskh Himalayas (HKH) region based on niche products.

Experience of Himachal Pradesh is worth emulating for development of horticulture. Our findings also support the hypothesis that higher area under horticulture helps restrict out-migration. It is, therefore important from policy point of view to promote this segment with an adequate support system.

Improving the asset base of the poor is crucial. The present research evidence has shown that poor farm households often lack assets (such as land, education and skill) that serve as important capacity variables for participating in RNF activities. However, in view of limited availability of cultivable land, it becomes an extremely difficult policy option to redistribute or distribute land to those who are landless or fall in sub-marginal category. Imparting appropriate education and marketable skills are, therefore other significant policy options for accessing employment in the skilled labour market.

The FGD technique was used to generate profiles of peoples' perceptions in selected villages with a view to identifying the potentials and constraints of such livelihood opportunities. The discussions were designed to elicit responses pertaining to the villagers' perception of livelihood issues—the assets, vulnerability, peoples' perception for improvement in access to livelihoods, and employment opportunities available (Annexure IX.1). Results have shown the availability of location-specific resources that have potential for providing sustainable employment and income opportunities. Policy interventions must be made with an understanding of assessing the location-specific resources and generating livelihood options through optimum exploitation of these resources. Also, voice of the poor has been captured through employing Participatory Rural Appraisal (PRA) technique in two villages with a view to incorporating the knowledge and opinions of rural people in the planning and management of development projects and programmes (Annexure IX.2).

(ii) Migration – a livelihood option

Out-migration is an important livelihood option in the region, even improved educational levels have not helped to restrict out-migration, rather it has accentuated the process owing to limited opportunities for the educated lots. Out-migration, which is indeed huge, has provided a much needed outlet for the excess labour and manpower. But this has obvious implications on the households and the local economy. High rates of out-migration have led to a significant change in gender roles with women increasingly having to undertake added responsibilities in both farm and household works that have tremendously increased their workloads and drudgery. Another related consequence is that there has been a significant increase in the number of female-headed households in the regions. Also, it has implications for the local labour market in the source area in terms of high sex ratio, tightening local labour market thereby raising the floor level wages, high female drudgery, involvement of children in cultivation and livestock rearing, long separation from the family and family insecurity etc. However, such a huge outflow of human resource has limited impact on the local economy in terms of promoting and accelerating development. Regression results show that long-term out-migration does not impact household income positively. It is important from the policy point of view to enhance the productive base of economy through diversification, industrialisation and focusing on the areas in which it has comparative advantages (horticulture, micro-hydel plants, tourism and other amenity services, for example).

(iii) Development of appropriate educational and skill structure

In spite of a relatively distinct resource base and potential for the development of numerous non-farm activities and enterprises in the state, its potential has not been fully exploited to the extent its resource base permit within the constraints of the fragile environment. There is a need for converting these physical resources into outcomes in terms of enterprises with value addition activities, capacity building and human resource development. Results of the present research clearly bring out at fore that technical skill among the workforce is abysmally low (about 1%) and almost half of the women workforce is illiterate. Transformation of physical resource base into real enterprise base would generate demand for numerous types of new skills and competencies, which would ultimately create employment and incomes in the productive activities. For this, education system has to be made relevant and this would require revamping of the existing educational system towards meeting the requirements of emerging skill structure. Relevance implies a correspondence between the nature of skills required by the enterprises and the type of skills provided by the educational and training institutions.

In this context, vocationalisation of education is of paramount importance with a focus on emerging and market driven trades. It is an essential measure in a rapidly changing economic environment that has profound impact on the production process, demand pattern and skill requirements. Such a change in the economic structure requires not only a huge capital investment but also a workforce that has the flexibility to acquire new skills for new jobs, as the structure of economy and occupation changes.

Vocational education is not only grossly inadequate in the state but seems to be less relevant to the needs of economy. Technical courses such as ITIs and Polytechnics suffer from the declining intake, obsolete trades, poor infrastructure and weak industry-education linkages. Although in recent years, many professional courses are mushrooming; but without corresponding to the emerging demand of economy in terms of skill and competency levels, they remain qualitatively at sub-optimal levels. Without any evaluation and impact assessment on regular basis, its efficacy to respond to the needs of the changing economic environment remains largely unknown. Such a situation might result in low returns, which would not be a viable form of investment in the long run, and this kind of situation needs to be corrected by setting some standards and benchmarking in order to improving the quality of these institutions.

The mismatch is largely due to lack of relevance of the course curriculum and inflexibility in education system which do not respond to the changing economic environment. Unless these technical and vocational courses are qualitatively improved to make them marketable, these would continue to become less relevant to the needs of the market.

There is a clear-cut policy message that the efforts to improve the relevant marketable skills are important for promoting high-income employment; and the importance of enhanced rural skill base for development of the RNF sector is incontrovertible. Our regression results clearly reveal that education and skills are the strong determinants for enhancing the household income.

(iv) Micro-Enterprises and its linkages

A substantively large majority of enterprises surveyed appear to be dominated by trade and household manufacturing activities with a narrow profile of activities. These kinds of enterprise-based activities have limited product lines, carried out on a small scale with little surplus for reinvestment. There are sizeable constraints in terms of scale and efficiency that result in weak linkage effects. Entrepreneurial activities suffer from numerous internal and external constraints, and as a result, over the years, these enterprises are languishing and operating at a low equilibrium trap with little product diversification and surplus. The major reasons for sickness of these enterprises can be attributed to both supply and demand side aspects.

Rural areas appear to be poorly equipped in terms of economic (roads, electricity, communication etc.) and social (vocational and training institutions, market information, access to credit institutions etc.) infrastructures. Some of these constraints are typically associated with hill specificities (inaccessibility and fragility, for example) that hinder the spur of entrepreneurial activities. As the survey results show, (a) education levels of entrepreneurs are low; (b) nearly one-fourth are illiterates and nearly half of the entrepreneurs have schooling up to high school level only. Also, those who are in the highest and lowest income groups scarcely participate in such activities.

Family labour is more prominent in the rural enterprises; nearly three-fourths employment constitutes family labour and one-fourth hired labour. Access to various supply side inputs (e.g. credit, technology and market) is low and most of the output of these enterprises is meant for the local markets. Demand is low primarily because of extremely low incomes and less purchasing power of those who demand the goods and services. In any case, this is an inadequate base for growth. But, if the demand for its output is to grow significantly, it is necessary to strengthen the market linkages. Input linkages are extremely weak for the local economy that generate little or no value addition to the enterprises. Mean earnings per man-day works out to be low with large variations across enterprises. The lowest mean earnings is noted for the weavers, which provides highest man-days of family employment but their earnings are observed to be below the casual wage earners. It is necessary to rejuvenate the weaving home-based enterprise through variety of promotional measures which has potential for generating strong forward and backward linkages to the local economy.

It is argued here that mountain areas should primarily focus on niche products in which the region has comparative advantage, rather than producing those products that do not have distinct advantage in terms of product and price competitiveness. However, there is a need for evolving special policies and support mechanisms to promote the micro and small enterprises taking into account the diversity and constraints in the regions.

The Government of Uttarakhand since its formation in November 9, 2000 has initiated several policy measures to promote industrialisation. The first industrial policy of the state was prepared in 2001 and later New Industrial Policy was announced in June, 2003. The New Industrial Policy provides various incentives for setting up industries in the state. The thrust industries identified in the state include floriculture, processing of medicinal plants and herbs, honey, horticulture and agro-based industries. The state government on its own has set up many development boards.

Integrated Industrial Policy was launched in February, 2008 with a view to accelerating industrial development in the hilly and remote areas through developing industrial infrastructures, and encouraging entrepreneurship development through variety of promotional measures. The policy focuses on industries in manufacturing and services sectors. These initiatives are in addition to the Industrial Policy, 2003 which aimed at providing a comprehensive framework for industrial development in the state.

Formation of an independent state has focused on the developmental problems in this region and some positive results are visible in terms of increased accessibility, communication and other development works; but unless the developmental issues are dovetailed within the hill perspective, most of the real issues will remain distant objectives. Employment has been one of the serious problems in the region and long-term employment growth has been abysmally low. Adequate employment opportunities cannot be generated unless productive base of the economy is enhanced. This would require sector-specific development strategies integrating environmental, economic and social components of sustainable mountain development. For this, a dētailed planning is a prerequisite for the region and within the regions due to enormous diversity in terms of suitability of land and other resources. In fact, land capability differs considerably according to the altitude and slope of the hills. Therefore, there is a need for appropriate land use patterns across regions and sub-regions.

Annexures

Annexure-I.1: Issues of Mountain Economies

European Mountains

Most of the European countries have some mountains. In the northernmost part there are Iceland and Scandinavia; the southernmost mountains are along the many mountainous islands of the Mediterranean. In the western side there are the mountains of Portugal, Spain, and the United Kingdom and Ireland. The most famous mountains are the Alps shared by France, Italy and Switzerland. There are other mountain chains in Western Europe, such as the Pyrenees, the Apennines etc. There are wide variations across these mountains, which include some very wealthy communities with highly industrialised and/or tourism-based economies in parts of western and northern Europe, and also very poor regions with subsistence based economies, particularly in southern and Eastern Europe (Mountain Areas in Europe, Final Report, Chapter1, Introduction). The Second Report on Economic and Social Cohesion (European Commission, 2001) notes, "Mountainous areas represent geographical barriers. While some mountainous areas are economically viable and integrated into the rest of the EU economy, most have problems, as witnessed by the fact that more than 95% of them (in terms of land area) are eligible for assistance under Objectives 1 or 2 of the Structural Funds." "Major changes are taking place in the uses of mountain land and water resources, effecting mountain livelihoods, downstream resources, and conservation of biological diversity. To a large extent, forces drive these changes external to the mountains (National and

European policies, urbanisation, migration, new economic activities)" (Price, 2000).

Appalachian Mountains

The Appalachian mountains are located in the Eastern North America, extending from Quebec to Georgia. Appalachian had fairly good growth of forests prior to 19th century but during 1890 and 1910, more than 90 per cent of forests were destroyed by lowland commercial interests. However, today Appalachian forests appear in relatively good condition. Most forestland is privately owned and timber extraction is an attractive alternative for rapid, short-term profits. Most of the profits from this resource extraction were removed from the mountain communities and little was replaced in the way of physical and social infrastructure. Haphazard land use and acid rain along with cutting of forests resulted in loss of cultural landscapes, and loss of biodiversity because of forest fragmentation (Byers, 2000).

African Mountains

African mountains present a shocking state of natural resources degradations. Ethiopian highlands reported enormous soil losses; water catchments of Wedza Mountain in Zimbabwe experiencing serious soil, water and vegetation resources degradation. Drought conditions being experienced in the lowlands surrounding Mount Kenya are partly attributed to the destruction of the water catchments. Grazing is expanding in the sub-pine and alpine grassland of Lesotho highlands while agriculture is extending higher up to 2,400-2,600 m. This has resulted in conflicts among different stakeholders of mountain areas. In Burundi, land use changes in favour of human utilisation of mountain ecosystems have resulted in loss of biodiversity. Some of the highest population densities in Africa are in mountain areas. As a result, population pressure on mountain resources is increasing. Poverty is one of the major contributory factors to unsustainable development in Africa. More and more people are experiencing drought and famine conditions, and therefore, food security remains one of the prime concerns for sustainable development of eco-system (Gichuki, 2000).

Latin American Mountains

As the longest cordillera across the continent, the Andes hold huge variation of ecosystems and societies adapted to cope with the mountain lifestyle. Sustainable communities are found in places where traditional knowledge is maintained and revitalised. However, threats from the globalisation process and ethnicity due to the encroachment of market forces in less competitive rural communities prompted to a reconsideration of research needs in the context of rapid socio-economic and ecological change (Sarmiento, 2000).

South West Indian Ocean

Major changes may affect mountain livelihoods, downstream resources, and conservation of biodiversity. Scarcity of water begins to be felt in the lowland zone. For a long time, mountain people have been marginalised. But they became the best keepers of their traditions and cultures, which are today a real richness of biological and original diversity (Ramamonjisoa, 2000).

The Hindu Kush Himalaya

Poverty alleviation and environmental conservation are the major development challenges for sustainable mountain development. For this, an integrated approach is required dovetailing economic, political, social and cultural priorities for a long-term and sustainable mountain eco-systems (Bhadra, 2000).

Annexure: II.1: Projected Outlay in the Tenth Plan

(Per cent)

Major development heads	*J&K*	*Himachal Pradesh*	*Uttarakhand*	*Sikkim*	*Arunachal Pradesh*	*Nagaland*	*Manipur*	*Mizoram*	*Tripura*	*Meghalaya*
I. Agriculture & Allied Activities	10.40	11.67	9.11	10.57	13.25	11.47	4.06	7.04	10.00	9.96
II. Rural Development	2.58	4.25	5.51	4.47	4.07	8.08	4.31	6.81	12.00	6.92
III. Special Area Programmes	5.32	0.20	0.05	1.81	1.67	2.00	0.82	1.76	7.00	1.49
IV. Irrigation & Flood Control	5.56	4.40	2.34	1.87	4.74	1.84	13.14	1.23	8.00	3.24
V. Energy	19.90	11.99	25.47	14.67	12.81	11.15	8.22	8.47	5.00	16.81
VI. Industry & Minerals	3.00	1.02	1.09	3.74	1.96	8.62	11.87	2.63	3.00	4.79
VII. Transport	11.32	15.88	14.27	16.00	21.20	7.65	7.97	20.95	11.00	17.96
VIII. Communication	-	0.02	-	-	-	-	-	-	0.20	-
IX. Science, Technology & Environment	0.25	0.06	0.81	0.66	0.12	0.20	0.61	0.23	0.30	0.26
X. Other General Economic Services	11.96	2.17	3.08	2.44	5.96	10.24	8.75	5.46	1.50	1.98
(i) Education	9.42	26.53	13.62	19.93	13.38	8.59	9.58	12.71	12.66	12.23
(ii) Medical & health	9.49	7.65	5.01	4.83	5.95	3.57	6.41	9.38	5.57	5.98
XI. Social Services & Education (Total)	27.70	47.51	37.23	40.24	31.87	33.15	36.80	41.60	40.50	34.38
XII. General Services	2.01	0.82	1.02	3.52	2.34	5.60	3.44	3.82	1.50	2.23
Grand Total (Rs. in lakh)	1450000 (100.00)	1030000 (100.00)	763000 (100.00)	165574 (100.00)	388832 (100.00)	222765 (100.00)	280400 (100.00)	230001 (100.00)	450000 (100.00)	300900 (100.00)

Source : Tenth Five-Year Plan, Planning Commission, Government of India, 2002.

Annexure III.1 : District-wise Indicators of Development in Uttarakhand State

Particulars	*Almora*	*Pithora-garh*	*Pauri Garhwal*	*Chamoli*	*Tehri Garhwal*	*Uttar-kashi*	*Bage-shwar*	*Rudra-prayag*	*Cham-pawat*	*Nainital*	*Udham Singh Nagar*	*Dehradun*	*Hardwar*	*Uttara-khand*
Percentage of net irrigated area from net cropped area (2008-09)	7.0	8.5	9.4	5.2	14.3	16.9	23.9	12.6	8.7	57.2	91.4	41.9	98.3	45.1
Percentage of cultivators and agri. labourers (2001)	74.77	67.70	67.06	64.36	69.85	75.10	69.91	75.78	74.67	42.03	29.72	18.64	22.63	49.77
Per capita NDDP (in Rs.) 2006-07 (Current prices)	23,829	230,40	22,365	25,675	26,478	21,088	18,332	19,423	22,802	33,164	27,968	33,917	40,967	29,373
Percentage of urban population to total population (2001)	8.56	12.14	12.95	13.43	9.67	7.79	3.13	1.20	14.58	35.36	32.65	52.94	30.86	25.59
Percentage of literate population to total population (2011)	81.0	82.9	82.6	83.5	75.1	75.9	80.7	82.1	80.7	84.8	74.4	85.2	74.6	79.6
Sex ratio: females per thousand males (2011)	1142	1021	1103	1021	1078	959	1093	1120	981	933	919	902	879	963

Sources : 1. *Statistical Diary*, Govt. of Uttarakhand, 2009-10. *Directorate of Economics & Statistics,* Ministry of Agriculture, Govt. of India, 2004-5.
2. Registrar General of India, *Census of India, Provisional Population Totals of Uttarakhand*, Paper 1 of 2001 and 2011, New Delhi.

Annexure-III.2 : Sampling Frame

District	*No. of blocks*	*Status*
I. Kumaon Region		
(i) Pithoragarh	12	Relatively developed
(ii) Nainital*	15	
(iii) Almora	14	Relatively backward
II. Garhwal Region		
(iv) Uttarkashi	6	Relatively developed
(v) Chamoli	12	
(vi) Tehri Garhwal	10	Relatively backward
(vii) Pauri Garhwal	15	
(viii) Hardwar*	6	
(ix) Dehradun*	6	

* Full or substantial part of the districts falling in the plain area.
Note : Districts taken before carving out new districts.

District and Block Selected for Investigation

District	*Block*	*Status*	*Remarks*
I. Kumaon Region			
(i) Pithoragarh (Relatively developed)	Kanalichhina		
	Didihat		
	Berinag	Relatively backward	Selected
	Dharchula	Relatively developed	Selected
	Pithoragarh		
	Gangolihat		
	Munakote		
	Munsiyari		
	Champawat*		
	Barakote*		
	Lohaghat*		
	Pati*		
(ii) Almora (Relatively backward)	Syaldey		
	Chaukhutia		
	Bhikiasen		
	Tarikhet		
	Salt	Relatively backward	Selected
	Dwarahat		
	Kapkot**		
	Bageshwar**		
	Garud**		
	Takula		
	Bhasiachhana		
	Hawalbagh	Relatively developed	Selected

(Contd...)

(Contd...)

	Lamgarha		
	Dholadevi		
II. Garhwal Region			
(i) Uttarkashi			
(Relatively developed)	Mori		
	Paraula		
	Naugaon		
	Dunda	Relatively backward	Selected
	Bhatwari	Relatively developed	Selected
(ii) T. Garhwal	Jaunpur		
(Relatively backward)	Chamba	Relatively developed	Selected
	Tholdhar		
	Bhilangana		
	Pratapnagar		
	Jakhanidhar		
	Jakholi***		
	Devprayag	Relatively backward	Could not be selected
	Kirtinagar		Selected (next relatively backward block in order)
	Narendranagar		

* Merged in newly carved out Champawat district.
** Merged in newly carved out Bageshwar district.
*** Merged in newly carved out Rudraprayag district.

Sample Distribution of Households

District/block	*Number*	*Per cent*
Almora	102	25.50
Pithoragarh	102	25.50
T. Garhwal	94	23.50
Uttarkashi	102	25.50
Blocks		
Berinag	52	13.00
Bhatwari	50	12.50
Chamba	44	11.00
Dharchula	50	12.50
Dunda	52	13.00
Hawalbagh	51	12.75
Kirtinagar	50	12.50
Salt	51	12.75
Total	400	100.00

Selection of Districts

District	% of horticulture area	% of index	Variation	% of non-food crop area	% of index	Variation	% of urban population	% of index	Variation
Uttarkashi	5.74	199.30556	0	3.86	57.698057	0.810842	7.2	31.074666	0.965687
Chamoli	3.3	114.58333	0.480315	0.96	14.349776	0.9780854	8.91	38.454899	0.927338
T.Garhwal	1.64	56.944444	0.807087	1.23	18.38565	0.9625144	5.67	24.471299	1
Dehradun	5.11	177.43056	0.124016	8.01	119.73094	0.571511	50.26	216.91843	0
Garhwal	0.66	22.297297	1	0.92	13.751868	0.9803922	11.89	51.316357	0.860507
Pithoragarh	2.96	102.77778	0.547244	1.05	15.695067	0.972895	7.43	32.067328	0.960529
Almora	1.61	55.902778	0.812992	0.58	8.6696562	1	6.39	27.578766	0.983853
Nainital	3.26	113.19444	0.488189	11.26	168.31091	0.384083	32.65	140.91498	0.394932
Hardwar	3.78	131.25	0.385827	17.92	267.86248	0	30.96	133.62106	0.432832
Total	2.88	100		6.69	100		23.17	100	

District	% of non-farm workers	% of index	Variation	% of Composite index	Rank %	Rank variation	composite index variation
Uttarkashi	18.38	85.968	0.882	93.51	4	4	0.335
Chamoli	19.64	91.861	0.830	64.81	5	5	0.196
T.Garhwal	15.56	72.778	1	43.14	8	9	0.057
Dehradun	39.57	185.079	0	174.78	2	1	0.826
Garhwal	25.42	118.896	0.589	51.56	7	7	0.142
Pithoragarh	21.08	98.596	0.770	62.28	6	6	0.187
Almora	16.97	79.373	0.941	42.88	9	8	0.065
Nainital	19.61	91.721	0.831	128.53	3	3	0.475
Hardwar	23	107.577	0.690	160.07	1	2	0.622
Total	21.38	100		100			1

A. Kumaon Region—Selection of Blocks

(Area in Hectare)

Almora district	*Total sown area*	*Area under potato*	*Percentage*	*Area under oilseeds*	*Area under tobacco*	*Area under rabi fodder*	*Total non-food*	*Percentage*	*Non-farm workers*
Blocks									
Syalde	15032	54	0.36	63	3	0	66	0.44	11.28
Chaukhutia	11835	87	0.74	82	2	1	85	0.72	16.35
Bhikiasen	12287	96	0.78	64	1	0	65	0.53	16.43
Tarikhet	13711	94	0.69	63	1	0	64	0.47	23.50
Salt	18239	41	0.22	78	3	1	82	0.45	10.88
Dwarahat	14972	147	0.98	88	2	1	91	0.61	17.03
Kapkot*	14687	141	0.96	59	1	0	60	0.41	13.78
Bageshwar*	12794	88	0.69	70	2	1	73	0.57	17.26
Garud*	12818	62	0.48	59	1	0	60	0.47	16.38
Takula	11127	96	0.86	63	1	0	64	0.58	22.27
Bhasiachhana	9088	87	0.96	64	2	0	66	0.73	16.96
Hawalbagh	11410	82	0.72	67	1	0	68	0.60	35.93
Lamgarha	11032	89	0.81	63	4	0	67	0.61	26.96
Dholadevi	11134	94	0.84	71	1	0	72	0.65	10.99
Total	180087	1258	0.70	954	25	4	983	0.55	16.97

1. Almora district	% of non-farm workers	% of index	Variation	% of area under potato	% of index	Variation	% of area under non-food crop	% of index	Variation	% Ranking	% Rank
Blocks											
Syalde	11.28	66.47	0.984	0.36	51.43	0.82	0.44	80.00	0.91	65.97	13
Chaukhutia	16.35	96.35	0.782	0.74	105.71	0.32	0.72	130.91	0.03	110.99	6
Bhikiasen	16.43	96.82	0.778	0.78	111.43	0.26	0.53	96.36	0.63	101.54	8
Tarikhet	23.5	138.48	0.496	0.69	98.57	0.38	0.47	85.45	0.81	107.50	7
Salt	10.88	64.11	1.000	0.22	31.43	1.00	0.45	81.82	0.88	59.12	14
Dwarahat	17.03	100.35	0.754	0.98	140.00	0.00	0.61	110.91	0.38	117.09	5
Kapkot*	13.78	81.20	0.884	0.96	137.14	0.03	0.41	74.55	1.00	97.63	11
Bageshwar*	17.26	101.71	0.745	0.69	98.57	0.38	0.57	103.64	0.50	101.31	9
Garud*	16.38	96.52	0.780	0.48	68.57	0.66	0.47	85.45	0.81	83.52	12
Takula	22.27	131.23	0.545	0.86	122.86	0.16	0.58	105.45	0.47	119.85	4
Bhasiachhana	16.96	99.94	0.757	0.96	137.14	0.03	0.73	132.73	0.00	123.27	3
Hawalbagh	35.93	211.73	0.000	0.72	102.86	0.34	0.6	109.09	0.41	141.22	1
Lamgarha	26.96	158.87	0.358	0.81	115.71	0.22	0.61	110.91	0.38	128.50	2
Dholadevi	10.99	64.76	0.996	0.84	120.00	0.18	0.65	118.18	0.25	100.98	10
Total	16.97	100.00		0.70	100.00		0.55	100.00		100.00	

* in Bageshwar district.

2. Pithoragarh district	% of Non-farm workers	Total sown area	Area under potato	% of area under potato	Area under oilseeds	Area under tobacco	Total non-food crops	% of non-food area
Blocks								
Kanalichhina	16.33	12514	284	2.27	182	11	193	1.54
Didihat	15.7	8308	59	0.71	61	0	61	0.73
Berinag	19.88	11126	56	0.50	45	3	48	0.43
Dharchula	31.2	6761	402	5.95	69	4	73	1.08
Pithoragarh	35.65	10266	93	0.91	100	1	101	0.98
Gangolihat	16.92	11384	66	0.58	86	11	97	0.85
Munakote	18.91	10827	100	0.92	101	9	110	1.02
Munsiyari	24.04	12786	114	0.89	33	9	42	0.33
Champawat*	16.54	9409	131	1.39	47	0	47	0.50
Barakote*	17.86	4283	87	2.03	57	13	70	1.63
Lohaghat*	19.95	10159	478	4.71	81	13	94	0.93
Pati*	14.05	6901	152	2.20	47	27	74	1.07
Total	21.08	114724	2021	1.76	909	101	1010	0.88

2. Pithoragarh district	% of non-farm workers	% of index	Variation	% of area under potato	Percentage	Variation	% of area non-food	Percentage	Variation	% Ranking
Blocks										
Kanalichhina	16.33	77.47	0.89	2.27	128.98	0.68	1.54	175.00	0.07	127.15
Didihat	15.7	74.48	0.92	0.71	40.34	0.96	0.73	82.95	0.69	65.92
Berinag	19.88	94.31	0.73	0.5	28.41	1.00	0.43	48.86	0.92	57.19
Dharchula	31.2	148.01	0.21	5.95	338.07	0.00	1.08	122.73	0.42	202.93
Pithoragarh	35.65	169.12	0.00	0.91	51.70	0.92	0.98	111.36	0.50	110.73
Gangolihat	16.92	80.27	0.87	0.58	32.95	0.99	0.85	96.59	0.60	69.94
Munakote	18.91	89.71	0.78	0.92	52.27	0.92	1.02	115.91	0.47	85.96
Munsiyari	24.04	114.04	0.54	0.89	50.57	0.93	0.33	37.50	1.00	67.37
Champawat*	16.54	78.46	0.88	1.39	78.98	0.84	0.50	56.82	0.87	71.42
Barakote*	17.86	84.72	0.82	2.03	115.34	0.72	1.63	185.23	0.00	128.43
Lohaghat*	19.95	94.64	0.73	4.71	267.61	0.23	0.93	105.68	0.54	155.98
Pati*	14.05	66.65	1.00	2.2	125.00	0.69	1.07	121.59	0.43	104.41
Total	21.08	100.00		1.76	100.00		0.88	100.00	0.58	100.00

* in Champawat district

3. Nainital district	*% of non-farm workers*	*Total sown area*	*Area under potato*	*% of area under potato*	*Area under non-food*	*% of area under non-food*
Blocks						
Ramnagar	17.41	22225	16	0.07	4400	19.80
Jaspur*	19.67	28757	101	0.35	2528	8.79
Kashipur*	21.22	26153	160	0.61	3282	12.55
Bajpur*	13.88	33906	251	0.74	5251	15.49
Kotabagh	12.31	9747	30	0.31	4456	45.72
Ramgarh	17.18	6639	433	6.52	286	4.31
Bhimtal	29.83	7748	562	7.25	284	3.67
Betalghat	19.33	6738	285	4.23	228	3.38
Dhari	7.77	5605	1038	18.52	222	3.96
Okhalkanda	9.82	10391	55	0.53	266	2.56
Haldwani	35.6	23062	3	0.01	6256	27.13
Gadarpur*	13.93	33597	26	0.08	1980	5.89
Rudrapur*	39.95	38400	63	0.16	4196	10.93
Sitarganj*	13.7	43397	21	0.05	2728	6.29
Khatima*	24.46	47736	55	0.12	2256	4.73
Total	19.61	344101	3099	0.90	38619	11.22

3. Nainital district	% of non-farm workers	% Index	Variation Index	% under potato	% Index	Variation Index	Area Under Non-food	% Index	Variation Index	% Ranking	% Rank	Variaton Rank	Variation Ranking
Block													
Ramnagar	17.41	88.78	0.70	0.07	7.78	0.997	19.80	176.47	0.60	91.01	10	6	0.23
Jaspur*	19.67	100.31	0.63	0.35	38.89	0.982	8.79	78.34	0.86	72.51	11	9	0.18
Kashipur*	21.22	108.21	0.58	0.61	67.78	0.968	12.55	111.85	0.77	95.95	9	6	0.23
Bajpur*	13.88	70.78	0.81	0.74	82.22	0.961	15.49	138.06	0.70	97.02	8	9	0.18
Kotabagh	12.31	62.77	0.86	0.31	34.44	0.984	45.72	407.49	0.00	168.24	5	3	0.39
Ramgarh	17.18	87.61	0.71	6.52	724.44	0.648	4.31	38.41	0.96	283.49	3	6	0.23
Bhimtal	29.83	152.12	0.31	7.25	805.56	0.609	3.67	32.71	0.97	330.13	2	4	0.37
Betalghat	19.33	98.57	0.64	4.23	470.00	0.772	3.38	30.12	0.98	199.57	4	7	0.20
Dhari	7.77	39.62	1.00	18.52	2057.78	0.000	3.96	35.29	0.97	710.90	1	5	0.34
Okhalkanda	9.82	50.08	0.94	0.53	58.89	0.972	2.56	22.82	1.00	43.93	14	11	0.03
Haldwani	35.6	181.54	0.14	0.01	1.11	1.000	27.13	241.80	0.43	141.48	6	1	0.48
Gadarpur*	13.93	71.04	0.81	0.08	8.89	0.996	5.89	52.50	0.92	44.14	13	10	0.09
Rudrapur*	39.95	203.72	0.00	0.16	17.78	0.992	10.93	97.42	0.81	106.31	7	2	0.40
Sitarganj*	13.7	69.86	0.82	0.05	5.56	0.998	6.29	56.06	0.91	43.83	15	10	0.09
Khatima*	24.46	124.73	0.48	0.12	13.33	0.994	4.73	42.16	0.95	60.07	12	8	0.19
Total	**19.61**	**100.00**	**0.63**	**0.90**	**100.00**	**0.952**	**11.22**	**100.00**	**0.80**	**100.00**			

* In Udham Singh Nagar.

B. Garhwal Region—Selection of Blocks

4. Chamoli district	*% of non-farm workers*	*Per cent*	*Variation*	*% of area sown potato*	*Per cent*	*Variation*	*% of area of non-food*	*Per cent*	*Variation*	*Index-1 %*	*Rank-1 %*	*Rank-2*
Block												
Joshimath	30.46	155.09	0.00	13.63	538.74	0.00	2	235.29	0.09	309.71	1	1
Ukhimath*	19.17	97.61	0.75	3.25	128.46	0.78	0.83	97.65	0.79	107.90	5	7
Augustmuni*	17.02	86.66	0.90	0.32	12.65	1.00	0.54	63.53	0.96	54.28	11	11
Karnprayag	30.02	152.85	0.03	1.59	62.85	0.90	0.47	55.29	1.00	90.33	8	4
Dasholi	24.22	123.32	0.42	2.61	103.16	0.83	0.79	92.94	0.81	106.47	6	5.5
Ghat	15.71	79.99	0.99	4.69	185.38	0.67	2.15	252.94	0.00	172.77	3	2
Narain Bazar	16.85	85.79	0.91	0.73	28.85	0.97	0.74	87.06	0.84	67.24	10	10
Gairsain	18.68	95.11	0.79	1.04	41.11	0.95	0.66	77.65	0.89	71.29	9	9
Tharali	24.17	123.07	0.42	1.78	70.36	0.89	1.22	143.53	0.55	112.32	4	3
Dewal	15.50	78.92	1.00	9.13	360.87	0.34	0.95	111.76	0.71	183.85	2	5.5
Pokhari	16.08	81.87	0.96	2.35	92.89	0.85	0.83	97.65	0.79	90.80	7	8
Total	19.64	100.00		2.53	100.00		0.85	100.00				

4. Chamoli district	Area under non-food crops (ha)												
	Total sown area	Area under potato	% of area under potato	Oilseeds	Sugarcane	Tobacco	Cotton	Rabi fodder	Kharif fodder	Jayad	Sanad	Total	% of Non-food
Block													
Joshimath	3095	422	13.63	62	0	0	0	0	0	0	0	62	2.00
Ukhimath*	4949	161	3.25	40	0	1	0	0	0	0	0	41	0.83
Augustmuni*	10749	34	0.32	58	0	0	0	0	0	0	0	58	0.54
Karnprayag	9289	148	1.59	43	0	1	0	0	0	0	0	44	0.47
Dasholi	6620	173	2.61	51	0	1	0	0	0	0	0	52	0.79
Ghat	3157	148	4.69	68	0	0	0	0	0	0	0	68	2.15
Narain Bazar	7019	51	0.73	51	0	1	0	0	0	0	0	52	0.74
Gairsain	8172	85	1.04	54	0	0	0	0	0	0	0	54	0.66
Tharali	4272	76	1.78	52	0	0	0	0	0	0	0	52	1.22
Dewal	2629	240	9.13	25	0	0	0	0	0	0	0	25	0.95
Pokhari	10184	239	2.35	85	0	0	0	0	0	0	0	85	0.83
Total	70135	1777	2.53	589	0	4	0	0	0	0	0	593	0.85

* in Rudraprayag district.

5. Dehradun district	Total sown area	Area under potato	% of area under potato	Oilseeds	Tobacco	Rabi fodder	Kharif	Jayad	Total	% of non-food crops	% of rural non- farm workers
Block											
Chakrata	11954	1005	8.41	230	22	0	0	0	252	2.11	11.08
Kalsi	10495	246	2.34	122	18	0	0	0	140	1.33	17.51
Vikasnagar	18717	15	0.08	649	0	405	491	13	1558	8.32	31.2
Sahaspur	17267	17	0.10	772	0	349	428	25	1574	9.12	47.83
Raipur	10640	38	0.36	219	0	274	493	118	1104	10.38	76.94
Doiwala	18633	43	0.23	709	0	420	754	71	1954	10.49	48.44
Total	87706	1364	1.56	2701	40	1448	2166	227	6582	7.50	39.57

5. Dehradun district	% of rural non-farm	% of index	Variation index	Area under potato%	% of Index	Variation index	Area under non-farm	% of index	Variation index	Rank %	Rank %	Rank variation	Rank variation
Block													
Chakrata	11.08	28.00	1.00	8.41	539.10	0.00	2.11	28.13	0.91	198.41	1	4	0.36
Kalsi	17.51	44.25	0.90	2.34	150.00	0.73	1.33	17.73	1.00	70.66	5	5	0.12
Vikasnagar	31.2	78.85	0.69	0.08	5.13	1.00	8.32	110.93	0.24	64.97	6	4	0.36
Sahaspur	47.83	120.87	0.44	0.1	6.41	1.00	9.12	121.60	0.15	82.96	4	3	0.47
Raipur	76.94	194.44	0.00	0.36	23.08	0.97	10.38	138.40	0.01	118.64	2	1	0.67
Doiwala	48.44	122.42	0.43	0.23	14.74	0.98	10.49	139.87	0.00	92.34	3	2	0.53
Total	39.57	100.00	0.57	1.56	100.00	0.82	7.5	100.00	0.33				

6. Hardwar district	% of non-farm workers	Total sown area	Area under potato	% of area potato	Area under non-food crop	% area non-food crops
Block						
Bhagwanpur	18.68	38519	133	0.35	8613	22.36
Roorkee	30.6	25320	77	0.30	5258	20.77
Nasan	26.21	33045	48	0.15	5650	17.10
Bahadrabad	23.94	40700	163	0.40	7825	19.23
Laksar	18.44	30177	23	0.08	4524	14.99
Khanpur	7.04	14059	23	0.16	1633	11.62
Total	23	181820	467	0.26	33503	18.43

6. Hardwar district	% of Index	Variation index	% of area potato	% of Index	Variation index	% of area non-food	% of index	Variation index	% of Ranking	% of Rank	Variation	Ranking variation
Block												
Bhagwanpur	81.22	0.51	0.35	134.62	0.16	22.36	121.32	0.00	112.39	3	3	0.78
Roorkee	133.04	0.00	0.30	115.38	0.31	20.77	112.70	0.15	120.37	2	1	0.85
Nasan	113.96	0.19	0.15	57.69	0.78	17.1	92.78	0.49	88.14	4	4	0.51
Bahadrabad	104.09	0.28	0.40	153.85	0.00	19.23	104.34	0.29	120.76	1	2	0.81
Laksar	80.17	0.52	0.08	30.77	1.00	14.99	81.33	0.69	64.09	5	5	0.27
Khanpur	30.61	1.00	0.16	61.54	0.75	11.62	63.05	1.00	51.73	6	6	0.08
Total	100.00	0.32	0.26	100.00	0.44	18.43	100.00	0.37				

7. Pauri Garhwal district	% of non-farm workers	Total area sown	Area under potato	%	Area under Potato	% area under non-crop
Block						
Kot	20.39	9723	9	0.09	83	0.85
Kaijikhal	19.6	8065	15	0.19	51	0.63
Pauri	21.47	7211	12	0.17	45	0.62
Pabo	18.51	7242	18	0.25	31	0.43
Khirsu	15.74	7050	23	0.33	44	0.62
Thalisain	20.75	9577	70	0.73	42	0.44
Birokhal	34.35	7963	20	0.25	38	0.48
Dhangu	42.71	16118	15	0.09	72	0.45
Dogadda	29.86	7913	20	0.25	385	4.87
Zahrikhal	48.82	8116	15	0.18	63	0.78
Ekeshwar	19.38	8527	23	0.27	80	0.94
Riknikhal	35.45	9599	21	0.22	41	0.43
Pokhra	23.58	9259	11	0.12	31	0.33
Yamkashwar	17.9	11137	18	0.16	35	0.31
Naunidanda	23.71	11292	23	0.20	53	0.47
Total	**25.42**	**138792**	**313**	**0.23**	**1094**	**0.79**

7. Pauri Garhwal district	% of non-farm workers	Per cent	Variation	Area under potato	Per cent	Variation	% of area under non-food	Per cent	Variation	% of Ranking	Rank-1%	Rank-2 Var.	Variation ranking
Block													
Kot	20.39	80.21	0.86	0.09	39.13	1.00	0.85	107.59	0.88	75.65	13	10	0.09
Kaijikhal	19.6	77.10	0.88	0.19	82.61	0.84	0.63	79.75	0.93	79.82	10	8	0.11
Pauri	21.47	84.46	0.83	0.17	73.91	0.88	0.62	78.48	0.93	78.95	11	7	0.12
Pabo	18.51	72.82	0.92	0.25	108.70	0.75	0.43	54.43	0.97	78.65	12	7	0.12
Khirsu	15.74	61.92	1.00	0.33	143.48	0.63	0.62	78.48	0.93	94.63	7	6	0.15
Thalisain	20.75	81.63	0.85	0.73	317.39	0.00	0.44	55.70	0.97	151.57	2	3	0.39
Birokhal	34.35	135.13	0.44	0.25	108.70	0.75	0.48	60.76	0.96	101.53	5	4	0.28
Dhangu	42.71	168.02	0.18	0.09	39.13	1.00	0.45	56.96	0.97	88.04	8	4	0.28
Dogadda	29.86	117.47	0.57	0.25	108.70	0.75	4.87	616.46	0.00	280.87	1	1	0.56
Zahrikhal	48.82	192.05	0.00	0.18	78.26	0.86	0.78	98.73	0.90	123.02	3	2	0.41
Ekeshwar	19.38	76.24	0.89	0.27	117.39	0.72	0.94	118.99	0.86	104.21	4	5	0.18
Riknikhal	35.45	139.46	0.40	0.22	95.65	0.80	0.43	54.43	0.97	96.51	6	4	0.28
Pokhra	23.58	92.76	0.76	0.12	52.17	0.95	0.33	41.77	1.00	62.24	14	9	0.10
Yamkashwar	17.9	70.42	0.93	0.16	69.57	0.89	0.31	39.24	1.00	59.74	15	11	0.06
Naunidanda	23.71	93.27	0.76	0.20	86.96	0.83	0.47	59.49	0.96	79.91	9	6	0.15
Total	25.42	100.00		0.23	100.00		0.79	100.00					

8. Uttarkashi district	% of non-farm workers	Total sown area	Area under potato	% of area under potato	Area under tobacco	Area under oilseed	Total area under non-food	% of area under non-food crops
Block								
Mori	9.6	5652	142	2.51	6	278	284	5.02
Paraula	15.76	5739	111	1.93	6	294	300	5.23
Naugaon	9.31	13043	609	4.67	15	375	390	2.99
Dunda	15.16	8909	179	2.01	2	191	193	2.17
Chinyalisaor	11.3	6206	146	2.35	2	183	185	2.98
Bhatwari	27.68	6708	559	8.33	4	199	203	3.03
Total	18.38	46257	1746	3.77	35	1520	1555	3.36

8. Uttarkashi district	% of non-farm workers	Per cent	Variation	% of area potato	Per cent	Variation	% of area non-food	Per cent	Variation	% of Index-1	Rank-1%	Rank-2	Variation Index-2
Block													
Mori	9.6	52.23	1.00	2.51	66.58	0.91	5.02	149.40	0.07	89.40	3	3	0.34
Paraula	15.76	85.75	0.66	1.93	51.19	1.00	5.23	155.65	0.00	97.53	2	2	0.45
Naugaon	9.31	50.65	1.02	4.67	123.87	0.57	2.99	88.99	0.73	87.84	4	4	0.23
Dunda	15.16	82.48	0.69	2.01	53.32	0.99	2.17	64.58	1.00	66.79	6	6	0.11
Chinyalisaor	11.3	61.48	0.91	2.35	62.33	0.93	2.98	88.69	0.74	70.83	5	5	0.14
Bhatwari	27.68	150.60	0.00	8.33	220.95	0.00	3.03	90.18	0.72	153.91	1	1	0.76
Total	18.38	100.00		3.77	100.00		3.36	100.00					

9. T. Garhwal district	% of non-farm workers	Total sown area	Area under potato	Per cent	Area under oilseeds	Tobacco	Total non-food crop	% of non-food crops
Block								
Jaunpur	10.72	11693	236	2.02	143	2	145	1.24
Chamba	22.13	9222	151	1.64	123	2	125	1.36
Tholdhar	18.76	11739	139	1.18	154	2	156	1.33
Bhilangana	9.96	10642	185	1.74	141	1	142	1.33
Pratapnagar	16.72	7915	81	1.02	126	1	127	1.60
Jakhanidhar	22	9514	103	1.08	120	1	121	1.27
Jakholi*	13.38	12113	198	1.63	150	1	151	1.25
Devprayag	13.21	15393	102	0.66	154	3	157	1.02
Kirtinagar	16.39	13315	96	0.72	129	3	132	0.99
Narendranagar	24.93	13082	148	1.13	131	1	132	1.01
Total	15.56	114628	1439	1.26	1371	17	1388	1.21

T.Garhwal district	% of non-farm workers	% of index	Variation	% of area under potato	% of Index	Variation	% of area non-food	% of index
Block								
Jaunpur	10.72	68.89	0.95	2.02	160.32	0.00	1.24	102.48
Chamba	22.13	142.22	0.19	1.64	130.16	0.28	1.36	112.40
Tholdhar	18.76	120.57	0.41	1.18	93.65	0.62	1.33	109.92
Bhilangana	9.96	64.01	1.00	1.74	138.10	0.21	1.33	109.92
Pratapnagar	16.72	107.46	0.55	1.02	80.95	0.74	1.6	132.23
Jakhanidhar	22	141.39	0.20	1.08	85.71	0.69	1.27	104.96
Jakholi*	13.38	85.99	0.77	1.63	129.37	0.29	1.25	103.31
Devprayag	13.21	84.90	0.78	0.66	52.38	1.00	1.02	84.30
Kirtinagar	16.39	105.33	0.57	0.72	57.14	0.96	0.99	81.82
Narendranagar	24.93	160.22	0.00	1.13	89.68	0.65	1.01	83.47
Total	15.56	100.00		1.26	100.00		1.21	100.00

* in Rudraprayag district

Annexure Table III.3 : Development Index of Surveyed Villages

Block	*Indicators of infrastructure*						*Value of index*					
	Villages	*Approx. distance from block Km.*	*PHC from block (km.)*	*Electricity availability (%)*	*Drinking water availability (%)*	*Literacy rate (%)*	*Distance from block (km.)*	*PHC from block (km.)*	*Electricity availability (%)*	*Drinking water availability (%)*	*Literacy rate (%)*	*Composite index*
Hawalbagh	Khunt	12	2.5	57	62	54	0.0004	0.9375	0.2692	0.7931	0.6842	0.46
	Champha	18	1	68	80	62	0.0006	1.0000	0.1282	0.1724	0.4737	0.65
	Hawalbagh	0.5	2	64	60	66	0.0004	0.9583	0.1795	0.8621	0.3684	0.53
	Salla Rautela	17	3	70	66	66	0.0006	0.9167	0.1026	0.6552	0.3684	0.59
	Dhamuakalan	12	3	50	65	56	0.0005	0.9167	0.3590	0.6897	0.6316	0.48
	Total										3.36	0.56
Salt	Talli Pokhari	16	6	52	65	48	0.0006	0.7917	0.3333	0.6897	0.8421	0.47
	Khumarh	5	2	55	68	54	0.0004	0.9583	0.2949	0.5862	0.6842	0.50
	Kane	11	4	54	69	50	0.0005	0.8750	0.3077	0.5517	0.7895	0.50
	Majherkhata	16	7	48	65	42	0.0006	0.7500	0.3846	0.6897	1.0000	0.44
	Nadoli	12	7	40	65	51	0.0005	0.7500	0.4872	0.6897	0.7632	0.46
	Total										2.41	0.40
Berinag	Nagore	18	3	56	62	48	0.0004	0.9167	0.2821	0.7931	0.8421	0.43
	Jakh	11	10	56	63	50	0.0005	0.6250	0.2821	0.7586	0.7895	0.51
	Baongarh	25	8	53	62	51	0.0005	0.7083	0.3205	0.7931	0.7632	0.48
	Shahgaron	2	5	70	70	58	0.0004	0.8333	0.1026	0.5172	0.5789	0.59
	Barsait	12	4	60	60	55	0.0004	0.8750	0.2308	0.8621	0.6579	0.47
	Total										2.49	0.50

Dharchula	Benia	12	6	58	68	53	0.0005	0.7917	0.2564	0.5862	0.7105	0.53
	Pangu	25	12	57	70	55	0.0008	0.5417	0.2692	0.5172	0.6579	0.60
	Binkane	5	6	60	75	50	0.0005	0.7917	0.2308	0.3448	0.7895	0.57
	Dhungatoli	10	5	56	68	45	0.0005	0.8333	0.2821	0.5862	0.9211	0.48
	Kuti	50	25	0	70	56	0.0000	0.0000	1.0000	0.5172	0.6316	0.57
	Total										2.75	0.55
Chamba	Jaripani	11	6	50	65	56	0.0005	0.7917	0.3590	0.6897	0.6316	0.51
	Nagerh	16	5	49	61	55	0.0005	0.8333	0.3718	0.8276	0.6579	0.46
	Sangaon	10	7	52	59	52	0.0005	0.7500	0.3333	0.8966	0.7368	0.46
	Thangdhar	15	8	68	60	50	0.0005	0.7083	0.1282	0.8621	0.7895	0.50
	Chamangaon	2	2	50	61	52	0.0003	0.9573	0.2947	0.5859	0.6576	0.43
	Total										1.93	0.48
Kirtinagar	Ranihat	4	14	30	50	48	0.0005	0.4583	0.6154	1.2069	0.8421	0.38
	Dhuret	13	15	47	68	52	0.0006	0.4167	0.3974	0.5862	0.7368	0.57
	Khola	20	15	45	56	42	0.0007	0.4167	0.4231	1.0000	1.0000	0.43
	Talli Rigoli	14	12	38	60	50	0.0006	0.5417	0.5128	0.8621	0.7895	0.46
	Upgarh	18	13	41	72	40	0.0006	0.5000	0.4744	0.4483	1.0526	0.50
	Total										2.34	0.47
Bhatwari	Bagori	30	5	55	70	50	0.0010	0.8333	0.2949	0.5172	0.7895	0.51
	Dharali	25	6	58	75	58	0.0008	0.7917	0.2564	0.3448	0.5789	0.61
	Pallavarsu	12	5	60	73	57	0.0010	0.8333	0.2308	0.4138	0.6053	0.58
	Kamakh	11	15	38	60	50	0.0007	0.4167	0.5128	0.8621	0.7895	0.48
	Malla	3	16	41	65	43	0.0007	0.3750	0.4744	0.6897	0.9737	0.50
	Total										2.68	0.54

Dunda	Barethi	11	6	50	60	50	0.0005	0.7917	0.3590	0.8621	0.7895	0.44
	Singuri	12	2	50	62	54	0.0004	0.9583	0.3590	0.7931	0.6842	0.44
	Malla-Patara	18	7	48	58	50	0.0005	0.7500	0.3846	0.9310	0.7895	0.43
	Brahma Makhal	22	8	40	62	50	0.0005	0.7083	0.4872	0.7931	0.7895	0.44
	Veerpur	4	2	55	68	55	0.0004	0.9583	0.2949	0.5862	0.6579	0.50
	Total										2.25	0.45

Source : Field Survey, 2004-05.

Annexure Table IV.1: Sectoral Distribution of Rural Workers in Uttarakhand* 1999-2000

Industry	*UPS*			*UPSS*		
	Male	*Female*	*Person*	*Male*	*Female*	*Person*
Agriculture	638280	668773	1307053	692468	1060395	1752863
Mining & quarrying	0	0	0	0	0	0
Manufacturing	89551	0	89551	89547	0	89547
Public utilities	5776	0	5776	5776	0	5776
Construction	147591	6056	153647	147584	25723	173307
Trade, hotel & restaurant	47308	0	47308	47306	0	47306
Transport etc.	46199	0	46199	46197	0	46197
Financial services & real estate	12281	0	12281	12281	0	12281
Public admin., community services etc.	81873	16222	98094	82494	16809	99303
Total workers	1068859	691051	1759910	1123652	1102927	2226579

* Excludes Hardwar.

Notes : Figures have been worked out using interpolated population and corresponding WPRs.

Annexure Table IV.2 : Sectoral Distribution of Rural Workers in Uttarakhand* 2004-05

Industry	*UPS*			*UPSS*		
	Male	*Female*	*Person*	*Male*	*Female*	*Person*
Agriculture	807907	903870	1711777	895734	1263736	2159470
Mining & quarrying	0	0	0	0	0	0
Manufacturing	71901	12317	84218	58451	14530	72981
Public utilities	5229	0	5229	5999	393	6391
Construction	149031	6632	155664	148010	7069	155079
Trade, hotel & restaurant	111120	0	111120	101277	393	101670
Transport etc.	50984	947	51932	53010	1178	54188
Financial services & real estate	13073	0	13073	13392	393	13785
Public admin, community services etc	98047	23686	121733	119134	21337	140471
Total workers	1307293	947453	2254745	1395007	1309029	2704035

* Excludes Hardwar.

Notes : Figures have been worked out using interpolated population and corresponding WPRs.

Annexure Table IV. 3 : Sectoral Distribution of Workers (at one-digit level) in Urban Uttarakhand, 1983 to 2004-05

Sectors	*1983*	*1987-88*	*1993-94*	*1999-00*	*2004-05*
Agriculture and allied activities	9.02	9.66	17.84	3.24	12.03
Mining & quarrying	0.00	0.00	0.69	0.00	0.04
Manufacturing	11.44	8.38	10.78	12.14	11.91
Electricity	0.61	3.32	1.09	4.41	1.27
Construction	5.23	8.98	2.59	10.80	10.27
Trade, hotels & restaurants	20.00	25.28	17.73	26.13	26.97
Transport, storage & communication	8.40	3.55	7.38	4.17	7.28
Finance, real estate & business	4.69	4.22	4.60	6.51	2.76
Pub. admn., edu., health & others	40.60	36.61	37.31	32.59	27.48
All	100.00	100.00	100.00	100.00	100.00
Urban Males					
Agriculture and allied activities	7.71	7.25	8.70	2.85	7.30
Mining & quarrying	0.00	0.00	0.87	0.00	0.00
Manufacturing	12.44	9.23	11.38	9.47	12.40
Electricity	0.67	3.90	1.38	5.28	1.50
Construction	5.76	10.13	3.27	12.94	11.80
Trade, hotels & restaurants	21.66	27.25	21.23	30.00	31.40
Transport, storage & communication	8.97	4.17	9.33	5.00	8.80
Finance, real estate & business	4.90	4.01	5.81	7.61	3.20
Pub. administration, education, health & others	37.89	34.07	38.02	26.86	23.60
All	100.00	100.00	100.00	100.00	100.00
Urban Females					
Agriculture and allied activities	22.15	23.70	52.43	5.23	33.40
Mining & quarrying	0.00	0.00	0.00	0.00	0.00
Manufacturing	1.45	3.44	8.48	25.64	9.70
Electricity	0.00	0.00	0.00	0.00	0.20
Construction	0.00	2.32	0.00	0.00	3.60
Trade, hotels & restaurants	3.32	13.80	4.46	6.61	7.10
Transport, storage & communication	2.68	0.00	0.00	0.00	0.63
Finance, real estate & business	2.59	5.41	0.00	1.00	1.03
Pub. Administration, education, health & others	67.82	51.34	34.63	61.52	44.34
All	100.00	100.00	100.00	100.00	100.00

Source : NSSO, household unit record data on employment and unemployment, various rounds.

Annexure Table IV. 4 : Workers at (one-digit Level) Rural Uttarakhand*

Industry	*1987-88*			*1993-94*			*1999-2000*			*2004-05*		
	Male	*Female*	*Total*	*Male*	*Female*	*Total*	*Male*	*Female*	*Total*	*Male*	*Female*	*Total*
Agriculture, forestry & fishing	779113	1191090	1970203	899240	1291070	2190310	692468	1060395	1752863	883039	1257976	2141016
Mining & quarrying	392	0	392	8961	0	8961	0	0	0	0	0	0
Manufacturing	77098	3225	80322	84671	6018	90689	89547	0	89547	72540	17017	89558
Electricity	862	0	862	3582	0	3582	5776	0	5776	5580	0	5580
Construction	115410	2901	118311	38409	3510	41919	147584	25723	173307	152056	6545	158601
Trade, hotels & restaurants	42775	1469	44244	67172	2735	69908	47306	0	47306	112996	0	112996
Transport, storage & communication	8581	0	8581	26952	0	26952	46197	0	46197	51615	1309	52924
Finance, real estate & business	4562	0	4562	5138	3171	8309	12281	0	12281	13950	0	13950
Pub admn., education, health & others	90868	9825	100692	80989	15359	96348	82494	16809	99303	103231	26181	129411
Total	1119661	1208509	2328170	1215116	1321864	2536979	1123652	1102927	2226579	1395007	1309029	2704035
Farm	779113	1191090	1970203	899240	1291070	2190310	692468	1060395	1752863	883039	1257976	2141015
Non-farm	340548	17419	357967	315876	30794	346669	431184	42532	473716	511968	51053	563020

* Excludes Hardwar.

Notes : Figures have been worked out using interpolated population and corresponding WPR (UPSS).

Annexure Table IV. 5 : Employment Growth Rate by Industry in Rural Uttarakhand*

Industry	*1983-88*			*1988-94*			*1994-2000*			*2000-05*		
	Male	*Female*	*Total*	*Male*	*Female*	*Total*	*Male*	*Female*	*Total*	*Male*	*Female*	*Total*
Agriculture, forestry & fishing	3.11	-1.83	0.46	2.42	1.35	1.78	-4.26	-3.23	-3.65	4.98	3.48	4.08
Mining & quarrying	-45.38	0.00	-46.76	68.48	0.00	68.48	-100.00	0.00	-100.00	0.00	0.00	0.00
Manufacturing	5.97	0.00	4.24	1.57	10.96	2.04	0.94	-100.00	-0.21	-4.12	0.00	0.00
Electricity	-2.55	0.00	-5.01	26.80	0.00	26.80	8.29	0.00	8.29	-0.69	0.00	-0.69
Construction	38.54	0.00	35.79	-16.75	3.23	-15.88	25.15	39.37	26.69	0.60	-23.95	-1.76
Trade, hotels & restaurants	11.07	-7.55	7.60	7.81	10.92	7.92	-5.68	-100.00	-6.30	19.02	0.00	19.02
Transport, storage & communication	-24.66	0.00	-26.56	21.02	0.00	21.02	9.40	0.00	9.40	2.24	0.00	2.76
Finance, real estate & business	-7.56	0.00	-9.89	2.00	0.00	10.51	15.63	-100.00	6.73	2.58	0.00	2.58
Pub. admn., education, health & others	-16.80	1.62	-17.66	-1.90	7.73	-0.73	0.31	1.51	0.50	4.59	9.27	5.44
Total	1.58	-1.70	-0.20	1.37	1.51	1.44	-1.30	-2.97	-2.15	4.42	3.49	3.96
Farm	3.11	-1.83	0.46	2.42	1.35	1.78	-4.26	-3.23	-3.65	4.98	3.48	4.08
Non-farm	-1.51	10.25	-3.45	-1.25	9.96	-0.53	5.32	5.53	5.34	3.49	3.72	3.51

* Excludes Hardwar.

Notes : Growth rate has been worked out using interpolated population and corresponding WPR (UPSS).

Source : Annexure Table IV.4.

Annexure Table IV. 6 : Sectoral Distribution of Enterprises, Workers and GVA in the Informal Sector in Uttarakhand, 1999-2000 (Rural)

Industry	*NIC 2digit*	*Enterprise*	*Workers*	*GVA*	*% Ent*	*%Workers*	*%GVA*	*Work/Ent*	*Productivity*
Manufacturing of food prod and beverages	15	11150	16741	208182971	8.43	9.52	6.03	1.5	12435
Manufacturing of textiles	17	2806	6303	104147691	2.12	3.58	3.02	2.2	16524
Manufacturing of wearing apparel	18	6588	8487	116862553	4.98	4.83	3.39	1.3	13770
Manufacturing of wood and wood products and cork	20	3986	5205	76342999	3.01	2.96	2.21	1.3	14667
Manufacturing of other non-metallic mineral	26	925	1850	11651850	0.70	1.05	0.34	2.0	6300
Manufacturing of fabricated metal products	28	2542	3338	37707105	1.92	1.90	1.09	1.3	11295
Manufacturing of machinery and equipment nec.	29	348	1008	15855952	0.26	0.57	0.46	2.9	15738
Manufacturing of electrical machinery etc.	31	275	1869	21733442	0.21	1.06	0.63	6.8	11625
Manufacturing of radio, television and community equipments	32	194	194	3243542	0.15	0.11	0.09	1.0	16740
Manufacturing of furniture nec.	36	842	1390	29965851	0.64	0.79	0.87	1.7	21558
Manufacturing (total)		**29654**	**46385**	**625693957**	**22.42**	**26.38**	**18.14**	**1.6**	**13489**
Construction	45	23726	25669	407436969	17.94	14.60	11.81	1.1	15873
Construction (total)		**23726**	**25669**	**407436969**	**17.94**	**14.60**	**11.81**	**1.1**	**15873**

Sale, maintenance and repair of motor vehicles	50	339	818	14667572	0.26	0.47	0.43	2.4	17934
Wholesale trade and commission trade	51	153	361	1816992	0.12	0.21	0.05	2.4	5039
Retail Trade, except motor vehicle etc.	52	43228	50538	1006379372	32.68	28.74	29.17	1.2	19913
Trade (total)		**43720**	**51717**	**1022863936**	**33.05**	**29.41**	**29.65**	**1.2**	**19778**
Hotel and restaurants	55	13849	18896	373841071	10.47	10.75	10.84	1.4	19784
Hotel & restaurant (total)		**13849**	**18896**	**373841071**	**10.47**	**10.75**	**10.84**	**1.4**	**19784**
Land transport etc.	60	11014	18295	743247420	8.33	10.40	21.55	1.7	40626
Post and telecommunication	64	427	869	8542243	0.32	0.49	0.25	2.0	9830
Transport storage (total)		**11441**	**19164**	**751789663**	**8.65**	**10.90**	**21.79**	**1.7**	**39229**
Renting of machinery and equipment	71	539	590	50295778	0.41	0.34	1.46	1.1	85288
Other business activities	74	1160	1160	41617799	0.88	0.66	1.21	1.0	35891
Financial intermediation (total)		**1699**	**1749**	**91913577**	**1.28**	**0.99**	**2.66**	**1.0**	**52543**
Education	80	1197	3507	32504167	0.90	1.99	0.94	2.9	9268
Health and social service	85	1546	1824	51825398	1.17	1.04	1.50	1.2	28407
Activities of member organisation	91	1255	1255	27873524	0.95	0.71	0.81	1.0	22212
Recreational, cultural activities	92	356	711	1770577	0.27	0.40	0.05	2.0	2490
Other service activities	93	3829	4954	62111034	2.89	2.82	1.80	1.3	12538
Services (total)		**8182**	**12251**	**176084700**	**6.19**	**6.97**	**5.10**	**1.5**	**14373**
Total		**132271**	**175831**	**3449623873**	100.00	100.00	100.00	1.3	19619

Source : Calculated from unit level data from CD of 55th Round NSSO, Survey of Informal Sector Non-agricultural Enterprises.

Sectoral Distribution of Enterprises, Workers and GVA in the Informal Sector in Uttarakhand, 1999-2000 (Urban)

Industry	*NIC 2digit*	*Enterprise*	*Workers*	*GVA*	*% Ent*	*%Workers*	*%GVA*	*Work/Ent*	*Productivity*
Manufacturing of food prod and beverages	15	1215	3118	91941232	1.26	1.98	2.21	2.6	29485
Manufacturing of textiles	17	6406	10496	48938616	6.67	6.67	1.18	1.6	4663
Manufacturing of wearing apparel	18	2850	5787	89311163	2.97	3.68	2.15	2.0	15432
Manufacturing of wood and wood products and cork	20	653	653	18902302	0.68	0.41	0.45	1.0	28938
Manufacturing of other non-metallic mineral	26	562	853	30361344	0.58	0.54	0.73	1.5	35602
Manufacturing of fabricated metal products	28	2170	2586	27429333	2.26	1.64	0.66	1.2	10607
Manufacturing of machinery and equipment (nec)	29	0	0	0	0.00	0.00	0.00	0.0	0
Manufacturing of electrical machinery etc.	31	820	1953	20525768	0.85	1.24	0.49	2.4	10511
Manufacturing of radio, television and community equipments	32	0	0	0	0.00	0.00	0.00	0.0	0
Manufacturing of furniture (nec)	36	1244	2821	92535936	1.29	1.79	2.22	2.3	32802
Manufacturing (total)		**15920**	**28267**	**419945693**	**16.57**	**17.96**	**10.09**	**1.8**	**14856**
Construction	45	8539	8851	259935071	8.89	5.62	6.24	1.0	29368
Construction (total)		**1491**	**7547**	**308101735**	**1.55**	**4.79**	**7.40**	**5.1**	**40827**

Sale, maintenance and repair of motor vehicles	50	1491	7547	308101735	1.55	4.79	7.40	5.1	40827
Wholesale trade and commission trade,	51	983	1399	20766720	1.02	0.89	0.50	1.4	14847
Retail Trade, except motor vehicle etc.	52	44118	63399	1901311983	45.91	40.28	45.67	1.4	29990
Trade total		**46592**	**72344**	**2230180438**	**48.48**	**45.96**	**53.57**	**1.6**	**30827**
Hotel and restaurants	55	6871	16749	445858624	7.15	10.64	10.71	2.4	26619
Hotel & restaurant		**6871**	**16749**	**445858624**	**7.15**	**10.64**	**10.71**	**2.4**	**26619**
Land transport etc.	60	3709	4745	125127942	3.86	3.01	3.01	1.3	26369
Post and telecommunication	64	820	1233	21467264	0.85	0.78	0.52	1.5	17418
Transport storage (total)		**4530**	**5978**	**146595206**	**4.71**	**3.80**	**3.52**	**1.3**	**24523**
Renting of machinery and equipment	71	308	720	26981085	0.32	0.46	0.65	2.3	37461
Other business activities	74	510	510	12485102	0.53	0.32	0.30	1.0	24466
Financial intermediation (total)		**818**	**1231**	**39466187**	**0.85**	**0.78**	**0.95**	**1.5**	**32072**
Education	80	2472	8095	254602378	2.57	5.14	6.12	3.3	31453
Health and social service	85	1023	1439	31676244	1.06	0.91	0.76	1.4	22019
Activities of member organisation	91	860	860	17633201	0.89	0.55	0.42	1.0	20503
Recreational, cultural activities	92	1432	2732	55497364	1.49	1.74	1.33	1.9	20314
Other service activities	93	5204	6947	144015051	5.42	4.41	3.46	1.3	20732
Services (total)		**10990**	**20072**	**503424238**	**11.44**	**12.75**	**12.09**	**1.8**	**25081**
Total		**96096**	**157404**	**4162766907**	**100.00**	**100.00**	**100.00**	**1.6**	**26446**

Source : Calculated from unit level data from CD of 55th Round NSSO, Survey of Informal Sector Non-agricultural Enterprises.

Annexure Table IV. 7 : Number of Enterprises, Workers and GVA in 1994-95 and 2000-01

	Number of Enterprises				
NIC Code	*Description*	*OAME*	*NDME*	*DME*	*Total*
20-21	Mfg. of food products	14024	1920	384	16328
23-24-25	Mfg. of beverages, tobacco & related products	1758	45	5	1807
26	Mfg. of textile products	1863	86	62	2011
27	Mfg. of wood and wood products	13428	189	746	14363
30	Mfg. of basic chemicals & chemical products (except products of petroleum & coal)	537	0	0	537
32	Mfg. of non-metallic mineral products	7760	5	186	7951
34	Mfg. of metal products and parts, except machinery and equipment	241	0	5	245
35-36	Mfg. of machinery and equipment other than transport equipment	147	0	0	147
38	Mfg. of other manufacturing industries	337	0	0	337
Total		40092	2245	1388	43725

	Number of Workers				
NIC Code	*Description*	*OAME*	*NDME*	*DME*	*Total*
20-21	Mfg. of food products	30,883	5,059	1,968	37,910
23-24-25	Mfg .of beverages, tobacco & related products	5,428	180	27	5,635
26	Mfg. of textile products	4,348	261	744	5,354
27	Mfg of wood and wood products	18,906	585	3,438	22,928
30	Mfg. of basic chemicals & chemical products (except products of petroleum & coal)	705	0	0	705
32	Mfg. of non-metallic mineral products	19,226	9	6,487	25,722
34	Mfg. of metal products and parts, except machinery and equipment	543	0	27	570
35-36	Mfg. of machinery and equipment other than transport equipment	184	0	0	184
38	Mfg. of other manufacturing industries	488	0	0	488
Total		80,712	6,094	12,692	99,498

GVA (constant prices)

NIC Code	*Description*	*OAME*	*NDME*	*DME*	*Total*
20-21	Mfg. of food products	352,846,997	38,253,193	19,590,996	410,691,186
23-24-25	Mfg. of beverages, tobacco & related products	24,064,005	2,857,010	79,224	27,000,239
26	Mfg. of textile products	12,759,098	1,591,502	10,191,204	24,541,803
27	Mfg. of wood and wood products	96,655,106	7,695,952	16,304,818	120,655,876
30	Mfg. of basic chemicals & chemical products (except products of petroleum & coal)	3,498,989	67,670	0	3,566,659
32	Mfg. of non-metallic mineral products	33,011,745	98,150	101,061,543	134,171,439
34	Mfg. of metal products and parts, except machinery and equipment	2,378,823	0	497,792	2,876,615
35-36	Mfg. of machinery and equipment other than transport equipment	999,370	0	0	999,370
38	Mfg. of other manufacturing industries	4,865,336	0	0	4,865,336
Total		531,079,469	50,563,477	147,725,578	729,368,524

Number of Enterprises, Workers and GVA in 2000-01

Number of Enterprises

NIC Code	*Description*	*OAME*	*NDME*	*DME*	*Total*
20-21	Mfg. of food products	17,095	1,287	738	19,120
23-24-25	Mfg. of beverages, tobacco & related products	79	0	0	79
26	Mfg. of textile products	20,906	1,285	0	22,192
27	Mfg of wood and wood products	5,781	203	48	6,032
30	Mfg. of basic chemicals & chemical products (except products of petroleum & coal)	16	8	0	24
32	Mfg. of non-metallic mineral products	2,223	0	477	2,700
34	Mfg. of metal products and parts, except machinery and equipment	1,739	87	26	1,851
35-36	Mfg. of machinery and equipment other than transport equipment	566	207	0	773
38	Mfg. of other manufacturing industries	724	0	0	724
Total		49,413	3,077	1,289	53,780

Number of Workers

NIC Code	*Description*	*OAME*	*NDME*	*DME*	*Total*
20-21	Mfg. of food products	38,227	4,160	5,247	47,635
23-24-25	Mfg. of beverages, tobacco & related products	79	0	0	79
26	Mfg. of textile products	29,376	3,853	0	33,229
27	Mfg. of wood and wood products	8,626	520	48	9,194
30	Mfg. of basic chemicals & chemical products (except products of petroleum & coal)	24	40	0	64
32	Mfg. of non-metallic mineral products	5,262	0	27,244	32,506
34	Mfg. of metal products and parts, except machinery and equipment	3,445	252	309	4,007
35-36	Mfg. of machinery and equipment other than transport equipment	738	450	0	1,187
38	Mfg. of other manufacturing industries	855	0	0	855
Total		86,632	9,274	32,849	128,755

GVA (constant prices)

NIC Code	*Description*	*OAME*	*NDME*	*DME*	*Total*
20-21	Mfg. of food products	178,875,785	41,764,346	28,932,301	249,622,432
23-24-25	Mfg. of beverages, tobacco & related products	81,936	0	0	81,936
26	Mfg. of textile products	70,389,660	28,967,009	0	99,356,670
27	Mfg. of wood and wood products	55,520,272	4,871,488	0	60,391,760
30	Mfg. of basic chemicals & chemical products (except products of petroleum & coal)	440,462	6,936,416	0	7,376,879
32	Mfg. of non-metallic mineral products	9,275,367	0	278,733,657	288,009,024
34	Mfg. of metal products and parts, except machinery and equipment	39,378,358	1,801,214	5,725,145	46,904,716
35-36	Mfg. of machinery and equipment other than transport equipment	2,479,027	852,789	0	3,331,816
38	Mfg. of other manufacturing industries	4,521,468	0	0	4,521,468
Total		360,962,336	85,193,263	313,441,103	759,596,702

Source: NSS 51st and 56th round Non-Agricultural Informal Sector Enterprise Survey.

Annexure Table IV. 8 : Distribution of GSDP Per Worker and Growth of Major Industry, Uttarakhand at 1993-94 Prices

Industry	*1993-94*			*1999-2000*			*2004-05*			*ACGR in per worker GSDP (%) 1993-94 to 1999-00*	*ACGR in per worker GSDP (%) 1999-2000 to 2000-05*
	GSDP (Rs. lakh)	*Workers UPSS*	*Per worker GSDP (Rs.)*	*GSDP (Rs. lakh)*	*Workers UPSS*	*Per worker GSDP (Rs.)*	*GSDP (Rs. lakh)*	*Workers UPSS*	*Per worker GSDP (Rs.)*		
Agriculture & allied activities	219713	2606421	8430	252265	2094893	12042	275983	2586849	10669	6.12	-2.39
Mining & quarrying	8272	11973	69090	10314	0	0	37105	321	11559190	0.00	-
Primary	227985	2618394	8707	262579	2094893	12534	313088	2587170	12102	6.26	-0.70
Manufacturing	80671	105494	76470	61122	178997	34147	117659	208074	56547	-12.57	10.61
Electricity, gas & water supply	12200	8971	135989	13740	33122	41484	34785	17305	201011	-17.95	37.11
Construction	39940	152220	26238	65001	271824	23913	156622	282578	55426	-1.53	18.31
Secondary	132811	266685	49801	139863	483942	28901	309066	507957	60845	-8.67	16.05
Trade, hotels & restaurants	44135	143752	30702	47378	211915	22357	77654	.364882	21282	-5.15	-0.98
Transport, storage & communication	24193	63676	37994	33153	80361	41255	70469	125584	56113	1.38	6.35
Finance, banking, insurance and real estate	63476	36773	172614	94860	53427	177550	138575	40241	344363	0.47	14.17
Community, social and other services	75957	399230	19026	107783	310459	34717	196883	383733	51307	10.54	8.13
Tertiary	207761	643431	32290	283174	656162	43156	483581	914440	52883	4.95	4.15
All	568557	3528510	16113	685616	3234997	21194	1105735	4009567	27577	4.67	5.41
State per capita income	7674			8290			12272				

Annexure Table IV. 9 : Distribution of GDP per Worker and Growth of Major Industry, All-India (at 1993-94 Prices)

ndustry	1993-94			1999-2000			2004-05			ACGR in per worker GDP (%) 1993-94 to 1999-00	ACGR in per worker GDP (%) 1999-2000 to 2000-05
	GDP (Rs. Crore)	Workers UPSS	Per worker GSDP (Rs.)	GDP (Rs. Crore)	Workers UPSS	Per worker GSDP (Rs.)	GDP (Rs. Crore)	Workers UPSS	Per worker GDP (Rs.)		
Agriculture & allied activities	241,967	239213130	10115	286,983	240033199	11956	314,180	262753712	11957	2.83	0.00
Mining & quarrying	20,092	2759529	72810	27,269	2167849	125788	34,700	2674804	129729	9.54	0.62
Primary	**262059**	**241972659**	**10830**	**314252**	**242201048**	**12975**	**348880**	**265428516**	**13144**	3.06	0.26
Manufacturing	125,493	39929724	31428	191,925	43733165	43885	265,712	56740485	46829	5.72	1.31
Electricity, gas & water supply	18,984	1433344	132445	28,401	1123742	252736	34,624	1318636	262574	11.37	0.77
Construction	40,593	11946574	33979	58,740	17444439	33673	78,724	26389380	29832	-0.15	-2.39
Secondary	**185070**	**53309642**	**34716**	**279066**	**62301346**	**44793**	**379060**	**84448502**	**44887**	4.34	0.04
Trade, hotels, transport, & communication	150,500	39241521	38352	255,807	55234554	46313	407,139	68929505	59066	3.19	4.98
Finance, banking, insurance and real estate	90,084	3650139	246796	145,863	4841002	301307	196,820	7877461	249852	3.38	-3.68
Community, social and other services	93,632	35970231	26030	153,379	33044162	46416	197,509	37854415	52176	10.12	2.37
Tertiary	**334216**	**78861891**	**42380**	**555049**	**93119718**	**59606**	**801468**	**114661382**	**69899**	5.85	3.24
All	**781345**	**374144193**	**20884**	**1148367**	**397622112**	**28381**	**1529408**	**464538400**	**32923**	**5.55**	**2.65**
Per capita income	**8742**			**11,438**			**13,787**				

Annexure-IX.1: Focus Group Discussion – People's Perception on Livelihood Options

Development initiatives, especially livelihood interventions, must be tempered with an understanding of location-specific perceptions of sustainable options. Rural households have over the years put in place and also refined livelihood adaptations and ignoring the same would compromise the responses to changing poverty paradigms. Since rural livelihoods entail economic, social and cultural aspects with people at the centre-stage gaining a holistic sense of all essential dimensions of the livelihood concerns is relevant – people's perceptions are integral to such an understanding.

Towards this end, the technique of Focus Group Discussions (FGD) was used to generate a profile of people's perceptions. One village from each block was selected for FGD. The FGD was carried out in eight villages which were randomly selected. The discussions were designed to elicit responses pertaining to the villagers' perceptions of livelihood issues—the assets, vulnerability, peoples' perceptions for improvement in access to livelihoods and employment opportunities available.

Panel : Sample Village Surveyed for Focus Group Discussion (FGD)

Sl. No.	*District*	*Block*	*Village*
1.	Almora	Salt	Garkote
2.	Almora	Hawalbagh	Bhanargaon
3.	Pithoragarh	Berinag	Garaon
4.	Pithoragarh	Dharchula	Champani
5.	Tehri Garhwal	Kirtinagar	Khola
6.	Tehri Garhwal	Chamba	Sabli
7.	Uttarkashi	Dunda	Barethi
8.	Uttarkashi	Bhatwari	Bagori

1. Village: Garkote (Salt Block in Almora District)

The village is about 8 km from the block headquarters with 52 households and about 10 per cent households belong to Scheduled Caste group. About 75 per cent population is educated. Agriculture is the main occupation of the people with animal husbandry being an integrated activity. Owing to general lack of development in this area, people do out-migrate to either Ramnagar which is the trading centre or Delhi for livelihood. Agriculture provides few months employment and therefore people depend on animal husbandry or some wage employment, particularly in construction works. Poverty is relatively higher in this area. Infrastructure facilities in terms of link road, health centres, educational institutions and training centres are not located nearby, as a result, people have to travel to avail these facilities. The area has an acute shortage of water both drinking as well as irrigation purposes. Land is also not fertile for field crops; however, the land appears to be suitable for growing chillies, ginger and some fruits (mango and banana). The area has potential for growing fruits, vegetables and medicinal plants, and forest based products. Wool-based enterprises can be set up in Saraikhet and tourists resorts in Manila.

Major Findings of the Focus Group Discussion

Assets	*Vulnerability*	*How to improve the access to livelihood? — peoples' perceptions*
1. Lack of fertile soil, lack of irrigation facilities. 2. Good prospects for dairying, chilli, mango, banana, ginger, vegetables, medicinal plants, mushrooms etc. 4. Enormous scope for developing tourist resorts (Manila). 5. Animal husbandry, goat keeping, poultry, forest products, wool (Saraikhet), minerals (limestone, sandstone). 6. River Ramganga with good potential for providing water for drinking and Irrigation purposes.	1. Scarcity of water. 2. Lack of better educational and training centres. 3. Lack of medical and health facilities. 3. Lack of connecting roads and communication. 4. Social evil like drinking of liquor among menfolks. 5. Landslides and damage to common properties. 6. Huge unemployment and limited employment opportunities outside farming. 7. Menace of forest animals.	1. Need for better educational, training and health facilities. 2. Better accessibility in terms of roads, communication and electricity. 4. Accountable and transparent administration. 5. Promotion of dairying, fruits, vegetables and processing units. 6. Promotion of different types of tourism and environment-friendly resort amenities. 7. Promotion of micro enterprises based on local niche products (fruits, vegetables, medicinal plants, non-timber forest based products etc.).

2. Village: Bhanargaon (Hawalbagh Block in Almora District)

This village is about 7 kilometres from the block headquarters Hawalbagh in Almora district. Majority of the people are engaged in agriculture and animal husbandry activities. Land is relatively productive here and fulfils food requirements of the full year. There are 59 households in the village of which three households belong to Scheduled Castes. In all, there are nine BPL households and two Antyodaya households and none of them are from Scheduled Caste. The Khastriyas dominate the village. But typically in agriculture, most of the men are engaged in specific activities of cultivation such as ploughing, sowing, hoeing, ditching, and threshing; while the women bear the major brunt of agriculture crop cultivation. The drudgery of hill women is enormous as they work for about 12-14 hours per day. This practice is most common in Uttarakhand hills. The village does not have road connectivity and no medical facilities; and often villagers have to rush to Hawalbagh for minor treatment. It is particularly children, women and aged people who often have to face lots of sufferings. Water scarcity has become an acute problem and long queue of children and women is mostly visible. There is one high school but no intermediate college, as a result, students have to go either Hawalbagh or Almora for intermediate education. Standard of education has deteriorated fast primarily because of the apathy of teachers to take up teaching seriously, and sometimes political interference also affects the teaching environment. Landslides are recurrent particularly in rainy seasons but no effective measures are being taken to prevent these. In many cases, regulations of forest department come in the way of the villager's usufruct rights that create a constant problem between the villagers and forest officials. In the village development works, corruption among officials seems to be rampant and they often demand for commission in getting the work sanctioned. Drinking of liquor has become another major social problem in the village, as it creates lot of tension in the families and women and children are the victims of this evil. A group of women called Mahila Mangal Dal is quite active in the village and has brought about certain reforms including ban on drinking of liquor in the village.

Major Findings of Focus Group Discussion

Assets	*Vulnerability*	*How to improve the access to livelihood? – peoples' perceptions*
1. Fertile soil, but lack of good irrigation facilities. 2. Good prospects for animal husbandry. 3. Active women's group.	1. Scarcity of water. 2. No intermediate college. 3. Lack of medical and health facilities. 4. No veterinary facilities. 5. Lack of connecting roads. 6. Corruption among officials in charge of development functions. 7. Social evil like drinking of liquor among menfolks. 8. Forest regulations are often anti-people. 9. Landslides and damage to common properties.	1. Need for better educational facilities. 2. Opening of primary health centre. 3. Better accessibility in terms of roads, communication and electricity. 4. Accountable and transparent administration. 5. Promotion of dairying.

3. Village : Garaon (Berinag Block in Pithoragarh District)

Garaon village is about 4 kilometres from the Berinag development block in Pithoragarh district. In all, there are 102 households of which 30 households are Scheduled Castes. About 60 are BPL households and all the Scheduled Caste households are declared as BPL. Brahmins are the better educated while the Scheduled Caste is either illiterate or educated up to higher secondary level. Majority of them have either migrated elsewhere or permanently shifted to plane areas. Even some of the families have shifted to Berinag town that provide them better opportunities for earning livelihood. More than half of the households have migrated from the village. Some of them have shifted nearer to the road-head that provide them better accessibility. Virtually few are pursuing agricultural related activities and most of the land remains either barren or leased out to others. There are better irrigation channels but they are not fully utilised. Generally, crop production is sufficient for meeting the food requirements of the full year. But in recent years, wild pigs have created menace and a large part of crops got destroyed. Condition of the Scheduled Caste families is worse as they do not have enough land to cultivate and most of the upper caste families have already migrated for whom they used to provide services (ploughing). There are no employment opportunities for them and they are mostly uneducated. Their vulnerability is due to the fact that they have neither enough land for cultivation nor they are educated.

Major Findings of Focus Group Discussion

Assets	*Vulnerability*	*How to improve the access to livelihood?– peoples' perceptions*
1. Potential for developing a tourist spot, as there is an ancient temple of Lord Shiva and 70 feet water-fall. 2. Immense potential for cultivation of Geranium plant (with high oil contents). 3. Good climate for growing fruits, vegetables, medicinal plants, spices and tea gardening.	1. No link road to village and motor road-head. 2. No primary health centre and veterinary hospital. For minor ailment villagers have to go to Berinag. 3. A small bridge over Kande-Kiroli tributary is must that will provide better accessibility and movement of people and cattle.	1. Providing roads to the village and linking it to main roads. 2. Provision of health facilities. 3. Development of horticulture, medicinal plants with marketing and extension support. 4. Promotion of tourist place that will provide better employment and income opportunities to the villagers.

4. Village: Champani (Dharchula Block in Pithoragarh District)

This village falls in Dharchula development block of Pithoragarh district. Ranthi is the second largest gram sabha after Baluakote. This gram sabha has 50 odd helmets spread over 1200 hectares' area. Champani is a helmet of about 52 households with no Scheduled Caste population, but it has four OBC households. Majority of households (40) are BPL families. Their main occupation is animal husbandry and agriculture. About 200 to 250 litre of milk is supplied daily to Dharchula town from this helmet. Most of the people make livings from selling milk and milk products. These milk vendors have to traverse about 10-12 kilometres steep height daily to sell milk, as there is no road connecting to Dharchula.

Major Findings of Focus Group Discussion

Assets	*Vulnerability*	*How to improve the access to livelihood? – peoples' perceptions*
1. Good prospects of milk and milk products; ghee	1. There is no road in the village and this makes the villagers most vulnerable.	1. There is the need for village road connecting to Dharchula town.

(Contd...)

from this area is famous. 2. Abundance of potato production. 3. Good potential for apple growing and tea gardening in the nearby places. 4. Potential for promoting tourist destination. 5. Potential for cultivation of medicinal plants and spices.	2. Lack of water for drinking and irrigation purposes. 3. No good medical and health facilities in the village. 4. Shortage of teachers in the high school. 5. No veterinary facilities.	2. Setting up of milk collection centre and dairy in the village. 3. Opening a veterinary centre in the village. 4. Availability of health and medical facilities.

5. Village: Sabli (Chamba Block in Tehri Garhwal District)

Sabli village is situated on Rishikesh road in Chamba block of Tehri Garhwal district. It is about 5 kilometres from the block headquarters. Being closer to Chamba town and Rishikesh, the village has better connectivity and other facilities. There are about 130 households in the village. The dominant social group is Brahmin; and 10 households belong to Scheduled Castes. About 25 to 30 households are such that have land-less than 0.025 hectares and most of them are BPL families. There is good number of educational institutions including higher education within a radius of 1-3 kilometres. Majority of the villagers (85%) are educated, and socially and politically conscious. The village has all the modern amenities like electricity, TV and telephone connections, tap water, cooking gas etc. Unemployment has become a major problem and traditional occupations are vanishing fast. Though, there is a provision for financial help for promotion of self-employment, yet availing the facility is difficult due to malpractices in sanctioning loan.

Major Findings of Group Discussion

Assets	*Vulnerability*	*How to improve the access to livelihood? – peoples' perceptions*
1. Good connectivity and better amenities and facilities. 2. Unique picturesque beauty and immense potential for developing tourist centres.	1. Lack of irrigation facilities. 2. High unemployment. 3. Fast disappearance of traditional occupations. 4. Widespread corruption in government departments. 4. About one-fourth house-	1. Providing irrigation facilities. 2. Promoting self-employment opportunities. 3. Promotion of activities that have good potentials for development in the area

(Contd...)

3. Good potentials for horticulture development, milk production, bee keeping, cultivation of medicinal plants. 4. Well-educated population.	holds have little or no land.	viz., horticulture development, milk production, bee-keeping, cultivation of medicinal plants and tourism.

6. Village: Khola (Kirtinagar Block in Tehri Garhwal)

Khola village is about 30 kilometres from Kirtinagar block. It is one of the most backward blocks in the Tehri Garhwal district. There are 35 households with majority of them belonging to Scheduled Caste (30 households), five families are Brahmins and another five families are Khastriyas. Nineteen households are BPL families, who belong mostly to Scheduled Caste. Large majority of the Scheduled Caste households have little or no land and they depend on casual wage labour.

Major Findings of Group Discussion

Assets	*Vulnerability*	*How to improve the access to livelihood? – peoples' perceptions*
1. Potential for dairying 2. Hardworking people.	1. Little land among Scheduled Caste households. 2. Low agricultural output and no irrigation facilities. 3. High unemployment among youth. 4. Menace of wild animals that destroy the substantial part of crops. 5. Low level of education that does not ensure any job. 6. Nepalese labourers are preferred than local people in road construction and related works. 7. No metalled roads connecting to main roads and frequent load shedding. 8. Distant place from the block. 9. No medical facilities.	1. Distribution of land to landless households. 2. Constructing irrigation channels. 3. Providing employment to people in public works. 4. Provision of better facilities like roads, medical facilities. 5. Government departments need to be sensitive to the needs of villagers.

7. Village: Barethi (Dunda Block in Uttarkashi District)

Barethi village is in Dunda block of Uttarkashi district. It has about 280 households, which in any case is a large sized village in the context of hilly region. About 250 households are from upper castes (Brahmins and Khastriyas) and remaining 130 are from the Scheduled Castes. About 141 families are such who belong to BPL families, mostly from Scheduled Castes. The village is about 4-5 kilometres from the district headquarters. Proximity to district headquarters has great impact on the village life in terms of provision of basic amenities and facilities. The village being closer to district headquarters, many people from outside have settled here, and as a result, land for agricultural purposes has become limited. Though the general level of crop production is satisfactory, yet limited land size has put severe constraints on the increase of production. Unemployment and poverty are serious problems in the village and there are no alternative employment opportunities except traditional crop cultivation and animal husbandry. Some of course get casual type of jobs in the district headquarters, but that too is available for a short time.

Major Findings of Group Discussion

Assets	*Vulnerability*	*How to improve the access to livelihood? – peoples' perceptions*
1. Proximity to district headquarters that provide some opportunity of livelihoods particularly to the poor. 2. Good potential for increased agricultural productivity. 3. Availability of basic amenities and other facilities. 4. Good market for milk and milk products and vegetables. 5. Potential for developing tourist centre.	1. Limited land particularly among Scheduled Castes. 2. Fast growth of market and consequent dispossession of land at thorough price has led landlessness among people. 3. Rampant unemployment among youth. 4. Debt burden is high as villagers have taken loan from the Government departments for purchasing buffaloes but somehow returns are too low.	1. Promotion of vegetable cultivation and animal. husbandry for milk and meat. 2. Development of tourist industry as this would provide employment opportunities to people. 3. Promotion of small units having potential for growth.

8. Village: Bagori (Bhatwari in Uttarkashi District)

Bagori is about 47 kilometres from the block headquarters Bhatwari in Uttarkashi district. It is one of the remotest areas bordering to China with a height of about 2500 meter and is one of the farthest villages of the block having harsh geographical conditions. It is situated on the way to famous Gangotri temple and trekking field. Majority of people are Scheduled Tribes and their occupation is sheep and goat rearing; knitting and weaving, and trading of woollen garments. Cultivable land is limited and whatever land is available is suitable for growing only limited crops like potato, *rajma* (kidney beans) and apple. There are about 245 households in the village among which 220 are Scheduled Tribes and remaining are Scheduled Castes. Nearly 40 households are BPL families, mostly with little or no land. During winter, people move to Veerpur near Dunda block along with sheep and goats. Sheep-rearing and weaving of woollen garments are their traditional occupations; but in the changed economic and social context, these occupations have been adversely affected. Cheap and fancy woollen products from the urban areas has made their traditional occupation most vulnerable. Lack of marketing support for their products has further added to their miseries; whatever they manufacture has to be sold at a minimum price. Earlier, these tribal people used to take their sheep for grazing near Rishikesh during the winter but now this traditional right has also been denied. Forest regulation has also come in the way of their usufruct rights of rearing animals.

Major Findings of Group Discussion

Assets	*Vulnerability*	*How to improve the access to livelihood? – peoples' perceptions*
1. Traditional skills of knitting and weaving and raw wool production. 2. Beautiful landscape and potential for	1. Remoteness and harsh geographical conditions. 2. Lack of cultivable land. 3. Declining traditional occupation. 4. Violation of traditional	1. Providing support to dying home based traditional knitting and weaving occupations. 2. Providing land to people for cultivation.

(Contd...)

developing tourist spots. 3. High potential for growing potatoes, *rajma* (kidney beans) and apples.	rights. 5. Drudgery of seasonal movement. 6. Insensitive governance to the problems of people; for instance, electricity has been disconnected in the village almost for about a year. 7. No road connection in the village. 8. Level of education is low due to frequent absence of teachers.	3. Providing usufruct rights to people for access to grazing land. 4. Providing extension facilities for growing vegetables and fruits.

Annexure-IX.1A : Employment Opportunities as Identified in FGD

Sector of employment	*Name of villages (District)*
I. Agriculture related	
(i) Vegetable cultivation	Bhanargaon (Almora), Barethi (Uttarkashi), Sabli (Tehri Garhwal), Champani (Pithoragarh)
(ii) Horticulture	Bhanargaon (Almora), Garaon (Pithoragarh), Sabli (Tehri Garhwal) Champani (Pithoragarh), Bagori (Uttarkashi)
(iii) Floriculture	Khola (Tehri Garhwal), Bagori (Uttarkashi),
(iv) Medicinal and Aromatic Plants	Bhanargaon (Almora), Garaon (Pithoragarh), Garkote(Almora), Champani (Pithoragarh) Bagori (Uttarkashi)
(v) Tea Plantation	Garaon (Pithoragarh), Champani (Pithoragarh),
II. Animal husbandry related	
(i) Poultry	Byasi (Pauri Garhwal), Bhanargaon (Almora), Barethi (Uttarkashi), Sabli (Tehri Garhwal)
(ii) Animal husbandry	Bhanargaon (Almora), Barethi (Uttarkashi)
(iii) Dairy	Bhanargaon (Almora), Champani (Pithoragarh), Barethi (Uttarkashi), Sabli (Tehri Garhwal)
III. Processing	
(i) Agro-processing	All villages
(ii) Processing of medicinal and herbal plants	Garaon (Pithoragarh)
(iii) Manufacturing of woollen garments	Bagori (Uttarkashi)
(iv) Knitting and weaving	Bhanargaon (Almora), Banethi (Uttarkashi) Bagori (Uttarkashi)
(v) Resin factory	Bhanargaon (Almora)
IV. Service sector	
(i) Tourism	Garaon (Pithoragarh), Champani (Pithoragarh), Garkote (Almora), Barethi (Uttarkashi), Bagori (Uttarkashi), Sabli (Tehri Garhwal)
(ii) Repair and maintenance	No one could identify the scope of such important activities

Source : Field Survey, 2004-05.

Annexure-IX.2: Voice of the Poor — A Tale of Uttarakhand

I. The Tales of the Poor – Some Evidences from the Field

Traditionally, Uttarakhand hill region has had a very strong system of mutual obligation and social security in which people of different social classes lived together and depended on each others, and this resulted in a closely knitted and cohesive society. This system has existed for a long time. The Scheduled Caste population, for instance, did not have enough land to cultivate and therefore they depended on the higher castes such as Brahmins and Thakurs (Kshatriyas) for crop share and livelihood. In turn, they provide services (Jajmani) like making agricultural implements and servicing them as well as performing other menial jobs. They also ploughed the fields of Brahmins, who in certain cases, themselves do not plough due to the high prestige held for them in society. This system has helped provide social and economic security to all castes and there has not been any hatred towards the Scheduled Castes, though they were still treated as untouchables, particularly by the Brahmins. Generally speaking, Scheduled Castes have been the poorest class, primarily because they have had little land to cultivate in comparison to other castes, and their levels of education have also been the lowest. The system has exploited the Scheduled Castes for a long time and in this process they did not get enough opportunity of education and better options for livelihood. It is not that they were discriminated against in the access to education or other facilities provided by the government, but somehow they were the victims of social deprivation for generations. However, this did not deter the social interaction between different social classes.

In a way, caste system has played an important role in determining the style of life, which distinguishes more sharply than others in certain points. For example, Scheduled Caste houses are small, often with thatched roof and located slightly in distance from other higher castes. The caste system is clearly ranked, and historically the upper castes generally monopolised certain advantages – the economic and social power – and the class endogamy tended to keep the rich as rich and the poor as poor. Also, Scheduled Castes have a distinct sub-system of kinship in which they interact in their own social groups for marriages, rituals and festivities. Upper castes do sometimes participate in their ceremonies like marriages, but abstain from having food at their place. Despite this distinct social hierarchy, by and large, there has not been any social strife and hatred among different classes barring a few isolated incidents. This kind of mutual obligation and cooperation existed since long time and has helped mitigate the problems of poverty, and in fact, none was perhaps reported having died of hunger. In spite of the absence of the absolute poverty, poor have been inflicted with variety of deprivations – social, economic and cultural. Hill women are more deprived than men folk primarily because women bear the brunt of cultivation and household chores, while males are the main breadwinners. The drudgery of hill women is enormous as they work for about 12-14 hours per day. Even the men-folk whose main activity is cultivation are relatively less burdened than their female counterparts as they perform the specific tasks of cultivation such as ploughing, sowing, hoeing, ditching and threshing.

With a view to understanding the conditions of the poor, their problems and perception about development, I visited four development blocks and about 20 villages in the Garhwal region during this summer. In this long and arduous journey, I had to encounter numerous difficulties by way of walking down long distances, climbing up hilly tracks, and crossing forests and rivers. I even had to face humiliation at times when villagers wanted to know from me how my visit would make any difference in their lifestyles and how I can improve their livings; if I cannot contribute towards improving their life, then what is the purpose of my visit. They also argued that at least over a dozen such people visit them every year from different agencies claiming to be the representatives of Central Government, State Government, NGOs, and sometimes from UN agencies. All come and make promises for the welfare of the people but they seem to end up writing some reports. The story goes on but the resentment is clearly visible among the villagers, who seem to have been bypassed by the development process in certain cases.

In this journey, I saw men, women, children, old, young, infirm, disabled, poor and also not so poor and witnessed the pathetic condition and misery of the poor. Their faces full of deprivation and hope still haunt me. I remember two particular instances when I visited Byasi (Thailisen block) and Kolinda villages (Birokhal block) in Pauri Garhwal district, where I had spent some time with the villagers. These two villages were selected with different perspectives in mind. In both types of villages, Scheduled Castes were chosen as the main social group for focused group discussion, primarily because they are the most deprived class subjected to various forms of discrimination. Also, class relations between the Scheduled Castes and the upper castes have far reaching implications for the society in terms of social security and livelihood as well as in terms of exploitative relations. The first village (Byasi), which is relatively poor and backward, has majority households belonging to Scheduled Castes and the second village (Kolinda) is relatively better-off, with Scheduled Caste population being the minority.

II. The Diversity in Village Economies

1. Byasi Village

In Byasi village, majority of households belong to Scheduled Castes with whom I had interacted in some detail. This village is located on Bungidhar road and is about 10 kilometers away from the block headquarters. Roads are commutable by jeeps but no buses ply on this road, the villagers have to depend on jeeps which are often irregular, and they ply only when they get sufficient passengers. This village has 88 families, of which, 51 families are Scheduled Castes and remaining 37 families belong to general category (Bisht Thakurs). The general caste households live on the upper portion of the village, while the Scheduled Castes live in the lower portion which is slightly distanced from the upper caste houses. Majority (71) of them belong to BPL families.

The main occupation of the villagers is agriculture combined with animal husbandry. By and large, hill agriculture is at a subsistence level. The terrace type of fields depending entirely on rains and with limitations in using any improved methods of cultivation, has kept the hill agriculture at a low level of equilibrium. Though everyone has some land which ensures food for a few months; yet the general castes own more land per household than the Scheduled Castes. Exchange of labour in crop cultivation is also common, wherein people help each other in their farming activities. The production is very low and often not sufficient to feed beyond few months in a year which in turn forces them to resort to a variety of livelihood strategies, and most often casual wage employment in construction, loading and unloading of material and off-farm wage work in agriculture seem to be the most common, howsoever low wages they offer. This is the major problem for a large majority of households and this in turn tells the story of how the people in the region cope with the challenges of livelihoods by often adopting multiple coping mechanisms. The major crops in the village are paddy, wheat, millet, (jhingura, madua, chaulai etc.) and barley. In addition, they cultivate variety of locally grown pulses (gahat, bhatt, urd, soyabean, masoor etc.) and mustard, potato, onion etc. The average production is very low by any standard. For example, the yield per nali (i.e, about 1/20th acre) is about 30-40 kg for paddy, 12-15 kg for wheat, 8-10 kg for madua and jhingura and the pulses range between 2-4 kg per nali. The yield of potato is about 70-80 kg and onion between 50-60 kg per nali. Generally, people do not make use of any fertilizers and HYVs. One of the reasons for this is that they cannot afford to purchase fertilizers and HYVs from the market due to cash crunch. There are only two minor irrigation channels (gool) in the village, which are not perennially active; often it dries up in the summers and benefits up to only 25 families of which six are from Scheduled Castes. The other major problems facing the villagers is soil insects (pests) which cause menace for crops; and a large part of crops is being devastated by these small creature in the soil. It harms the crops, which are particularly grown in non-irrigated areas. This problem has become more acute during the last three to four years. Some people even approached the block development office (crop protection unit) for their help to eradicate the menace of insects but of no use. Sometimes, block officials advise them to use insecticides but the cost of insecticides is very high and as a result the poor villagers cannot use them. Also, wild animals such as monkeys, bears and wild pigs have been causing substantial crop losses.

Almost all the people are engaged in the crop and livestock production as their principal livelihood, which do not ensure food for the year, and at best, the foodgrains are sufficient to last for a few months. Out of 51 Scheduled Caste families, 30 are ironsmiths, making agricultural implements and 15 families are such who make baskets for carrying cowdung in the fields, storing grains and bringing fodder from the jungles for the upper castes in lieu of crop share. As usual in the state, the Scheduled Castes own little land as compared to other castes; therefore, they have to depend on other coping mechanisms for livelihood, and in most cases through working in construction and off-farm activities on daily wage. The prevailing wages range between Rs. 50–60 per day in the case of male members, and Rs. 30–40 per day for females with usual minor benefits attached, like two-times tea, and in some cases, breakfast consisting of *chapatti* and cooked vegetables. But such work is neither perennially nor easily available around the nearby villages. In some cases, male members have to travel even 8-10 km from their homes to seek casual work. If work is available for a longer duration say, 15-20 days, then they even go to Baijro – a small town which is about 32 km away. They stay there along with other co-workers and return after the work is over. In any case, no work is available for them for more than 3-4 days on an average in a month in the nearby vicinity. No one was in government service among Scheduled Castes, though a few among the upper castes were in government jobs. Savitri Devi (w/o Guna Ram), Gram Pradhan of the village explained that earlier there was only one gram sabha for three villages, namely, Kunet, Marora and Byasi and no work (government schemes) was got done through gram pradhans. During the last one year, three gram sabhas were created separately for these villages. As a result, the Government schemes are being implemented through gram pradhans. This has provided some relief, as the villagers get a few days' casual employment within the village. But this is a temporary relief and the villagers have to find other means of livelihoods.

There is an acute unemployment among the youth and they have to desperately move out from their homes to earn a living. About 15-20 male members are such, mostly young boys, who have moved out to planes in search for jobs. Majority of them have gone to Chandigarh, Ludhiana, Delhi and Dehradun and are engaged in petty jobs in restaurants as wash-boys or helpers, domestic servant in the houses and *kothis*, and some are employed in the factories as security guards. Their jobs are casual and they earn Rs. 800-1,000 per month depending on the length of their service and relevant experience. They send back a part of their earnings to their homes in order to meet the cash requirements mostly for daily consumption needs. They flock into the cities primarily because of acute unemployment in the region, and there are little or no opportunities of jobs in the local area. Most of them who move on to cities for jobs are illiterates or educated up to primary or in some cases, upper primary levels, that too without any skills. This increases their vulnerability to find jobs. The women, on the other hand, bear the brunt of crop cultivation and livestock production, bring the headloads of fodder from the far-off jungles for which they have to walk down 4-5 km on an average, and also look after children, cook food and fetch water. For them, the day starts at 5 AM in the morning and continues till 10 PM. They, therefore, entail the extraordinary burden of cultivation and household activities. Strenuous activities, lack of nutrition and healthcare make their conditions worst.

The system of mutual obligation has provided some kind of social security to different social classes and this has perhaps been the reason for social harmony and bondage. The jajmani system has however been attenuated over time. Nevertheless, there has been no overt class-conflict among them. This system has inherent exploitative relationship between the upper caste and the Scheduled Caste. The exploitative relationship existed primarily because the latter had lack of access to assets (e.g., land, education and better jobs etc.) and it has increased their dependence on the former for livelihood. In this particular village, class relationship is not that antagonistic because majority of the households are poor and the Scheduled Castes are in majority. There is also no perceptible variation in terms of assets and wealth across classes. It seems that greater the unequal distribution of assets, the more exploitative relations develop between the two classes. Since the village head belongs to the lower caste and therefore they enjoy greater autonomy and power in decision-making process in the village level development activities.

The literacy level in the village is abysmally low, unlike other parts of the state. There is one primary school in the upper part of the village where the general caste people reside. The school was built in 1970 and its condition is very bad. At present, there are 88 students in the school with a single teacher. There is little or no teaching in the school and often the teacher remains absent. The mid-day meal attracts a lot of children to school, particularly children from the lower castes. Scheduled Caste children also get some amount of scholarship, but the uniform is compulsory, the cost of which has to be borne by the parents and in most cases, the poor families cannot afford it. This causes great hardship to the poor families. In some cases, very poor children are not going to school. During 2000, one junior school (VI to VIII) was started which is about a half kilometer distance from the village and this has provided great relief to the villagers. Earlier the children had to walk down to Bagwadi, which was about 4 km for the junior school. One so-called public school (up to primary level) named Children's Paradise Academy was started in 2003 where slightly better-off households, mostly among the upper castes, send their children. Still, the level of education is very low, half of the girls are illiterate and some are literate only up to primary level. No girl was found in the village having qualified with high school education for aganwadi programme among the BPL families. As a result, the programme could not be started. Girls help in the cultivation related activities, fetching water, rearing animals and bringing fodder from the jungle. This precisely leads to illiteracy among the girl children and they mostly drop-out from the school.

There is an acute shortage of health facilities in the village. Most of the people in the village depend on quacks for minor ailments or in some cases go to the nearby shop, which keeps some general medicines. The primary health centre is located at Thalisen, which is about 10 km from the village. Though Auxiliary Nurse Midwife (ANMs) visit the village once in a month or so, but it is more like a ritual. For major ailments, the villagers have to go to Thalisen, and in most cases there is no medicine in the Primary Health Centre (PHC), and the doctors often prescribe the medicine which the villagers have to purchase from the market. For serious illness, people generally go to Ramnagar or Delhi. This further accentuates hardship – they have to borrow money for treatment or in some cases mortgage or sell the jewellery. There is no maternity facility in the village and all the expecting mothers depend on the local *dai*, Bhadi Devi – a 65 years old woman for delivery. The *dai* does not charge any fee for delivery as such, but she generally gets Rs. 200 per delivery. Ladies in particular hide their illness and shy away from visiting doctors because of lack of money. As a result, the illness sometimes turns into serious ailment and there are instances where women have died in the village under such circumstances. The misery of women does not end here – the men drink, smoke and gamble. Though gambling is occasional, yet money is needed for it. Whatever money is earned through casual works, a part of it gets dissipated into it and the women have to suffer torture and humiliation from the men. This sometimes leads to quarrel and hatred which again has to be borne by the women. But life has to go on – as usual, their day starts at 5 a.m. and continues till 10 p.m. The pradhan however reports that the incidents of quarrelling after drinking have drastically reduced in recent years because of intervention by the senior village people. Not only this, in every household men folk take all the decisions including the matter of sale and purchase of any item, and women don't have any say in household decisions.

There an acute shortage of drinking water and villagers often have to fetch water from distant places, either from natural streams or from the river for which they have to travel 1 to 2 km. But now they get tap water under the scheme, Swajal Dhara. There are 13 water stand posts, 10 in the area of upper castes and three in the Scheduled Castes' area. But there are no latrines; though some money was given for construction of latrines under the Ambedkar and Swajal Yojana, but somehow the villagers are neither used to these nor these are in usable conditions.

Though electricity was given in the village at some 8-10 years ago, yet only seven families have availed the connection and another 20 families have availed the connection under Kutir Jyoti Scheme for the BPL families for which Rs.140 and 25 are charged from the families respectively. But, villagers often complain of faulty meter-reading and thus overcharging. Their complaints to the authorities have not yielded any desired result.

There is one Public Distribution System (PDS) shop nearby run by Keshar Singh from where the villagers have been getting foodgrains, sugar and kerosene oil. But surprisingly, for last about one year no one is getting any foodgrains from this shop despite the fact that there are 71 BPL families in the village.

Government programmes such as Swa Rozgar Yojana (SRY), Jawahar Rozgar Yojana (JRY) XI Finance Commission and Indira Awaas Yojana (IAY) have been providing some relief to the villagers through construction of pathways, repair of village by lanes, boundary wall of school, bathing place for pregnant women, pond for irrigation facilities etc. Savitri Devi is the Gram Pradhan; but in real sense, she is the *de jure* Pradhan, while her husband Guna Ram is *de facto* Pradhan. Whenever any scheme comes to the village, Guna Ram consults the villagers and every household is taken into confidence; only then employment is given to each member for certain number of days. Though these schemes provide only some temporary relief to the villagers, yet it is an important source for meeting immediate cash requirement of the poor people. There was an NGO working in this village by the missionaries called World Vision, which has done many good works in the area. One big water tank for drinking purpose was constructed in the village in 1998-99 which provided a lot of employment to the villagers during its construction, though they also have to mobilise free labour (shramdan) for at least two days in a month. This institution has done excellent work in the field of healthcare, particularly for children. Regular free check-up camps were organised and in certain cases when the condition of the children was serious, this NGO had given free treatment in the referred hospital in Lucknow. But somehow, the villagers lost their trust in this NGO, since they believe that it is doing the charity not on humanitarian ground but for the cause of promotion of Christianity. As a result, the NGO had to leave the area. Villagers however still remember the good work done by the NGO. Unfortunately, none of the elected representatives visit the village excepting at the time of election, and this is very much common in most cases.

There is a gram sabha with six members and majority of them are women. They meet once in a month and discuss the implementation of employment schemes and other village problems. All disputes related to land and other problems are discussed and sorted out mutually. The meeting takes place in the panchayat bhavan. The panchayat bhavan is in bad shape and needs a repairing. This is being used by the primary school for cooking mid-day meal for the children.

As regards the wealth ranking, majority of people in this village are very poor and some are slightly better-off than others, but none has good economic background. The size of land, income from wage employment, remittance, pension, owning shop or animal wealth and 3-4 room-house are considered some of the indicators of slightly better-off households. The villagers who have been identified as slightly better-off are Keshar Singh, Mohan Singh, Bhagat Singh, Chandra Singh, and Khushal Singh. According to the villagers, Shri Keshar Singh is the richest man, who has 3 acres of land, owns the PDS shop, receives pension and has a four-room house. On the other hand, the poorest are those who have little or no land, no earning sources and those who are widow, infirm, too old etc. Some of the poorest people in the village are: Aushoni Lal, Seklu Lal, Jagat Lal, Prem Lal and Jhapli Devi.

The Untold Misery of Aushoni Lal and Bhagat Lal

Among all, the condition of Aushoni Lal is most pathetic and miserable. Aushoni Lal is an old man of about 70 years and has almost lost his vision and cannot even come out from his house without someone's help. He has 0.1 acre (2 nali) land and depend solely on ironsmithy, but due to poor eyesight and ageing factor, he could not continue it for long and for last 4-5 years he has completely stopped working. Aushoni Lal was doing ironsmithy for eight upper caste families and used to get grains after every crop; and this was his only source of livelihood. Sometimes he used to get casual work mainly in the road works, but such work is rarely available barring a few days. His wife died 15-16 years ago and he has one son Bhagat Lal. He is about 35 years old but he looks like an old man of 60 years. Bhagat Lal's wife also died four years ago and has two sons Dinesh (6 years) and Ramesh (5 years). Ramesh remains most of the time ill as bowel erupts in his body every now and then and also his vision is poor and he needs constant caring. He has no money for treatment, whenever some para-medical person visits the village they give some medicine but of no use. For Aushoni Lal and Bhagat Lal feel that this is their destiny and they have to live with this problem for ever. Bhagat Lal is somehow managing household chores – looks after children and his father, cooks food, and also brings firewood from the jungle for cooking. He is not a skilled ironsmith as his father was and this has made him more vulnerable. Since there is not much work in the village, Bhagat Lal has to do whatever work is available and manage with whatever he earns from that work. When some scheme comes in the village, good fortune appears before him as he gets foodgrains and some cash. They can't remember having bought any clothes in their lifetime; they have been solely depending on others for old clothes. Villagers are kind enough to this family and they have been giving them old clothes, particularly those migrants who come home in the vacation from the planes. Villagers have also been giving them corn or food when they have nothing to eat. He has a one-room house which is in a bad condition. There are some old utensils in which Bhagat Lal cooks food for the family. He has to cook something to feed the children but he himself and his father can hardly afford to eat two times. It rarely alleviates the family's constant hunger pains. Many times they have to sleep hungry and this is not new to them. When I talked with Aushoni Lal and Bhagat Lal, they became happy and narrated their misery and despair. Aushoni Lal told that for them life has no meaning; they would have died long ago had the villagers not come to their rescue in difficult times. Villagers told me that Bhagat Lal has been suffering from acute psychological disorder, as he constantly worries about how to feed the little children and what will happen to his infirm father. He did not talk much with me and remained quiet. But clearly, whatever little he talked, he talked about his children and old father. Suddenly, he went out and promised me that he would come soon, but he never came and later I was told that he had gone to the jungle for collection of firewood, otherwise the little children would have to sleep hungry. It was already 6 PM and the darkness gradually enveloping, and I was wondering how Bhagat Lal has gone to jungle at this time, but perhaps he has been living in the darkness of despair and poverty and it has become usual for him. Aspirations for better days seem to be a mirage for the poor Aushoni Lal and Bhagat Lal.

Major Findings of Group Discussion

Assets	*Vulnerability*	*Livelihood strategies*	*How to improve the access to livelihood –peoples'perception*
1. Land 2. Livestock 3. Labour 4. Mutual obligation and social security	**I. Land** (i) Small sizes of land holding. (ii) Food insecurity. (iii) Pest diseases. (iv) Menace of wild animals. (v) Lack of irrigation **II. Livestock** (i) Low quality of cattle. (ii) No market for disposal of milk. (iii) Drudgery involved in fodder collection. **III. Labour** (i) Majority are BPL families. (ii) Lack of work available around. (iii) Low wages. (iv) No regular wage employment. (v) Lack of literacy and skill. (vi) Lack of health facilities. **IV.Mutual obligation and social security** (i) Less exploitative relation across the classes (ii) Attenuating values of *Jajmani* system **V.Insensitive governance** (i) Callous attitude and lack of accountability on the part of Government officials.	**Multiple coping strategies** (i) Crop cultivation. (ii) Livestock production. (iii) Crop share under *Jajmani* system. (iv) Non-farm wage employment. (v) Off-farm wage employment. (vi) Dependence on remittance.	(i) Urgent need for pest disease control. (ii) Opening of milk collection centre. (iii) Opening of Aganwadi Kendra. (iv) More teachers in primary school. (v) More job opportunities in nearby areas, particularly in lean season. (vi) Setting up of primary health sub-centre. (vii) Making responsive administration. (viii) Adequate medical facilities at the block office. (ix) Regular availability of ration in PDS. (x) Setting of skill training centre for unemployed youth.

2. Kolinda Village

Kolinda village is about 45 kilometers away from the Birokhal block headquarters and it is the last village of the block; thereafter the boundary of Thailisan block starts. The village is located on Birokhal–Thalisen motor road and along the Purvi Nayaar river about 2 km away from the roadside and situated slightly on the elevated plane. Majority of the households are Brahmins followed by Thakurs and Scheduled Castes. There are about 104 families in the village of which 76 are Brahmins, 18 are Thakurs and the remaining 10 families are Scheduled Castes.

Agriculture is the main occupation in the village along with animal husbandry, barring for the Scheduled Caste families who do not have land and therefore depend mostly on wage labour either in the fields of upper castes or in the casual works in non-farm activities. Among the general castes, a good number of people are in job either in the government or in private sector. Agriculture is totally rainfed and there are no irrigation facilities, though the nearby Purvi Nayaar river flows perennially. Here paddy, wheat, jhingura, madua and pulses like gahat, bhatt, urd, soyabean, masoor etc. are grown. Production of wheat is comparatively less than paddy due to cold climate. If rain is normal then crop is also normal but for most of the families the crop is sufficient only for few months in the year. This is the usual pattern with the hill crops. But due to monkey menace and insect problems, a lot of crops get devastated year after year. There is no respite from the monkey menace despite the efforts made by the villagers to stop it with the squad of dogs. As told by Madhavanand Semwal, monkey menace is a problem since the recent past (10-15 years) and this is primarily because of the aforestation programme of the Forest Department particularly of growing pine trees. Pine plantation, in particular, have many disadvantages as it drastically reduces the water tables and draws out the surface water. As a result, all the natural streams have dried up causing an acute water shortage for the animals and people in the forest. The other related problem is recurrent fire in the pine trees.

Among the upper castes, many inhabitants are working for salaried jobs; some are in the government departments, while a good majority of them are in the private sector. Private jobs are not available locally, hence they migrate to plane areas. Most of them are engaged in petty jobs in factories, private houses, restaurants etc. for a meagre salary. These migrants maintain strong linkages to their homes through regular visits and remittance. The Scheduled Castes, on the other hand, have no land (barring one or two families) and they plough the fields and cultivate the land of upper castes and in return get a crop share. In certain cases, they get Rs. 400-500 per season for ploughing. Since majority of males among the general castes have migrated, these households have to depend on the Scheduled Castes for ploughing and related activities. No one among the Scheduled Castes is in the government jobs and some have been doing petty jobs in restaurants as wash-boys in Dehradun and Delhi. Most of the Scheduled Castes in the village are doing off-farm activities and casual works on daily wages in construction, loading and unloading works etc. The average wages are Rs. 50 to 60 per day for males, and the females generally work in others' farm and in return they get foodgrains. There are seven families among the Scheduled Castes who do ironsmithy and three families do the tailoring work for the villagers and in return get a fixed amount of crop share under the jajmani system. But in winters and in the rainy season, there is no work around and they have to face lot of difficulties to eke out their livings. In the road works they do not get any work, as the contractors prefer the Nepalese; even in agriculture related works, Nepalese are preferred primarily because of their dexterity and hard work. The women are most burdened in the cultivation and livestock rearing, fetching water and in other household activities. They bring fodder from the forest (Deewa Daanda), which is 7-8 km away from the village. These women often go early in the morning and come back only in the evening. They normally go to the forest two to three days in a week in the winters as well as in summers.

In this village, class conflict between the upper castes and the Scheduled Caste seems to be more apparent. One of the principal reasons for this conflict is the landlessness among the latter class, which makes them highly dependent on the upper castes and vulnerable to exploitation. Not only this, there is a sharp inequality in terms of other assets like status of houses, livestock, level of education, jobs in the government departments etc. Scheduled Caste households have virtually no land for cultivation, no livestock, small houses (kutchha) with one room and no jobs in government departments, and majority of them are uneducated. Their vulnerability is due to the fact that they have to depend on the upper castes for their livelihood in the form of crop share in lieu of their labour power. In this process, they are exploited since they have no option but to work for the survival. Exploitation takes various forms. Firstly, no cash wage is paid for performing the off-farm activities and labourers are given some foodgrains, which is not proportionate to their labour efforts. This is most common in the case of women working in their fields. Secondly, the male members who plough the fields of the upper castes on contract basis for a cropping season usually get very low wages. It comes just half of what an unskilled labourer gets as a daily wage. Thirdly, the majority of households are upper castes (asset-owning class) and therefore the Scheduled Caste is ignored in common decision-making process for the village development activities. Fourthly, it has been observed in certain cases that Nepalese labourers are preferred to the local people among the Scheduled Caste for various agricultural activities because of their dexterity and hard work.

The upper caste people are better educated while those belonging to lower castes are mostly illiterates. Most of the parents in the lower castes have now been sending their children in the nearby primary school as the children get free meal and scholarship. Despite free education, some parents have withdrawn their children because they cannot afford to spend money on their school uniform. Primary school is located nearby and there is no problem sending the child there, but the middle and high schools are located in Jaspur Khal, which is about 4 km away from the village and children have to climb up steep hill. But for 11th and 12th classes, the villagers have to send their children either to Thalisen or Baijron, which are about 15 km away from the village for which they have to necessarily stay there. It becomes very difficult to send girls to this distant place; as a result, they cannot continue their education beyond high school and therefore after high school girls start working and helping in cultivation and animal husbandry. Among the Scheduled Castes, the drop-out rate is much higher especially for girls.

There are no health facilities in the village; the PHC is either at Baijron or at Birokhal, which are located at about 15 and 24 km distance respectively. It is not possible for villagers to go to these far-off places. For minor ailments they have to depend on the local chemists. But even when they have to go to these health centres for major ailments, there are no doctors available and if doctors are at all available there is no medicine. Doctors often prescribe the medicines, which the poor villagers have to purchase from the market. During my visit to this village, many of the villagers were suffering from a sort of flue with high fever but no one from the PHC visited this village. Though a sub-centre was set up in this village 12-14 years ago and one ANM was appointed, unfortunately most of the ANMs have been either on leave for the most part of their tenure or managed to get their posting elsewhere. The present ANM posted in the village is absconding for last one year. Villagers even reported this matter to the District Chief Medical Officer, but of no use. There is no maternal facility in the village and the expecting mothers have to depend on the village *dai* (Hira Devi, 63 years old) for childbirth, for which she never charges anything.

There is shortage of water in the village; particularly it becomes an acute problem in summer. The main reason for scarcity of water is due to drying up of natural streams as a result of plantation of pine trees, which do not conserve water but draws out it. Also, lack of maintenance of pipelines by the water department leads to frequent breakdowns. There are 9-10 water stand posts in the village but often few are working. There are no sanitation facilities for the villagers barring few well-off families who have constructed latrines at their own houses. But none of the Scheduled Caste families has any such facility.

Though there is electricity in the village yet frequent load-shedding is most common. Only 18-20 families have taken connections. Others have not taken connection either because they are not in a position to afford billing, or because of the problems associated to the department and their callous attitude. The villagers complaint that the electricity department does not heed to their problems nor do they visit for meter reading and often send inflated bills. Only two meters are functioning while others are either not functioning or jammed since long. None of the Scheduled Caste families has electricity connection, not even under Kutir Jyoti Scheme meant for BPL families, because they cannot afford the cost of electricity.

There is one PDS shop at Bhera about 4 km from the village. Most of the Scheduled Caste families bring ration from there as they are listed under BPL Cardholder, but the quality of ration is poor as reported by Bhagat Ram. They get wheat at Rs. 5.50 and rice at Rs. 7.00 per kg. Many of the families cannot even afford to bring the ration regularly due to cash crunch.

There is no connecting road in the village despite the fact that sometimes ago the government had sanctioned construction of road linking Jaspur Khal to Kulinda but nothing has been done so far. Also, one hanging bridge over Purvi Nayaar river too had been sanctioned by the government almost 10 years ago, but since then nothing has been done tells Pitamber Datt. Lalmani tells that about a year back construction of a community hall was undertaken in the village from the local MLA funds but no one from the village was consulted in its construction and the Block officials appointed the contractor. But after some work it was stopped and the structure still remains incomplete. The schemes that are implemented through the village panchayat are more effective because the villagers are taken into confidence in every stage of activities. There has been a callous attitude of government departments towards development activities in the village. Also, there is no veterinary centre nearby and for that villagers have to go either to Thalisen or Birokhal. People have surplus milk which is an important source for cash requirement but there is no dairy where people can sell milk. There is no aganwadi progarmme in the village nor are there any training activities for girls and ladies, whereas in other villages some schemes like tailoring, embroidering, weaving and pickle making etc. are being promoted. There is no health visitor in the village and the women have to suffer the most, as they cannot afford to extricate themselves from their daily routines to go to far-off places for getting medical attention. Being the last village of the block, no one visits this place and it has remained neglected for long, tells Janaki Devi (head, Mahila Mangal Dal). None of the elected representatives has visited the village since the election was held last time.

Ganesh Prashad is the Gram Pradhan and with the help of other members he carries out the village schemes like construction of village pathways, repairing of tanks, panchayat ghar, taps and related works in which villagers are also given works for certain number of days. There is gram samiti in the village, which has been continuing for time immemorial. This is an important village institution where villagers collectively work in the ceremonies; help each other in difficult times. The villagers have assets worth Rs. one and half lakh in the form of utensils and other community articles. The villagers use these assets, irrespective of caste, in marriage and other social ceremonies with reasonable user charges.

One can distinctly notice the glaring inequality in the village in terms of size of land, job opportunities, educational attainments and pucca house and other assets. Every family in the upper caste has land and livestock and some source of income, howsoever small it is, but most of the Scheduled Caste families do not have land, livestock and employment. They have small houses, often kutchcha with one room. Mostly, they depend on casual wage employment either on others' fields or working as construction labourers. But the work is not available regularly around the village or nearby places. The traditional jajmani occupations, which they have been pursuing for generations, are no longer sufficient to eke out their livings. Gobind Ram tells that landlessness among the Scheduled Castes is the most tragic aspect of their life and without land they have to virtually beg from the upper caste for every now and then, and as a result, they have to accept whatever little they get in return of their hard work. The government has not done anything for them in this regard and their misery has in fact increased over the years. Bachi Ram tells that the upper caste people are exploiting them principally because they have no land and other assets. The upper caste people are monopolising most of the common benefits meant for the village. To Kali Charan, the richest people in the village are: Madhavanand (having sufficient land, good house, three sons in the government jobs), Ram Prashad (sufficient land, income from the pension, son in government job), Chintamani (income from the pension, son in government job, good house and sufficient land), Satyendra Prashad (son in the job, good house and sufficient land) and Kundan Lal (son in the job, good house and sufficient land). The poorest lot is from Scheduled Castes and the most poor among them are Chankhi Ram and Bhagat Ram who have no means of livelihood and they are just subsisting in extreme poverty and helplessness.

Sufferings of Chankhi Ram Auji

Chankhi Ram is 77 years old and is the poorest man in the village. Since he belongs to a drum beating family and therefore they are known as auji. They beat drums in the marriages and other auspicious occasions in the village and in lieu of that they used to get some money and foodgrains. This has been the family occupation of the auji's. He has almost negligible (0.05 acre) land. Chankhi Ram has two daughters and a wife, but he cannot work because of ill-health and poor eyesight. His father died when Chankhi Lal was one year old and his mother somehow managed the livings of the family by working in others' field. He had three sisters and Chankhi Ram was the youngest among all. When Chankhi Ram grew older he learned drum beating and started to earn something for the family and married the sisters. He somehow wanted to learn his ancestral occupation of tailoring but there was none in the village from whom he could learn this skill. But he had an obsession to learn tailoring. Once he had Rs.2.25, which he earned through drum beating in the village marriage. He thought to run away from home and he immediately boarded the bus, after covering some distance on foot, and somehow reached Dehradun. He was then 13 years old. There, he had an encounter with a Sardarji, who fortunately had a shop of tailoring and Sardarji agreed to keep Chankhi Ram as a helper. Chankhi Ram became extremely happy and gradually he learned tailoring. He did not inform anybody in the village nor wrote any letter to his mother about his whereabouts because he did not know the postal address. After three years, Chankhi Ram returned home and his mother became very happy to see him. Chankhi Ram got married and he wanted to start tailoring but he had no money for purchasing the sewing machine. His mother begged the money from the villagers for whom she used to work and purchased the sewing machine for Chankhi Ram. He saw good times again and managed the livings through tailoring and drum beating. But good days did not continue for long for his mother. His mother was worried all the time, as Chankhi Ram had no child even after many years of marriage. She died when Chankhi Ram was 45 years old. Chankhi Ram's wife was also unhappy as she had no issue. Villagers pressurised Chankhi Ram for second marriage, as there will be no auji in the Scheduled Caste community if he does not have an issue. For the sake of offspring, he had a second marriage from which he had two daughters named Sampati and Sarita. Life continued for Chankhi Ram but after 7-8 years his second wife died in a fire accident at home. He worked hard and earned living for the family but gradually he had developed eyesight problem. He got them operated twice in free camps organised in nearby places. But the problems still persisted and his vision deteriorated gradually. Then difficult time started for Chankhi Ram as he became old and frail and could not continue tailoring due to his poor eyesight. His worry was how to marry his daughter Sampati who then became 17 years old. With the help of relatives, his daughter got married in June last year. Now his first wife and younger daughter are with him. His wife is also 66 years old and has become frail and cannot work much. The daughter goes to the nearby school but she would probably not continue for long. Villagers are very kind to Chankhi Ram. Whenever any marriage takes place in the village, Chankhi Ram arrange for drumbeaters from other village of his community and gets some money. Both have become now old and helpless. Constant worry haunts them how their 12 years old daughter Sarita would be married. There is no old-age pension for this couple despite promises made to them by some officials. They became very happy when I met them in their house. Perhaps they thought that their pension has been sanctioned. They are constantly being eluded by the hope of getting old-age pension.

Major Findings of Group Discussion

Assets	*Vulnerability*	*Livelihood strategies*	*How to improve the access to livelihood –peoples' perception*
1.Land 2. Livestock 3. Labour 3. Mutual obligation and social security	**I. Land:** (i) Landlessness among Scheduled Caste. (ii) Food insecurity intense among the Scheduled Caste. (iii) Pest diseases. (iv) Menace of wild animals. (v) Lack of drinking water and irrigation. (vi) No connecting roads. (vii) Remote village from the block headquarters. (viii) Recurrent fire in the pine trees. (ix) No schools beyond primary within the radius of 4 km. **II. Livestock** (i) Low quality of cattle. (ii) Drudgery involved in fodder collection. **III. Labour** (i) Lack of work available around. (ii) Low wages. (iii) No regular wage employment. (iv) Lack of literacy and skill. (v) Lack of health facilities. **IV. Mutual obligation and social security** (i) Exploitative relation with upper castes. (ii) Attenuating values of *Jajmani* system. **V. Insensitive governance** (i) Callous attitude and lack of accountability on the part of Government officials.	**Multiple coping strategies** (i) Crop cultivation. (ii) Livestock production. (iii) Crop share under Jajmani system. (iii) Non-farm wage employment. (iv) Off-farm wage employment. (v) Dependence on remittance.	(i) Urgent need for pest control. (ii) More job opportunities in nearby areas particularly for the Scheduled Castes. (iii) Setting up of primary health sub-centre. (iv) Making responsive administration. (iv) Adequate medical facilities at the block office. (vi) Regular availability of ration in PDS. (vii) Setting of skill training centre for unemployed youth and ladies.

References

Allan, N.J.R., G.W., Knapp and C.Stadel (eds.) (1988), *Human Impacts on Mountains,* New Jersey, Rowman and Littlefield.

Awasthi, I.C. (2009), Rural Non-Farm Employment in Uttarakhand: A Case of Gender Biased Work Structure, *Manpower Journal,* Vol. XLIV, No.3, July-September, Delhi.

—., (2010), Migration Patterns in Hill Economy of Uttarakhand: Evidence from Field Enquiry, *The Indian Economic Journal,* January-March, Vol.57 (4), New Delhi.

—., R.P. Mamgain and Balwant Singh (2005), Employment in Uttaranchal: Issues and Challenges, *The Indian Economic Journal,* Vol.53, Number 2, July-September, New Delhi.

Badhani, K.N. (1998), "Enterprise-based Transformation of Hill Agricultre : A Case Study of Vegetable Growing Farmers in Garampani Area, Nainital District, India", Discussion Paper, Series No. MEI, 98/5, International Centre for Intergrated Mountain Development (ICIMOD), Kathmandu, Nepal.

Bardhan, B.K., (1979), "Labour Supply Functions in a Poor Agrarian Economy", *Amercian Economic Review,* March.

Basant, Rakesh (1993), "Diversification of Economic Activities in Rural Gujarat : Key Results of a Primary Survey", *The Indian Journal of Labour Economics,* vol. 36, No. 3.

—, B.L. Kumar and R. Parthasarathy (1998), *Non-Agricultural Employment in Rural Gujarat,* Rawat Publications, Jaipur.

Banskota, Mahesh (2000), "The Hindukush Himalayas : Searching for Visible Socio-economic and Environmental Options", in *Growth in Poverty Alleviation and Sustainable Resource Management in the Mountain Areas of South Asia,* Banskota, *et al.* (eds.) ICIMOD, Kathmandu.

—, Trilok Singh Papola and Jurgen Rishter (eds.) (2000), *Growth in Poverty Alleviation and Sustainable Resource Management in the*

Mountain Areas of South Asia, International Centre for Integrated Mountain Development (ICIMOD) and German Foundation for International Development, Kathmandu, Nepal.

Batzing, W., M. Perlik and M. Dekleva, (1996), "Urbanisation and Depopulation in the Alps", *Mountain Research and Development,* vol. 16, No. 4.

Bhalla, Sheila (1990), "A Theoretical Framework for a Study of Rural Labour Markets", *The Indian Journal of Labour Economics,* Vol. 33, No. 2.

—, (1993), "Tests of Some Propositions about the Dynamics of Changes in the Rural Workforce Structure", *The Indian Journal of Labour Economics,* vol. 36, No. 3.

— (1997), "The Rise and Fall of Workforce Diversification Process in Rural India", in *Growth, Employment and Poverty,* G.K. Chadha and Alakh N. Sharma (eds.) Indian Society of Labour Economics, Vikas Publishing House, New Delhi.

—, (1998), "Trends in Poverty, Wages and Employment in Rural India", in *Empowering Rural Labour in India – Market, State and Mobilisation,* R. Radhakrishna and Alakh N. Sharma (eds.), Institute for Human Development, New Delhi.

Binayak, Bhadra, *The Hindu Kush Himalaya, Alpin Forum: Moving Towards Worldwide,* Newsletter (2), Bergamo.

Binswanger, H.S., Khandker and M. Rosenzweig (1989), *How Infrastructure and Financial Institutions Affect Agricultural Output and Investment in India?* World Bank, Working Paper 163, Washington, DC.

Bhati, J.P. (1990), "Development Strategies in Himachal Pradesh", Discussion Paper, ICIMOD, Kathmandu.

Bora, R.S., (1986), "Migration for Survival", *The Economic Times,* Special Silver Jubilee Issue Feature, December, 19.

—, (1986), "Extent and Causes of Migration from the Hill Region of Uttar Pradesh, in *Migrant Labour and Related Issues,* Vidyut Joshi (ed.), Oxford and IBH Publishing Company, New Delhi."

— (1996), *Himalayan Migration : A Study of the Hill Region of U.P.,* Sage Publications", New Delhi.

—, (2000), "Arresting out-migration : Some Policy Consideration for Uttarakhand", *The Indian Journal of Labour Economics*, vol. 43, No. 2.

Breman, J. (1978), "Seasonal Migration and Cooperative Capitalism : Crushing of Cane and Labour by Sugar Factories of Bardoli", *Economic and Political Weekly*, October 13, pp. 31-33.

— (1985), *Of Peasants Migrants and Paupers : Rural Labour Circulation and Capitalist Production in Western India*, Oxford University Press, New Delhi.

Byers, Alton C. (2000), *The Appalachians, Alpin Forum : Moving Towards Worldwide*, Newsletter (2), 2000, Bergamo.

Census of India (2001), "Provisional Population Totals", Paper of 2001 Series 6, New Delhi.

Census of India (2011), "Provisional Population Totals", Papers 1 and 2.

Chadha, G.K., (1993), (ed.) Editor's Introduction in Special Issue on Non-farm Sector in the Rural Economy of India, *The Indian Journal of Labour Economics*, vol. 36, No. 3.

— (1994), *Employment, Earnings and Poverty : A Study of Rural India and Indonesia*, Sage Publications, New Delhi.

— (1997), "Access of Rural Households to Non-farm Employment : Trends, Constraints and Possibilities", in Chadha, G.K., and Alakh N. Sharma (eds.), *Growth Employmnt : Trends, Constraints and Possibilities – Change and Continuity in Rural India*, Vikas Publishing House, New Delhi.

— (2002), "Rural Non-farm Employment in India : What Does Recent Experience Teach Us?", *The Indian Journal of Labour Economics*, vol. 45, No. 4, October-December, (Conference Issue).

— and Alakh N. Sharma (1997) (eds.), *Growth Employment : Trends, Constraints and Possibilities – Change and Continuity in Rural India*, Vikas Publishing House, New Delhi.

Chand, Ramesh, (1995), *Agricultural Diversification and Employment in the Hill Region : A Study of Himachal Pradesh*, Institute of Economic Growth, Delhi.

— (1996), "Diversification through High Value Crops in Western

Himalayan Region : Evidence from Himachal Pradesh", *Indian Journal of Agricultural Economics,* vol. 51 and No. 4.

Chand, S.P. and B. Thapa (1992), "Mountain Agricultural Technology Development and Diffusion : The Pakhribas Model, Nepal", in *Sustainable Mountain Agriculture : Farmer's Strategies and Innovative Approaches,* vol. 2, N.S. Jodha, M. Bankskota and Tej Partab (eds.)

Chakravarty, Sukhamoy (1988), "The Logic of Employment-Oriented Planning in Developing Countries", G.L. Mehta Memorial Lecture delivered at Madras.

Choudhury, Dhrupad, (2004), "Agricultural Transformations in the Uplands of Northeast India : Where Are We Heading?", Paper presented in a National Seminar "Transforming the Hill Economy of North-East Region : Emerging Challenges and Opportunities", during November, 26-28, 2004, Itanagar.

Connell, J., B. Dasgupta, R. Laishley, and M. Lipton (1976), *Migration from Rural Areas : The Evidence from Village Studies,* Oxford University Press, New Delhi.

Das, Gurudas and Rajesh Datta (2004), "Structural Transformation of the Hill Economics of India's North East : Some Policy Implications", paper presented in a National Seminar on "Transforming the Hill Economy of North-East Region : Emerging Challenges and Opportunities", during November, 26-28, 2004, Itanagar.

Das, Kalyan (2004), "Population Growth and Dynamics of Labour Market in Hill Areas of North East India : Opportunities and Constraints in the Present Economic Environment", Paper presented in a National Seminar on "Transforming the Hill Economy of North-East Region : Emerging Challenges and Opportunities", during, November 26-28, 2004, Itanagar.

Davies, S. (1996), *Adaptable Livelihood : Coping with Food Insecurity in the Malian Sahel,* Macmillan Press, London.

Dayal, H. and A.K. Karan (2003), *Labour Migration from Jharkhand,* Institute for Human Development, New Delhi.

Denniston, D. (1995), "Sustaining Mountain People and Environments", in *The State of the World,* World Watch Institute

Report on Progress Towards a Sustainable Society, W.W. Norton Company, New York.

Deshingkar, Priya and Sven Grimm (2004), "Voluntary Internal Migration : An Update", paper commissioned jointly by the Urban and Rural Change Team and the Migration Team within the Policy Division of the British Government's Department for International Development.

Deshingkar, P. and D. Start (2003), *Seasonal Migration for Livelihoods, Coping, Accumulation and Exclusion,* Working Paper No. 220, Overseas, Development Institute, London.

Duraisamy, P. (2000), *Changes in Returns to Education in India, 1983-34 : By Gender Age Cohort and Location,* Centre Discussion Paper No. 815, Economic Growth Centre, Yale University.

Eapen, Mridul (1994), "Rural Non-Agricultural Employment in Kerala : Some Emerging Tendencies", *Economic and Political Weekly,* vol. 29, no. 21.

— (1995), "Rural Non-Agricultural Employment in Kerala, Inter-district Variations", *Economic and Political Weekly,* vol. 30, No. 13.

Earth Summit in Rio de Janeiro (1992), *Managing Fragile Ecosyterms : Sustainable Mountain Development,* Agenda 21, Chapter 13.

Ellis, Frank (2000), *Rural Livelihood and Diversity in Developing Countries,* Oxford University Press, New York.

European Commission (2001), *Unity, Solidarity, Diversity for Europe its People and its Territory,* Second Report on Economic and Social Cohesion, European Commission, Brussels.

Farooque, Nehal A. and D.S. Rawat (1997), *Development Dilemma, Indian Scenario and Rural Himalaya,* Gyanodaya Prakashan, Nainital.

Fei, John, C.H. and Gustav Ranis, (1964), *Development of the Labour Surplus Economy : Theory and Policy,* Irwin Homewood, III.

Friedman, John and William Alonso (1964), *Introduction in Regional Development and Planning – A Reader,* The MIT Press, Cambridge.

Ghosh, Jayati (1995), "Employment and Labour under Structural

Adjustment in India since 1991", *The Indian Journal of Labour Economics,* vol. 34, Issue, 4.

Ghosh, P.P. and A.N. Sharma (1995), "Seasonal Migration of Rural Labour in Bihar", *Labour and Development,* vol. 1, No. 1, July-December.

Gichuki, Francis N. (2000), *The African Mountains and Highlands, Alpin Forum : Moving Towards Worldwide,* Newsletter 2000 (2), Bergamo.

GIDS (1999), *Uttarakhand Update,* Giri Institute of Development Studies, Lucknow.

Gordon, Ann and Catherine Craig (2001), *Rural Non-farm Activities and Poverty Alleviation in Sub-Saharan Africa, Centre for Sustainable Development,* Natural Resource Institute, DFID, Policy Series, 14, UK.

Goswami, Homeswar and Jayanta Kr. Gogoi (2004), "Regional Disparities in India with Special Reference to Hill States of Northeast India", paper presented in a National Seminar on "Transforming the Hill Economy of North-East Region : Emerging Challenges and Opportunities", during November 26-28, 2004, Itanagar.

Government of India, *Tenth Five-Year Plan,* 2002-07, Planning Commission.

— (2002), *National Human Developmentr Report* (2001), Planning Commission.

Government of Uttarakhand, *Sankhikiya Patrika,* 2002 and 2003, Dehradun.

—, *Tourism Master Plan for Tehri Dam Project Area,* Final Report, 2002, (Chapters 4 : Proposed Draft Tourism Master Plan), Dehradun.

— (2007), Directorate of Economics and Statistics, Dehradun.

— (2011), *Statistical Diary Uttarakhand, 2009-10,* Dehradun.

Haan, Arjan De (1999), "Livelihoods and Poverty : The Role of Migration – A Critical Review of the Migration Literature", *The Journal of Development Studies,* vol. 36, No. 2, December, Sussex, UK.

Harris, John, (1991), *Agriculture and Non-Agriculture Linkages and the Diversification of Rural Economic Activities : A South Indian Case Study Transformation in Asia,* Oxford University Press, Delhi.

Hazell, P.B.R. and S. Haggblade (1991), Rural Growth Linkages in India, *Indian Journal of Agricultural Economics,* vol. 46 (4). Himachal Pradesh Human Development Report (2002), Government of Himachal Pradesh.

Husain, T. (1992), "The Aga Khan Rural Support Programme : An Approach to Village Management System in Northern Pakistan", in Jodha *et al.* (eds.) *Sustainable Mountain Agriculture : Farmer's Strategies and Innovative Approaches,* vol. 2.

Huddleston, B. Ergin Ataman, SDRN, Paola de Salvo, Marina Zanetti, Mario Bloise, Judith Bel and Gianluca Franceshini; and Luca Fé d'Ostiani (2003), *Towards a GIS-based Analysis of Mountain Environments and Populations,* FAO, Rome.

IDFC, (2002), *An Agenda for Development,* Industrial Development Finance Company, Mumbai.

Institute for Human Development, (2005), *Employment Generation in Uttarakhand : Constraints and Opportunities* (sponsored by the Planning Commission), New Delhi.

Islam, N. (1997), *The Non-Farm Sector and Rural Development – Review of Issues and Evidence, Food, Agriculture and the Environment,* Discussion Paper 22, IFPRI, Washington, DC.

Islam, Rizwanul (1987), "Rural Industrialisation and Employment in Asia : Issues and Evidence", *Rural Industrialisation and Employment in Asia,* (eds.) ILO/ARTEP, New Delhi.

Ives, D. Jack (1997), "Comparative Inequalities – Mountain Communities and Mountain Families", in Messerli, B. and J.D. Ives (eds.), *Mountains of the World : A Global Priority,* The Parthenon Publishing Group, New York and London.

— and Bruno Messerli (1989), *The Himalayan Dilemma – Reconciling Development and Conservation,* The United Nations University, Routledge, London and New York.

— Bruno Messerli and Robert E. Rhoades (1997), "Agenda for Sustainable Mountain Development", in Messerli, B. and J.D. Ives (eds.) *Mountains of the World : A Global Priority,* New York : The Pantheon Publishing Group.

Jayaraj, D. (1994), "Determinants of Rural Non-Agricultural Employment", in Visaria, Praveen and Rakesh Basant (eds.) *Non-Agricultural Employment in India : Trends and Prospects*, Sage Publications, New Delhi.

Jodha, N.S. (1992), "Mountain Perspective and Sustainability : A Framework for Development Strategies", in Jodha *et al.* (eds.) Sustainable *Mountain Agriculture : Perspectives and Issues*, vol. 1, International Centre for Integrated Mountain Development (ICIMOD), Oxford and IBH, New Delhi.

— *et al.*, (eds.) (1992), *Sustainable Mountain Agriculture : Perspectives and Issues*, vol. 1, International Centre for Integrated Mountain Development (ICIMOD), Oxford and IBH, New Delhi.

— (1992), *Sustainable Mountain Agriculture : Farmer's Strategies and Innovative Approaches*, vol. 2, International Centre for Integrated Mountain Development (ICIMOD), Oxford and IBH, New Delhi.

— M. Banskota and T. Pratap (1992), "Strategies for the Sustainable Development of Mountain Agriculture : An Overview", in Jodha *et al.*, (eds.) (1992), *Sustainable Mountain Agriculture : Perspectives and Issues*, vol. 1, New Delhi.

— (1992), "Mountain Perspective and Sustainability : A Framework for Development Strategies", in Jodha *et al* (eds.), *Sustainable Mountain Agriculture : Perspectives and Issues*, vol. 1, ICIMOD, Oxford and IBH, New Delhi.

— (1997), *Highland-Lowland Economic Linkages*, 1997/8, ICIMOD, Kathmandu.

— (2000), "Poverty Alleviation and Sustainable Development in Mountain Areas : Role of Highland-Lowland Links in the Context of Rapid Globalisation", in Banskota, *et al.*, (eds.), *Growth in Poverty Alleviation and Sustainable Resource Management in the Mountain Areas of South Asia*, ICIMOD, Kathmandu.

Joshi, B.K. (2001), "Statehood and Beyond : Revisioning the Future of Uttarakhand", in Pandey *et al.*, (eds.) *Economy of Uttarakhand : Profile and Dynamics of Change*, Anamika Publishers and Distributors, New Delhi.

Joshi, P.C. (1980), "Perspective of Planners from Above and People's

Perceptions from Below : The Problem of Bridging the Hiatus", paper presented in a Seminar "Development of the Hill Areas", Giri Institute of Development Studies, Lucknow.

— (1995), *Uttarakhand : Issues and Challenges,* Har-Anand Publications, New Delhi.

— (1999), "Looking Beyond Statehood - Uttarakhand : Search for a New Agenda", *Economic and Political Weekly,* December, 11-17.

Kapos, V.J., Rhind, M. Edwards, M.F. Price, and C. Ravilious (2000), *Developing a Map of the World's Mountain Forests,* in Price, M.F. and N. Butt (eds.), *Forests in Sustainable Mountain Development Report for 2000,* CAB International, Wallingford, UK : 4-9.

Karan, A. (2003), *Changing Patterns of Migration from Rural Bihar in Migrant Labour and Human Rights in India,* (Iyer, G.Ed.), Kanishka Publishers, New Delhi.

Kashyap, Pradeep (2001), "From Micro Finance to Micro Enterprise : Employment Road Map for Rural Women", paper presented in Workshop on "Rural Transformation in India : The Role of Non-farm Sector", September (mimeo).

Khanka, S.S. (1988), *Labour Force, Employment and Unemployment in a Backward Economy,* Himalaya Publishing House, New Delhi.

Kuznets, S. (1966), *Economic Growth of Nations : Total Output and Production Structure,* Belknap Press of Harward University Press, Cambridge.

Lal, Deepak, (1976), Supply Price and Surplus Labour – A Review Article, *World Development,* vol. 4, No. 9.

Lanjouw, P. (1999), *Policy Options for Employment in the Rural Non-farm Sector : Rural Development,* Note No. 4, Washington, DC, World Bank.

Lanjouw, P. and A. Shariff (1999), "Rural Poverty and Non-farm Employment in India : Evidence from Survey Data", Department of Development Economics, Free University of Amsterdam (mimeo).

— and Abusaleh Shariff (2002), *Rural Non-Farm Employment in India : Labour, Access, Income and Poverty Impact,* Working

Paper No. 81, National Council of Applied Economic Research, February.

Libiszewski, Stephen and Gunther Bachler (1997), "Conflicts *in Mountain* Area – A Predicament for Sustainable Development," in Messerli, B. and J.D. Ives (eds.), *Mountains of the World : A Global Priority,* New York : The Pantheon Publishing Group.

Lanjouw, P. (1999), *Policy Options for Employment in the Non-Farm Sector, Rural Development,* Note No. 4, Washington DC, The World Bank.

Lanjouv, P. and A. Shariff (1999), *Rural Poverty and Non-farm Employment in India : Evidence from Survey Data,* Department of Development Economics, Free University of Amsterdam (mimeo).

Lee, E.S. (1966), "A Theory of Migration", *Demography,* volume, 3, No. 1.

Lewis, Arthur (1954), *Economic Development with Unlimited Supplies of Labour,* Manchester School of Economics and Social Studies, vol. 22, pp. 131-91.

— (1979), *The Dual Economy Revisited,* Manchester School of Economic and Social Studies, September, pp. 212-216.

Lipton, M. (1968), "Strategy for Agriculture urban : Urban Bias and Rural Planning in Streeten", Paul and M. Lipton, (eds.), *The Crisis of Indian Planning,* Oxford University Press, London.

— (1980), "Migration from Rural Areas of Poor Countries : The Impact on Rural Productivity and Income Distribution", *World Development,* vol. 8.

Mac Gee, T.G. (1971), "Catalysts of Careers? The Role of Cities in Asian Society" in L. Jakobson and V. Prakash (eds.), *Urbanisation and National Development,* Sage Publications, Beverley Hills.

McDowell, Christopher and Arjan de Haan (1997), *Migration and Sustainable Livelihoods : A Critical Review of Literature,* IDS Working Paper 65, Sussex, UK.

Mahajan, Vijay and B. Yerram Raju (2005), "Institutional Framework and Enabling Environment for Rural Non-farm Sector", in Nayyar, Rohini and Alakh N. Sharma, (eds.), *Rural Transformation in India,* op. cit.

Mahendra Dev, S. (1990), "Non-agricultural Employment in Rural India—Evidence at Disaggregate Level", *Economic and Political Weekly*, vol. 25, No. 28, July, 14.

Maithani, B.P. (2004), "Land Policy and Land Management : Key to Transformation of Northeastern Hill Economy", paper presented in a National Seminar on Transforming the Hill Economy of North-East Region : Emerging Challenges and Opportunities, November 26-28, 2004, Itanagar.

Mamgain, Rajendra P. (2004), "Employment, Migration and Livelihoods in the Hill Economy of Uttarakhand", Ph.D. Thesis submitted to Jawaharlal Nehru University, New Delhi.

Mathew, E.T. (1995), "Unemployed and Self-Employed : Job Preferences and Employment Perspectives", *Economic and Political Weekly*, vol. 30, No. 44.

Mehta, G.S. (1997), *Development Experiences and Options in a Hill Region : The Case of Uttarakhand*, U.P. ICIMOD, Kathmandu, Nepal.

Meier, Gerald M. (1975), "External Trade and Internal Development", in Pet Duignan and L.H. Gann (eds.), *Colonialisation in Africa*, 1870-1969, vol. 4, New York.

Mellor, J.W. (1976), *The New Economics of Growth*, Cornell University Press, Ithaca, New York.

— (1986), *Agriculture on the Road of Industrialisation : Development Strategies Reconsidered*, Overseas Development Council, USA.

Meybeck, M., P. Green, P. and C.J. Vörösmarty, (2001), "A New Typology for Mountains and other Relief Classes : An Application to Global Continental Water Resources and Population Distribution", in *Mountain Research and Development*, No. 21, pp. 34-45.

Micevska, Maja and Dil Bahadur Rahut (2008), *Rural Non-farm Employment and Incomes in the Himalayas*, Working Paper, No. 205, ICRIER, February.

Mittal, Surabhi, Gaurav Tripathi and Deepti Sethi (2008), *Development Strategy for the Hill Districts of Uttarakhand*, Working Paper No. 217, ICRIER, July.

Mountain Areas in Europe - Final Report, (2004), Analysis of Mountain Areas in EU Member States, Acceding and other

European Countries, Conclusions from the National Interviews and Reports (Chapter 9), Nordregio Report, 2004.

Myrdal, Gunnar (1957), *Economic Theory and Under-development Regions,* Duckworth, London.

Narayanamoorthy, A., Queenne Rodrigues and Ashwani Phadnis (2002), "Determinants of Rural Non-farm Employment : An Analysis of 256 Districts", *The Indian Journal of Labour Economics,* vol. 45, No. 4.

National Commission for Enterprises in the Unorganised Sector (2007), *Report on Conditions of Work and Promotion of Livelihood in the Unorganised Sector.*

Nayyar, Rohini and Alakh, N. Sharma (eds.) (2005), *Rural Transformation in India : The Role of Non-farm Sector,* Institute for Human Development, New Delhi.

Negi, Aparna and Pyare Lal Verma (2004), "Himachal Pradesh : A Model for Hill Development", paper presented in a National Seminar on Transforming the Hill Economy of North-East Region : Emerging Challenges and Opportunities, November 26-28, 2004, Itanagar.

North Eastern Region : Vision 2020, Peace, "Progress and Prosperity in the North Eastern Region", *Sectoral Strategies for the Region,* vol. II.

Oberai, A.S. and H.K. Manmohan Singh (1983), *Causes and Consequences of Internal Migration : A Study in the Indian Punjab,* Oxford University Press, New Delhi.

Organisation for Economic Co-operation and Development (OECD) (2001), *Policies to Enhance Sustainable Development,* OECD, Paris.

Pande, P.N. (1996), *Drudgery of the Hill Women,* Indus Publishing Company, New Delhi.

Papola, T.S. *et al.,* (eds.) (1983), *Introduction* in *Development of Hill Areas : Issues and Approaches,* Himalaya Publishing House, Bombay.

— (1987), "Rural Industrialisation and Agricultural Growth : India", in Rizwanul Islam (eds.) *Rural Industrialisation and Employment in Asia,* ILO/ARTEP, New Delhi.

— (1992), "Rural Non-farm Employment : An Assessment of Recent Trends", *The Indian Journal of Labour Economics*, vol. 35, No. 3.

— (1996), "Integrated Planning for Environment and Economic Development", in *Mountain Areas : Concepts, Issues and Approaches*, ICIMOD, Kathmandu.

— (2000), "Enterprise Development or Poverty with Sustainable Resource Management : Trends, Experience and Policies in the HKH Region", in Papola T.S. *et al.*, (eds.), *Poverty Alleviation and Sustainable Resource Management in the Mountain Areas of South Asia*, ICIMOD, Kathmandu.

— (2002), *Poverty in Mountain Areas of the Hindu Kush Himalayas : Some Basic Issues in Measurement, Diagnosis and Alleviation*, ICIMOD, Kathmandu.

— (2003), "Development and Livelihoods in Sikkim : Towards a Comparative Advantage Based Strategy", Paper prepared for UNDP, New Delhi (mimeo).

— and D.N. Awasthi (2005), *Enterprise Development in Mountain Areas : Guidelines for Entrepreneurs Promotional Agencies and Policy Makers*, Himalaya Publishing House, New Delhi.

— and Alakh, N. Sharma (2005), "Towards a Policy Agenda for Rural Non-Farm Secotr", in Nayyar, Rohini and Alakh N. Sharma, (eds.), *Rural Transformation in India : The Role of Non-Farm Sector*, Institute for Human Development, New Delhi.

Perloff, Harvey and Lowdon Wingo Jr. (1964), *Natural Resource and Economic Growth in Regional Development and Planning – A Reader*, The MIT Press, Cambridge.

Pound, B. K., Budathoki and B.R., Joshi (1992), "Mountain Agricultural Technology Development and Diffusion : The Lumle Model, Nepal", in *Jodha et al., (eds.), Sustainable Mountain Agriculture : Farmers Strategies and Innovative Approaches*, vol. 2.

Planning Commission, (1985), *Working Group on Hill Area Development, for the Seventh Plan* (1985-90), Government of India, June.

Planning Commission, (2002), *10th Five-Year Plan (2002-2007)*, Chapter 4, Special Area Programmes, Government of India.

Pokhriyal, H.C. (2004), "Mountain Development : Lesson Learnt and Strategic Initiatives", paper presented in a National Seminar on "Transforming the Hill Economy of North-East Region : Emerging Challenges and Opportunities", November, 26-28, 2004, Itanagar.

Price, L.W. (1981), *Mountain and Man : A Study of Process and Environment,* Berkeley, University of California.

Price, Martin (2000), *The European Mountain, Alpin Forum : Moving Towards Worldwide,* Newsletter, 2000 (2), Bergamo.

Radhakrishna, R. and Alakh N. Sharma (1998), (eds.) *Empowering Rural Labour in India : Market, State and Mobilisation,* Institute for Human Development, New Delhi.

Rajasekhar D. (2005), "Micro-finance and Rural Non-farm Sector : Some NGOs Experiences", in Nayyar, Rohini and Alakh N. Sharma, *op. cit.*

Ramachandra, H. *et al.* (2002), "Correlates of Non-farm Occupations : A Study of Rural Haryana", *Manpower Journal,* vol. XXXVIII, Nos. 2 and 3, July-December.

Ramamonjisoa - Amma, Joselyne (2000), *South West Indian Ocean, Alpin Forum : Moving Towards Worldwide,* News-letter, 2000 (2), Bergamo.

Rao, U. (1994), *Palamoor Labour : A Study of Migrant Labour in Mahabubnagar District Hyderabad,* C.D. Deshmukh Impact Centre, Council for Social Development, Southern Regional Centre Hyderabad.

Ravenstein, E.G. (1885), "The Laws of Migration", *Journal of the Royal Statistics,* vol. 48, No. 2.

Reardon, T. (1997), "Using Evidence of Household Income Diversification to Inform Study of the Rural Non-farm Labour Market in Africa", *World Development,* 25 (5).

— (1999), "The State of Food and Agriculture", *Rural Non-farm Income in Developing Countries,* Food and Agriculture Organisation (FAO), Rome.

— *et al.* (1998), "The State of Food and Agriculture", part III, *Rural Non-farm Income in Developing Countries,* FAO, Rome.

— (2000), "Effects of Non-farm Employment on Rural Income Inequality in Developing Countries : An Assessment Perspective", *Journal of Agricultural Economics* (51-52).

Regmi, Gopal and Clem Tisdell (2002), "Remitting Behaviour of Nepalese Rural-to-Urban Migrants : Implications for Theory and Policy", *The Journal of Development Studies,* vol. 38, No. 3, February.

Rieder, Peter and Jorg Wyder, (1997), "Economic and Political Framework for Sustainability of Mountain Areas", in Messerli, B. and J.D. Ives (eds.) *Mountains of the World : A Global Priority New York: Parthenon Publishing Group.*

Rodan, Rosenstein, P. (1943), "Problems of Industrialisation of East and Southeast Europe", *Economic Journal* (June-September).

Rosenzweig, M.R. (1978), "Rural Wages, Labour Supply and Land Reforms : A Theoretical and Empirical Analysis", *American Economic Review.*

Sachdeva, Gulshan (2004), "Fiscal Governance in the Northeast", paper presented in a National Seminar on "Transforming the Hill Economy of North-East Region : Emerging Challenges and Opportunities", November, 26-28, Itanagar.

Sadhu, A.N. and Falendra K. Sudan (2004), "Experiences of Jammu and Kashmir Hill Economy and its Lessons for North-East", paper presented in a National Seminar on "Transforming the Hill Economy of North-East Region : Emerging Challenges and Opportunities", November 26-28, Itanagar.

Saith, A. (1992), *The Rural Non-farm Economy : Process and Policies,* ILO, Geneva.

Sen, Abhijit (1996), "Economic Reforms, Employment and Poverty", *Economic and Political Weekly,* vol. 31.

— (1997), "Structural Adjustment and Rural Poverty : Variables that Really Matter", in Chadha, G.K. and Alakh N. Sharma (eds.) *Growth Employment and Poverty,* Vikas Publishing House, New Delhi.

— (1997), "Agricultural Growth and Rural Poverty", in Chadha, G.K. and Alkah N. Sharma, *op. cit.*

— (1998), *Rural Labour Markets and Poverty* in Radhakrishna, R. and Alakh N. Sharma, *op. cit.*

— and Praveen Jha (2005), "Rural Employment : Patterns and Trends from National Sample Survey", in Nayyar, Rohini and Alakh N.

Sharma (eds.), *Rural Transformation in India : The Role of Non-farm Sector,* Institute for Human Development, New Delhi.

Sen, A.K. (1966), "Peasants and Dualism, With and Without Surpus Labour", *Journal of Political Economy.*

Sen, Amartya, (1975), *Employment, Technology and Development,* Oxford University Press.

Sarmiento, Fausto O. (2000), *The Latin Amercian Mountains, Alpin Forum : Moving Towards Worldwide,* Newsletter 2000 (2), Bergamo.

Shah, S.L. (1996), *Agricultural Development in Hilly Areas : Constraints and Potential* (ed.), New Age International, New Delhi.

Sharma, Alakh, N. (1997), *People on the Move : Nature and Implications of Migration in a Backward Economy,* Vikas Publishing House, New Delhi.

— *et al.* (2001), "Rural Non-farm Employment in India : An Overview", paper presented in a workshop on "Rural Transformation in India : The Role of Non-farm Sector", September 19-21, 2001, New Delhi (mimeo).

Sharma, H.R. (1996), *Mountain Agricultural Development, Processes and Sustainability—Micro Evidences from Himachal Pradesh,* ICIMOD, Kathmandu.

— (2005), "Rural Non-farm Sector in Himachal Pradesh : Patterns, Processes and Implications", in Nayyar, Rohini and Alakh N. Sharma, (eds.), *Rural Transformation in India : The Role of Non-farm Sector,* Institute for Human Development, New Delhi.

— and E. Sharma, (1997), *Mountain Agricultural Transformation Processes and Sustainability in the Sikkim Himalaya,* ICIMOD, Kathmandu.

Sharma, P. (2000), "Tourism and Livelihood in the Mountains : Regional Overview and the Experience of Nepal", in Papola, T.S. *et al.* (eds.), *Poverty Alleviation and Sustainable Resource Management in the Mountain Areas of South Asia,* ICIMOD, Kathmandu.

Sharma, R.K. (1980), *Factors Affecting Fertilizer Use in the Hill Region of Uttar Pradesh,* Research Study 80/2, Agricultural Research Centre, Delhi University.

Sharma, S. (1997), *Agricultural Transformation Processes in the Mountains of Nepal : Empirical Evidences from Ilam District*, ICIMOD, Kathmandu.

Shukla, Vibhooti, (1992), "Rural Non-Farm Sector in India : Issues and Policies", *Economic and Political Weekly*, vol. 27, No. 28.

Singh, A.K. (1994), "Change in the Structure of Rural Workforce in Uttar Pradesh", in Visaria, Praveen and Rakesh Basant (eds.) *Non-Agricultural Employment in India*, Sage Publications, New Delhi.

— (1997), *Socio-Economic Development Status at the District Level in Uttar Pradesh (India)*, Giri Institute of Development, Studies, Lucknow.

Singh, Surjit, (2001), *The RUDA, Model : Carpet Weaving Training in Rajasthan*, Paper presented in Workshop on "Rural Transformation in India : The Role of Non-farm Sector", September (mimeo).

Srivastav, Nirankar and Amaresh Dubey (2002), "Rural Non-farm Employment in India : Spatial Variations and Temporal Change", *The Indian Journal of Labour Economics*, vol. 45, No. 4.

Srivastava, R.S. (1999), "Rural Labour in Uttar Pradesh : Emerging Features of Subsistence, Contradiction and Resistance", *The Journal of Peasant Studies*, vol. 26, Nos. 2-3.

— (2005), "Internal Migration Links with Poverty and Development", country paper presented at the Regional Conference on Migration and Development in Asia, Lan Zhou, China, March, 14-16.

Srivastava, R.S. and S.K. Sasikumar (2003), "An Overview of Migration in India, its Impacts and Key Issues", Paper presented at the Regional Conference on "Migration, Development, and Pro-Poor Policy Choices in Asia", Dhaka, June, 22-24.

Stark, Oded (1980), "On the Role of Urban Rural Remittances in Rural Development", *The Journal of Development Studies*, vol. 16, No. 3.

— (1991), *The Migration of Labour*, Harvard University Press, Cambridge, MA.

Sundaram, K. (2001), "Employment-Unemployment Situation in the Nineties : Some Results from NSS 55th Round Survey", *Economic and Political Weekly*, March, 17.

Tankha, Ajay (2001), "Community Organisations in Micro-Finances : The Role of Self Help Groups in Poverty Alleviation and Rural Transformation", Paper presented in Workshop on "Rural Transformation in India : The Role of Non-farm Sector", September (mimeo).

Thorat, Sukhadeo (1993), "Land Ownership Structure and Non-farm Employment of Rural Households in India", *The Indian Journal of Labour Economics,* vol. 36, No. 3.

— and Nidhi Sadana Sabharwal (2005), "Rural Non-farm Employment and Scheduled Castes : Activities, Education and Poverty Interlinkages", in Nayyar, Rohini and Alakh, N. Sharma, *op. cit.*

Todaro, M.P. (1969), "A Model of Labour Migration and Urban Unemployment in Less Developing Countries", *The American Economic Review,* vol. 59, No. 1.

Tulachan, P.M. (1997), "Ensuring Local Food Security : An Example from the Mountains of Nepal", in *Mountain Development,* 97 (1), ICIMOD, Kathmandu.

— (1999), "Trends and Prospects of Sustainable Mountains Agriculture in the Hindu Kush Himalaya Region", in *Mountain Development,* (99) (2), ICIMOD, Kathmandu.

— (2000), "Mountain Agriculture in the Hindu Kush Himalaya : Trends and Sustainability", in Papola, T.S. *et al.* (eds.), *Growth in Poverty Alleviation and Sustainable Resource Management in the Mountain Areas of South Asia,* ICIMOD, Kathmandu.

Unni, Jeemol (1991), "Regional Variation in Rural Non-agricultural Employment – An Exploratory Analysis", *Economic and Political Weekly,* vol. 26, No. 3, January, 12.

— (1998), "Non-Agricultural Employment and Poverty in Rural India – A Review of Evidence", *Economic and Political Weekly,* March 26-April 3.

— (2000), *Sustainable Development and Social Security : Role of Non-Farm Sector,* Vikas Publishing House, New Delhi.

— and Uma Rani (2005), "Gender and Non-farm Employment", in Nayyar, Rohini and Alakh, N. Sharma, *op. cit.*

Upendranath, C. (2005), "Training and Capacity Building in Micro

Finance and Micro Enterprise Sector", in Nayyar, Rohini Alakh N. Sharma, *op. cit.*

UNDP, (1996), *Human Development Report,* Oxford University Press.

Vaidyanathan, A. (1986), "Labour Use in Rural India : A Study of Spatial and Temporal Variation", *Economic and Political Weekly,* vol. 21, No. 52.

— (1994), "Employment Situation : Some Emerging Perspectives", *Economic and Political Weekly,* vol. 29 No. 50.

— (1997), *Report on the Workshop to Evolve an Agenda of Research on Rural Non-Agricultural Employment,* Workshop Proceedings, *Indian Journal of Agriculture Economics,* vol. 52, No. 1, Jan.-March.

Verma, Binoy N. and Neelam Verma (1995), "Distress Diversification from Farm to Non-farm Rural Employment Sector in the Eastern Region, *Indian Journal of Agricultural Economics,* vol. 50, No. 3, July-September, pp. 422-29.

Visaria, Praveen and Rakesh Basant (1994), *Non-Agricultural Employment in India : Trends and Prospects,* Sage Publications, New Delhi.

World Bank (2000), "The Rural Non-farm Economy", Report on Presentation on Discussion at the World Bank, Washington, May 15-17 (mimeo).

(WSSD), (2002), International Partnership for Sustainable Development, in Mountain Regions, *World Summit on Sustainable Development,* Bali, 3 June.

Yadava, K.N.S., S.S. Yadava, and R.K. Sinha (1996-97), "Rural Out-migration and Its Economic Implications on Migrant Households in India – A Review", *The Indian Economic Journal,* vol. 44, No. 2.

Zhaoguang, Liu and Wu Ning (1992), "A Local Resource - Centred Approach to Rural Transformation : Agro-Based Cottage Industries in Western Sichuan, China", in Jodha, *et al.* (eds.) *Sustainable Mountain Development,* Vol.I, Oxford and IBH, New Delhi.

Index